UNCERTAIN EMPIRE

STANFORD STUDIES IN JEWISH HISTORY AND CULTURE
Edited by Jessica Marglin and Daniel Schwartz

UNCERTAIN EMPIRE

Jews, Nationalism, and the Fate of British Imperialism

ELIZABETH E. IMBER

STANFORD UNIVERSITY PRESS
Stanford, California

Stanford University Press
Stanford, California

© 2025 by Elizabeth E. Imber. All rights reserved.

No part of this book may be reproduced or transmitted in any form or by any means, electronic or mechanical, including photocopying and recording, or in any information storage or retrieval system, without the prior written permission of Stanford University Press.

This book has been partially underwritten by the Peter Stansky Publication Fund in British Studies. For more information on the fund, please see www.sup.org/stanskyfund.

Library of Congress Cataloging-in-Publication Data
Names: Imber, Elizabeth E., author.
Title: Uncertain empire : Jews, nationalism, and the fate of British imperialism / Elizabeth E. Imber.
Other titles: Stanford studies in Jewish history and culture.
Description: Stanford, California : Stanford University Press, [2025] | Series: Stanford studies in Jewish history and culture | Includes bibliographical references and index.
Identifiers: LCCN 2024042801 (print) | LCCN 2024042802 (ebook) | ISBN 9781503642430 (cloth) | ISBN 9781503642447 (paperback) | ISBN 9781503642454 (ebook)
Subjects: LCSH: Zionism—History—20th century. | Jewish nationalism—History—20th century. | Anti-imperialist movements—History—20th century. | Jews—Great Britain—Colonies—History—20th century. | Jews—Politics and government—20th century. | Palestine—History—1917–1948.
Classification: LCC DS149 .I463 2025 (print) | LCC DS149 (ebook) | DDC 941/.004924—dc23/eng/20241231
LC record available at https://lccn.loc.gov/2024042801
LC ebook record available at https://lccn.loc.gov/2024042802

Cover design: Michele Wetherbee
Cover photograph: British and Zionist flags at the Jubilee Forest planted in honor of King George V, Mandatory Palestine, 1935. Photo by Zvi Oron, from the collections of the Central Zionist Archives, Jerusalem (NZO\633673)

For my parents

Contents

Acknowledgments		ix
	Introduction	1
1	Wanderers Between Two Worlds	23
2	Zionists and the British Question	54
3	An Uncertain Alliance	97
4	Between Empire and Nation	134
5	Legacies of Empire and Imagining the Postcolonial	162
6	Realism, Refugees, and the British Horizons of War	200
7	The Eve of Empire	250
	Conclusion	276
	Notes	281
	Bibliography	335
	Index	357

Acknowledgments

Although this is a book about empire and global politics, at its heart lies a network built on the ties of friendship and family. I am grateful to have the chance to thank my own—similarly scattered and global in reach—here.

I am grateful to teachers and mentors who encouraged me from the start. Rabbi Henry Zoob, Cantor Louise Treitman, and Nancy Mollitor created a haven and nurtured my fascination with the Jewish past. Judith Solar gave me Jewish books and told me to keep writing. At Brandeis University, Chae-Ran Freeze, Antony Polonsky, and Jonathan Decter provided intellectual inspiration and professional direction. Jonathan Sarna told me to go into the archives during a semester abroad in Scotland, and I have not wanted to emerge since. His palpable love of Jewish history made me want to become a Jewish historian. I am so grateful for his continued mentorship. A special thanks to Rosanna Hertz and Fran Malino for their guidance.

This book project began at Johns Hopkins University, where I had the great good fortune to study with Judith Walkowitz and Kenneth Moss. Judy modeled for me what it means to think both critically and empathetically, both seriously and imaginatively. I am so grateful for her dedicated mentorship and for her commitment to training me as a writer and thinker. It is an honor to have been her student. Ken is an unfailingly generous mentor and my most important reader. This book has been shaped more than anything by his vast knowledge of Jewish history, his immense intellect, and his generosity of spirit. I am deeply grateful to be able to continue learning from him and for his friendship. He embodies what it is to be both a true scholar and *mentsh*.

I have been fortunate to have two wonderful academic homes while writing this book. My colleagues Mee-Ae Kim, Steve Maughan, Jeff Snyder-Reinke, and Mark Smith at the College of Idaho gave me my start and modeled what it is to be good colleagues and friends. I am forever grateful. Working and teaching at Clark University, which has been my home for the past five years, is a privilege, and I am grateful each day to be surrounded by such wonderful friends and colleagues in the History Department. Thank you to Wim Klooster, Doug Little, Nina Kushner, Ousmane Power-Greene, Thomas Kühne, Frances Tanzer, Lex Lu, Nana Kesse, Drew McCoy, Janette Greenwood, Taner Akçam, and last but most certainly not least, Amy Richter, for whose wisdom and support I am truly grateful. I am thankful to share the hallways of Jefferson with my colleagues in Political Science and Sociology. A special thanks to Diane Fenner for all that she does. Finally, I am deeply grateful to Michael and Lisa Leffell for their support.

James Loeffler and Milton Shain offered essential feedback on the entire manuscript. Eitan Bar-Yosef and Arie Dubnov have been crucial interlocutors on Jews and the British Empire from the beginning. A very special thanks to Liora Halperin and Sunny Yudkoff for their support for many years now. Nina Kushner and Gohar Sidiqi have been indispensable writing partners and the best company as I finished this book. Countless other colleagues, teachers, and friends have read drafts, allowed me to share my work, provided critical feedback, helped with research logistics, and supported this work in myriad other ways. It gives me great pleasure to thank them here: Elissa Bemporad, Rachel Biale, Janine Blumburg, Michael Brenner, Dina Danon, Joseph Davis, Donna Robinson Divine, Ofer Dynes, David Feldman, Talia Fishman, Federica Francesconi, Shirli Gilbert, Jonathan Gribetz, Alma Heckman, Katie Hindmarch-Watson, Hilary Falb Kalisman, Alexander Kaye, Zachary Lockman, Nathan Lucky, Adam Mendelsohn, Yehudah Mirsky, David Myers, Pamela Nadell, Derek Penslar, Katherine Radburn, Nick Radburn, Gail Twersky Reimer, Judith Rosenbaum, Marina Rustow,

Naomi Seidman, Yoram Sharett, Eugene Sheppard, Gideon Shimoni, Rebecca Shimoni-Stoil, Dimitry Shumsky, Valerie Sperling, Ora Szekely, Frances Tanzer, Amy Weiss, Shayna Weiss, Ronald Zweig, and my longtime friend and coconspirator Geoffrey Levin.

I owe a huge debt of gratitude to the archivists and librarians at the Central Archives for the History of the Jewish People, the Central Zionist Archives in Jerusalem, the London Metropolitan Archives, the Middle East Centre Archive at St Antony's College, the National Library of Israel, the University of Cape Town Libraries Special Collections, and the Women's Library at the London School of Economics; without them, I could not have written this book. Thank you to the Moshe Sharett Heritage Society, the Central Zionist Archives, and GandhiServe India for making it possible to include the photographs in this book. I am also grateful to the archivists at the Anglo-Jewish Archives at the University of Southampton's Hartley Library, the British Library, the Harpenden & District Local History Society, the KKL-JNF Photo Archive, the Manchester Central Library, the National Archives (United Kingdom), and the Schocken Institute for their assistance in the course of my writing this book. A special thanks to Yochai Ben-Ghedalia, Juan-Paul Burke, Rachel Misrati, and Daniel Payne for their help. The wonderful librarians at Clark University's Robert H. Goddard Library have likewise made my research possible. A very special thank you to Laura Robinson, Lawrence Bolduc, and Katie Stebbins. Thank you finally to the Brandeis University Library for allowing this appreciative alumna to borrow books.

This book is actually a book thanks to the wonderful editorial team at Stanford University Press. Thank you to Margo Irvin for envisioning this project as a Stanford book and deftly guiding a first-time author through the process. My sincere thanks also to Kate Wahl, Thane Hale, Natalie Gabriela Rovero, Chris Peterson, Melissa Jauregui Chavez, Joe Abbott, and Fred Kameny. A heartfelt thanks to the series editors of Stanford Studies in Jewish History and Culture, Sarah Abrevaya Stein and David Biale. Sarah's scholarship has been foundational, and her historical imagination, deftly moving across borders and oceans, has inspired my work. I was privileged and am grateful to have experienced David's intellectual energy, deep kindness, and generous mentorship from this project's inception. I will miss him greatly.

ACKNOWLEDGMENTS

Writing this book has been a joy, made all the sweeter by the love and support of dear friends. Katherine Radburn is a kindred spirit, constant confidant, and the dearest of friends. Thank you to Kate Fischl, Brian Rayburn, Sarah Edelsburg, Adam Aviv, Nick Radburn, Sydnee Chavis, and Harrison Kessler for their friendship and support. Ellen Rothman has gone from great boss to cherished friend. John Fidler, Lisa Zalkind and Sarah Grimaud, the Insoft family, Annette Tolomeo, and Lorenzo Berra are the family you choose. A true blessing of this work has been the research and the places and people it has brought me back to: I am so grateful that trips to Israel meant spending precious time with Veronique Hassid and Simona Vainberg and that I had the company of Susanna Klosko in Jerusalem. Katrina Smith Kennedy has been watching out for me for a very long time, indeed, and gave me a home away from home in Scotland during my earliest archival pursuits.

My greatest thanks are to my family. I am grateful to my Ettenger and Imber cousins for their love and support. So much of my instinct as a historian and my reverence for the past was nurtured by my beloved grandparents, Frankie and Erwin Ettenger and Flip and Herman Imber, of blessed memory. I am in awe to witness the next generation now take shape. I thank my brother, David, for his love. And most of all, I thank my parents, Amy and Jonathan Imber, for loving and supporting me through it all. My mother has been my most steadfast champion and true north. My father, my blueprint, read every word on these pages and long before that, instilled in me a deep love of books, learning, and a good story. I am so proud to follow in his footsteps. I dedicate this book to them, with love and gratitude.

This book was made possible through the generous support of the Posen Foundation; the Social Science Research Council's International Dissertation Research Fellowship, with funds provided by the Andrew W. Mellon Foundation; the Association for Jewish Studies; the Leonard and Helen R. Stulman Jewish Studies Program at Johns Hopkins; the Johns Hopkins Department of History; the American Academy for Jewish Research; the Howard Berger-Ray Neilsen Endowed Chair of Judaic Studies at the College of Idaho; the Clark University Department of History; and the Michael and Lisa Leffell Chair in Modern Jewish History at Clark University.

Introduction

FROM HIS NEW STATION in Aleppo in January 1918, Moshe Shertok (later Sharett), then a twenty-three-year-old soldier in the Ottoman army, thought anxiously about the uncertain course of the war and what it would mean for Jewish futures in Palestine. The previous fall, the Middle Eastern theater of World War I had seen renewed action when the British Empire's Egyptian Expeditionary Forces broke through Ottoman lines in Beersheba, ending a six-month stalemate in southern Palestine. Two days later, on November 2, 1917, the British government had issued the Balfour Declaration. Conveyed in a letter from Foreign Secretary Arthur Balfour to the Anglo-Jewish leader Walter Rothschild, the short statement expressed Britain's intention to help facilitate the establishment of a "national home for the Jewish people" in Palestine. In December, British troops had taken Jerusalem.

Born in 1894 in the Russian Empire in the port city of Kherson, Shertok immigrated to Ottoman Palestine as a child with his family in 1906. After living for two years in the Arab village of Ein Siniya, where the young Shertok learned Arabic, the family relocated to Jaffa. Shertok was a member of the first graduating class of the Herzliya Hebrew Gymnasium, and like many of his classmates and other young Zionist leaders at the time, he believed that the future of the Yishuv, the Jewish community in Palestine, depended on cooperation with the Ottoman state. In pursuit of this goal, Shertok continued his studies at the University of Constantinople, where he acquired Turkish and became acquainted with the emerging leaders of the Labor Zionist movement, including David Ben-Gurion. While Shertok was on a visit home to Jaffa in the fall of 1914, the Ottoman Empire entered the war on the side of the Central Powers; unable to return to Constantinople, Shertok taught Turkish at the Herzliya Gymnasium before eventually enlisting in the Ottoman army in April 1916. When his impressive linguistic abilities became known to his superiors, Shertok was seconded to German forces in the region as an interpreter. In January 1918, he was assigned to Aleppo, which sat at the crossroads of the Ottoman Empire's overtaxed rail system. There, Shertok spent his days working for the German military in transportation logistics, translating documents between Turkish and German, an assignment he found monotonous and mind-numbing.[1] He longed for the war to be over so that he could return to Palestine and his family.

British military advances in the region had expanded the scope of possible postwar outcomes for the Yishuv. Many Jews who found themselves on the British side of the front had welcomed the army as liberators. News spread that Britain would create a new battalion made up of Jews from Palestine to join the already existing Jewish Legion. More and more young Jews who had enlisted in the Ottoman army, including some of Shertok's closest friends, defected, choosing to risk execution—the punishment for desertion—in order to aid in the British war effort. But Shertok believed the outcome of the war was still uncertain. In a January 1918 letter to Tzippora Meirov, his future wife, who was in Haifa at the time, Shertok expressed worry that Jews in Palestine were ill-prepared for what might transpire. "You pin all your hopes on only one option," he wrote, referring to British victory over all of Palestine, "and cast out ... the rest of the possibilities and combinations that are not to your liking." Shertok explained that he wanted to be prepared for all potentialities. If 90 percent of Jews hoped for the "good option," then 10 percent needed to prepare for grimmer outcomes. "And should there be only 10 of us, there will at least be one prepared for disaster," he reasoned.[2]

As winter stretched into spring and spring into summer, fighting on the western front forced Britain to slow its offensive in Palestine. Amid this impasse, Shertok wondered if the Ottoman Empire might break with Germany in order to negotiate a better settlement with the Allies; perhaps Palestine, or at least its northern portion, might remain in Ottoman hands. Then again, perhaps the British might take all of Palestine; but would one imperial ruler be better than another? Shertok had deep concerns about the Yishuv's ability to harness and assert power in whatever future arrangement transpired. He worried that recent developments, including the formation of the Zionist Commission in March, were still ultimately under British control.[3] "All the grand initiatives are not in our hands and we are but beggars in them, and the ones that are in our hands are small and inconsequential just as before, and maybe even more than before," he feared.[4] Despite these misgivings, Shertok decided to add English to his linguistic repertoire—his eighth language by that point—obtaining a language-instruction book and dedicating his free time to study. If the British conquered the rest of the region, English would become an essential language, and he wanted to be prepared.

In September, the British renewed their offensive, pushing north, capturing the rest of Palestine, and eventually reaching Aleppo on October 25, 1918. Five days later, the Ottoman Empire officially surrendered, and war in the Middle Eastern theater came to an end. Shertok, who burned his Ottoman uniform and dressed in civilian clothes for fear of being sent to Constantinople with the retreating army, was finally able to return to his family in Palestine, now entirely under British military occupation. In a letter to Tzippora, Shertok shared that after thinking about the future and trying to anticipate what would happen for so long, he yearned to live in the present. "Nevertheless, to write about this present before it has taken shape and been determined, is indeed once again to relent to hopes and aspirations," he admitted.[5]

Even in these early, formative years as an Ottoman soldier, Shertok evinced a kind of political sensibility and calculation that would become a critical part of the Jewish political imagination over the next three decades. That political thought was based on the fundamental assumption that the Yishuv and Palestine would remain, at least for the foreseeable future, under some form of imperial control. That assumption, in turn, produced an anticipatory outlook, bound up in two intertwined questions: what would empire, in this period of flux, mean for Jewish futures in Palestine? And given the fact of imperial oversight, what might Jews do—what power or

FIGURE 1 Moshe Shertok (standing, center) in his Ottoman uniform with fellow enlisted Herzliya Hebrew Gymnasium students in 1916. Courtesy of the Moshe Sharett Heritage Society.

agency might they be able to grasp—to shape their own destiny, not only for Jews already in Palestine but, increasingly as the years wore on, for the masses of Jews still in Europe?

In the ensuing years and decades, Shertok would come to play a central role in navigating Jewish relationships with the British Empire. But his uncertainty over what any relationship would mean for Jewish futures, bound up as it was in these questions and their undetermined answers, would remain. The reconstruction of that uncertainty and the kind of political thought it provoked lies at the heart of this book.

After more than two years of military administration in Palestine—the Ottoman Empire vanquished—Allied powers assigned to Britain a League of Nations Class A mandate for Palestine in April 1920. Designed as a provisional legal measure to guide former Ottoman territories toward eventual independence, the mandate brought Palestine—and Jewish national aspirations along with it—into the British imperial fold. The British Empire not only came to encompass a new, burgeoning Jewish population in the wake of World War I, but as the administrator of a potential Jewish national home in Palestine, Britain also assumed a pivotal role in determining Jewish political futures both in and beyond the empire.

Palestine, and the solutions to the Jewish predicament in Europe that Zionism proposed, came to appeal to a diverse array of Jews, with varying and often clashing politics, for a broad range of reasons. This book follows the political thought of figures typically understood as belonging to three very different political camps. I examine dedicated ideologues, including Moshe Shertok, as well as Chaim Arlosoroff, important leaders and political functionaries in the Zionist movement; their commitment to the creation of a Jewish national home in Palestine—to the systematic creation of Jewish settlement, society, and polity—stemmed from their deeply held nationalist convictions. But I also look at Jews, including Norman Bentwich, the Anglo-Jewish attorney general of Mandate Palestine, who supported the building of a Jewish cultural center in Palestine but imagined they might realize that goal while safeguarding Jewish-Arab relations and without seeking separate Jewish political sovereignty. Finally, I also examine Jews, including Helen Bentwich (Norman Bentwich's wife), who felt compelled to think about Zionism and Palestine not because of their own deeply held political or cultural commitments—in other words, not because they considered themselves to be Zionists—but because of exigency. Whether it was the upheavals of World War I, periods of unrest in interwar Palestine, or, most significantly, the crisis and catastrophe of the Nazi rise to power and the Holocaust, exigency propelled "non-Zionist" Jews to turn to Palestine as a possible solution—if not for themselves, then for imperiled Jews. What these diverse Jews all had in common was a shared commitment to a politics of improving the global Jewish condition and an accompanying conviction (with different geneses to be sure) that Palestine represented the best possible option—or at the very least, an essential part of the answer—to the tribulations of modern Jewish life.

Beyond the protagonists of this book, this "turn" to Palestine also held true for the Jewish masses of Eastern Europe, as well as for those in Central and Western Europe, even though commitments to Zionism were ever shifting and variegated, waxing and waning depending on the situations in both Palestine and Europe. In Eastern Europe, the heartland of Jewish nationalist thought, Palestine seemed to many to offer the best possible avenue toward a more secure life. Following the passing of restrictive quotas in 1921 and 1924, immigration to the United States—a solution taken up by more than two and a half million Jews since 1881—was no longer a possibility for the vast majority of the millions of Jews now living in the new and expanded nation-states of post–World War I Eastern Europe, including Poland and Romania. Other political visions offering solutions *in* Eastern Europe to the Jewish dilemma, including diaspora nationalism and Yiddishism, suffered the successive blows of World War I, the Russian Revolution and Civil War, and the rise of Nazism and resurgent antisemitism. Driven as much, or more, by disillusionment and mounting fear as by nationalist ideals and agendas, more and more Jews who had previously supported these paths would look elsewhere in desperation for answers.[6] With the Nazi rise to power in early 1933 and the subsequent Nazification of German society, many Jews who found themselves at the center of the crisis would likewise turn to Palestine as an escape, even when they had previously felt little connection or attraction to Zionism.[7]

In Western Europe, as well as in the United States, Jews who had championed the liberal promise of integration would also grow to regard Palestine as a solution, not for themselves but for the Jews in jeopardy to their east. Western Jews, including the well-off, well-integrated Anglo-Jewish establishment, had a long practice of intervening on behalf of persecuted Jews in other reaches of the globe. Yet the tradition of Jewish *internationalism*, epitomized by Moses Montefiore and Adolphe Crémieux's efforts during the Damascus Affair, did not translate easily into enthusiasm for Jewish *nationalism*.[8] Many Anglo-Jewish elites, for example, worried that support for Zionism would call into question their patriotism and loyalty to Britain—that hard-won political and social integration ever accompanied by an anxiety over its precariousness.[9] But as the upheavals of the early twentieth century made it increasingly challenging for any Jew committed to Jewish welfare to ignore Palestine and Zionism, a group of Western Jewish elites emerged who were neither Zionist nor anti-Zionist. Rather, these non-Zionist Jews would come to regard a Jewish home in Palestine not as a political ideal but as the only rational option left for much of the world's Jewish population. To be sure, in the relationship between the Zionist movement and these essentially liberal integrationist Western Jewish actors, there were periods of more intense cooperation and periods of more pronounced disagreement, mirroring the ups and downs of the era: the calamity of World War I, the relative quiescence of the 1920s, the Nazi-imposed "social death" of German Jewry, the increasingly catastrophic economic and political outlook facing Jews in Eastern Europe in the 1930s, and the destruction of European Jewry and its aftermath in the 1940s. In those periods of cooperation, marked by exigency and crisis, Western Jewish non-Zionists would come to find themselves working in concert with Zionists, their differing politics secondary to the exigencies of the time. Thus, for Zionism's ideologues, but for many who had been indifferent or even critical toward Zionism, Palestine emerged as perhaps the best possibility—in an increasingly narrowing range of options—for a safe future.

But the growing centrality of Palestine to a broad range of Jews is only the point of departure for this book. The fact of that centrality—that Palestine and Zionism became so vital for so many Jews—meant that Britain and its empire after 1917 likewise became crucial. And for that reason—and here is where this book begins conceptually—Jews living across the British Empire, from Palestine to India and from South Africa to the British metropole, came to occupy a unique position in global Jewish political life. A diverse coterie of Jews—Eastern European Zionists who had immigrated to Palestine, Baghdadi Jewish elites in India navigating the volatile line between imperial loyalty and anticolonial liberation, South African Jewish elites with a variety of relationships to the Jewish community and to Zionism, and British Jewish non-Zionists, among others—suddenly found themselves at the center of Jewish politics in the post–World War I era. They alone were forced to confront the question of Jewish political futures while living in the empire that now held the mandate for Palestine, the territory at the center of Jewish political aspirations.[10] To complicate the picture further, the development of Jewish nationalism occurred against the backdrop of the growth of general anticolonial and nationalist ferment across the British Empire. In the same moment that Zionism was expanding and maturing as a movement, so, too, were Pan-Arabism, the pan-Islamic Khilafat movement, and the Indian independence movement. Just a week after the Twelfth Zionist Congress convened in Carlsbad, Czechoslovakia, in September 1921, Gandhi made the historic decision to divest himself of his cap and vest and to don only the loincloth that would come to symbolize India's struggle against British colonial rule. Jews across the British Empire thus found themselves navigating their identities as Jews, Zionists, locals, and British imperial subjects across a profoundly plastic political landscape, their own uncertain futures—and potentially the future of Jews the world over—bound up in the uncertain fate of the British Empire.

This book examines how Jewish elites and leaders from four sites—Mandate Palestine, India, South Africa, and metropolitan Britain—strove to understand and navigate the changing and potentially conflicting relationships of British imperialism, Zionism, and anticolonial national and transnational political movements from 1917 to 1948, the period of British rule in Palestine. I reconstruct how the British Empire and the consideration and negotiation of its many possible fates—from the persistence of imperial rule to the triumph of anticolonial political movements—moved from the margins to the center of the Jewish political imagination. Jews from Palestine, India, South Africa, and Britain imagined Jewish political futures that would take shape within the context of an enduring British Empire. They imagined that Palestine might join the ranks of the British Commonwealth of Nations as an autonomous dominion, such as Australia, South Africa, and Canada. These Jewish elites also viewed Britain and the British Empire as wellsprings of cultural and political ideals and ideas, as models and inspiration for Jewish political life—particularly in Palestine.

But those same Jewish elites and leaders also envisioned Jewish political futures that might break from the British Empire. They anticipated the potential victory of anticolonial nationalisms across the empire and worked to build ties with the leaders of those movements, including Muslim and Hindu nationalists in India. This negotiation of any number of potential outcomes produced a range of political behaviors, strategies, practices, and vocabularies that on first glance seem paradoxical. Leaders of the Baghdadi Jewish community in Calcutta forcefully asserted their European cultural identity in their dealings with colonial authorities but at the same time remained deeply embedded in local elite Indian and Jewish worlds. Chaim Arlosoroff, a prominent Labor Zionist leader in interwar Palestine, became a steadfast proponent of the Zionist-British partnership, and though he eventually abandoned his dedication to the alliance, he remained entrenched in British social circles in Palestine and developed a close friendship with British High Commissioner Arthur Wauchope. In South Africa, a small group of both Zionist and non-Zionist Jews who had befriended Gandhi during his time in the country became the chief mediators between the Zionist movement and Indian nationalism in the 1930s. And while these South African Jews supported Indian independence, they also defended Zionist ties with the British Empire. Likewise, Moshe Shertok, who became responsible for directing Zionist foreign policy beginning in the mid-1930s, insisted on maintaining productive relations with Britain while simultaneously working to build ties with anticolonial leaders in other parts of the empire, particularly India.

Within the frame of its reconstruction of the centrality of the British Empire, including its anticolonial horizons, to the Jewish political imagination, this book argues that these ostensible contradictions and incongruities were, in fact, all part of a broad, shared horizon of uncertainty—uncertainty over Jewish national futures (varied and malleable as those visions were), uncertainty over the future of Jewish life in Europe, and uncertainty over British imperial futures amid the rise of anticolonial nationalisms. This book's conception of politics sits uneasily in classic typologies and represents a departure from the way historians most often approach the question of modern Jewish politics.[11] For example, Jewish historians have long examined Jewish relationships to a political idea or movement—for instance, the Jewish involvement in radical leftist politics or the Jewish engagement with Revisionist Zionism.[12] More recently, historians have taken a cultural-historical approach, examining Jewish relationships to a public or civic identity promoted by a state or empire.[13] I offer a third approach: the politics in this case were not the expression of a fixed ideology or the result of synthesis or acculturation with a non-Jewish society, even though the British Empire figures at the center of this story. Rather, I reconstruct a politics of uncertainty—a politics of trying to envision and navigate any number of undetermined futures that could produce drastically different consequences for the Jewish community.

Critically, the *kind* of uncertainty that shaped Jewish political strategy and outlook depended greatly on the period. This book moves through three profoundly different decades of the Jewish experience. The relative stability of the 1920s produced an uncertainty of possibility, a broad array of visions of what Palestine might become—a dominion, a binational state, a federal state—if always visions still tempered by realities on the ground. The 1930s became a decade of narrowing options and increasingly untenable life circumstances for millions of Central and Eastern European Jews. Zionists and non-Zionists in Palestine and across the British Empire, as they worked desperately to find solutions to the growing crisis, experienced the uncertainty of an impending but yet-unknown catastrophe and the cruel momentum of time, measured not in days or years but in immigration certificates granted and refugees saved. At the same time, however, and in contrast to the increasingly circumscribed agency of Jews under threat in Europe, Jews in Palestine in the 1930s confronted the growing crisis in Europe and rising tensions with Britain in a period when Jewish military and economic power in Palestine was actually *stronger* than it had ever before been; this fact, as chapter 6 explores, changed their political calculations vis-à-vis Britain. Beyond the Jewish world, uncertainty over the British Empire's fate, particularly the question of Indian independence, also opened new political possibilities and alliances for Jews in the empire. The uncertainty of the 1940s was of yet a different kind. As Jews in the empire confronted the destruction of European Jewry and worked to rescue the surviving remnant, another reckoning was unfolding: the postcolonial world seemed imminent, but its contours were yet to be determined. India and Palestine each faced an unclear constitutional future: would they remain as unitary states or be partitioned? For Jews in the empire, anticipating and preparing for this unknown future, with so many political variables, proved a daunting challenge, one that forced them to confront their own uneasy place in the postcolonial world-to-come. This politics of uncertainty was provoked both by exigency *and* by possibility, both by a sense of narrowing options *and* by a context of expanding power. It was at once an emotional state *and* a political logic that gave life to an astonishing array of plans of action and aspirations.[14]

The geographic sites that frame this project were distinct imperial spaces. Palestine, as a League of Nations Class A mandate, was governed by Britain by international sanction, with the intention that the local population would eventually take over the country's administration. India, the cornerstone of the British Empire, was administered by direct Crown rule. South Africa, by contrast, functioned as a self-governing, autonomous dominion. Finally, the British metropole, hub of the empire, was both home to its own Jewish community and host to imperial elites from around the empire, including to Jews from Palestine. After World War I and the creation of the British mandate, Britain also emerged as the center of Zionist political and diplomatic activity in the interwar and immediate post–World War II period. These four sites represent more than simply a comparative constellation chosen for examination by virtue of their distinct attributes. Rather, this spatial framework reflects how historical actors understood the political geographies that defined their lives and work.

The Jewish elites who lived in and moved between these locales were equally distinct. This project examines four different groups of them: British Jews who spent long stretches in Palestine, including mandatory officials and their families; Zionist leaders in Palestine, especially members of the Jewish Agency, the country's official representative Zionist leadership body; Baghdadi Jewish elites in India, immensely wealthy from their participation in global trade and commerce, who directed Jewish communal life in Calcutta and Bombay; and Jewish cultural and communal elites from South Africa, particularly those who developed friendships with Gandhi during his long tenure in the country (from 1893 to 1914). These individuals were very different types of Jews and, indeed, very different types of elites, reflecting the diverse range of ethnic backgrounds, cultural and religious practices, politics, professional pursuits, and socioeconomic statuses among the heterogeneous Jewish communities living throughout the empire. Critically, they espoused a broad range of attitudes toward Zionism, a movement that itself contained many distinct and sometimes opposing visions. Some Jewish elites in the British Empire identified as cultural Zionists, believing that Palestine should be a center for cultural, spiritual, and psychical regeneration that would benefit—and not negate—the worldwide Jewish diaspora. Others supported political Zionism, seeing national development in Palestine as the solution to the increasingly untenable state of Jewish life in Europe. Political Zionists in the British Empire identified with a range of Zionist parties and positions, including the Labor, General, and Revisionist branches of the movement. Both among and within these Zionist parties, Jews in the British Empire—especially in Palestine and South Africa—hotly debated what type of government should eventually be adopted in Palestine and what role both Palestinian Arabs and the British should play in that future polity. By contrast, though many Jews in India ultimately came to support Zionism, they never divided into competing political parties. Instead, for many Baghdadi Jews, religious and romantic attachment to the Land of Israel inspired their commitment. Finally, other Jews in the British Empire did not identify as Zionist at all.

Despite their varied backgrounds, these Jewish elites shared common attributes. They all served as intermediaries between their Jewish communities and British and local authorities, while simultaneously confronting Jewish nationalist ideas. Many of them also personally knew each other; they corresponded about issues facing the Jewish community, studied in the same schools and universities, spent time as neighbors in London, and even married one another. More abstractly, these Jewish elites were all linked by a common consideration of Jewish political futures in an empire in flux, amid imperial retrenchment and rising anticolonial sentiment. Despite their diverse backgrounds, their varied relationships to the British metropole, and—most significantly—their wide-ranging attitudes toward Zionism, these elites ended up working together to secure Jewish political futures against this shared horizon of uncertainty and change. This book, in other words, explores not only what *Zionism* came to mean but also what *non-Zionism* functionally meant in a period when the uncertainty and, furthermore, the exigencies of the era—namely crisis and catastrophe in Europe and the concomitant fact of limited options for Jewish rescue and refuge—practically demanded that politically conscious Jews, no matter the substance of their politics, consider Palestine as a solution.

This book also helps us rethink the role of the state and state power in modern Jewish history. Jews across the British Empire—cultural Zionists, political Zionists, and non-Zionists alike—promoted numerous and shifting visions of Jewish political futures for Palestine that variously embraced, rejected, and tabled the political model of the state. Yet many of these British imperial Jews, though they had vastly different political commitments and ideas about the state, collectively assumed that Palestine would become a British dominion. Of course, Palestine never did become a dominion; we can view dominionization, then, as a member of the pantheon of "roads not taken" by the Zionist movement, along with binationalism, federalism, and autonomism. In examining these visions, historians more recently have revealed the capaciousness of the interwar Zionist political imagination and, in doing so, have challenged the teleology of national independence—that is, the long-standing tendency in the historiography to assume that all Zionist activity before 1948 was geared toward the establishment of an independent Jewish nation-state.[15] But the dominion idea differed intrinsically from these other "nonstatist" visions. Though dominion status appealed to some Jews in the British Empire because it created space for cultural autonomy while abjuring political sovereignty, the idea interested other Zionists precisely *because* it would give the Yishuv state-like power. For instance, Palestine's attorney general, Norman Bentwich, saw the dominion idea as a constitutional option that could accommodate both Jewish and Arab cultural autonomy without separate political sovereignty. But Chaim Arlosoroff, by contrast, found dominionization appealing because it would allow the Yishuv to direct land development, secure major international loans, and control immigration—the last of which, in particular, became all the more pressing following the Nazi rise to power.[16] These abilities were all critical elements of state power; other dominions in the British Commonwealth, including Canada and Australia, possessed these powers. The dominion idea, then, became a receptacle of both nonstatist and statist visions; commitments to imperial belonging, Jewish-Arab rapprochement, and Jewish national independence were all vectored through it. Put differently, to frame Zionist political visions along a simple binary of statist and nonstatist ideas risks losing sight of a much more complex middle ground in which imperial subalterns worked to harness what power they could, using existing imperial models, to effect their political goals. Indeed, Jews were not the only ones in the British Empire thinking about dominionization. In the same moment, some Indian independence leaders, including Gandhi—in a strategy that played to both Indian nationalist ambitions and British imperial interests—proposed dominion status for India.

My approach to analyzing Jewish politics in the British Empire is twofold. First, the project assesses the intellectual-historical question of how Jewish elites actively thought about and approached the changing relationships between Zionism, British imperialism, and local anticolonial nationalisms. How did Jews frame their political relationship to the imperial state? How did they reconcile Zionism with other nationalisms? Second, I examine the sociocultural question of how quotidian practices, convivial spaces, and affective ties served as sites of political formation and expression for Jewish elites in the empire. How did the friendships they formed, the parties they attended, and the civic and cultural activities in which they participated shape and reflect their politics? While this dual intellectual-historical and sociocultural approach is useful for understanding politics in any setting, the payoff is especially high in assessing imperial contexts where structures of power and racial hierarchies were created and maintained just as much through social ties and daily practices as they were through laws. In these settings, where one lived, how one dressed, what one read, how one ate, and which clubs one frequented all mattered—and mattered *politically*.[17] In reconstructing these convivial spaces and affective ties, I argue that close, personal relationships played a central role in shaping Jewish political outlook and strategy. These personal ties took diverse forms with distinct gendered dimensions, including companionate marriages, intense homosocial male friendships, and female-led volunteer networks made up of individuals who had known each other often for decades. Taken together, these relationships show that the public face of Zionism and broader Jewish political activism often concealed a more intimate reality, one shaped by abiding ties and gender dynamics not typically identified with the world of politics.[18]

This book is the first monograph to consider twentieth-century Jewish political actors from across the British Empire and to assess Jewish politics in a multisite, British imperial context. It yields critical new insight into modern Jewish history, British imperial history, and the history of Israel/Palestine, as well as the histories of Zionism and nationalism. My research builds on and contributes to a growing literature that explores the experiences of Jews in modern imperial contexts. It is part of a scholarly effort to expand the Jewish historiographic geographical imagination that has been limited by the Eurocentric tropes of modern Jewish history, especially emancipation, secularization, acculturation, assimilation, and antisemitism.[19] More specifically, modern Jewish historiography and British imperial historiography are two fields that, despite important historical overlap, have only recently begun to engage one another. British imperial historians have largely avoided Jewish topics, perhaps in part, as David Feldman suggests, out of a fear of reproducing associations between Jewish finance and imperialism made by some late nineteenth- and early twentieth-century critics of empire. Likewise, Jewish historians, even Anglo-Jewish historians, have with few exceptions mostly ignored the British Empire.[20] Beyond the British Empire, recent work on Jews in the Ottoman and French empires has expanded our understanding of the modern Jewish experience and furthered the development of important theoretical foundations for assessing the relationship between Jews and empire. Yet much of this scholarship has focused on the ways that Jews experienced colonialism specifically *outside* the context of Israel, Palestine, or Zionism.[21] Finally, a new crop of scholarship on the global dimensions of modern Jewish politics, particularly in relation to the issues of minority rights, human rights, and humanitarianism, has done essential work recasting the geographic, temporal, and conceptual frameworks of Jewish political imagination and activity.[22] Much of this work has emphasized the *international* and *transnational* aspects of this history—for example, by looking at the League of Nations and the new international politics it represented as a locus of Jewish political strategy—but has generally conceived of the *imperial* as of waning or secondary importance.[23] In these accounts, the British Colonial Office, for example, is but one of many satellites in the international orbit of modern Jewish political activism. The Jewish historical actors in this book, by contrast, understood the British Empire—both its enduring imperial and anticolonial potentialities—as *the* central broader political framework of their life's work.

A book that examines the relationship between British imperial Jews and Palestine, as well as Zionists and British imperialism, obviously finds itself in the maelstrom of debate on how to talk about Zionism, Palestine/Israel, and colonialism. Scholarly inquiry into these topics immediately puts into play many tension-laden historiographical impulses and legacies. More recently, historians have framed Zionists in mandate-era Palestine variously as agents and subaltern servitors of British imperialism;[24] as part of a settler colonial movement, with similarities to settler colonial societies elsewhere in the British Empire, as well as other overseas European empires;[25] and as historical actors whose lives were textured in various ways by the presence of a colonial regime but who also possessed their own ideas about European imperialism and Orientalism that informed their encounter with Palestinian Arabs, as well as non-European Jews.[26] Much of this work has developed alongside scholarship outside of Jewish history and the history of Zionism that assesses Mandate Palestine as an explicitly *colonial* space or frames Palestine in comparison with other British colonial spaces, particularly in terms of settler colonialism and partition.[27] There are many reasons to understand Zionists in Palestine, in their relations to the British Empire and in their experience of British imperialism, as distinct from Palestinian Arabs and other colonized peoples—whether because of their relation with the colonial regime, the power they were able to wield, their conceptions of and commitments to European modernity, or their (often ambiguous or contested) identity as European or white (or, rather, "white but not quite").[28] At the same time, Zionists in Palestine were still subordinate to mandatory authorities and British oversight. Jewish land development and immigration, although supported by the British at times during the interwar period, were also sometimes steeply curtailed; Zionists were unable to set those terms on their own, though they worked to influence them through intense lobbying and ultimately illegal tactics. The goals of building a new society and new settlements and facilitating immigration—the success (or failure) of which shaped the Zionist sense of power and powerlessness—also set them apart from colonized peoples in other reaches of the empire. Zionist concerns may have overlapped with other subalterns in some ways (for example, in the realm of nation building broadly construed) but also differed substantially (for instance, in navigating the logistics of importing an increasingly imperiled stateless nation into another land). Yet these goals and concerns also set Zionism apart from colonial movements, with metropolitan centers and much more powerful sponsors. My book steps into this historiographic space not to challenge one approach or champion another (indeed, I build on each) but rather to argue that the historical actors I examine (both Zionists and non-Zionists) were thinking about these very questions *in real time*. Jews in the British Empire worked to harness British imperial power but also grappled—in ways that transformed their political strategies and outlooks—with the recognition that there were limits to that endeavor; they looked to settler colonial societies in the British Empire as models but also worked to build ties with anticolonial leaders in India. What this book examines, then, is how Jewish political actors in the British Empire sought to negotiate the reality of imperial control in Palestine and all that it might mean for Zionism, coupled with the growing possibility that the empire might collapse as anticolonial movements near and far gained traction.

This book features Jewish political thinkers who grappled with the question of polity and considered seriously futures for Palestine beyond the nation-state. Some readers may anticipate, then, that the book will leave them with lessons gleaned from the "paths not taken": what might have been had a Zionism devoid of politics or one that abjured the idea of the sovereign nation-state prevailed? This is also a book about empire and the Zionist movement's relationship to it. For that reason, some readers might likewise expect to learn a history of Zionism *as* colonialism: can we locate in the history here colonial genealogies still reverberating and manifest in Israel/Palestine today? The limitations of transposing lessons derived from the mandate era to the post-1967 political landscape aside, neither expectation—neither question—captures what this book is, in fact, about and the lessons I hope to offer. Here, the reader will encounter historical actors who thought seriously about state power not because they revered the state as an ideal or were committed to a politics of Jewish supremacy but because they ultimately concluded that Jewish security and survival, in Palestine and beyond, depended on Jews being able to wield state-like power or, at the very least, critical elements of it. And while they had diverse relationships to Britain and to questions of imperialism, the historical actors I examine were committed to working with the British Empire for similar reasons—because it was a global power and it controlled Palestine. As the mandate years wore on and the Jewish situation in Europe became increasingly perilous, political Zionists, cultural Zionists, binationalists, and non-Zionists alike understood that saving Jews meant cooperating with the British Empire. This book, then, is also a history of political actors intensely aware of the limitations of their own power and keenly attuned to global power dynamics. The world of the British Empire reconstructed here is long past, so a great deal of this history is now foreclosed. But perhaps this book can still prompt readers to think seriously—like the historical actors in these pages—about the purpose of state power, the place of (now American) global power in the region, and the relationship between the two.

The first chapter examines the experiences of Helen Bentwich, a social worker, and her husband, Norman Bentwich, the Anglo-Jewish attorney general of Mandate Palestine, as they negotiated their identities as Britons, colonial actors, Jews, and Zionists in interwar Jerusalem. Over the course of more than a decade in Palestine (1919–30), Helen came to find herself more at home with new Jewish friends than in British circles. A committed feminist and socialist and a resolute non-Zionist, Helen's attitudes toward Zionists and the Zionist movement—initially so hostile—also shifted. Resentful of British colonial standards of femininity and increasingly disturbed by rising antisemitism among the British in Palestine, Helen came to empathize (though never fully identify) with Jewish nationalism and found herself working on behalf of Jewish-led organizations in Palestine, particularly in the realm of social welfare efforts. In contrast to his wife, Norman arrived in Palestine already an ardent Zionist. This chapter shows how his support for binational, autonomist Zionism was informed by his British Labour ideals and British conceptions of nationhood. As Norman built ties with binationalists in Palestine, particularly with intellectuals and academics affiliated with the Hebrew University, he was forced to disentangle his role as a British mandatory official with his visions of Jewish political futures. Drawing on a vast collection of personal correspondence and memoirs, this chapter both synthesizes and challenges the historiography of elite British sociability in the empire and the growing body of work on the diversity of interwar Jewish nationalist expression. Through an examination of Helen and Norman Bentwich's marriage—a companionate and egalitarian partnership—the chapter explores the complex convergence of interwar Zionist and non-Zionist visions of Jewish political futures in the context of the British Empire.

Chapter 2 recovers the British horizons of Zionist politics by examining the ways that Zionist leaders in Palestine thought about the "British Question"—that is, Zionism's relationship with Britain and the role that relationship would play in the future of the Yishuv. The chapter focuses on the Labor Zionist leader Chaim Arlosoroff, whose extensive political writings and daily work on behalf of the Zionist Organization capture the myriad ways interwar Zionists thought about the British Question. Arlosoroff believed that the ideals and lessons derived from British culture and history represented worthy models for the Yishuv, and he pioneered efforts to make knowledge of the British Empire accessible to a Hebrew-reading public. He also believed that long-term cooperation and understanding between the Yishuv and Britain were critical to realizing Zionist aspirations. Most significantly, he thought seriously about possible future political formations for Palestine that would take shape within the framework of the British Empire, including the prospect of dominion status. By examining Arlosoroff's own grappling with nonstatist *and* statist Zionist futures—with the dominion idea encompassing elements of each—this chapter shows how the British Empire remained at the center of both disparate political visions.

Chapter 3 shows that at the nadir of Zionist fortunes in the early 1930s, a profound uncertainty about the viability of the Yishuv compelled Chaim Arlosoroff, Norman Bentwich, Gershon Agronsky, and others to disentangle their visions of Zionist and British futures in distinct ways. The question of Jewish immigration and land development provoked bitter debate; Zionists had lost faith in Britain's commitment to the terms of the Balfour Declaration; Jewish-Arab relations appeared equally bleak; and, most significantly, the rise of Nazism in Germany meant that Palestine might soon need to accommodate thousands of Jewish refugees and face the potential of another global conflict. Arlosoroff, whose transformation was the most radical, argued that Zionism's only hope for survival might be to overthrow by force British mandatory authorities and establish a minority government in Palestine. Long a champion of the Zionist-British partnership, Arlosoroff now questioned the fundamental tenability of Zionist futures in the British Empire. Norman Bentwich was forced to abandon his work on behalf of mandatory authorities; he could no longer be both a British official and a Zionist. Amid the rise of Pan-Islamist movements, Gershon Agronsky, a journalist working for the Jewish Agency, decided that rather than turning to British imperial powers, Zionists should build ties with moderate Muslim activists in India. The chapter frames the impulse to divorce Zionist and British futures against the actual social landscape of Jerusalem at the time, a space in which Zionist and British elites continued to dine together, attend parties and performances, and develop close, communicative friendships.

Leaving the setting of Mandate Palestine, chapter 4 moves to British India, exploring how Baghdadi Jewish elites navigated the potentially conflicting pulls of British imperialism, Indian nationalism, and Zionism. Focusing on the lives of Rachel and David Ezra, a Baghdadi Jewish couple from Calcutta, the chapter examines two disparate sites of political formation: first, a memorial campaign led by David Ezra to have his Baghdadi community classified as European in the Bengali electorate and, second, the quotidian practices and affective ties that shaped the Ezras' embeddedness in elite Indian and Jewish cultures. In this second space, the Ezras expressed a tentative hopefulness about the prospect of Indian self-rule and continued to support Zionism, even as British attitudes toward Jewish nationalism were becoming increasingly hostile. The two sites of political formation examined in this chapter each generated distinct political vocabularies, categories, and concerns. The chapter argues, however, that both sites were informed by a single political horizon: a growing uncertainty about Jewish futures in India amid the rise of Indian nationalism and the changing terms of British imperial rule.

Chapter 5 journeys across the empire, beginning in South Africa and moving to Britain, Palestine, and India. As Zionist leaders in Palestine and Britain became increasingly convinced in the 1930s that imperial and anticolonial politics in India mattered a great deal to Jewish futures in Palestine, South African Jews emerged as uniquely capable of navigating this issue. During his time in South Africa, from 1893–1914, Gandhi developed close relationships with a number of South African Jews, particularly Hermann Kallenbach and Henry Polak. Both Kallenbach—who became a Zionist—and Polak—who remained a committed non-Zionist—endeavored to convince Gandhi to support the development of the Jewish national home and worked to establish connections between Zionist and Indian leaders. Although they held different opinions on Zionism and possessed distinct relationships to the Jewish community, both Kallenbach and Polak understood Jewish political fates to be bound up in Indian ones. More broadly, this chapter shows how Zionists saw transnational and transimperial relationships as crucial to the future of the Zionist movement and how the British Empire persisted in shaping Zionist geopolitical thought on the eve of world war.

Chapter 6 assesses Jewish relationships with the British Empire during World War II, questioning and revising the commonly accepted paradigm, as articulated by David Ben-Gurion, that Jews would fight the war as if there were no white paper and fight the white paper as if there were no war—in other words, that Jews would simultaneously fight on behalf of the Allied war effort *and* work to end restrictive British immigration policies in Palestine. Although the period of World War II is commonly understood to be the era in which the Zionist movement began to view the United States (increasingly in place of Britain) as the world power that could help effect its goals, this chapter shows that Britain and its empire necessarily remained a central focus of Jewish activity across the Zionist and non-Zionist political spectrum throughout the war. This chapter weaves together the continuing stories of Norman and Helen Bentwich, on the one hand, and Moshe Shertok, who had succeeded Chaim Arlosoroff as head of the Political Department, on the other. Norman Bentwich, who had worked on behalf of the League of Nations High Commission for Refugees, traveled across the British Empire attempting to secure entry for Jewish refugees from Nazi Europe. Helen Bentwich, meanwhile, played an essential role in organizing the Kindertransport. Moshe Shertok, who was often the highest-ranking Zionist official in Palestine during the war, led the charge to revive a Jewish battalion in the British Army, which had previously existed during World War I. Furthermore, he maintained that Zionists must continue their relationship with Britain, not just in the context of the war but for an anticipated postwar era. Though the Bentwiches and Shertok were deeply divided in their politics over the questions of partition, where Jewish refugees should settle, and the future polity of Palestine, they shared the fundamental assumption that the British Empire represented the last best hope for Jewish futures amid utter catastrophe. Born out of sober political realism and narrowing options, this attitude was also accompanied by deep cynicism and frustration with the British government and British policy. This chapter makes clear that commitment to the British Empire often existed alongside fierce condemnation and critique, as Zionist political behavior began consciously to mirror anticolonial political movements in other reaches of the empire.

Facing a stark new reality after the Holocaust, Jews across the globe were forced to rebuild Jewish life in the wake of utter destruction. Jews in the British Empire confronted this unprecedented terrain as the fate of the empire was at long last revealed. The seventh and final chapter frames postwar Jewish relationships to the British Empire in the context of broader empire-wide partition politics, growing intercommunal violence and anticolonial resistance, and emergent postcolonial state politics. The chapter examines efforts by Yishuv leaders once again to bolster ties with India and other emerging postcolonial nations, tracing the activities of the ten-member delegation from the Yishuv that attended the Asian Relations Conference in Delhi in March and April 1947. Convened by Nehru, the conference hosted delegations from across the continent to discuss the shared social and economic challenges faced by Asian nations as they transitioned from colonial to independent states. While this new mission echoed Yishuv outreach to India of the previous decade, the stakes were now higher, with an impending UN decision on Palestine and the charged prospect of newly independent states emerging from the empire. With so much uncertainty about both Palestine's and India's futures—would they remain unitary states or be partitioned?—the Jewish delegation struggled to determine the appropriate allies and most effective strategy to serve the Yishuv. And though their mission was shaped by the forward-looking imperatives of a UN vote and a potential independent Jewish state, on the eve of partition, the delegates discovered that their political prospects were still very much shaped by their colonial past.

ONE

Wanderers Between Two Worlds

IN LATE 1923, AFTER NEARLY five years in Jerusalem, Helen Bentwich (1892–1972) identified a remarkable change in herself. She had been born into one of the most prominent Jewish families in Britain but had decided in her youth to reject the "distasteful" and inegalitarian religious orthodoxy of her father, in favor of atheism and socialism.[1] In 1915, Helen Franklin married Norman Bentwich, then a law lecturer at the University of Cairo and soon after a commissioned officer in the British Army. Helen joined Norman in Egypt until 1916, when his post in the Camel Transport Corps took him farther from Cairo, into the Sinai. Helen returned to Britain, where she worked as a factory foreman at Woolwich Arsenal in southeast London, until she was fired for trying to organize a women's trade union. She then joined the Women's Land Army, serving as a welfare officer and riding across southern England to site visits on an unruly motorbike.[2] In 1919, Helen left Britain to join her husband in Palestine, where he had been appointed director of public prosecutions with the British military administration and would later go on to serve as attorney general under the mandate. She arrived determined to put her socialist ideals and training as a social worker to practical use, confident that cross-cultural cooperation—particularly among women—could help alleviate some of Palestine's pressing social welfare issues. Living through World War I had convinced her of the destructiveness of ethnonationalism, and she disliked the attitude and demeanor of the Zionists she initially encountered. She perceived them as brusque, intransigent, and infuriatingly un-English, an assessment shared by many British officials in Palestine. Despite her husband Norman's long-standing commitment to Zionism, Helen Bentwich was resolutely *not* a Zionist.

Less than five years later, Helen realized that many of her opinions—about the feasibility of intercommunal collaboration, about Zionists, and about her place in the British colonial scene, which she experienced as increasingly antisemitic—had changed. In October 1923, she wrote:

> I find I have got much more sympathy with, & desire for friendship towards, the Jewish people here than before. It's largely, too, due to their attitude towards me. Formerly, it was Hebrew or nothing; now they are all prepared to talk to me in English, or apologize if they can't.... They want to learn English & meet the English people. When we first came here, the Jews were exclusive & kept to themselves—now it's the English that do that, & are narrow & bigoted, & the Jews are liberal & progressive. They are, too, the persecuted & downtrodden here in every way, & I feel I like to champion them in the same way as I would Labour at home. They *are* the most interesting people here; it's a real joy to talk to men like Rutenberg or Joshua Gordon or Dr. Magnes or Ben Zvi—or Fred [Kisch] & Nurock & Sacher—instead of the ordinary British official & his inanities.[3]

This circle of friends, with whom Helen had come to find an unanticipated kinship, felt far more familiar to her husband, Norman. Born in northwest London into a religiously observant family, Norman grew up around a circle of Jewish intellectuals, friends of his father, Herbert Bentwich, who included Solomon Schechter, Israel Zangwill, Moses Gaster, and Lucien Wolf. Herbert, who also practiced law, became an ardent supporter of Zionism in the 1890s and helped to establish the Chovevei Zion movement in England.[4] He imparted this passion to his children; seven of the eleven Bentwich siblings eventually settled in Palestine, including Norman's sister Rosalind "Nita" Lange, who built a large, castle-like estate with her husband, Michael Lange, in Zichron Ya'akov in 1912. The house became the center of

Bentwich family affairs in Palestine, and Norman thought it proved "perhaps better than any other house in Palestine" that a country home there could be just "as beautiful and as restful" as one in Europe or the United States.[5] In addition to Zionism, early defining commitments for Norman included the law, Labour politics, and social work. He spent two summers while in university at the famous settlement house Toynbee Hall, and after being called to the bar as a lawyer in 1906, he and several friends established a Jewish settlement branch in Whitechapel.[6] Though the effort was short-lived, Norman credited his time with the settlement movement for pushing his political leanings "steadily away from the Liberal Party to more radical views."[7] He and some of his fellow settlement workers, including Leon Simon and Harry Sacher, became disciples of Ahad Ha'am, who had settled in London in 1907.[8] Norman's growing affinity for Labour politics and the influence of Ahad Ha'am were key factors in the maturation of his Zionism, marked by a commitment to the revival of Jewish culture and a rejection "of the demand of each nationality for political sovereignty."[9] A friendship with Judah Magnes, whom he had first met in 1909 while visiting Solomon Schechter in New York, brought Norman further into the circles of Zionist Jews who supported binational and autonomist programs. During his time as attorney general, Norman developed close ties to the binationalist group Brit Shalom, dedicated to Jewish-Arab cooperation, and later became involved in the binationalist political party Ihud. Even into the 1930s and 1940s, when binational and autonomist schemes were attacked as anti-Zionist, Norman argued that "cultural and social autonomy, rather than separate sovereignty, [was] coming to be recognized as the healthy expression of a national idea which can form part of a stable world-order."[10]

Over the course of Norman's legal career in Palestine, from 1918 to 1930, it became more and more challenging for him to embody simultaneously the roles of Zionist and British official. Arriving in Palestine in December 1917, on the heels of General Allenby, Norman served first as director of public prosecutions under the British military administration. After the transition to a civilian administration in 1920, he was named legal secretary, a post that became attorney general following the official enactment of the British Mandate for Palestine in 1923. Norman remarked that at the beginning of the civilian administration, "in those days of determined hopefulness, the

British Government was willing to appoint to senior positions several British Jews."[11] But throughout the 1920s, Norman faced increasingly vicious criticism from Jews, Arabs, and British alike, fielding accusations of disloyalty, betrayal, and partiality from all sides. While on leave in England in late 1930, Norman experienced mounting pressure from the Colonial Office to resign as attorney general; refusing, he was "retired" in 1931. For a year, the Bentwiches resumed civilian life in London. Norman took up barrister's chambers, while Helen became involved in local and national Labour politics. In early 1932, an offer for Norman to join the faculty at the Hebrew University allowed the couple to return part-time to Jerusalem. With the rise of Nazism, both Helen and Norman became involved in Jewish refugee work, the subject of chapter 6. Norman worked for the Council for German Jewry, while Helen helped spearhead the Kindertransport.[12]

Norman, an Anglo-Jewish Zionist and the attorney general of Mandate Palestine, makes an obvious choice of focus for a project examining the centrality of the British Empire to the Jewish political imagination. As will become apparent in this chapter, as well as in chapter 3, Norman was forced to disentangle his role as a British mandatory official with his visions of Jewish political futures, all the while basing those visions on British Commonwealth models of nationhood. But it is Helen—a non-Zionist—who emerges as the heart of this chapter. Helen's long, vivid, and expressive letters home to her mother, which she wrote regularly over the course of nearly twelve years in Jerusalem, provide a window into the tensions she and Norman experienced in Palestine as they negotiated their relationship to the Zionist movement and navigated their identities as Jews, Britons, and colonial actors. While Norman wrote in his memoirs about the challenges of "wandering between worlds," Helen's letters went beyond abstraction, detailing the ways that everyday life—friendships, daily routines, meetings, committees, lunches, teas, clubs, and recreational sports—shaped this journey. In this companionate and egalitarian (as well as childless) marriage, Helen prided herself on being a modern, educated, and politically active woman.[13] She was a keen observer of British mandatory society in Palestine and an impassioned critic of British colonial standards of femininity. Through Helen's voice, we are able to recover the textured, daily aspect of her and Norman's shared experience as Anglo-Jews in Palestine confronting Jewish national ideals amid a shifting British imperial landscape. Helen's letters, written from daughter to mother, exude a quality of intimacy and read like an ongoing, animated conversation. At the same time, there is little doubt that Helen hoped that her letters—which emphasized her political convictions, her frustrations with the norms of 1920s femininity, and (eventually) her exasperation over British antisemitism in Palestine—would reflect a sense of her own exceptionality for posterity. She and Norman later included many excerpts from the letters in their coauthored memoir, *Mandate Memories*.[14]

Helen's lively and insightful letters reveal how gender transformed the ways she—as a colonial wife, social worker, and supporter of Labour—experienced British and Jewish, as well as Arab, society in Palestine. Her fierce commitments to gender equality, socialism and the Labour Party, and social work—which shaped her time in Palestine—developed at a young age. In her memoir, Helen recalled being a "troublesome child" who "resented the differences made" between her three brothers and herself. She daydreamed about being a boy and, when reprimanded for disobedience, would retort, "I'd be all right if I were a boy." Helen's older sister, Alice Franklin (1885–1964), an active feminist and suffragette, served during Helen's youth as honorary secretary of the Utopians, led by H. G. Wells. Helen, then an "untidy schoolgirl," would "creep in at the back, unnoticed," to watch the meetings, instead of doing her homework. At fourteen, she declared herself a socialist, too, and grew self-conscious of bringing friends home to such "unnecessary opulence."[15] Helen's brother Hugh Franklin (1889–1962), a militant suffragist active in the Women's Social and Political Union, served stints in prison for attacking Winston Churchill in 1910, for throwing stones at Churchill's house in 1911, and for setting fire to a railway carriage in 1912. Along with his wife, Elsie Duval, Hugh undertook hunger strikes in prison and was subjected to force-feeding. The couple—with Hugh dressed as a woman—escaped to continental Europe to avoid further arrests before World War I.[16]

Helen's early forays into social work and community volunteering were directed by her sister Alice, who set Helen up as a Girl Guides leader at a school next door to Toynbee Hall. Helen later enrolled at Bedford College in a four-term course in social hygiene and subsequently worked at the West Central Jewish Girls' Club in Soho, founded by her cousin Lily Montagu.[17] Helen felt "deeply shocked" by prostitution in Soho, an issue she would encounter again in Jerusalem.[18] At the beginning of the war, before marrying Norman and joining him in Cairo, Helen continued working for the West Central Club, teaching and performing home visits. In a letter to Norman, Helen wrote that in "Relief Work" in London, "the resultant mixture of old-fashioned charity and an attempt at socialism is really comic." At the West Central Club, about one thousand girls, who otherwise would have been unemployed, did garment work and received Trades Board wages. The club was forbidden from taking private orders and had "to take any girls the Labour Exchange" sent. "That is all Socialism," Helen explained. But middle- and upper-class women also volunteered, occupying positions that could easily have been filled by "out-of-work professionals," and did work in "cosy little suburban groups" that should have been done in the urban workrooms.[19] This convergence of old-fashioned charity and socialism was, in fact, integral to Helen's own Labour politics. While Helen was troubled by class inequality and was at times self-conscious of her family's wealth, she was chiefly concerned with bringing efficient, modern administration to the work of managing vulnerable populations and organizing women rather than the end of capital.[20]

Norman's own writings indicate that he agreed with Helen on many issues of women's equality. He was adamant, for instance, on gender equality in Jewish ritual and prayer, and he also encouraged his wife in her political activism (which progressed in earnest after the couple's return to Britain in 1930). Norman acknowledged that during the 1920s, Helen had been permitted to be only a "passive socialist, restrained by [his] official trammels."[21] Not insignificantly, Norman married Helen knowing she supported her brother Hugh, whose militant activism caused tremendous embarrassment to Helen's parents and resulted in detectives being posted outside their home.

Helen's record of her time in Jerusalem does not merely fill in the picture or provide a more detailed, multidimensional, nuanced lens into her shared story with Norman, however. Born into a family that included Herbert Samuel, the Zionist first high commissioner of Palestine, and Edwin Samuel Montagu, the anti-Zionist secretary of state for India, Helen traveled along the interstices of Anglo-Jewish attitudes toward Jewish nationalism. Traversing non-Zionist, anti-Zionist, Labor Zionist, cultural Zionist, and binationalist Zionist circles, her experience was emblematic of the tight, interconnected, and contentious nature of Jewish nationalist politics in Britain. During her time in Palestine, Helen came to find herself more at home in Jewish circles than in British circles. And despite continuing to identify as a non-Zionist, she grew to empathize with Zionism (particularly the binationalist Zionism of her husband) and support Zionist efforts, especially in the realm of social welfare work. This personal background and journey—which Helen did not share with Norman—stands as testament to the complex convergence of mandate-era Zionist and non-Zionist visions of Jewish political futures, especially in the space of the British Empire, where Jews with diverse political convictions confronted the same horizon of uncertainty amid the rise of anticolonial nationalisms.

Along their journey, the Bentwiches became important participants in, and astute observers of, Zionist circles that did not consider the "state" to be the primary goal of Zionism or that even shunned the statist ideal altogether.[22] In their manifestations in Palestine, these nonstatist visions included various versions of federalism, autonomism, and binationalism. Whereas scholars have previously stressed the Central European origins of nonstatist and binationalist Zionism, the Bentwiches represent an entirely different path to these politics, forged out of British Labour ideals and British Commonwealth conceptions of nationhood.[23] Their visions of Jewish political futures were incubated in a space where the warring parties of Herzl and Ahad Ha'am, encapsulating the divide between political and cultural Zionism, found common followers;[24] where single families—like Helen's—embodied the spectrum of Jewish nationalist sentiment; and where ties to British Labour made for unexpected Zionist connections. On this latter point, for example, the Bentwiches and the Revisionist Zionist leader Ze'ev Jabotinsky (1880–1940)—despite their very different Zionist politics—shared a friendship with Colonel Josiah Wedgwood (1872–1942), a Labour MP who proposed that Palestine become a British dominion.[25] Studying the Bentwiches' connection to Zionism—and its British geneses—helps to reverse the Jewish historiographical trend that treats Britain as unimportant to Jewish political and intellectual development.[26] As this chapter and larger project show, Britain—its history, culture, language, gender dynamics, and politics—played a critical role in the ways that Zionists imagined Jewish political futures. Beyond its British and nonstatist features, the Bentwiches' relationship to Zionism—indeed, their marriage itself—reflected the surprising convergence of non-Zionist and Zionist visions.

SOCIAL WORK AND SOCIAL WORLDS

When Helen Bentwich reached Jerusalem in late January 1919—one of the first British wives to join her husband—she immediately began investigating what pressing social welfare issues she might address. The war had disrupted the networks of economic support on which civilians in Palestine relied. Forced expulsions by the Ottomans had left civilian populations from Gaza, Jaffa, and Tel Aviv scattered and living in squalor. Hunger and disease were rampant across the country. By the time General Allenby marched on foot into Jerusalem in December 1917, the city had been living in desperate conditions for four years.[27] Following the conquest, Ronald Storrs (1881–1955), the military governor of Jerusalem, organized food distribution and rationing, and groups including the Syrian Relief Fund, the American Zionist Organization, and the American Red Cross helped supply further aid, which eased the immediate humanitarian crisis. When Helen arrived just over a year later in January 1919, she was pleased to note that Jerusalem appeared on the track toward modernization, with "motor cars & lorries tearing through the streets day & night; clean & decent bazaars inside the walls; and law & order everywhere."[28] Only a year earlier, there had not been a single private car in the city.[29]

Despite these improvements, there was no shortage of urgent welfare needs. Soon after her arrival, Helen set up a meeting with Annie Landau, the Anglo-Jewish headmistress of the Evelina de Rothschild School in Jerusalem, to discuss where Landau thought Helen might be most useful.[30] Landau, whom Helen had first met in 1914, was regarded as a fixture of Jerusalem life. "Miss Landau is the one feature of Jerusalem that has undergone no change," Helen wrote to her mother. Landau had come to Jerusalem in 1899 to take a teaching position at the Anglo-Jewish Association's Evelina de Rothschild School, the city's first school for girls, and had been appointed its headmistress the following year. The school accepted both Ashkenazi and Sephardi students of diverse economic backgrounds and offered a modern curriculum taught in Hebrew and English, to the disapproval of both Orthodox Jews (who opposed the secular curriculum) and secular Zionists (who wanted only Hebrew instruction). Exiled in Alexandria during the war, Landau had returned to Jerusalem in February 1918—the first foreign woman allowed to reenter the city—determined to reopen the school she had been forced to shutter the previous year. Many of the students who had attended the school on scholarship were left unsupervised; some were forced to live on the streets. Landau came back armed with several tons of food and clothing—donations from the school's benefactors Jack Mosseri and Sir Elly Kadoorie.[31] With the help of Ronald Storrs, Landau reopened her school three months after her return, reenrolling five hundred girls. At the ceremony marking the occasion, Storrs was given an English poem, written by the students, which gave thanks to Britain for its wartime sacrifices:

> We love our land of Palestine
> And England we love too,
> The land that's fighting hard to make
> A home for every Jew.[32]

At the event, where he witnessed the students' impressive knowledge of English, Storrs became convinced that graduates of Landau's school would make excellent clerks at the offices of the military government, known as the Occupied Enemy Territory Administration (OETA); as a result, Landau began offering her students a course on shorthand. It was the beginning of a long partnership between Landau and British authorities that moved beyond the professional into the convivial; as we will see, her parties became a locus of elite Jerusalem life during the mandate period.

Landau, an Englishwoman committed to girls' education and protection and who had ties to the OETA, made an obvious first contact for Helen in Jerusalem. At their meeting, which lasted "2 hours nearly" as Landau "poured forth conversation," Helen learned that "a Rescue home . . . [was] badly needed for the bad girls in Jerusalem to be sent to."[33] Hunger, homelessness, and the thousands of occupying British troops stationed in Jerusalem meant that prostitution had become a major concern in the city.[34] In 1919, there were approximately five hundred prostitutes in Jerusalem, the majority of whom were Jewish.[35] Though feminist efforts led by Josephine Butler successfully repealed the Contagious Diseases Acts in the British metropole in 1886, legalized regulated prostitution was still permitted in other reaches of the empire. British authorities were confident that the policing of women's bodies would both accommodate soldiers' needs and control the spread of venereal disease.[36] In Jerusalem, Major General Alfred, head of the OETA, identified the neighborhood of Nahalat Shiv'a and the Milner Houses in Mea Shearim, both near the Evelina de Rothschild School, as regulated sites for prostitution. Jewish responses to the situation varied; some ultra-Orthodox Jews in Jerusalem vehemently denied the very existence of Jewish prostitutes, while Chaim Weizmann and other Zionist leaders acknowledged a need to deal with the issue.[37] Mirroring nineteenth-century efforts by nonconformist middle-class English women to repeal the Contagious Diseases Acts, elite Jerusalem women from different communities came together to form the Social Service Association (also known as the Welfare Society), which aimed at putting an end to legalized prostitution and alleviating the causes. The effort was spearheaded by Salmah Salameh, an Orthodox Christian Palestinian Arab; Marianne Hoofien, a Dutch Jew married to the director of the Anglo-Palestine Bank; and Bertha Spafford Vester, leader of the American Colony.[38]

Helen soon joined the group, and while she was emboldened by the cross-cultural cooperation, she initially felt frustrated at what she perceived to be the group's lack of concrete action. Efforts had been stymied by lack of funding; Helen had approached the Zionist Commission only to be told there was no money to spare. "So there's nothing to do but talk & talk & talk," she reported. At a meeting of the Social Service Association in June 1919 hosted by Janet MacInnes, the wife of the Jerusalem Anglican bishop, Helen observed that "females from all sects & communities in Jerusalem" were present to discuss the rescue home and plans to file a request with the OETA to "stop licensing bad houses."[39] But "as usual here, it was mostly talk," she wrote, adding, "I didn't do any, because nearly all the talk was done by Jewish women, & I wanted to show that one, at least, could keep quiet." When Janet MacInnes went on leave to England, Helen took over her work. She reported to her mother in July 1919 that "we are hoping to open a rescue home quite soon—undenominational, but all run kosher, with an English or American head." Instead of seeking substantial funding from a sponsoring organization, the Social Service Association switched tactics, "trying to collect funds from the population... asking for a minimum of [two shillings] a month from everyone."⁴⁰ Finally, the rescue home was opened in the fall of 1920, with Helen in the role of chair of the association. The home also included a large garden, where Helen eagerly put her wartime Land Army experience to practical use (though she experienced the frustration of plants "growing *down* instead of *up*" during periods of drought).⁴¹

Helen's social work activities in Palestine represented both a manifestation of her British Labour values and practices learned in the metropole and a contravention of expected British colonial standards of femininity. Returning to many of her wartime pursuits in Palestine (specifically farming and social work), she also once again donned more masculine clothing. During the war, Helen had traveled around the country sporting rain slacks, a waterproof cape, and a sou'wester hat; in Palestine—despite her mother's chiding—she resolved to wear breeches, which she found best suited for "gardening and long walks."⁴² Helen's work in Palestine made her feel that she was not "just existing as a useless female," as she once put it in a 1914 letter to Norman.⁴³ Just as Norman had understood his involvement in the settlement movement to be the critical factor in his political conversion to Labour, Helen, too, saw her social work activities as manifestations of her commitment to British Labour and women's rights. Yet the female networks that Helen encountered through her social work in Palestine had largely been established before British rule and included Christian missionaries, the wives of businessmen working for Zionist enterprises like the Anglo-Palestine Bank, and urban Arab elites. Helen was notable among the wives of British officials in Palestine for participating in efforts that moved her beyond the spheres of colonial domesticity and leisure.⁴⁴ British women's domestic roles in the empire, operating as keepers of their home in charge of a cast of native servants, were critical to maintaining and reproducing colonial power.⁴⁵ In contrast to Helen, the average *memsahib* (white woman in India) not only did not participate in social work but also had little knowledge of, or was expressly unsympathetic toward, contemporary women's political movements.⁴⁶ Helen found these societal expectations imposed on her as the wife of a British official to be trying. "It is rotten that just because you marry your whole atmosphere has to get bounded by a house & domestics. They monopolize one's life & interests," she complained in a letter to her mother.[47] "I find I have no drawing-room conversation," she reported in another missive, "so I entertain my guests chiefly with what it feels like to be a factory-hand, & the easiest way of hoeing turnips."[48] After begging her mother to send her a "manual on social etiquette," she eventually felt that she could "manage most of the ladylike business."[49] "But afternoon-tea at home with callers beats me," she wrote. "I always retreat into the kitchen to see if the water is boiling."[50] Helen's social work activities also reflected her elite Anglo-Jewish upbringing. "There was a strong tradition . . . that members of the wealthier families should devote some of their time to helping those who were less fortunate," she wrote in her memoir.[51] These efforts, which saw wealthy Jews from west and northwest London volunteer in the city's East End, were replicated by Jews in other reaches of the empire, though on a smaller scale. Wealthy Baghdadi Jews in Calcutta and Bombay, for instance, helped to settle and provide for Jewish refugees from Europe who began to arrive in India in the 1930s. These charitable practices were pursued in part to alleviate the embarrassing presence of poor, unassimilated Jews. But as we have seen, British Labourites like Helen and Norman considered volunteering in the East End to be important social work with political underpinnings. These metropolitan Anglo-Jewish efforts developed in tandem with Zionist discourses about the westernizing, modernizing power of hygiene.[52] Helen's early social work in Jerusalem, which relied on similar discourses around hygiene and modernity, took place in a window of time when British power was still being solidified in Palestine, when elite networks established before the British conquest still had considerable agency, and when the development of Jewish and Arab nationalisms had not yet precluded crosscultural cooperation. Later, British mandatory authorities' unwillingness to invest in these welfare initiatives and their inclination to delegate work to independent agencies, meant that Zionist and Arab social welfare infrastructures would become increasingly bifurcated and insular.

Helen's experiences with Zionists during her first few years in Jerusalem confirmed many of her negative preconceived attitudes. Soon after her arrival, she paid a visit to the Zionist Commission, hoping to speak with Dr. David Eder about welfare schemes. A British psychoanalyst from a well-to-do Anglo-Jewish family and a cousin of Israel Zangwill, Eder had been appointed by Chaim Weizmann to the newly formed Zionist Commission the previous year. Norman considered him an "old friend" from his youth.[53] Any expectation of speaking with a familiar like-minded countryman about the welfare of girls was dashed when Helen learned that Eder was away in London. Instead, she was confronted with a Zionist official whose bedraggled state and lack of English-language skills likely immediately elicited her disdain. "I had a long talk with a hairy old man called Kahn through an interpreter," she wrote to her mother, "he saying I must learn Hebrew first, & me saying that the lives of babies & the souls of girls were more important, & that I meant to get going on that right away."[54] Helen found Zionists' insistence on using Hebrew—which she did not speak—to be a significant frustration. When her social work with girls commenced, she wrote to her mother, "I know I should talk to the girls in Hebrew, but I don't seem to be able to learn any. What with having learnt an Ashkenazi pronunciation before, & some Arabic since, I can't get hold of this Hebrew here at all. So—prepare for a shock—I find I get on quite nicely in Yiddish."[55]

Helen saw the insistence on Hebrew as reflective of what she considered to be broader Zionist political intransigence, disorganization, and self-defeating behavior—the very opposite of the modern, streamlined welfare management on which she considered herself an expert. She found the Zionist Commission to be "the *worst run organization* with the *most unsuitable personnel* it has ever been my lot to strike. They have no records of relief, no proper investigators, no proper division of the city, no correlation between the departments of giving relief to orphans, men, girls, widows, or medical, & so there is absolute chaos, & much wasting of money."[56] When the Bentwiches attended a concert given by the OETA in March 1919, Helen reported on "the usual 'incident' without which nothing [in] Jerusalem is able to take place." At the end of the concert, the British in attendance expected the orchestra to play "God Save the King" and so rose from their seats in anticipation. When the song ended up being the Zionist anthem "Hatikvah," General Money ordered his men to sit down. "Of course, Britishers only stand up for 'God Save the King,'" wrote Helen, "or else they'd be always on their feet what with Ireland, Judea . . . & all these other self-determined nations."[57] Annie Landau, who was seated next to a group of British officers "sat down automatically with them" though "entirely by accident." Marianne Hoofien, one of the founding members of the Social Service Association, and other Zionists "were so incensed" by this (unintentional) slight that they "decided to boycott" Landau's upcoming party.⁵⁸

Helen lamented that "nothing can be done here without politics," referring to the contentiousness developing between competing Jewish and Arab nationalist claims. Her "aim & object in life [was] to keep out" of politics, she wrote to her mother, but she found her work continually thwarted by political disagreements.⁵⁹ During a period of drought, when Helen tried to find suitable employment for Jerusalem girls in a sector besides gardening, she decided to rule out factory work because it was "so hard to get a Jew & Moslem & Christian to work side by side." After meeting with C. R. Ashbee (1863–1942), the English designer and Jerusalem civic planner, to discuss postdrought garden plans, Helen bemoaned the challenges of social work in Palestine: "I'm keen to take part, but since then politics & other difficulties have thrust themselves in so I may have to back out.... I'll dig & plant for them, with pleasure, if it can only be done on a simple, straightforward footing but it's awfully hard to do anything here, & I think, as an official's wife, I'd have done best to have kept absolutely clear of everything, & not attempted any work. The others have done that, & it seems the wisest course."⁶⁰

The frustration Helen experienced over dealing with competing nationalist politics during her first year in Palestine was soon eclipsed by the upheavals and changes of 1920: the fallout from the Nebi Musa riots and the announcement of the British Mandate for Palestine in April; the arrival of Helen's uncle Herbert Samuel as high commissioner at the end of June; the beginning of the civilian administration in Palestine, replacing the military one, in July; and Helen's ever-increasing awareness of antisemitism among the British in Palestine. The Bentwiches had spent the first four months of 1920 on leave in England and were away from Palestine during the Nebi Musa riots. On the first day of the unrest, Ze'ev Jabotinsky and Pinhas Rutenberg had approached Ronald Storrs to demand that Jewish defense forces be allowed into the Old City to protect Jewish homes and shops from Arab rioters.⁶¹ Storrs learned at the time that both men were armed. The following day, as the riots continued, British authorities searched Weizmann's private residence and the Zionist Commission; two days later, on the final day of the riots, authorities found a small weapons cache in Jabotinsky's home. Nineteen members of the Haganah, the fledgling Jewish paramilitary force, were arrested, as was Jabotinsky. In a typical British conflation of Zionism and Bolshevism, a subsequent military inquiry accused Jabotinsky, whose Zionism was anything but socialist, of stirring up insidious Bolshevist passion. Jabotinsky initially received fifteen years of penal servitude; the nineteen Haganah members were each sentenced to three years. After a public backlash in Palestine and Britain, the sentences were reduced to one year for Jabotinsky and six months for the other men.[62] Helen and Norman returned to Palestine at the end of April 1920. They arrived on the very day the assignment of the mandate to Britain was announced at the San Remo Conference, as Jewish anger toward the British flared, spurred on by a sense of betrayal for what had transpired during and after the riots.

Helen criticized the British response to the riots, particularly the lessening of prison sentences, and compared the whole situation to Ireland, then in the midst of its War of Independence. "One day Jabotinsky . . . gets 15 years imprisonment for having arms, & many others 3 years each—& today we hear he's gone down to 1 year, & the others 6 months—& all will probably be commuted," she wrote. "It's undignified of the British to get the wind up in this way—but it's Ireland over again, only too plainly. 'We are not ruled by murderers, but only by their friends,'" she concluded, quoting Rudyard Kipling's poem "Cleared!"[63] The poem was written in response to the Parnell Commission (1888–89), the judicial inquiry into whether the Irish MP Charles Stewart Parnell was guilty of condoning the assassination of two British officials in Dublin (known as the Phoenix Park Murders). When evidence against Parnell was determined to have been forged, he was acquitted of the more serious charges—a decision that Kipling protested in his poem and that Helen implicitly compared to the lessening of Jabotinsky's sentence.[64] Helen's dislike of Zionists in Palestine certainly colored her assessment of the riots, though she also did not object to the use of military force more broadly. Of her service during the war, Helen wrote that while she was a socialist, she was "never a pacifist."[65] Furthermore, her criticism of weak-willed British imperial policy and even her outright championing of Kipling was hardly anathema to Labour supporters in England, many of whom had condoned the British response to the Easter Rising in Ireland four years earlier and had failed to see the struggle as anti-imperialist. During the ongoing Irish War of Independence, when worry gripped Britain that the loss of Ireland could be a bellwether for the rest of the empire, most British Labourites held fast to the older Liberal Party line on Home Rule; that is, they supported Irish self-government within the empire but not complete sovereign independence.[66]

Helen felt increasingly concerned that the volunteer commitments that had occupied her time before her leave in England, hindered as they often were by disagreement and inaction, were not truly contributing to Palestine. "I am very tired of all the charity work," she told her mother. "It's not a *real* life for a wife—only for the men who are actually doing things. Petticoat influence . . . is not much my line, is it? I hate not being something *myself*— only being it as Norman's wife. In England one is not like that, but it's always that here," she wrote.[67] Helen was pleased at the arrival of her aunt and uncle Beatrice and Herbert Samuel in the summer of 1920 and hoped that Herbert would use his position as high commissioner to encourage women to work together on important issues. "If he gives us women a status—not social, but public & national—apart from our husbands, we will bless him for evermore," she wrote to her mother. "After all, you're not 'Arthur Franklin's wife' in Aylesbury, are you? I'm always 'Col. Bentwich's wife' here."[68] With the beginning of the civilian administration in July 1920, Norman went from Colonel Bentwich to "plain Mr Bentwich" when he was appointed legal secretary.[69] With the realization that they would remain in Palestine for the foreseeable future, Helen redoubled her efforts to organize women. The influx of British administrators and their wives created a more robust colonial social scene in Palestine, giving rise to clubs and societies that resembled associational life elsewhere in the empire.[70]

That summer, Helen helped to found one such club—the Jerusalem Ladies' Club, for which she served as chair. Though she objected to the name—"I hate being branded a lady," she wrote—she hoped that the club might serve as a space where women of different cultural backgrounds (though of similar social standing) could come together.[71] "It'll make all the difference to the women to have something in common," she wrote, "& after I've given them a few home truths at the next meeting, the lions & the lambs, I am sure, will never get up from lying together."[72] The "usual difficulty over languages" presented itself, but Helen reported that "we've decided to be officially tri-lingual."[73] The club's newspaper, the *New Jerusalem*, was published in Hebrew, Arabic, and English. The membership demographic resembled that of the Social Service Association—an assortment of Jews, missionaries, and various other Europeans and Americans, with Arab women harder to attract. Helen noted that only "one Moslem lady" but "lots of Jewish ones" came to a lunch she hosted in November 1920.[74] Over the next year, she became frustrated by growing complaints from the European and British contingent that the club was becoming "too Jewish." One club committee member even resigned as a result, an act Helen put down to jealousy and prejudice. "It's all because I was elected chairman & she wasn't last year," Helen wrote. "We are too Jewish because we had a Hebrew lecture (they forgot about the Moslem one too) & because so many Jewish people & not 'British' ones come to them. There are such a lot of English people one can't meet on equal terms now, because of their antisemitism," she bemoaned.[75]

Antisemitism among the British, what Helen referred to as "pureblind bigotry," became increasingly apparent to her in this period; it was often in these new social spaces such as the Ladies' Club that anti-Jewish bias became most apparent. Helen complained to her mother that "most of [the British] are so very outspokenly anti-Jewish now, that it makes it rather difficult.... The things they say are too absurd.... They can't believe that what they think isn't the right thing for English people to think."[76]

In December 1920, Helen returned her focus to social work when she proposed forming a "Council of 8"—a committee of eight democratically elected Jerusalem women tasked with advising the British Administration on welfare issues and acting as "an intermediary & progressive body, between the government & charities."[77] To Helen's delight, the idea received the support of Beatrice and Herbert Samuel.[78] The first meeting was held in January 1921. Women from various organizations across Palestine were asked to participate. Helen reported that the "usual language question" inspired a lively meeting; her Aunt Beatrice, who was in the chair, "weathered it well."[79] In addition to Beatrice, Marianne Hoofien, Henrietta Szold, and Sophia Berger (later Mohl), an American who worked with the Red Cross and with Szold at Hadassah, were the Jewish women elected to the Council.[80] The others included Effie Newton, a missionary from Haifa who had been in Palestine since the Ottoman period and whom Norman called "incurably anti-Jewish"; Bertha Vester of the American Colony; Janet MacInnes, the wife of the Anglican bishop; and Jane Hope Grierson, a Scottish missionary and teacher at the Tabeetha School in Jaffa.[81] Helen was pleased with the parity of election results—"Most fortunately 4 of each"—but found her appointment as honorary secretary "rather a stiffer job than [she] bargained for."[82] At a later date, two Arab women—one Muslim and one Christian—were elected to the council. The issue of languages continued to cause conflict even when a trilingual policy of English, Arabic, and Hebrew was observed. Helen created a letterhead for the group with the "National Council of Women of Palestine" written in the three languages, where the Hebrew translation used *Eretz Yisrael* (Land of Israel) instead of Palestine. "Immediately there was a violent outcry from Miss Newton, who threatened to resign," Helen recounted. Beatrice suggested that only English be used on the letterhead because most correspondence would be sent abroad, to which the other women—"with some demur from the Jewish members"—agreed. The group picked the issue of prison reform to tackle first. They also concerned themselves more broadly with the issue of women's status in Palestine and were consulted by the British Administration over relevant laws. Helen reported that reaching a consensus among women with such different cultural backgrounds was challenging. Fixing the age of consent, for example, proved contentious.[83]

For Helen, the year following the beginning of the civilian administration in July 1920 was filled both with new efforts to organize women and with an increasing awareness of the challenges of intercommunal work and of growing antisemitism among the British. She resented that gossip was becoming ever more endemic to elite life in Palestine, particularly in the tight-knit British community. "Any unusual remark one makes is repeated everywhere & comes back on every side," she told her mother. Though she cursed the fact that "nothing can be done here without politics" when she first arrived in Palestine, Helen came to resent the difficulty of discussing her political commitments with the British. Talk often veered into antisemitic territory, and the conflation of Bolshevism and Zionism was a well-worn theme. "Never to say what you think of politics, or you'll be called a Bolshevik; hardly ever to mention a good book or poem without being called an 'intellectual' or 'highbrow'; never to rag or you are called unconventional & undignified," she vented in a letter.[84] The year was also marred by personal loss for the

Bentwiches. In July 1920, while on a relief mission for the American Jewish Joint Distribution Committee, Norman's brother-in-law Israel Friedlander and Rabbi Bernard Cantor were murdered in western Ukraine by Red cavalry units, who mistook them for Polish officers.[85] Norman's widowed sister Lilian and her six children would move to Palestine two years later, following another tragedy—the death of Norman's sister Nita Lange—to take over Nita's estate in Zichron Ya'akov. But the year had occasion for celebration, too—an engagement and a marriage. In October 1920, Norman's sister Thelma, who had recently moved to Palestine, announced her engagement to Eleazar Yellin, the eldest son of education pioneer David Yellin, one of the first prominent figures of the "Old Yishuv" to announce his support of Zionism.[86] In December, Edwin Samuel, Herbert and Beatrice Samuel's son and Helen's cousin, married Hadassah Grasovsky. The bride, who was raised in Jaffa, was born into a prominent Zionist family that had come to Palestine in 1887 during the First Aliyah. Her father, Yehuda Grasovsky (later Gur), an early advocate of Hebrew alongside Eliezer Ben-Yehuda, had worked with David Yellin to compile Hebrew dictionaries. Edwin Samuel had come to Palestine before his father, serving as the liaison between the British Army and the Zionist Commission.[87] Thelma's engagement and Edwin's marriage served to embed the Bentwiches further into Yishuv society, into a tight-knit social circle of Palestine's Zionist elite, in a period when they were feeling increasingly ostracized and frustrated by British antisemitism.

In May 1921, while Helen's parents Caroline and Arthur Franklin were on a visit to Palestine, riots erupted in Jaffa. A May Day procession of Jewish communists marching from Jaffa to Tel Aviv clashed with a separate group of Labor Zionist Ahdut ha-Avodah supporters.[88] Police fired into the air to try to stop the fight, causing nearby Arabs to think the Jews were firing at them. Riots ensued in Jaffa over the next three days, particularly in the mixed Jewish and Arab quarter of Manshiyya. Later the unrest spread to surrounding *moshavot* (rural Jewish settlements), where Jews responded to Arab attacks with armed resistance. Eleazar Yellin's colleague was killed in Petah Tikvah. After a week of violence, casualties were listed at 47 Jews and 48 Arabs killed, and 146 Jews and 73 Arabs wounded—far exceeding the fatalities and injuries during the Nebi Musa riots the previous spring. The majority of the Arab casualties resulted from clashes with British police.[89]

In the immediate wake of the riots, Norman traveled back and forth between Jerusalem and Jaffa, and his efforts to try to restore order—as well as his character in general—were subjected to virulent attacks in both the Arab and Jewish presses. "I believe the only point on which the Jews & Arabs agree is that neither of them wants Norman here—a good tribute to his impartiality!" Helen wrote. "The Arabs say *of course* he favours the Jews, & the Jews say they expect him to but he doesn't! It's all rather black otherwise," she concluded.[90] The next week Helen wrote, "The Arab press is starting to go for Norman very strongly, calling him a 'Militant Zionist.' Poor Norman being a militant anything!"[91] Helen reported to her mother, who had by then returned to England, that Thomas Haycraft, Chief Justice of the Supreme Court in Palestine, had been appointed to head up a commission of inquiry to investigate the unrest.[92] In its findings, the Haycraft Commission identified Arabs as the primary "aggressors" during the violence. But it maintained that "Bolshevik" Jewish provocation and Zionist arrogance, as well as Arab economic and political upset over continued Jewish immigration to Palestine (Jews made up around 10 percent of the population at the time), represented important factors in the unrest.

Helen's response to the 1921 riots represents a remarkable departure from her assessment of the Nebi Musa unrest of the previous year. In 1920, she had accused Britain of a weak-willed response to the riots when they had lessened the sentences of Jabotinsky and other Haganah men, comparing the affair to Ireland and invoking Kipling's poem "Cleared!" A year later, she was angered over what she considered an inane British obsession with rooting out alleged Jewish Bolshevism, and she expressed understanding and sympathy with the need for armed Jewish defense. "The worst thing we have to contend against is the 'military mind,' which is following the scent of Bolshevism to the exclusion of everything else, & who arrest the most respectable Jews & threaten to hang them for just having fire-arms in self-defense," she wrote.[93]

The British response to the riots put mandatory authorities in "rare agreement" with Arab leaders, who likewise identified Jewish Bolshevism and the threat of Jewish immigration to Palestine as key grievances.[94] British officials in the aftermath of the riots aimed to deescalate the situation. Herbert Samuel temporarily suspended Jewish immigration and gave a speech the month after the riots in which he argued that future Jewish immigration to Palestine needed to be determined based on the economic absorptive capacity of the entire country. Arab unemployment, in other words, needed to be a central factor in determining the number of Jews who would be permitted into Palestine. In his speech, Samuel also tried to assure Arabs that the British had "never consented and will never consent to such a policy" that would take Muslim and Christian holy sites away in an effort to build a Jewish national home in Palestine.[95] Arabs, as well as Jews, responded negatively to the speech. The Arabic newspaper *Filastin* published a critique that argued that Samuel had not given any true assurances that the terms of the Balfour Declaration would protect Palestinian Arabs. An openly Zionist high commissioner, the article argued, would never defend Arab interests in the country. A War Office memo to the Colonial Office noted this grievance, expressing concern that the Arabs were demanding the resignations of both Herbert Samuel and Norman Bentwich, the two highest-ranking Jews in the mandatory government.[96] Zionists, for their part, believed that Samuel's new policy position represented a betrayal of the Balfour Declaration. The ensuing Churchill White Paper (issued in June 1922) attempted to walk the line; it maintained Britain's commitment to help foster the establishment of a Jewish national home in Palestine, but it made the principle of absorptive capacity, which Samuel had articulated in his speech, an official policy of the Palestine government.

Angered by the British response to the 1921 riots in Jaffa, dismayed by their obsession with Bolshevism, and frustrated with the challenges of intercommunal work, Helen found herself in the summer of 1922 hoping that the League of Nations would delay official confirmation of Britain's mandate for Palestine. "If it goes through, [we] will have to stay to see things straight—if it doesn't, we will probably get home in a few weeks. That would be very nice," she told her mother.[97]

Helen's wish was not to be. The League confirmed Britain's mandate for Palestine on July 24, 1922, and the Bentwiches accepted that their tenure in Palestine would continue for the foreseeable future.

"A RABBI & A REGULAR INDIAN ARMY SOLDIER": FINDING A HOME IN PALESTINE

Helen entered the autumn of 1922 acutely aware of her unusual status in Palestine, an isolating feeling that she was not fully part of British society by virtue of her Jewishness; nor was she truly comfortable in Yishuv society—her Englishness, non-Zionism, and inability to speak Hebrew setting her apart. For Norman, this shared reality meant that he continued to face mounting criticism from multiple fronts. "One of the trials of official life in Palestine, particularly for a Jew in office," he wrote, "was to be all the time watching one's step. . . . I was a special target because of my Zionist history." Norman expected attacks against him in the Arab newspapers but found denunciation "more difficult to bear" when it came from Jewish circles. "A part of the Jewish people, both within and without Palestine," he wrote, "failed . . . to reconcile themselves to the essential position of Sir Herbert Samuel and of any Jew in the Administration, that they were officials of the British Government and must maintain administrative uprightness and hold the balance fairly between Jewish and Arab claims. . . . The honourable position inevitably was to displease both communities."[98]

The arrival in Palestine of Frederick Kisch and Judah Magnes, both in November 1922, transformed the Bentwiches' social landscape and provided them with a fledging cohort of like-minded Jewish friends—Jews who played critical roles in the development of the Yishuv but had personal backgrounds, Anglo-cultural orientations, and hopes for Jewish political futures that separated them from the Yishuv mainstream. Over the next several years, as we will see, Helen's attitudes toward Zionism shifted and warmed, while Norman found a circle of intellectually minded Zionists committed to binationalism and Jewish-Arab rapprochement, where his own distinct ideas about Jewish national futures found expression.

Frederick Kisch (1888–1943) was born to Anglo-Jewish parents in Darjeeling, India, where his father, the colonial civil servant Hermann Kisch, was postmaster general of Bengal. The family eventually returned to England, where Kisch attended Clifton College and the Royal Military Academy. In 1909, he joined the Royal Engineers and was posted back to India, where he put his childhood knowledge of Hindustani to practical use. During World War I, Kisch served in France and the Middle East and later was a member of the British Delegation to the Paris Peace Conference. In 1921, he received a telegram from Weizmann, whom he had met only once years earlier, asking him to represent the Zionist Organization in Jerusalem. "The invitation came to me out of a clear blue sky," he remembered.[99] Around the same time, as his work in Paris drew to a close, Kisch was denied entry to Staff College, a qualification necessary to reach higher ranks in the British Army. In light of this professional setback, he contemplated joining the newly formed League of Nations, a position with the Suez Canal Company, or a job in civil engineering. Ultimately, however, he agreed to Weizmann's proposal. According to Kisch, the Zionist leader "pressed upon me the point of view that the Zionist Organization had no one available who could negotiate with high British officials in Palestine on equal terms, while he also explained the urgent need of systematic efforts towards reconciliation with the Arabs, a task which greatly appealed to me, having regard to my many associations with India where I was born and where I had passed the early years of my military service."[100] Kisch arrived in Palestine in late November 1922 to take up his post as head of the Zionist Executive in Jerusalem, as well as head of its Political Department—a position that made him chief liaison between the Yishuv and British mandatory authorities.[101] "Fred Kisch turned up yesterday," reported Helen. "He has come out to run the Zionist Executive, & is a great asset. I think we'll like him very much. He'll go down well with the English people, being regular Army, & knowing India & the War Office things," she predicted.[102]

Helen's approval of the Zionist movement grew under Kisch's leadership. "It's a good thing to have an ex-military man at the head of Zionist affairs.... It does make their shows punctual & well-organized," she quipped. Zionism became a movement that felt increasingly less foreign to Helen. She began identifying common cause between her own Labour ideals and those of Zionism—shared connections that were obvious for many Labor Zionists. For instance, in the summer of 1923, Helen began devising a plan to establish a training kibbutz in England for young Jewish men and women, an idea she proposed to Kisch. "It would be a great publicity catch, I believe, as people would think of Palestine as something actually relieving our labour market, & removing those 'undesirable' aliens. And it would prevent all this talk of only Bolshevist Jews going there," she explained.[103] The idea reflected Helen's growing admiration for Zionist models of labor in Palestine, as well as her new inclination to conceive of British Jewry within the broader Zionist fold, something that many Anglo-Jewish elites and she herself had been hesitant to do. The idea was also a departure from Helen's previous work—both in England and in Palestine—that focused primarily on women and girls. Here, in line with the kibbutz movement in Palestine (as well as the training kibbutzim or *hakhsharot* of continental Europe), Helen imagined Jewish men and women from Britain working together.

Judah Magnes (1877–1948), an American rabbi and outspoken pacifist during World War I, also moved to Jerusalem with his wife, Beatrice, and three sons in November 1922. Born in San Francisco, Magnes received his rabbinical ordination from Hebrew Union College, the Reform rabbinical seminary in Cincinnati, and afterward pursued doctoral work in Semitics and philosophy in Germany. While in Berlin, Magnes became a Zionist and, like Norman, was greatly influenced by the ideas of Ahad Ha'am. Imagining Palestine as a spiritual and cultural center of Jewish life resonated with Magnes, who was concerned with reconciling Jewish nationalism with universalist ideals. On his return to America, Magnes settled in New York and helped to found the American Jewish Committee. He also established the New York Kehillah, the organization that represented and unified the city's rapidly multiplying Jewish synagogues, communal institutions, and other organizations. During World War I, Magnes became a leading pacifist voice and served as the first chairman of the People's Council of America for Democracy and Peace. When Britain issued the Balfour Declaration, Magnes warned fellow Zionists that the success of Jewish life in Palestine depended on mutual understanding and cooperation with the Arabs.[104]

The Bentwiches quickly became close friends with Magnes, who shared their commitment to universalism and opposition to ethnonationalism. The two families had weekly Friday lunches together, and Norman and Magnes launched a plan to establish a new Reform congregation in Jerusalem. "I've lunched with the Magneses & had a long talk about the new congregation on Western lines he & Norman mean to get up, & attended a meeting between them & some very orthodox young men who are English & American but don't believe in the equality of the sexes which Norman & Magnes insist on," Helen wrote to her mother.[105] Despite Helen's early commitment to atheism, she found herself regularly—and not unhappily—attending Shabbat services led by Norman and Magnes.

Proposing English kibbutz schemes and attending religious services represented a remarkable change for Helen, a fact that did not escape her. "I find that... partly as a reaction against the unfair & pro-Arab partiality of all the British officials & Army here; & mostly as a result of getting so bored with the English people, & partly also perhaps Fred [Kisch]'s influence—anyway, I find I have got much more sympathy with, & desire for friendship towards, the Jewish people here than before," she wrote.[106] This coalescing circle of friends and family—Kisch, Judah and Beatrice Magnes, Edwin and Hadassah Samuel, and Thelma and David Yellin—provided the Bentwiches with a small but meaningful group of confidants in Palestine with whom the challenges of balancing both Jewish and British identities could recede—if only temporarily. "All the English Christians are so awfully nice in not telling us what they *really* feel about Jews; & all Jewish non-English are so nice in not telling us all they feel about the English," Helen explained to her mother. "But one knows so well what it is, & that it's there—on both sides. Often it is only with the English Jews, like Fred, that we can feel really at ease," she wrote.[107]

Helen began an annual tradition of hosting a "Jewish" Christmas party for the group. "They were a little sniffy about Xmas at first," she noted with regards to their inaugural holiday together in 1923. "It had to be all very ordinary, & no special food or decoration," she explained. But the night progressed to more serious revelry, with Mrs. Magnes first suggesting a balloon game where everything got "terribly rowdy & excited," followed by a round of dancing the Virginia reel, and ending with Judah Magnes teaching everyone to play poker. "We sat in a ring on the floor & played for matches till midnight, being instructed by a Rabbi & the head of the Zionist Executive," Helen told her mother, referring to Magnes and Kisch. Thinking of both, she wrote, "It's upsetting all my preconceived notions that the two nicest men here should be a Rabbi & a Regular Indian Army soldier."[108] The following Christmas ensued in similar fashion; Helen recorded that "Dr. Magnes was the rowdiest, with Norman a close second."[109]

During the relatively peaceful tenure of Lord Plumer as high commissioner, from 1925 to 1928, Norman's Zionist vision fully matured, his ideas about Jewish nationhood based on British dominion models and his commitment to Jewish-Arab cooperation finding expression in the binationalist program supported by Judah Magnes and members of Brit Shalom. In his role as attorney general, Norman pushed for commercial reform that he believed would advance a modern, progressive, prodevelopment agenda in line with Labour principles, help the Zionist cause, and protect Jewish-Arab relations.[110] Norman's economic reforms represented a program distinct from the "determined policy" of the Histadrut (the organization of Jewish workers in Palestine) that "Jewish public bodies . . . employ only Jewish workers," the concept known as *'avodah 'ivrit* (literally "Hebrew labor"). He thought this strategy, which he would later call "economic apartheid," was one of the main causes of antipathy between Arabs and Jews.[111] Norman's visions of Jewish political futures had a distinctly British genesis. He was introduced to Ahad Ha'am's conception of Jewish national culture in London; his progressive, universalist principles, a critical factor in his Zionism, were nurtured in the settlement movement in Britain; and his ideas about autonomist nationhood were based on British dominion models, which had given "a place for the realization of national ideals independent of political sovereignty." The Scottish, Welsh, Irish, Canadian, South African, and Australian nationalities were, "like the Hebrew, essentially cultural," according to Norman. His cultural conception of nationhood—based on a shared "traditional heritage, a language, literature, and aspirations for the future"—also depended critically on a "physical home." "The lack of the home had been hitherto the tragic weakness of the Jew," he argued.[112] Palestine, then, would become for the Jews what Scotland was for the Scottish. While Norman saw these British "nations" as useful models for a Jewish nation without political sovereignty, other Zionists would invoke these British dominion models precisely because of the autonomy they afforded (even without complete independence). As we will see in the next chapter, Chaim Arlosoroff looked toward Australia and South Africa after the inauguration of the British Commonwealth of Nations in 1926, as model nations that had achieved political autonomy but still benefited from being part of a larger empire.

Norman arrived, then, at binationalism by a notably different route than did most of Brit Shalom's founders, including Martin Buber (1878–1965), Hugo Bergmann (1883–1975), and Hans Kohn (1891–1971), who came out of a particular Central European cultural milieu (though Norman shared many of their fundamental conclusions). Founded in 1925, Brit Shalom opposed the creation of an independent Jewish state and, instead, supported the idea of a binational state in which Jews and Arabs would receive equal representation. Other important members included Gershom Scholem (1897–1982), Ernst Simon (1900–1988), and Robert Weltsch (1891–1982). While neither Norman nor Magnes ever officially joined Brit Shalom (both because of their professional positions), the two men openly supported the group's aims and have often been identified subsequently as members. Both also later helped to establish the binationalist party Ihud in the 1940s.[113]

The Hebrew University, founded in 1925, became the center of binationalist activity in Palestine, with several of Brit Shalom's members serving on the faculty.[114] Magnes was appointed chancellor, while Norman served as

FIGURE 2 Helen and Norman Bentwich (front row, second and third from right) with chief rabbis Abraham Isaac Kook (front row, fourth from right) and Yaakov Meir (front row, fifth from right) during a visit to Bikur Cholim Hospital in Jerusalem. Photograph by Tsadok Bassan. From the collections of the Central Zionist Archives, Jerusalem (PHG\1026569).

vice-chancellor and treasurer. Although the university (and Brit Shalom) would become the focus of increasing controversy in the 1930s, as we will see in chapter 3, its early years succeeded in bringing together an impressive cross section of Palestinian society. At the opening ceremony in April 1925, Helen noted that "all the English, & quite a number of non-Jewish Palestinians were there, including a number of Bedouin sheikhs from Beisan." She was relieved that "a more orderly crowd you couldn't conceive," but the ceremony itself "failed to impress" her. In his speech, the Ashkenazi Chief Rabbi Abraham Isaac Kook "began & wouldn't stop"; Weizmann spoke "inadequately"; and Helen was even "awfully disappointed" in Arthur Balfour's speech.[115] By contrast, Norman would years later remember the ceremony as "the greatest occasion of the many great occasions in the 30 years of the British mandate for Palestine which I was privileged to witness."[116] Her critique of the opening ceremony aside, Helen would soon come to appreciate the atmosphere at the Hebrew University. At a Jewish Studies reception given by Magnes and Norman the following December, Helen observed delightedly that Jewish students with different levels of religious observance were able to come together in the university setting—evidence, in her eyes, of modern progress for the Yishuv. It was "a very nice show," she wrote, "where bearded & hatted orthodox men & short-haired, short-sleeved, short-skirted girls, all met on equal terms, as students."[117] On a short trip to Cyprus in 1928, Helen contrasted her circle of friends at the Hebrew University with the colonial service members she met on the island. "I don't think any of them ever read a book, or think seriously of anything beyond qualifying for a pension," she wrote, "and though our Palestine officials may be as bad . . . we have our Jewish & Continental intelligentsia as a refuge."[118]

RIOTS AND RELIEF WORK

That sense of refuge was shattered on August 23, 1929. While Norman and Helen were on leave in England, a long-simmering conflict between Muslims and Jews over access to the Western Wall erupted in riots. Arab attacks on Jewish communities spread from Jerusalem across the country over the next several days. The majority of victims were Jewish members of the "Old Yishuv," the community of mostly non-Zionist Jews who had lived in Palestine before the advent of Zionist immigration. The Jewish communities in Hebron and

Safed suffered significant loss of life and extensive property damage. A serious internal refugee situation developed as Jews from affected areas fled their homes. British authorities, who had maintained limited military and police power in Palestine since 1926, struggled to quell the violence. Many British Jewish subjects in Palestine, including Norman's younger brother Joseph, demanded that they be allowed to arm themselves. Chief Secretary Harry Luke, serving as acting high commissioner at the time, forbade it.

The Bentwiches made plans to return to Palestine as soon as they heard reports of the unrest. Arriving in early September, Helen approached Dr. Chaim Yaski (1896–1948), the medical director of Hadassah Hospital, to ask if she could help organize relief work. Yaski welcomed Helen's assistance and placed her, along with Sophia Berger Mohl (one of the Jewish women elected to the "Council of 8"), on his organizing committee. Helen and the committee agreed that, as much as possible, Hadassah funds should be preserved for later reconstruction work and that the government should be responsible (at least financially) for immediate relief. "At present the Government only feed about 400 people from Hebron here in Jerusalem, & the Safed people," wrote Helen, "but there are 2000 here, in various schools and lodgings, from unsafe places." She wanted mandatory authorities to identify villages to which displaced Jews could safely return so that those who were not able to go back could be provided with adequate food and shelter. "There's fear of an epidemic if it goes on in this crude way," she reported.[119] Helen took the request to British authorities, likening it to "[holding] a pistol" to their heads. "We said they must ensure safety for the people to return to their homes . . . or else they must be prepared to feed everyone who had left their homes in fear," she recalled. Much to her surprise, authorities conceded to the committee's request: funds to feed twenty-five hundred in Jerusalem, fifteen hundred in Tel Aviv, two thousand in Haifa, and two thousand in Safed.[120]

Helen helped to organize volunteers across the country, calling on a network of Jews with ties to Britain. In Haifa, efforts were led by Marie Hyamson, wife of Albert Hyamson, the director of the mandate's Immigration Department and, like Norman, one of the few Anglo-Jews in a high-ranking position in the government.[121] Selene Millstein, an Anglo-Jewish clerical officer for mandatory authorities, and her staff were "lent" to the Hadassah committee for a week and assisted families in Jerusalem who needed food and housing. Cyril Henriques, the Anglo-Jewish engineer who the following year would be appointed vice president of the Jewish National Fund, was visiting Palestine at the time and proved an "invaluable" help with relief work, according to Helen. Helen implored her mother to show "such people as you may meet who pooh-pooh the seriousness of the riots here" her letters, which contained descriptions of the carnage and destruction. "I went round the hospitals & saw some of the wounded. All the children have fractured skulls, if nothing worse. One woman had her child killed on her lap & her fingers cut off," she wrote.[122] When Helen went to Safed in late September to survey the wreckage, a representative of the government traveling with her "declared that the only thing he had ever seen at all comparable" was the carnage of the Battle of Ypres during the Great War.[123]

In October 1929, relief work was taken over by the Palestine Zionist Executive. According to Helen, the entire effort became more about including all the different Zionist parties—with only male representatives—rather than efficient relief work. "Fred [Kisch] 'took charge' in a rather overbearing way, without a word of thanks to us, or even telling us he *was* taking charge. He appointed a relief & reconstruction committee—without a woman on it!" Helen told her mother. "It has all got so 'political' since Fred took it on, with rabbis & labour people & agudath & everyone represented on the committee, & not a soul who understands relief work," she bemoaned.[124] Helen's frustration with Kisch—who, granted, was a close personal friend—and with the Zionist Executive more broadly, was reminiscent of the exasperation she felt toward the Zionists soon after arriving in Jerusalem. Yet the way Helen approached relief work in her efforts with Hadassah in the month before the Executive took charge was also emblematic of the change she had undergone over the course of the previous decade. In earlier social work schemes, Helen had labored to bring together women from different communities, believing that cross-cultural collaboration was critical to solving Palestine's welfare ills. The British Labour values that had animated Helen's social work from the start continued to inspire her involvement in welfare matters, but by 1929, she had abandoned any pretense of intercommunal work. Joining up with Hadassah and calling on Anglo-Jewish contacts around the country to contribute to relief efforts, Helen found that Jewish-organized social work had become the space in which she could enact her Labour commitments in Palestine. Though she remained critical of the Zionist Executive's disorganized and all-male management of relief work, Helen's own participation in social work through a Jewish organization and her reliance on Jewish networks meant that her approach had aligned in a significant way with the Zionist presumption that education, health, and welfare services would be separated by community.[125]

Helen's attitude toward the British authorities in Palestine, shaped by years of experiencing antisemitism and by increasing dismay over their governance, had arrived at outright shame and disapproval. Following the 1929 riots, Helen was "left with no respect for the English Government here." "You can't realize what it feels like to be so ashamed of one's country as one feels here," she wrote.[126] Without referencing the first time she had invoked the poem in 1920, Helen told her mother in October 1929 that she had recently read Kipling's "Cleared!," which "seems an excellent prophecy." She had once drawn comparisons between the "undignified" handling of Irish nationalists and Zionists, criticizing the British for being too lenient in doling out punishment. In 1929, in a remarkable inversion, she interpreted "Cleared!" in the context of her expectation that the upcoming British Shaw Commission would refuse to hold accountable the *British* mandatory authorities, who had failed to stop the riots. "I very much fear that one or two minor officials will be scarified," she wrote, "& the rest 'cleared.' "[127]

The 1929 riots have been marked by historians as a major moment of reckoning in the history of Zionism and Palestine. The upheavals worked to solidify mainstream Labor Zionists' statist goals and commitment to a defensive ethos.[128] For the Brit Shalom leader Hans Kohn, his assessment of Zionism's path—away from any hope of reconciliation with the Arabs in the wake of the riots—caused him to cut ties with the Zionist movement and even eventually to leave Brit Shalom.[129] For the Bentwiches, however, 1929 only reinforced their particular vision of Zionism, which fused British Labour ideals and conceptions of nationhood with a commitment to Jewish cultural development. Increasingly excluded from British circles in Palestine, but still fundamentally opposed to statist claims of political sovereignty, Helen and Norman found themselves entrenched more deeply in a community of like-minded Jews who maintained hope for a binationalist future for Palestine.

TWO

Zionists and the British Question

LATE IN THE EVENING ON August 18, 1929, just days before the riots in Palestine erupted, Chaim Arlosoroff sat alone in a rented room in a London boardinghouse and began a letter to his wife, Sima.¹ "It is Sunday, the Library is closed, and I am lonely," he wrote, thinking he would fight his solitude with a note detailing what he had witnessed earlier that evening.² After more than a year and a half of travels across North America and Europe at Chaim Weizmann's behest, the young Labor Zionist leader was in London for a few weeks—an interlude between the Sixteenth Zionist Congress in Zurich, which Arlosoroff had attended the previous month, and a meeting of the Zionist Actions Committee planned for early September in Geneva.³ On days when the British Museum was open, Arlosoroff put in as much research as he could on a project of personal interest—a planned biography of Julius Vogel (1835–99), the London-born Jewish politician and author who served as premier of New Zealand during the 1870s. The previous day, Arlosoroff sat in the museum's reading room, listening to "the faint rustling of a thousand sheets of paper, books, manuscripts, magazines, [and] writing-pads," in awe of the hallowed space. "Here so many of the very great have sat and worked," he reflected. "Marx on his 'Kapital,' Kropotkin on his 'Mutual Aid,' Eduard Bernstein on his 'History of the English Revolution.' And here I am sitting now and digging myself into the life of a strange country, a strange man and a fascinating period of colonization."[4] Arlosoroff, who sported heavy, round horn-rimmed glasses, generally donned a wool suit, and was wont to smoke a pipe, appeared more sartorially suited for life in British academia than politics in Palestine.

But earlier on that lonesome Sunday, to distract himself from the absence of wife and work, Arlosoroff wandered over to Speakers' Corner in Hyde Park and observed a sight he found most remarkable. In his letter to Sima, Arlosoroff recounted: "I cannot but respect and admire what should of right be called a national institution of the English. Once more I have been standing and listening to their community singing, out in the open.... I looked into the serious almost solemn faces of the motley crowd, that had gathered to sing, middle-aged women, churchgoers and young lads, apparently newcomers to London from the counties who had found in Hyde Park the lost atmosphere of their parish church, schoolboys and lower middle class gentlemen with derbies and umbrellas, singing and singing."[5]

As Arlosoroff continued his walk through the park, he came to a platform with a sign for the "National Secular Society." A ruddy-faced gentleman with a monocle and moustache stood on it proclaiming the fraud of Christianity and all religion: "There was never a man Jesus Christ alive," he declared. "There is not the slightest evidence for the existence of God. Do not waste your time on such foolish things." The crowd around him—about two hundred people—listened "attentively, not interrupting him, not hooting." Arlosoroff found this noteworthy, particularly since he assumed that some of the hymn singers from nearby must have been among the listeners, who were all, as he put it, respectfully "lending their ears to argument." Farther on, Arlosoroff came to the Open Socialist platform. A seasoned socialist himself, he was rather unimpressed with the banality of this speaker, an "exceptionally weak one," by his account, who was reciting the "old song" of "'Capitalism restricts production' and so on." But all these vignettes taken together—what he identified and admired as "a national institution of the English"—made a significant impression on Arlosoroff. "I cannot get away from the idea," he wrote, "that very much of national psychology is revealed here, in the singing as well as the listening, in the argument as well as the silence."[6]

Arlosoroff's ideas and writings, as well as his daily work on behalf of the Zionist Organization and the Jewish Agency, capture the myriad ways Zionists in Palestine in the mandate period thought about the "British Question"—that is, the relationship between the Yishuv and the British Empire. Indeed, of all the prominent Zionist leaders of the time, Arlosoroff thought most widely about this relationship and the role it could play in the future of the Yishuv. As his 1929 dispatches from London attest, Arlosoroff respected British political and civic culture and admired the unique place Britain held in the histories of socialism and colonization. He felt that the ideals and lessons derived from British culture and history represented worthy models for the Yishuv, and he pioneered efforts to make knowledge of the British Empire accessible to a Hebrew-reading public. More broadly, he believed that long-term cooperation and understanding between the Yishuv and Britain were critical to realizing the Zionist dream. Quite apart from feelings of admiration or affinity, Arlosoroff could also approach the question of Yishuv-British relations with clinical, sociological scrutiny. He soberly assessed the complex and contentious nature of the Jewish-British relationship in Palestine, identifying causes of tension and recommending remedies for the future. He also carefully considered different political options for Palestine, contemplating nonstatist federative and dominion possibilities that would take shape within the framework of the British Empire.

Arlosoroff was not alone among Zionist leaders in thinking about nonstatist futures for Palestine. Ideas such as autonomism, federalism, binationalism, and dominionization (and various combinations and syntheses of these visions) represented important early interwar tenets across the Zionist political spectrum.[7] This was especially true within Labor Zionism, where leaders, including David Ben-Gurion, Berl Katznelson, and Shlomo Kaplansky, articulated a range of federative and binational visions for Palestine in the 1920s and 1930s that sought to stabilize Jewish-Arab relations. Revisionist Zionists, too, considered nonstatist options. Jabotinsky trumpeted the Seventh Dominion Scheme, an effort to make Palestine part of the British Commonwealth of Nations—an idea, as we will see, that Arlosoroff also examined.

Yet Arlosoroff never completely eschewed the state—or more aptly, the sovereignty it afforded—as a compelling concept. In his confidential June

30, 1932, letter to Chaim Weizmann (discussed in chapter 3), Arlosoroff suggested that a Jewish revolution that would overthrow mandatory authorities and establish a Jewish state by force, despite an Arab majority, might eventually become the Yishuv's only option for survival.[8] Even in times, both before and in the year after his famous 1932 missive, when Arlosoroff espoused more moderate views toward British mandatory authorities, he maintained an appreciation of state-like apparatuses as levers of power that could effect real control—particularly over issues critical to the Zionist movement, such as immigration and land development. This conception of state and state-like power shaped Arlosoroff's determination to promote cooperation between Jews and the British in Palestine. Although the Jews of Palestine had built an impressive, self-governing society, Arlosoroff feared that they risked locking themselves out of future political arrangements by refusing to participate actively in the mandatory government.[9] Furthermore, a central appeal of the dominion idea was precisely that it would afford the Yishuv levers of state-like power.[10] Thus, just as Arlosoroff's rich understanding of nonstatist politics pushed him to consider the benefits of belonging to the British Empire, his appreciation of the state apparatus prompted him—more often than not—to insist on the importance of protecting and improving Yishuv-British relations.

Arlosoroff is a singular figure in Yishuv history not because other Zionists did not engage with the "British question"—they certainly did—but because no other contemporary Zionist leader thought so comprehensively and penetratingly about the subject. Unique in scope and depth of consideration, encompassing both admiration and dispassionate analysis, Arlosoroff's ideas and their development serve as a springboard for understanding more broadly how the Yishuv navigated its relationship to the imperial power that held the mandate for Palestine. This chapter traces the path of Arlosoroff's diverse ideas about Britain: Britain as a civic and political model for the Yishuv; as an international center of both imperial and labor development; as the mandatory authority with an imperfect, human workforce; as the leader of the British Commonwealth of Nations that could one day include the Jewish national home; and as the political power at the center of his own evaluation of nonstatist ideals and the appeal of state sovereignty. Weaving these ideas into broader debates and discourses—of which Arlosoroff was a key participant—this chapter reframes the relationship between Zionism and Britain and between the Yishuv and the British Empire. Beginning with Arlosoroff's early years in Palestine as a member of the Zionist Actions Committee, the chapter concludes in 1931 on the eve of Arlosoroff's appointment as head of the Jewish Agency's Political Department. In this capacity, Arlosoroff served as the chief liaison between the Yishuv and British mandatory authorities. He held the position from 1931 until his murder on a beach in Tel Aviv in 1933, leaving a nation reeling and wondering who Arlosoroff might have become and what might have been had he lived.[11]

EARLY YEARS

Arlosoroff was born in 1899 in the city of Romny in Ukraine. His father, Saul, the son of a rabbi and Talmudic scholar, worked in the wheat and lumber industries and provided a comfortable middle-class life for his family. Russian was spoken at home—Arlosoroff went by the name "Vitaly" as a young child—and both parents also knew German. In October 1905, amid the mass social and political upheavals of the 1905 Russian Revolution, Jewish communities across the Russian Empire were attacked in a wave of pogroms.[12] The day after Nicholas II issued the October Manifesto, violence erupted in Romny, lasting two days.[13] Eight Jews were killed, and dozens were injured; the city's two synagogues, the Jewish schools, and Jewish-owned shops were burned; and many Jewish homes—including the Arlosoroffs'—were attacked. In the wake of the violence, the then six-year-old Arlosoroff and his family fled Romny, living first in a small East Prussian border town before finally settling in Königsberg in 1912. Arlosoroff, who assumed the German name "Viktor," enrolled in a gymnasium, where he excelled in his studies, as well as in athletics. At home, he received private tutoring in Hebrew and Jewish subjects.

At the outbreak of World War I, the Arlosoroff family—as Russian subjects and thus enemy aliens—faced potential deportation. The family relocated to Berlin, however, where they were allowed to remain. Yet Saul Arlosoroff did not stay in Germany for long. The war had disrupted his business, and in an attempt to recover some of his assets, he returned to Russia. The young Arlosoroff would never see his father again. Blocked from returning to Germany because of the war, Saul Arlosoroff ultimately contracted cholera and died in June 1918, five months before the armistice. During the war years, the young Arlosoroff continued his studies, embracing the culture of his adopted country. Grateful for the refuge Germany had provided his family and enamored with the writings of Goethe, Kant, and Schiller, Arlosoroff tried at the beginning of the war to enlist in the German army—an honor he was, as a Russian subject, denied. Shlomo Avineri argues that it was the psychological dislocation and tragedy of the war that pushed Arlosoroff, like many in his generation, toward the socialist and universalist ideals that would henceforth shape his political thinking.[14] What is more, it was during the war that Arlosoroff began to think seriously about the predicaments of modern Jewish life—particularly in wartime—and to believe deeply in the promise of Zionism. He became a disciple of Martin Buber, who was then living in Berlin. The philosopher acquainted the young Arlosoroff with the writings of Gustav Landauer (1870–1919), the social anarchist influenced by Kropotkin, whose agrarian communitarianism inspired the kibbutz movement.[15] Buber also introduced Arlosoroff to the ideas of A. D. Gordon, the founder of Hapoel Hatzair in Palestine. This non-Marxist, moderate socialist Zionist group became a focus of Arlosoroff's life in Germany.[16] While at the University of Berlin, where he studied economics, Arlosoroff served as one of the central leaders of Hapoel Hatzair and edited its German-language mouthpiece, *Die Arbeit*. The group recognized an enduring capitalism and rejected class struggle, differentiating it from other left-wing Zionist parties, including Ahdut ha-Avodah (with which it would later merge in 1930 to form Mapai). It was committed to manual labor, particularly agricultural work, as a means of Jewish political, national, and spiritual rejuvenation. Many of the individuals who joined Hapoel Hatzair in Germany were influenced by Max Weber, Werner Sombart, and other members of the Verein für Socialpolitik, particularly their idea that state involvement in the economy would stimulate growth.[17] In a broader socialist climate that often rejected the state, this moderate influence made German Labor Zionists far more amenable to the notion of state-like power—a fact that would have significant bearing on Arlosoroff's politics later in Palestine.

During his studies, Arlosoroff published his first treatise *Der jüdische Volkssozialismus* (1919), a critique of Marxist attitudes toward nationalism that advocated a synthesis between class consciousness and national consciousness. He also penned an essay in 1921 on Peter Kropotkin's social anarchism, a concept that Arlosoroff understood to be fundamental to his own emerging vision of a nonstatist, libertarian, socialist society—in contrast to Marx's socialist state—which he hoped could manifest itself in the Yishuv through the kibbutz.[18] But when Arlosoroff traveled to Palestine for the first time that same year, his most affecting experience turned out not to be socialist farming but rather urban unrest. He had decided to spend the Passover holiday in Jaffa with Yosef Aharonovitch (1877–1937), a leader of Hapoel Hatzair and editor of its Hebrew-language paper in Palestine. The day after the holiday ended, on May 1, 1921, riots erupted in Jaffa. Arlosoroff stood in armed defense of the Jewish neighborhood of Neve Shalom in northern Jaffa, which was besieged by Arab rioters until British forces intervened and evacuated the community. Comparing the Jaffa riots to Eastern European pogroms became a widespread trend within Zionist circles. Arlosoroff's host, Aharonovitch, saw the 1921 riots as a continuation of the bloodthirst and savage plunder that had marked the outbreaks of violence against Eastern European Jews, not as evidence of an emerging, coherent Palestinian Arab political movement.[19] Arlosoroff, however, who had witnessed both, objected to the analogy. Instead, the experience instilled in Arlosoroff the importance of taking emerging Palestinian Arab nationalism seriously. He acknowledged—what many of his Zionist peers argued—that no Arab nationalist movement existed in Palestine in the way that nationalist movements existed in Poland or Italy, for example, or in other parts of the British Empire, such as Egypt and India. In those countries, developing capitalist economies, diminishing social divides, and increasing educational opportunities—none of which existed in Palestine—provided the preconditions of classical nationalism. But after witnessing the Jaffa riots, Arlosoroff felt that this empirical observation was largely beside the point, likening it to a doctor who denies that his patient, "wallowing in the heat of fever," is ill because the microbes from the patient's blood look unlike anything he has previously seen under a microscope. Arlosoroff also believed that the concomitant impulse to blame British authorities—as many labor Zionists, including Aharonovitch and Ahdut ha-Avodah members Ben-Gurion and Katznelson, did—also missed the crux of the problem. In an essay he authored after the riots, Arlosoroff argued that Zionists must understand that the "Arab question" was a political one—not a "sociological, economic-historical-ethnographic, or moral" one. They needed to recognize the existence of an Arab national movement, even if that movement's genesis seemed atypical, and abandon "strong hand" policies which relied on British might for security. Ultimately, Arlosoroff asserted, Zionists and Arabs must pursue a path toward "mutual understanding," an effort that would be made possible through the robust support of British authorities—efforts already evidenced, according to Arlosoroff, through the work of High Commissioner Herbert Samuel.[20]

This essay reflected Arlosoroff's insistence in the wake of the riots that Hapoel Hatzair move away from the policy of Hebrew labor ('*avodah 'ivrit*), which insisted on the hiring of Jewish rather than Arab workers, and instead promote long-lasting understanding between the two communities in Palestine. That understanding would be based not on neighborly cooperation or mutual economic interest but on a carefully negotiated *political* agreement (the nature and structure of which were yet to be determined, but certainly autonomist and federative governments were options). Furthermore, Arlosoroff questioned the Zionist movement's insistence on establishing a "Jewish majority" or at least its insistence on bombarding Arabs with the slogan "ten times a day."[21] Arlosoroff's stance—his recognition of Arab nationalism; his refusal to blame the British for the riots nor to rely on them to enforce policy through military power; his challenge to Zionist conventional wisdom and policy—set him apart from Jabotinsky and the Revisionists, Ahdut ha-Avodah, and even members of his own political party, Hapoel Hatzair. Indeed, in response to Arlosoroff's essay, Aharonovitch issued his own statement, in which he argued that no Palestinian Arab nationalist movement existed in the classical sense, a position that he fervently maintained even after the riots of 1929.[22] Arlosoroff's thoughts on the use of force and his ideas about a Jewish majority and Hebrew labor shifted over the course of his short lifetime. But as we will see, his conviction that Arabs would necessarily be part of any political future in Palestine and that the British would play a key role in the development of that polity remained largely constant.

After his eventful and formative trip to Palestine, Arlosoroff returned to Berlin and to his studies, completing his doctoral dissertation on Marx's theory of class struggle in 1923. Though offered a university assistantship by

Werner Sombart (his doctoral adviser), Arlosoroff declined; his ambitions and heart lay elsewhere. That same year, at the Thirteenth Zionist Congress, in Carlsbad, Arlosoroff was elected to the Zionist Actions Committee, the body responsible for managing Zionist affairs between congresses. A year later, Arlosoroff moved to Palestine with his first wife Gerda and their young daughter, Shulamit.[23]

THE NEW INTERNATIONAL POLITICS AND EMPIRE

When Arlosoroff arrived on the scene in Palestine in 1924—this time to stay—he already had a reputation as the wunderkind of the Zionist movement. At only twenty-five years of age, he was more than a decade younger than the majority of Zionist leaders at the time. He was recognized as a forceful orator, noted not for his rhetorical style or ostentation but for his dynamic arguments and impressive depth and breadth of knowledge. Indeed, Arlosoroff was perhaps the only prominent Labor Zionist leader who could have been considered a European-educated intellectual of the highest quality—with a doctorate—who produced original, sophisticated theoretical writings. Within two years, he had established himself as a central leader of Labor Zionism and had been appointed and elected to leadership positions of Hapoel Hatzair, the Histadrut, the Assembly of Representatives, and the Va'ad Leumi (the Jewish National Council and executive of the assembly). In 1926, the Va'ad Leumi selected Arlosoroff to participate in a delegation to represent the Yishuv at the Ninth Session of the Permanent Mandates Commission of the League of Nations, scheduled for June in Geneva.[24] The delegation, which also included Meir Dizengoff, the mayor of Tel Aviv, and B. Z. Uziel, the city's Sephardic chief rabbi, would not have official status in Geneva, barring it from closed meetings. The Permanent Mandates Commission, the League body responsible for overseeing the mandates created at the end of World War I, recognized only one official representation from each mandate: the mandatory government.

Although the three men left a relatively peaceful Palestine—the country had not seen any significant unrest since the riots in 1921—the international scene on which they descended was anything but serene. The Permanent Mandates Commission had experienced a significant crisis of legitimacy over France's response to the broad-based anticolonial uprising in Mandatory Syria and Lebanon. The brutality of the French aerial bombings of Damascus in October 1925, which killed more than fourteen hundred civilians, left many in the international community convinced of the indefensibility and inhumanity of French rule in the Levant. Moreover, the League had ostensibly put the French mandate in place to guide the residents of Syria and Lebanon toward political self-determination—not to crush a nationalist movement vying for independent government. In short, the French mandate began to seem much more like occupation than custodianship. British leaders worried that supporting the legitimacy of French mandatory authority at the expense of Syrian nationalism could engender resentment and anger among Muslims in Britain's own empire. But disrupting the balance of power in the Middle East could be equally if not more disastrous. One failed mandate could cause the rest to topple like dominoes.[25]

In the end, the latter concerns won out. At the Eighth Session of the Permanent Mandates Commission, a special meeting held in Rome in late March and early February 1926 to discuss the situation in Syria and Lebanon, international representatives resolved to uphold the legitimacy of the French mandate. They determined that the essential role of the Permanent Mandates Commission was to "cooperate" with mandatory authorities, not manage them. Syrian nationalists would find the swiftest path toward self-determination by cooperating with the French. This decision was in essence an affirmation by the Permanent Mandates Commission of the limitations of its own power; the mandatory authority itself—in this case, France—ultimately had control. Supporters of Syrian nationalism, humanitarians, and some strict interpreters of the mandates system alike condemned the decision, considering it a failure of the new international order. Two months after the meeting in Rome and a month before the Ninth Session of the Permanent Mandates Commission was set to open in Geneva, any hope that the recently installed French High Commissioner Henry de Jouvenel would adopt a more measured and less militaristic approach to the uprising was dashed. The French resumed aerial bombings in May, resulting yet again in catastrophic loss of civilian life. In response, a Syrian delegation—which, like the Yishuv's delegation, had no official status at the Permanent Mandates Commission—planned to issue a petition at the meeting.

Arlosoroff thus set off for Geneva in a moment when the international imbroglio of competing political interests—between Britain and France, between European empires and the League, between public opinion and governments, and between emerging national movements and mandatory powers—had been thrown into stark relief. The League's ineffectiveness in managing the mandatory authorities it had created was especially apparent to Arlosoroff. In an essay entitled "Wall of Glass," which he published in advance of his trip to Switzerland, he noted that Stanley Baldwin's Conservative government in Britain—which had ousted the Labour government led by Ramsay MacDonald in 1924—"defended at all costs" the local power of its colonial administrations, including mandatory ones. Arlosoroff believed that Baldwin's government was unlikely to abide by League intervention in its affairs; indeed, the League had proven powerless not only to stop the recent French aerial bombings of Syria but in 1920 had "given England full freedom of action in Mesopotamia"[26]—action that included indiscriminately dropping 97 tons of bombs and firing 183,861 rounds of ammunition in an effort to stop the Iraqi revolt against British rule.[27]

Given this record, Arlosoroff felt that his delegation could hardly expect to address the Yishuv's grievances—for instance, over issues of land settlement, the use of public works funds, and police service—by going to Geneva to create a "tactical basis for a war against the British administration."[28] In other words, there would be no solution in readying a lawsuit against the British mandatory government or in asking the League to intervene. Those efforts would undermine public opinion of Zionism, and when they almost assuredly failed, they would leave the Yishuv even further surrendered to the "arbitrariness of the local bureaucracy."[29] Instead, though it would make clear the Yishuv's grievances with the British administration, the delegation would do so with "coolness and patience."[30] Any political action would be moderate and measured, and would not follow the tactic—as Zionists had often done previously—of leading with final demands and starting negotiations with ultimatums.

Arlosoroff, Dizengoff, and Uziel reached Geneva on May 31, 1926. On the train ride to the city, Arlosoroff found a copy of the (London) *Times* that included news of his delegation's expedition with the disheartening headline "Palestine Jews' Complaints."[31] In his diary, Arlosoroff lamented that the Zionists had "been signed and sealed as a people who had come to complain," not as "an ally participating with equal rights in a joint enterprise." The delegation's arrival proved no more encouraging. No one came to greet their train, so the three men made their own way to the hotel through pouring rain.[32] Accommodations had been booked at the Hotel England, partly "for patriotic reasons," Arlosoroff wrote jokingly in his diary, but also because it suited the delegation's character (or more likely, its modest budget). Their fellow guests—"hardly a single Englishman" in sight—included representatives to the Mandates Commission from Portugal and Greece, as well as a fascist group attending the League of Nations International Labour Conference.[33] On its first night in town, the Yishuv delegation received a visitor who warned Arlosoroff ominously, "What do you want? The League of Nations is England!" The encounter, which Arlosoroff conceded contained a "core of truth," further reinforced for him that the Permanent Mandates Commission would likely have no more power in provoking policy change in Palestine than it had in Syria and Lebanon.

Before he arrived in Geneva, Arlosoroff had thought about the situation in Syria and Lebanon mostly within the context of international mandatory politics, as part of his assessment of the League's power and effectiveness. But attending the Ninth Session of the Permanent Mandates Commission alongside the delegation from Syria inspired Arlosoroff to reconsider the conflict specifically in the context of French imperialism and to question the nature and moral cost of French-Zionist relations. After Jouvenel publicly denounced the Syrian delegation at the opening meeting of the commission, the delegation's representatives published a manifesto stating their objection to French activities in Syria and Lebanon. "The letter has aroused many thoughts in my mind," wrote Arlosoroff. Days before Jouvenel arrived in Geneva, he had appeared onstage with Chaim Weizmann at the Palais du Trocadéro in Paris at a large Zionist rally.[34] Arlosoroff struggled to understand how Zionists could accept Jouvenel's support after he had been responsible for ordering—"not a fortnight before"—the aerial bombardments that had killed noncombatant women and children. "To stand at this moment, in times of national distress in Syria and tyrannical rule by the French, openly alongside this imperialism—is it not too high a price for the affection for Zionism?" asked Arlosoroff.[35]

Arlosoroff's critique of violent French imperialism and his sense of the moral and ethical dilemma of accepting Jouvenel's support for Zionism, without any allusions to a British parallel, may well have reflected disconnection or hypocrisy. He had previously acknowledged before the Geneva trip that Britain had done in Iraq what France was doing in Syria. While he did not yet support Zionist-British cooperation as emphatically as he would even a year later, Arlosoroff already felt in 1926 that the Yishuv could not afford to antagonize the British and would have to work together to achieve constructive political change. In other words, he knew that to criticize the practices of French imperialism, as opposed to British imperialism, held far fewer dangers to Zionism. But in his failure to hold Britain to the same moral standards as France, Arlosoroff was not alone.[36] As France carpet-bombed Damascus, memory of when Britain had done the same in Iraq faded, eclipsed by the successful negotiation of the Anglo-Iraqi Treaty (1922), which scrapped the Mesopotamia mandate plan and set up British ally Faisal as king. Members of the international community held up this path as a potential model for the French in Syria and Lebanon. Britain had become no less than an exemplary mandatory power with a lesson for France.[37] Arlosoroff's increasing inclination that the Yishuv should depend on the British was further bolstered by his dawning comprehension not only of the League's administrative feebleness but of its precarious moral authority. If the first wave of French bombings in Damascus reflected an organizational failure of the League, its ultimate refusal to address the continued violence represented a dire moral failure.[38]

Before the conclusion of their trip, the Yishuv delegation submitted an official memorandum on behalf of the Va'ad Leumi. The document reflected Arlosoroff's vision for the delegation to Geneva: to express constructive criticism of the mandatory government, to demand realistic solutions, and to make clear the desire for a better partnership with Britain.[39] The results of the Permanent Mandates Commission's official discussion on Palestine—held on June 22 and 23 behind closed doors—proved satisfactory enough. The commission had requested the mandatory government "take steps to provide land for Jewish colonization" and that it "substantially increase" funding for Jewish schools.[40] Arlosoroff likely understood that the commission's request was only just that; Zionists would have to turn to Britain to make concrete political progress.

THE SEVENTH DOMINION

In November 1926, while Arlosoroff was on a tour across America on behalf of the Zionist Organization, another international meeting convened in London. Leaders from Australia, Canada, the Irish Free State, Newfoundland, New Zealand, and South Africa—the British Empire's six dominions—met at Westminster for the Seventh Imperial Conference.[41] Leaders from India, a potential future dominion, also attended. At the conclusion of the conference, after the fate of the dominions and their status within the British Empire had been discussed, another Balfour Declaration was issued. Named, as its predecessor had been, for Arthur Balfour, this 1926 declaration affirmed that the dominions were "autonomous Communities within the British Empire, equal in status, in no way subordinate one to another in any aspect of their domestic or external affairs, though united by a common allegiance to the Crown, and freely associated as members of the British Commonwealth of Nations."[42]

The creation of a Commonwealth of Nations—neither bound by a single constitution nor inferior to the metropole—opened up a new avenue of political possibility for Palestine, one that would have a dramatic effect on the ways that Chaim Arlosoroff, and others, imagined potential futures for the Jewish national home. Before the Balfour Declaration of 1926, Arlosoroff believed that positive Jewish-British relations in Palestine were important, but he remained focused on securing a broad international coalition in support of Zionism and viewed the League of Nations as the obvious locus of that effort. After the inauguration of the British Commonwealth, Arlosoroff became increasingly focused on Britain and the possibilities that its imperial network might hold for Palestine. He threw himself into the study of British colonial history, became dedicated to sharing that knowledge with a Hebrew-reading public, and thought seriously about the prospect of dominion status for Palestine.

The idea of making Palestine into a British dominion was first proposed by Col. Josiah C. Wedgwood, a British Labour politician and fervent imperialist who was touring Palestine with his wife, Florence, when the Seventh Imperial Conference convened in London.[43] The couple met Norman and Helen Bentwich in Jerusalem. Helen found the Colonel "very nice" but a "bit pugnacious"; they would go on to become friends.[44] Wedgwood had a reputation for impassioned advocacy of Zionism, a sympathy that stemmed from a distinctly English Protestant evangelical zeal and from his personal friendships and experiences with Jews. Wedgwood first encountered Chaim Weizmann in December 1914 at a meeting held by David Lloyd George and was impressed with the Zionist leader's message.[45] During the Gallipoli Campaign, in which Wedgwood was injured in the service of the Royal Navy, he met and developed great respect for the Jewish volunteers of the Zion Mule Corps, led by Joseph Trumpeldor.[46] After Wedgwood returned home to Britain from his 1926 visit to Palestine, he published an essay in the *Palestine Bulletin* outlining his idea for the country to join the newly inaugurated six-member British Commonwealth. While the nations of the Commonwealth (with the exception of Ireland) originated as British crown colonies with substantial European settler populations, their inhabitants were not exclusively of English extraction. "We have in Lower Canada a French partner; in Ireland a reluctant Irish partner; in South Africa a Dutch partner; and in India, Ceylon and Burma we expect and hope to have some day quite non-European partners in that new Union into which the Imperial Conference of 1926 has converted the Empire," wrote Wedgwood. Jews, he argued, would also make valuable members of this Commonwealth enterprise. As the "Clapham Junction of the Commonwealth," Palestine represented a strategic imperial holding.[47] The Jews there would be of "real political and economic service to the Empire," Wedgwood argued. And while many perhaps thought of Jews as foreign, they were in fact quite similar to the English. Both were inclined to lend money and take risks, both had a "passion for wandering over the earth," both detested working for a master, and both had a preference—albeit a "lamentable" one—for the Old Testament's doctrine of "hit him first and hit him hard" rather than the pacifism of the New Testament. As part of the British Commonwealth, Jews in Palestine would benefit from the protection of a powerful empire, a valuable security in light of Mussolini and the "Roman fasces." And critically, reasoned Wedgwood, "protection [was] no longer humiliation" since the 1926 Balfour Declaration. Jews could now enjoy the safety of being part of an empire "without destroying independence or self-respect." Just as Arlosoroff had weighed the differences between a Zionist alliance with Britain compared to one with the League of Nations, Wedgwood also recognized this choice and warned his fellow countrymen that they would be wise not to drive the Jews into the arms of the League. "Plain realists" should recognize, he argued, "that moral as well as commercial advantages may well repay and balance the risks of protecting Palestine."[48] In February 1928, Wedgwood published an expanded version of his essay as a small book entitled *The Seventh Dominion*.[49]

According to Frederick Kisch, Wedgwood's fervent advocacy bordered on the problematic. In a private letter to Chaim Weizmann, Kisch wrote that "Wedgwood has had his innings with the Secretary of State and told him that most of the Government officials in Palestine are Egyptianised loafers and that they have done nothing to Anglicise the country!"[50] Kisch acknowledged that Wedgwood's combined passions for British imperialism, Labour politics, and Zionism held extraordinary value, but "such accusations . . . can only embitter the officials here who latterly have really been behaving rather well."[51] The positive attitudes of British clerks could be attributed to the guiding influence of High Commissioner Herbert Plumer, who "always recognises the duty of the Government to help us in our aims as much as possible, subject only to the Government acting rightly by the Arab population," wrote Kisch. "Fear of Arab criticism does not enter his mind as it always did with [High Commissioner Herbert] Samuel," he noted, "but merely the question of whether he himself is acting rightly in regard to the second part of the Balfour Declaration as well as the first"—that is, protecting the rights of the non-Jewish inhabitants of Palestine, while also facilitating the establishment of the Jewish national home.[52]

At the end of July 1928, Plumer concluded his term as high commissioner, and John Chancellor, the governor of Southern Rhodesia, was appointed to replace him. He would not, however, take up the post until December. In the interim, Harry Luke, the former assistant governor of Jerusalem and most recently the colonial secretary of Sierra Leone, was appointed acting high commissioner. Even with the economic recession experienced by the Yishuv in 1926, Plumer's tenure had been regarded by the Jewish community as one of peace and fairness in Palestine, with no major outbreak of violence. David Ben-Gurion believed Plumer had been a "first class" high commissioner. "I do not mean that he always did what we asked him to do, though his relations with us were very good," Ben-Gurion recalled, "but he was a firm and wise governor."[53] Luke, on the other hand, was remembered in Palestine for his participation in the Haycraft Commission in the wake of the 1921 Jaffa riots.[54] The commission, which blamed "Bolshevik" Jews for inciting the unrest, had driven Helen Bentwich (previously keen to criticize Zionists in Palestine) into a fury against the British "military mind," which justified the arrest of even the "most respectable Jews" simply for self-defense.[55] Arlosoroff, though he had not been arrested, had stood—armed—in defense of a Jewish neighborhood in Jaffa during the unrest.

In October 1928, against the backdrop of this changing guard, Arlosoroff wrote his second major consideration of the British question in Palestine. Entitled "British Clerks and the National Home," the piece appeared in Hebrew in *Hapoel Hatzair*. Though he would pen a lengthy response to Wedgwood's dominion scheme a year later, Arlosoroff first made reference to the idea of the "Seventh Dominion" in this 1928 essay. Understanding the British and addressing any of their negative attitudes toward Jews and Zionism was, he reasoned, "much more a way to the Seventh Dominion than all the decisions about a Jewish state."[56] The essay argued that promoting positive Zionist-British relations was imperative and would remain so indefinitely. "The partnership of the Jews and the British in Palestine is not limited in advance, as one might think, to a few years or even to the present generation alone," wrote Arlosoroff. "I think—and to tell the truth I will say it—that this partnership is more than temporary." [57]

Arlosoroff recounted that while reading an issue of the London weekly the *Near East and India*, he had come across the following line, which he felt perfectly encapsulated the problem of Jewish-British relations in Palestine: "The Arab in the Land of Israel effortlessly and without much difficulty secures the understanding and affection of the English, while at the same time, the Jew seems to the Englishman to be a mystical creature, irksome and unclear—precisely as he was perceived by the Roman official eighteen centuries ago."[58] This image of the enigmatic, intractable Jew, muddying established British colonial order, echoes themes from Arlosoroff's 1926 essay "Wall of Glass"; however, in "British Clerks and the National Home," Arlosoroff offered not the general prescriptions for moderation and cooperation that he had in 1926 but a detailed, sociological typology of British clerks in Palestine and concrete recommendations for addressing their biases. Arlosoroff argued that understanding and promoting positive relations with

FIGURE 3 Chaim Arlosoroff at the Fifteenth Zionist Congress in Basel, Switzerland, in 1927. From the collections of the Central Zionist Archives, Jerusalem (PHG\1091441).

British clerks by dispelling the image of the troublesome Jew—particularly among the rank and file of the mandatory government—was critical to the success of Zionism. The Yishuv had learned, as the British had long known, that an administration was just as important as a constitution. At times an administration even willingly contravened a constitution. Moreover, according to Arlosoroff, "the administrative nature of the country might be affected much more strongly by choosing postmen and police officers than by choosing a high commissioner or an attorney general." In other words, having Zionists such as Herbert Samuel and Norman Bentwich in high places still would not determine the character and attitude of a government administration.[59]

Arlosoroff outlined three major types of British clerks in Palestine, explaining each group's attitude toward Jews and Zionism. The first included about 10 percent of the British bureaucracy, mostly high officials with positive attitudes toward Zionism, some of whom arrived in Palestine already as bearers of those "ideas and ideals" and others who reached them while serving in the mandatory government. "This does not mean, of course, that they start talking or acting like they were members of the Zionist General Council," wrote Arlosoroff. In fact, these individuals, as stalwart imperialists, generally protected "the prestige of administrative justice," sometimes at the expense of the Jews. Arlosoroff included Wyndham Deedes; Brigadier General Gilbert Clayton; High Commissioner Plumer; and Major J. E. F. Campbell, the district commissioner of the southern region of Palestine, in this group.[60]

The second type of clerk resembled the first in their high level of education and culture; but these administrators were unfriendly toward Jews and Zionism, in part owing to a Christian religious fear of Jewish control over holy sites. "More than they oppose the Jews," however, wrote Arlosoroff, "they tend to the side of the Arabs." The English had a long, storied practice of celebrating the national cultures of other countries. For instance, "in no other poetry is there a sense of closeness and understanding of Italy as in English lyrics," Arlosoroff claimed.[61] In a convergence of orientalism and liberalism, this tradition had, in turn, shaped an English instinct to defend other nationalist movements and to criticize British imperialism. "No natural-born Egyptian attacked British rule in Egypt like Wilfrid Scawen Blunt," observed Arlosoroff, and "in the first ranks of the fighters for the national freedom of Indians to this day, we find Annie Besant and Gandhi's English advisors."[62] This impulse explained how a "pro-Arab idealistic movement" had developed among British officials. Such idealists included Gertrude Bell, St John Philby, Percy Cox, and Palestine's own Ernest Richmond, the assistant civil secretary and later director of antiquities for the Mandate Government.[63] Helen Bentwich, who considered Richmond a friend when he first arrived in Palestine, noted that by 1922, he had become more partisan toward the Arabs. An event honoring the king's birthday (the birthday itself had fallen on a Saturday) had been moved to a Monday out of deference to Jewish Sabbath observance. According to Helen, many Muslims refused to take part as a result. "So the mufti & his friends sulked, including Richmond who absented himself from everything too. . . . Oh, how I loathe all this squabbling & discord here," she lamented.[64]

The final group included the majority of British clerks in Palestine: individuals among the middling and lower ranks who staffed the police and the postal service, engineers in the Department of Public Works, and clerks in the Land and Health Departments. "We must take into account that under the conditions of the Land of Israel, all these officials have great importance," argued Arlosoroff. For instance, a post office director could decide whether Hebrew would be used in practice; a police officer could prevent Jews from visiting certain holy sites; an engineer from public works could decide how many Jews he would hire; and a British judge could decide who was to blame for unrest. Arlosoroff cited the prosecutions of the Jaffa riots of 1921 as a specific example of British justice meted out to the detriment of the Jewish community.[65]

On arrival in Palestine, these clerks held no particular feeling toward Jews. "The Jewish question throughout the world preoccupies them like last year's snow," wrote Arlosoroff. While the Jewish press had a tendency to condemn the British in Palestine for endemic antisemitism (Arlosoroff believed the fact that no administrator escaped accusation was proof of the preposterousness of the blanket charge), the majority of British clerks formed opinions of the locals in Palestine much in the way they did in "Iraq, Rhodesia, or . . . some other country." They arrived "groping in the dark" until they "finally [found] their way."[66]

Eventually, Arlosoroff argued, many British clerks developed pro-Arab sympathies. Certainly antisemitism existed to an extent within the British administration—and that made the problem "more complex"—but it did not, to his mind, explain the widespread tendency for the bulk of British clerks to support and identify ultimately with the Arabs.[67] Instead, Arlosoroff offered an explanation that evidenced his growing awareness and consideration of British imperial dynamics. The majority of these clerks, like their Roman counterparts eighteen hundred years before, gained administrative experience in other British colonies before coming to Palestine. Those who served in Iraq, Sudan, and Egypt learned Arabic and became familiar with Arab cultures. Had Palestine been inhabited only by Arabs (and perhaps the occasional European tourist), these clerks would have been content. Jews, however, represented a "perversion undermining the existing routine" of colonial administration.[68] They seemed "inorganic, complex, mystical and unusual" to the British. Why would Jews have left their developed countries to live in a provincial backwater like Palestine?[69] Arlosoroff imagined a situation in which a British public works engineer had to deal with Jewish laborers. A motley crew of former students, tailors, and shoemakers who only recently learned how to build buildings and roads, these Jewish workers—and their sense of sublime purpose—would stupefy their boss. "They say, that at the base of a historic process, they came to this country and became construction workers," the British engineer would muse, befuddled. "So what do I have to do with historic processes?!"[70]

Arabs, by contrast, fell into familiar imperial categories for the British, argued Arlosoroff. From images of primitive simplicity to exotic romanticism, Arabs in Palestine satisfied a British orientalist fantasy. Narrow alleyways, the muezzin's call to prayer, and bustling marketplaces recalled *One Thousand and One Nights* and Kipling's poetry (never mind, quipped Arlosoroff, that "after a more thorough examination," garage owners in Ramle and shopkeepers in Jaffa were in reality no more exotic than their counterparts in Britain).[71] "And into this idyll," wrote Arlosoroff, "Jews introduced dissonance and incompatibility." Even Jews' particular brand of Europeanness, wrapped up as it was in the "worry and restlessness" of Jewish life in Eastern Europe, was confusing and unidentifiable to the British. Jews were neither British enough nor Arab enough, neither part of the civilized metropole nor part of the mysterious wilds of the Middle East. "The pendulum from the beginning swings to one side. And not to our side," concluded Arlosoroff.[72]

So what was to be done? Arlosoroff maintained that neither the Jews nor the British would change their natures and that the contradictions in those clashing temperaments produced powerful disagreements. "Our aim in the Land of Israel demands from us that we abstain as much as possible from these arguments," urged Arlosoroff. A legislative body—despite Zionist objections that it would place them in an official minority position—would have at least given Jews in Palestine a direct point of mediation with the British. Instead, the people of Palestine found themselves governed by an "autocratic colonial bureaucracy." To counter this, argued Arlosoroff, Jews needed to create an English-language newspaper of "high cultural and presentation value" that, in place of a parliament, would represent Jewish opinion to the British.[73]

Arlosoroff then made his boldest assertion: this publication, as policy, would insist that Zionist-British cooperation was not a temporary aim but rather "a political aim that defines the nature of our national existence," both in the present *and* in a planned future when Jews would be the majority in Palestine. In other words, a partnership between the Yishuv and the British was not a means to an end, not a way to an independent state, but a fundamental and enduring ideal of the Jewish national home. "The good, idealistic Jewish national home must be open to the English," Arlosoroff concluded. Cooperation across cultures would prove difficult—indeed, even within the Jewish community, diverse backgrounds often provoked tenacious disagreement. But Arlosoroff believed that striving for positive Zionist-British relations was the only way forward. "We need to get to know each other," he implored, reasoning that "it is only in the wake of understanding that affection will come." And that intentional, cultivated understanding—more so than any dramatic political pronouncements from on high—was decidedly a surer way to a Seventh Dominion.[74]

While Arlosoroff felt that the prospect of dominion status could only be broached after many intermediate steps, others were willing to move more quickly toward political ends. Of all the major Zionist leaders at the time, Ze'ev Jabotinsky took up the idea of dominion most enthusiastically, viewing it as a streamlined path toward Jewish self-determination.[75] On learning of Wedgwood's scheme in 1927, the Revisionist leader wrote to the British MP to learn more about his ideas. "Of course the country should be governed from London for quite a long period yet," Jabotinsky began in his letter. Like Arlosoroff, Jabotinsky understood that further development in Palestine—chiefly substantial Jewish immigration that would place Jews in the majority—needed to occur before new political configurations, including dominion status, could be enacted. Any current attempt at representative government—a fixture of dominion countries—would be to the detriment of Jews in Palestine given the demographic imbalance. But Jabotinsky—unlike Arlosoroff, as we will see—favored immediate action, legislated from the metropole, that would put Palestine on the road toward dominion status. He told Wedgwood that he would not "shrink from something like direct annexation, fixing the status of the country forever as part of the British Commonwealth, now a [Crown Colony] and in the end a Dominion."[76] Wedgwood's unbridled criticism of the mandatory government in Palestine also appealed to Jabotinsky, who maintained his admiration for Britain and its metropolitan government but believed that British authorities *in* Palestine were ruining any prospect of constructive Zionist-British cooperation.[77]

The idea of dominion status also received attention in the Yishuv beyond the upper echelons of its leadership, particularly during the summer and fall of 1928, when Plumer's departure as high commissioner opened wide the prospect of change. In August 1928, the publisher and bookseller Yechezkel Steimatzky informed Jabotinsky that he had sold two hundred copies of Wedgwood's book in his Jerusalem and Jaffa shops—a "colossal" success, in his opinion. Moreover, the popularity of the book meant "a lot in a country where just the intelligentsia hardly know any English." Steimatzky thought a Hebrew translation of *The Seventh Dominion* would "be a little avalanche." Jabotinsky even offered to write a new introduction for the Hebrew-language edition, but no translation was ever produced.[78] The scheme also received coverage in the press, including the English-language *Palestine Bulletin* and the right-leaning *Doar Hayom* (whose editorship was taken over by Jabotinsky in December 1928). The *Bulletin* reproduced the preface of *The Seventh Dominion* for its readers; covered speeches given by Wedgwood in Berlin at a Poale Zion conference and at a meeting of Revisionist leaders; but also published a scathing critique of the dominion scheme written by the British politician and academic Ernest Bennett.[79] Peretz Dagan, the assistant editor of *Doar Hayom*, wrote favorably about the dominion scheme in his column "Parshat ha-Yom," arguing that one benefit would be increased Jewish immigration. Rather than impeding immigration as the mandatory government had, he reasoned, the new dominion government would encourage immigration, just as the dominion governments of New Zealand, Canada, Australia, and South Africa had.[80] Local meetings in Palestine were also held to discuss the idea. For instance, *Davar* reported that Klivnov and Finkelstein[81] gave talks on the Seventh Dominion scheme to an audience in Haifa, where debate ensued.[82]

Amid this summer buzz, Jabotinsky, who was on holiday in the French Pyrenees, wrote a letter to Wedgwood. In the note, he imagined what might be possible if the Revisionists were to sweep elections at the upcoming Sixteenth Zionist Congress and a "Seventh Dominion League"—a society promoting the dominion idea for Palestine—were to be formed. "It will give you and the rest of our close friends an element of actual everyday influence in Palestine," he predicted, continuing, "I feel confident that in a years [sic] time the League can become a noticeable force in British Middle East politics."[83]

The Seventh Dominion scheme initially received support from other Revisionist Zionists. The Third Revisionist World Conference held in Vienna in December 1928 voted that "no contradiction" existed between the goals of a Jewish national home in Palestine and dominion status in the British Commonwealth.[84] Two months later, on February 26, 1929, Wedgwood officially inaugurated the Seventh Dominion League at Central Hall Westminster, with himself as chair. In May of that year, Jabotinsky accepted the chair of the chapter established in Jerusalem.

Between the establishment of the London and Jerusalem League chapters, Arlosoroff finally issued his own direct response to Wedgwood's plan, which he published in the *New Palestine* in April 1929.[85] The article reflected Arlosoroff's Weizmannian insistence on slow, gradual development. Though Wedgwood's book contained compelling arguments, Arlosoroff thought the entire proposal "somewhat precipitate." Any discussion of Palestine's political future or Zionism's ultimate aims was premature and would be to the detriment of the movement. The viability of different political proposals was entirely contingent on "the actual balance of political power in Palestine." At present, Jews constituted roughly only 15 percent of the total population, with Palestinian Arabs making up the majority. Given this reality, the Yishuv needed to focus on the day-to-day work of building up its society and economy and had to resist the inclination to fantasize about the "forty-ninth and fiftieth" steps toward its goal rather than the immediate tasks at hand.

"The Jew, and for that matter the Zionist," wrote Arlosoroff, "thinks too much of the Jewish State and too little of the average annual yield of his cow which may help him establish a profitable dairy, and, progressively, systematic immigration, and, ultimately the Jewish State."[86]

His concerns with regard to timing established, Arlosoroff moved to the central question of his article: Were Zionist aspirations and dominion status fundamentally compatible, potentially in a "far-off future" scenario? "It is my opinion," he declared, "that from the point of view of Zionist ideals, the Seventh Dominion scheme does not offer the slightest contradiction." The political aim of Zionism—to achieve the right of national self-determination for the Jewish people within the boundaries of Palestine—allowed for a broad range of possible constitutional forms, he argued. And although it was too early to know what specific form that would eventually be, a dominion was certainly just as plausible as a Soviet republic or even "a monarchy under Ussishkin's dynasty," he suggested in jest.[87] But in seriousness, continued Arlosoroff, more than being simply one of many potential constitutional options equal in merit, dominion status in fact boasted several "conclusive arguments in its favor."[88]

Arlosoroff proceeded to outline a series of arguments in favor of dominion that he based on a careful assessment of the economic and political conditions in Palestine. His "not at all sentimental" analysis (in contrast to the Anglophile Jews who favored close relations to Britain based on "purely psychological factors, like gratitude or sympathy") first explored the economic question. No longer confined to the borders of "limited national states," successful modern economies instead flourished in larger supranational networks. Commonwealth and "imperial combines" such as the United States, the British Empire, and the Soviet Union were "much better equipped to meet the requirements of our economic age," wrote Arlosoroff. States such as France, Germany, and Italy "though basking in the sun of sovereignty," suffered economically for their independence as they faced growing trustification, increasingly cumbersome economic legislation, and the mess of coordinating tariff and trade agreements. Smaller independent nations like Poland and the Baltic states made the reality of modern economies "a thousand times more obvious."[89]

Palestine, a small country and not "one too richly endowed with monopolies of any kind," had always been part of a larger Levantine economic system. But treaties signed in the wake of World War I had disrupted those long-standing economic ties, cutting off the fertile Hauran plateau from British Palestine and blocking access to the trade ports of Jaffa and Haifa for the rest of the region. Writing against the backdrop of the growth of Arab nationalisms, Arlosoroff envisioned that over the course of the next few decades, independent Arab states would begin to emerge around Palestine and would likely form economic alliances or a federation. "Palestine will then be a self-sufficient and secluded unit, in the economic sense, even less than at present," he noted. While Arlosoroff, like other Zionists, including Ben-Gurion and Katznelson, thought seriously about the possibility of a federation, he feared that a broader economic federation of Arab states represented a bleak option in comparison to the prospect of official ties with "one of the outside powers of the supra-national type." Membership in the British Commonwealth, "one of the most advanced and highly developed political organisms, commanding a modern system of production and transportation and wide markets," would afford Palestine more economic opportunities and would counteract the "naturally gravitating" inclination of the country's Palestinian Arabs toward other Arab states. When presented with the choice between "independence within the field of gravitation of an Arab federation" versus "Dominion status within the British Empire," Arlosoroff argued that "the answer, from our standpoint . . . can hardly be doubted." Canada, with strong economic ties to its southern neighbor and a French-Canadian population resistant toward the dominion's "British allegiance," represented a close parallel to Palestine's situation.[90] Though Arlosoroff did not state so explicitly, he implied with the Canadian comparison that Palestinian Arabs would become citizens of a Palestine dominion. Jabotinsky and Wedgwood, in contrast, repeatedly spoke of a *Jewish* dominion and did not address what would happen to the Arab population.

With regard to politics, Arlosoroff believed that dominion status would enlarge Palestine's political standing and sphere of influence far beyond what its size and resources could permit independently. An aspiration for international influence did not reflect outsized ambitions or naive hopes, like "the foolish desire of a small boy to step into his big uncle's trousers." Rather, argued Arlosoroff, building up the Yishuv's international standing was a political imperative of Zionism, "the logical conclusion of our nationalism." With greater influence came a better ability to safeguard international peace—potentially preventing another conflict in which Jews had to face each other on the battlefield. Dominion status could also invest Palestine with the diplomatic power to advocate for Jewish political and civic interests across the diaspora.[91]

Despite Arlosoroff's belief that any discussion of Palestine becoming a dominion was at that time premature, the theoretical adoption of a dominion scheme would allow for several developments favorable to the Zionist movement. As Peretz Dagan pointed out in *Doar Hayom* and Jabotinsky also understood, once Palestine became a British crown colony (an intermediate step on the way to dominion status), the new government would establish a colonialization department. This body would undertake—on an enlarged scale—the work of immigration and settlement, previously the sole responsibility of the Palestine Zionist Executive. Arlosoroff believed that the dominion plan, fundamentally different from a mandate, would also improve British attitudes toward the Yishuv—ever his central concern. No longer "[sweating] for other people's interests . . . their own ends no less than those of the Jews," British officials would help to establish a long-lasting dominion rather than toil through the transient custodianship of a mandate. Finally, any discussion over the nature of parliamentary institutions and proper representation of Jews and Palestinian Arabs—"one of the most intricate, delicate and unsolvable issues"—would, at least in the interim, "be dropped from the agenda" once Palestine became a crown colony.[92]

Notwithstanding these hypothetical benefits, Arlosoroff believed the dominion scheme also had several drawbacks and weaknesses. Wedgwood had argued that his scheme, in order to succeed, needed the support of both Britain and the Jews. Arlosoroff had his doubts, despite the attention Wedgwood's plan received in the British press, that Britain would actually take the idea of a Palestine dominion seriously—"as seriously as, say, the naval base in Singapore."[93] As to the second half of Wedgwood's formula for success, Arlosoroff acknowledged that the scheme had already gained the support of Jabotinsky and the Revisionists. It "might succeed in winning us [Labor Zionists] over as well," he suggested. Yet even if the Zionist Congress were to commit to the scheme, they could neither compel the population of Palestine to follow it nor force their decision to have any weight in international politics without Britain's full support. "How, indeed, can people dispose of things which they do not, as yet, possess?" Arlosoroff asked.[94]

These obstacles aside, "there exists one argument, momentous and grave, which weighs heavily against the idea of Palestine gradually growing into a British Dominion," wrote Arlosoroff. The very nature of the Jewish diaspora, scattered across the globe, which made the idea of a British dominion with its concomitant international standing and influence so politically expedient, also made it potentially dangerous: "This scattered and split up nation—the House of Israel divided against itself—has undertaken to build a national center, a homeland for the people as a whole, a homeland for its national genius and civilization. As soon as Palestine accepts membership among the Dominions of the British Empire, this national homeland becomes part and parcel of one of the existing political spheres of interest. In a certain sense it becomes partisan, it sides with one of the powers."[95]

Any set of hypothetical antagonisms—a British-Russian conflict or even a British-American one—could burden millions of Jews with accusations of conflicting loyalties and allegiances. This represented a serious hypothetical problem, conceded Arlosoroff, but avoiding "political spheres of interest" was likely impossible, regardless of Palestine's political future—the country did not exist in a geopolitical vacuum. "What is called 'Pax Britannica' may be not the worst guarantee for Palestine.... The dominion program is, after all, the safest road," he concluded.[96]

A measured and logical tone, divorced from sentimentality about Britain, pervades Arlosoroff's discussion of the dominion scheme. While he concluded that a dominion might ultimately be "the safest road," he did so with little to no praise for British civic and political culture or for British imperialism, the type of rhetoric characteristic of British Labour imperialists, including Wedgwood.[97] Dominion was, by its very nature, an encroachment on Jewish national autonomy—rather than a means to achieve it, as Jabotinsky saw it—but total independence had far more serious political and economic disadvantages. In Arlosoroff's assessment, dominion was the best compromise among a series of compromised choices.

Arlosoroff was unique among his Labor Zionist peers for publicly considering the dominion scheme—even more so for offering it his tentative support. Despite Wedgwood's Labour politics, most Labor Zionists refrained from commenting altogether on the question of dominion. Indeed, the scheme elicited unease from most Zionists who were not Revisionists. Kisch worried about the damaging effect of Wedgwood's criticism of the mandatory government.[98] Ben-Gurion, though he considered Wedgwood a great friend of Zionism, also thought that his enthusiastic machinations endangered Labor Zionism's commitment to cautious development.[99]

Although Jabotinsky's hopes for the founding of a Seventh Dominion League were realized, his dream of a Revisionist takeover at the Sixteenth Zionist Congress was not to be. In late July and early August 1929, the Zionist Congress convened in Zurich, and far from a sweeping Revisionist success, delegates, in fact—despite passionate Revisionist protestation—voted to include non-Zionists in the newly inaugurated Jewish Agency for Palestine (formerly the Palestine Zionist Executive).[100] At the conclusion of the Congress, Arlosoroff left for London—the last stop on a long journey that had taken him across North America and Europe. He arrived determined to find out all he could about Julius Vogel, New Zealand's Jewish prime minister, and to deepen his knowledge about the history of British colonialism through research at the British Museum.

IN THE WAKE OF THE RIOTS

Five days after Arlosoroff's walk through Hyde Park, recounted at the opening of this chapter, riots broke out in Palestine. Like the Bentwiches, who were on leave in England at the time, Arlosoroff found himself forced to process news of the violence—which arrived piecemeal in devastating blows with the morning, afternoon, and evening papers—from thousands of miles away. On Saturday, August 24, 1929, the morning after the first day of rioting, Arlosoroff leisurely strolled to the British Museum, unaware of what had transpired in Palestine. He admired the charm of Bloomsbury, particularly the neighborhood's beautiful enclosed squares, musing that the streets were reduced to "mere accessories" against the verdant luster of the gardens. But a morning newspaper quickly shattered his reverie. "I stood face to face with the calamity that occurred the day before in Jerusalem, and the consequences of which it is impossible to foresee even in this moment," he related in a letter to his wife. The afternoon paper was a greater shock, with a sensational headline—"Warships to Palestine!"—and reports of extensive casualties. "The worst thing is nobody is nowhere [sic]," wrote Arlosoroff. Not a single member of the Zionist Executive was in Palestine—Isaiah Braude, the Executive's bookkeeper, had been left in charge. High Commissioner Chancellor, too, was away. London, in that final stretch of August, was hardly any better. Louis Lipsky, the head of the Zionist Organization of America, had arrived in town the previous night, but when Arlosoroff saw him on Saturday, the American had no idea anything had happened. British officials in London were also inaccessible. The Colonial Office had cleared out for the weekend and the under-secretary of state for the colonies was unreachable.[101] Newspapers from Palestine had been suspended and telegrams censored. "God knows what is going on there," worried Arlosoroff, "and what is it all about? And what good is it all? That damned Wailing Wall-issue is a complete deadlock, no way out, and it will cost us so much: blood, peace, nerves, good-will, prestige, constructive possibilities, relations so difficult to cement, confidence of the Jews."[102]

Following the riots, leaders of the Yishuv believed they were facing down an unprecedented moment of rupture in Palestine. The violence had heralded a new reality of Palestinian Arab nationalism, shattering Zionist hopes of establishing a Jewish national home while the movement was still in its infancy. Some Labor Zionists initially hoped that the recently formed British Labour government, led once again by Ramsay MacDonald, would intervene, condemn Arab violence, and reiterate Britain's commitment to the Jewish national home. But two investigative commissions and a white paper policy statement later, many Zionists believed that hope had been defeated. Zionist-British relations, it seemed, had undergone irreparable damage.[103] Wedgwood's scheme also suffered a crushing blow. Convinced the lofty goal of the Seventh Dominion League was now wishful thinking, its members disbanded.[104]

Arlosoroff regarded the riots as a moment of reckoning and trauma that demanded a reevaluation of Zionist policy and tactics—chief among them a rededication to the idea of auto-emancipation and an understanding of Zionism as a movement for "self-liberation" that required state-like levers of power to achieve its aims. If Revisionists had created a "nationalism full of phraseology, possessed perhaps of power, but without means or possibility of implementing that power," Zionists on the opposite side of the political spectrum had given life to something far more damaging. In an essay he published just days before the Shaw Commission arrived in Palestine in late October 1929, Arlosoroff argued that "the psychological influence of the extreme pacifist agitators, especially among certain groups of intellectuals, has resulted in the creation of a spirit of disbelief in our own powers, however limited they may be."[105] Zionism in 1929 had no time for the "defeating ideology" of Brit Shalom, which "virtually repudiates the theory of auto-emancipation," he wrote. Indeed, no space even existed for the ideas of Ahad Ha'am. Rather, Zionists must realize, Arlosoroff insisted, that their movement was "based upon the principle of self-liberation." All the spiritual and cultural development in the world could not mitigate the need for "continuous immigration, systematic colonization, self-defense and political organization." Zionists needed to believe that they themselves could secure these aims and wield levers of state-like power. "A movement which is nurtured in a sense of powerlessness must inevitably go down in disappointment," Arlosoroff concluded.[106]

But alongside these forceful political pronouncements, the riots did not prompt disillusionment in the Zionist-British relationship but rather inspired Arlosoroff to redouble his commitment to understanding and improving the partnership. Over the next tumultuous two years, though he categorically condemned the actions of British mandatory authorities, Arlosoroff threw himself doggedly into cementing strong, productive Zionist-British ties, particularly between Labor Zionists and British Labourites. He also worked to make knowledge of Britain and its empire accessible to a Hebrew-reading public and continued his personal research on Julius Vogel and the history of British colonization. Thus, as Arlosoroff grew increasingly convinced that state-like power was critical to Zionist aims, he also intensified his dedication to the Zionist-British partnership. What is more, the ideas of state-like power and self-liberation, on the one hand, and a commitment to a continued relationship with the British Empire, on the other, represented not disjointed, distinct lines of thought in Arlosoroff's mind but, as we will see, intimately intertwined ones.

When Arlosoroff returned to Palestine in mid-September 1929, the Yishuv was still reeling from the riots. Helen Bentwich, who wrote that "everyone is a raw mass of nerves," had just begun organizing relief efforts for Hadassah.[107] Antagonism toward High Commissioner Chancellor, widely regarded not only as unsympathetic to Zionism but also as prone to antisemitism, was particularly acute. Facing accusations of his administration's unpreparedness and partiality, Chancellor argued that while most of the violence had been carried out by Arabs, the cause of the unrest stemmed from Jewish immigration and land purchases. In the same October 1929 essay in which he articulated Zionism's need for concrete power and commitment to self-liberation, Arlosoroff joined in the criticism of Chancellor's administration. The old challenges in the Zionist-British relationship in Palestine persisted, as they always had, explained Arlosoroff. British authorities, for instance, continued to be confounded by those Jewish "former students who talk in seventy tongues but have no experience in their trades." But the relationship had reached a marked level of "retrogression" in the aftermath of the riots. Now a "bitter feeling of disappointment, desertion and betrayal" pervaded the Yishuv, whose members believed British authorities employed a "daily routine of annulment defeating every constructive plan for the upbuilding of the National home in Palestine." This sad state of affairs was all the more striking for the fact that "a deep loyalty, a feeling of honor for British culture and government," and a "love for the British flag" had developed among Jews in Palestine and around the world in the wake of World War I. In his jaunts through Hyde Park and his awestruck wonder in the hallowed halls of the British Museum, Arlosoroff undoubtedly experienced these affinities himself. But "the precious principles of justice and righteousness in administration inherent in the 'Pax Britannica' have been weakened," he argued. "Jews have learned that there is one standard of Justice between 'gentlemen' and another between 'gentlemen' and those who are not 'gentlemen.'"[108]

Arlosoroff also recognized that the sorry state of Zionist-British relations reflected factors far removed from the minutiae of workaday realities in Palestine. For instance, while "the massacre of seminary students, the slaughter of old men and children, under the British flag, made a powerful impression" on the British public, sympathy for Zionism had failed to follow, "perhaps because it is generally difficult in time of war to find sympathy for the Jew and his cause," Arlosoroff wrote with eerie prescience.[109] More broadly, an indifference—even antagonism—among Britons toward imperial activity had developed since the war and had only sharpened after the onset of a worldwide economic crisis. "England is now beset with difficult economic problems, with a million and a quarter unemployed for years and coal mining districts in a state of paralysis," he wrote. These financial hardships had empire-wide ramifications:

> The people do not feel that the Dominions are making any special effort to come to their aid by opening the doors to immigrants and inaugurating broad colonization programs. The working class and its leaders are farther than ever from turning aside from the oppressive questions of the day and allowing themselves the luxury of dreaming about new conquests that would involve new expenditures. Here again it must be stressed that the political literature of England deals only incidentally with the actual ties that bind the Empire to Palestine; so that it appears that whatever England is doing is being done for the sake of the Jew.[110]

Here, Arlosoroff presented a new understanding of dominion status, the political possibility for Palestine that he had cautiously endorsed only earlier that year. Then, he had thought a dominion could correct the unbalanced, custodial nature of the mandate.[111] Now, he observed, an enmity in Britain existed toward all the dominions for a perceived failure to uphold their end of the partnership.

Factors in other reaches of the British Empire—especially India—also shaped the Zionist-British relationship. "The British Empire today is the largest Moslem power in the world," wrote Arlosoroff. "Its relation therefore with other Moslem lands is one of the chief problems of an empire which includes parts of India, Afghanistan, Baluchistan, Persia, Mesopotamia, Arabia, Egypt and the Soudan, besides Palestine." India—home to 60 million of the 110 million Muslims living under the British flag—sat at the epicenter of communication with "all the lands of Islam." In the past, argued Arlosoroff, conflict between Jews and Arabs in Palestine had revolved around "local economic and political" issues and had not been of tremendous concern to Muslims in other parts of the empire. "But as soon as religious motives are involved, as in the incident of the Wailing Wall, it becomes a political problem of the first magnitude from the view point of the Empire," he wrote. "In its action England has stressed this factor."[112]

British "action" also reeked of double standards, according to Arlosoroff. While he praised the immediate response of the British Labour government to the riots in Palestine (in contrast to that of the local mandatory administration), he argued that Labour's broader imperial policy—principally disarmament and, most important, the introduction of self-government—had not been extended to Palestine. This was an era in which Britain ended the Egyptian protectorate; installed Faisal as king in Iraq and negotiated the country's eventual entry into the League of Nations; "dared to announce" that India might receive dominion status even before the conclusion of the Simon Commission;[113] and worked to reduce armaments at the naval base in Singapore. "Amidst all this," wrote Arlosoroff, "the policy of a 'strong hand' in Palestine, the method of governing without popular representation and the suppression of every movement among its inhabitants, seems a glaring contradiction."[114]

Arlosoroff continued this comparative line of critique in his response to the Shaw Commission, demonstrating his expanding knowledge of the British Empire. After investigating the August riots, the Shaw Commission upheld High Commissioner Chancellor's opinion that Jewish land purchases and immigration were the root cause of the unrest. The investigation also cleared the British administration of any wrong doing. Helen Bentwich, "confident of [the commission's] entire futility," had been right in her prediction that a British commission would fail to hold a British administration responsible.[115] In his response, Arlosoroff noted that whereas the royal commissions tasked with public inquiry in Britain and the dominions were "usually composed of resident members of the local parliament who have an exact knowledge of their respective countries," the Shaw Commission contained not a single resident of Palestine—Arab, Jew, or otherwise.[116] He also criticized the commission's idealization of prewar economic practices in Palestine, specifically the example of Jewish-owned citrus farms employing Arab workers.[117] Though the commission held this up as a model of cross-cultural cooperation between Jews and Arabs, Arlosoroff objected to the depiction. "What the Report calls 'co-operation' is actually a system of exploitation . . . of the mass of the population by a minority," he wrote. After World War I, Hebrew labor—the employment of Jewish workers, even though Arab workers often represented cheaper labor—had become a central tenet within mainstream Labor Zionism. "The Shaw Commission seems not to have heard that a system of colonisation built upon the exploitation of a native population by an immigrant minority of European origin has been rejected by leading authorities on colonisation, on social as well as political grounds," argued Arlosoroff, citing a recently published study on settlement and economic development in Australia.[118] Unrest in 1921 and again in 1929, which swept cities like Petach Tikvah and Hebron, where Jewish and Arab "co-operation" had been the prewar norm, proved that the model was untenable, Arlosoroff claimed.

In a 1927 essay published in *Hapoel Hatzair*, Arlosoroff had looked to another site in the British Empire—South Africa—as a parallel to the economic situation of Jews and Arabs in Palestine. Instead of stressing the issue of exploitation, as he would in 1929, Arlosoroff focused on the impact that a joint Jewish-Arab economic sector would have on Jewish wages and, in turn, the development of the Jewish national home. He prefaced his discussion with the caveat that he was not presenting South Africa as a political model for Palestine but rather only wanted to "compare the polar points in the economies of both countries." In terms of percentages of white European workers, on the one hand, and non-European and native workers, on the other, South Africa represented a close contemporary parallel to Palestine. Facing competition from Indians and Africans, who worked for cheaper wages, white supporters of the South African Labour Party and trade unions had successfully campaigned for the imposition of a color bar, which excluded nonwhites from higher-level positions and created two distinct (though interdependent) economic sectors. "It does not matter if we reject these politics," Arlosoroff reasoned. Instead, he argued the main point was "to emphasize the economic motives and social relations that, justly or not, led to the adoption of the color bar law." He explained that in the case of Palestine, European Jewish immigrants would only remain in the country if they were able to find decent wages. In a similar dynamic to South Africa, the competition of Arab labor in the context of a joint economy in Palestine would drive Jewish wages down, resulting in reverse immigration and the deterioration of the Yishuv.[119] Joint organization (that is, a joint Jewish-Arab labor union) could not overcome the realities of an enduring capitalism. Thus the solution in Palestine, Arlosoroff argued, was to create two separate economies—by implication, one for Jews featuring higher wages for skilled labor and another for Arabs with lower-wages for unskilled labor.[120]

These positions on labor signified a departure for Arlosoroff. In the aftermath of 1921, he had criticized the policy of Hebrew labor because it offered an *economic* solution to Jewish-Arab relations in Palestine, when he believed that the only solution was a *political* one. In 1927 and again in 1929, with a deepening awareness of colonization, colonialism, and the British Empire, Arlosoroff defended Hebrew labor on economic grounds by pointing to parallels in other reaches of the empire. Though Arlosoroff recognized Palestinian Arab nationalism as a significant political force much earlier than his Labor Zionist peers, his assessment of the economic situation in Palestine after the recession of 1926 prompted him to support labor policies that fundamentally violated universalist labor principles. Arlosoroff surely recognized the controversy into which he was wading by invoking South Africa and the color bar; his equivocating language of "justly or not" and his insistence on avoiding a political comparison indicate as much, though they hardly constitute a condemnation of the racist policies in South Africa that would eventually be institutionalized as apartheid in 1948. The 1927 essay was never translated and published in English, while the 1929 essay, which referenced only Australia—a far more palatable comparison for British Labour supporters than South Africa—subsequently appeared in English translation.

While Arlosoroff did not hesitate to criticize British policy in Palestine, the nature and content of his critique reflected just how immersed he had become in questions about Britain and its history, empire, politics, and culture. What is more, alongside this criticism—indeed, sometimes in the very same essay—Arlosoroff continued to insist on the utter importance of defending and improving Zionist-British relations, often at the expense of Jewish-Arab cooperation. In his 1929 essay published before the Shaw Commission, Arlosoroff concluded that "despite the difficult relations" and the "embittered feelings of disenchantment ... there is no Zionist task today as important as the strengthening of our relations with England." It was precisely because the relationship to Britain was so "complicated and involved" that Zionists needed to approach it as their "one chief task." They needed "to elucidate it, to unravel the snarls, correct mistakes and overlook a great many things that may seem important now, but are nothing compared to the essential." For Arlosoroff, that essential work included identifying a "common program of activity in the future"; organizing "methodological propaganda" in London; and, finally, developing a plan for some type of representative legislative body. Such a body would hold the mandatory power "to public account every day"; otherwise, the British, according to Arlosoroff, would "always follow the path of the least resistance" in their administration of Palestine.[121] A year earlier, in his essay outlining a typology of British administrators in Palestine, Arlosoroff had suggested that a high-quality English-language paper might function in place of a legislative body in representing Jewish opinion to the British.[122] After the riots, successfully conveying the Jewish position no longer seemed enough; a truly effective Zionist-British partnership demanded British mandatory accountability.

BRINGING THE EMPIRE TO PALESTINE

Other Zionists maintained faith in Zionist-British relations up until the release of the Shaw Commission's report in March 1930, but Arlosoroff is notable for insisting on the continued importance of the partnership and for working actively to cultivate it even during the height of the crisis: the publication of the Passfield White Paper in October 1930.[123] For instance, after the January 1930 founding of Mapai (a merger between the Labor Zionist parties Ahdut ha-Avodah and Hapoel Hatzair), Arlosoroff focused particular attention on strengthening ties between his new party and the Labour Party in Britain, whose shared politics presented an obvious opportunity to develop a "common program of activity."[124] The merger—in which Arlosoroff played a key role—signified the weakening of the divisions that had previously separated the two parties, particularly Ahdut ha-Avodah's historic emphasis on class struggle and Hapoel Hatzair's repudiation of it; on that matter, the latter's position prevailed. Arlosoroff understood that British Labour—a stronghold for reformist ideas that moved away from the notion of an impending revolution and recognized a potentially enduring capitalism—could be a beacon for the new moderate Mapai Party as a participant in an international socialist effort. After the merger, Arlosoroff assumed the role of editor of the journal *Ahdut ha-Avodah* (which retained its title) and, in that capacity, reached out to a range of British Labour figures to invite them to author articles for the publication.¹²⁵ "We are most anxious to keep the contacts between the Palestinian workingman and social and cultural developments abroad close and alive," wrote Arlosoroff in a form letter to several Labour figures in April 1930, a month after the Shaw Commission's report was published. "Whatever is going on in the British Commonwealth of Nations and, particularly, in the ranks of British Labour is . . . of special importance to us," he continued, explaining that the journal would now have a section dedicated to "problems of the British Empire from Labour's point of view." Arlosoroff reached out to Labour figures who were already established allies of the Zionist cause, as well as to some individuals who would later become supportive. For instance, he wrote to Wedgwood and Joseph Kenworthy, another MP and champion of the Seventh Dominion Scheme.¹²⁶ Three years earlier in New York, Arlosoroff had partnered with Kenworthy to raise funds for the United Palestine Appeal.¹²⁷ Arlosoroff also contacted Norman Angell, the British MP and writer who was a close friend of Weizmann; Susan Lawrence, one of the first women Labour MPs and later a supporter of Zionism;¹²⁸ the MP and philanthropist Charles Buxton, who had been an early proponent of Zionism;¹²⁹ and Harold Laski, the Fabian leader and academic (and brother of Anglo-Jewish communal leader Neville Laski), who became more involved in Zionism in the wake of the 1930 Passfield White Paper.¹³⁰

For Arlosoroff, providing these perspectives in Hebrew translation represented a key way to educate the Yishuv about British Labour and the empire. It was often challenging, however, to convey back to the non-Hebrew reading authors the effect of their articles. After mailing G. T. Garratt¹³¹ a copy of the issue in which his article "The Indian Imbroglio" had appeared, Arlosoroff apologized for not translating the several interesting reader comments he had received in response to the piece. In reply, Garratt gave his "kind opinion of the journal." Arlosoroff thanked him, conceding that his generous assessment had necessarily been limited to the journal's appearance. "As to the contents," wrote Arlosoroff, "you know the rendering of the phrase 'It's all Greek to me' in French is: 'C'est [de] l'hébreu pour moi!'"¹³² Garratt would write more for *Ahdut ha-Avodah*: an article entitled "The Labour Party and the Empire" and a piece on the first Round Table Conference, held in London from November 1930 to January 1931 to decide on future constitutional reforms for India.¹³³

Outside of his journal, Arlosoroff brought other work on British and British imperial topics to the attention of the Yishuv. In 1930, he published a Hebrew translation of Basil Williams's 1928 book *The British Empire*, a short, readable volume that recounted a triumphalist story of imperial expansion with particular attention to economic development.[134] The preface to the Hebrew edition explained that the book was a celebration of the imperial enterprise, written out of "a belief in the power of life and development which is still apparent in the British Empire."[135] Also in 1930, Arlosoroff published a review of *The Dominions and the Colonial Offices* (1926), written by the former permanent undersecretary of state George Fiddes.[136] Arlosoroff argued that Fiddes's book, though one of many published on the topic of British imperialism, offered a unique and vivid insider's view of the upper echelons of the Colonial Office. He recommended the text as a kind of guide—an "anatomy of the administration of the British Empire, with all its sections and branches"—that could shed light on a labyrinthine institution so often viewed by the public as one of those "mysterious forces of nature whose activity is shrouded in darkness."[137]

While immersing himself in writing about the British Empire and working to make that information available to the Yishuv, Arlosoroff continued to pursue a related project of personal interest: his planned biography of Julius Vogel. After his first research trip to London in August 1929 was cut short because of the riots in Palestine, Arlosoroff resolved to move ahead with his examination of the "life of a strange country, a strange man and a fascinating period of colonization."[138] Vogel was indeed an unusual historical figure—and one, Arlosoroff realized, who had been left remarkably unexamined and "underestimated" by historians.[139] Born in London in 1835 into a family of middle-class Ashkenazi Jews, Vogel was raised in the home of his maternal grandfather, who ran a merchant firm in the City of London.[140] Vogel was educated in Ramsgate (at the school promoted by Moses Montefiore) and later at the Royal School of Mines, where he studied chemistry and the material sciences. In 1852, he left England bound for Australia, joining the migration of young adventurers hoping to make their fortune in the goldfields of Victoria. There, he worked as a newspaper editor and ran unsuccessfully for the Victorian Parliament. In 1861, he settled in Otago on the South Island of New Zealand, where he wrote for a local paper and made his first successful foray into politics. After serving as a member of the New Zealand Parliament for ten years, Vogel was elected premier of the country in 1873. He held the post for two years and again in 1876, during which he spearheaded a major public works scheme. Vogel was also notable for supporting women's suffrage (New Zealand eventually became the first country to give women the vote in 1893) and for penning New Zealand's first science fiction novel, *Anno Domini 2000, or, Woman's Destiny*. The novel imagined a future in which the British Empire had become an imperial federation, and women held the most prominent positions of power.

Arlosoroff, who planned to call his book *Sir Julius Vogel and the Colonization of New Zealand*, was particularly interested in the premier's public works scheme. In a letter to a contact in Dunedin, Arlosoroff reported that his book would "be an economic analysis of the era of the Public Works Policy and its importance for the development of New Zealand, centering around Sir Julius' personality and achievements."[141] New Zealand in the 1870s had navigated many of the same challenges faced by the Yishuv in the interwar period. Vogel's ambitious and controversial scheme, made possible by massive borrowing from Britain, promoted large-scale immigration and settlement and revolutionized New Zealand's infrastructure, building up the country's railways, roads, ports, and telegraph lines (often through the acquisition of Māori land). Vogel's Jewishness and the role it played in his political career also intrigued Arlosoroff. Though Vogel married a non-Jewish woman from Dunedin, he never converted to Christianity, identified as a Jew his entire life, and was buried in a Jewish cemetery in London (in contrast to his contemporary Benjamin Disraeli). He also had been "exposed to many slanderous attacks on account of his being a Jew," which Arlosoroff thought made it unlikely that "he should have ignored [his Jewish identity] altogether."[142] Arlosoroff returned to London in November 1930 and continued research on Vogel in his spare time. "Today and to-morrow (Saturday) are my relatively free days," he wrote to his wife. "I am spending them, of course, in the British Museum Reading Room, dipping back to Sir Julius Vogel's life. It still interests me very much."[143]

Arlosoroff had been called back to London in November 1930, at Weizmann's behest, to participate in negotiations with the British government following the fallout of the Passfield White Paper. Issued the previous month, the white paper articulated a new British policy of dual obligation to both Jews and Arabs. It maintained the Shaw Report's recommendation that Jewish land purchases should be curtailed and that further Jewish immigration should abide by a principle of absorptive economic capacity, which took into account all of Palestine, not solely the Jewish economy. In effect, this meant that Arab unemployment constituted grounds for restricting Jewish immigration to Palestine. The white paper also made clear that the recently restructured and enlarged Jewish Agency, which now included non-Zionists, held no political power in Palestine. Finally, the policy statement announced Britain's intention to establish a representative legislative assembly in Palestine, which (because of the population makeup in Palestine) would necessarily have an Arab majority. Weizmann resigned as president of the Zionist Organization in protest over what he saw as the white paper's fundamental betrayal of the Balfour Declaration and in recognition that his policy of Zionist-British cooperation had come to be regarded as a failed one in Zionist circles. Zionists and legal experts alike argued that the policy laid out in the Passfield White Paper contravened the terms of the mandate. The issuer of the white paper, Colonial Secretary Sidney Webb (Lord Passfield), faced backlash not only from Liberal and Conservative politicians but also from his own Labour colleagues. Fear, too, of rebuke from the League of Nations Permanent Mandates Commission loomed large over Whitehall. Consequently, the British government entered negotiations with Zionist leaders (including Weizmann, who had continued to direct the Zionist Organization until a successor could be appointed at the next Zionist Congress) and ultimately issued a letter from Prime Minister Ramsay MacDonald clarifying the policy of the white paper. Published on February 13, 1931, the MacDonald Letter—branded the "Black Letter" by Arabs—reaffirmed Britain's commitment to Jewish immigration and land settlement in Palestine, in essence reversing the policy of the Passfield White Paper. In response, Weizmann decided to reverse his resignation.

The entire saga of the Passfield White Paper—the events leading up to it and the debates in its wake—unfolded as major questions regarding the future of the British Empire were debated. While Arlosoroff and other Zionists participated in negotiations with British politicians in London, Indian and

British leaders convened nearby for the first Round Table Conference to decide on constitutional reforms for India. How would Britain respond to demands for self-determination and self-rule in the empire? Would representative government be introduced? Might India and British crown colonies become dominions? The various threads of Arlosoroff's political thought at this time—his increasingly forceful articulation of the Zionist need for state-like power; his growing focus on questions of self-determination and representation in imperial settings; his fascination with the history of British colonization and his regard for it as a model for the Yishuv; and his continued dedication to the upbuilding of an international labor politics—took shape against this horizon of political uncertainty. Labour proponents and socialists across the British imperial world—including Arlosoroff—were forced to reconsider how their left-wing politics fit into an empire wrestling with the rise of nationalism. Arlosoroff looked toward the British Empire—its history, politics, and the possibilities it held for the future—as a means and model through which Jewish self-determination, continued Zionist settlement, and socialist ideals might all find expression.

But Arlosoroff did so while other left-wing thinkers struggled more and more with the entanglement of nationalism, colonization, and socialism—and while many increasingly insisted on their incompatibility.[144] For instance, at the beginning of his tenure as colonial secretary in June 1929, Sidney Webb expressed a measure of admiration for the Zionist movement, a sentiment based not on approval of Zionism's national-political aims but on its settlement efforts.[145] This position of supporting constructive settlement was in keeping with Webb's Fabian socialist ideology, formulated in his response to the Boer War three decades earlier.[146] Then, he and other Fabians had argued that imperial expansion and the spread of socialism could work in tandem. But outside of this modicum of admiration, Webb objected to Labor Zionism for its efforts to combine socialism and nationalism—even as independence leaders from Trinidad to India used socialism as an ideological basis for their national struggle.[147] Most famously, Jawaharlal Nehru promoted Indian nationalism and vociferously criticized British colonial rule, positions he understood to be inextricably linked to his socialist (indeed, Fabian socialist) politics.[148]

Examining the British imperial context of Arlosoroff's political thinking also reveals something about Zionism's complex relationship to the state.

With the inauguration of the British Commonwealth of Nations in 1926, the idea of dominion offered a political option that fit squarely into neither a statist nor nonstatist mold. It provided the economic and political advantages (and risks) of being part of a larger global network but also came with many of the virtues of independence and self-determination: the ability to undertake major international loans, the power to control immigration, and the security of diplomatic standing. As we will see in the next chapter, after Arlosoroff was appointed head of the Jewish Agency's Political Department in the summer of 1931 and spent his days actively managing the Zionist-British partnership, he continued to grapple with Zionism's relationship with state-like power—a question made all the more pressing with the rise of Nazism.

THREE

An Uncertain Alliance

IN JUNE 1932, DESPAIRING THAT the Zionist movement had reached a near hopeless crossroads, Chaim Arlosoroff sent his famous confidential letter to Chaim Weizmann. In it, he proposed that Zionism's only hope might be to revolt—to overthrow British mandatory authorities and establish a minority government in Palestine by force. At the time he wrote the letter, Arlosoroff had spent nearly a year as head of the Political Department of the Jewish Agency, a position akin to foreign minister of the Zionist movement; one of his chief responsibilities was liaising with British authorities in Palestine. Over the course of that year, he had witnessed the nadir of Zionists fortunes. Immigration and land development had become intractable challenges. Zionists had lost faith in Britain's commitment to the Jewish national home. Jewish-Arab relations seemed equally hopeless. And, most significantly, the Nazi climb to power in Germany meant that Palestine might soon need to accommodate thousands of Jewish refugees and face the prospect of another world war.[1] This profound uncertainty about Zionist futures, shaped out of an assessment of the increasingly limited *time* the movement might have left to effect its goals, compelled Arlosoroff to defy central principles of labor politics and convinced him that the Zionist movement had to achieve state power. This uncertainty also pushed Arlosoroff—

long a steadfast champion of the Zionist-British partnership—to question the fundamental tenability of Zionist futures in the British Empire.

This chapter traces how the uncertainty and anxiety of the 1930s compelled Zionists, including Arlosoroff, Norman Bentwich, and Gershon Agronsky, the journalist in charge of public relations for the Political Department of the Jewish Agency, to disentangle their visions of Zionist and British futures in diverse ways.[2] Norman, as we will see, was forced to abandon his work on behalf of mandatory authorities; he could no longer be both a British official and a Zionist. Amid the rise of Pan-Islamist movements, including Khilafat, which sought a restoration of the caliphate, Gershon Agronsky decided that rather than turning to British imperial power, Zionists should work to build ties with moderate Muslim leaders in India. The broad horizon of uncertainty did not produce one singular response, and the impulse to divorce Zionist futures from the British Empire remained complicated by the realities on the ground in Palestine. As this chapter shows, Arlosoroff built ties with Jewish elites throughout the British Empire, participated in British-oriented social circles in Jerusalem, and developed a close, candid friendship with High Commissioner Arthur Wauchope—all while he grew increasingly frustrated with the broader state of Zionist-British relations. These divergent and even contradictory paths, however, all emerged out of a shared consideration of the broad range of possible futures of the British Empire, spanning from the persistence of imperial rule to the triumph of anticolonial independence movements. These visions reflect a politics of uncertainty—uncertainty over both Zionist and British imperial futures—that characterized the early 1930s.

A year before Arlosoroff's famous letter to Weizmann, the Zionist movement had been beset with upheaval. At the Seventeenth Zionist Congress in Basle in the summer of 1931—the first congress since the 1929 riots—Revisionists, Mizrachi (Religious Zionists), and a contingent of American Zionists waged a bitter protest against Chaim Weizmann's leadership. In a vote of 118 to 48, delegates determined not to reelect Weizmann and, in his place, chose the veteran Zionist and Hebrew journalist Nahum Sokolow as president. Fifteen years Weizmann's senior, Sokolow had worked closely with the latter in London since World War I. Though Weizmann's loss reflected endemic Zionist frustration with the ousted leader's policy of British cooperation, the election results of the Seventeenth Congress far from heralded a new regime of Zionist-British antagonism. On the contrary, on his election, Sokolow announced that Zionist-British cooperation would be an essential policy of the newly elected Zionist Executive. And on that new Executive now sat Arlosoroff, long the defender of Zionist-British cooperation. Congress had also appointed Arlosoroff to replace Frederick Kisch as head of the Political Department, a job in which he felt determined to uphold this policy.

The British government experienced its own tumult and turnover that summer. Unable to reach an agreement on austerity measures in the face of economic depression, the Labour Government dissolved on August 24, 1931. A coalition National Government was formed in its place by Conservative and Liberal politicians, along with a small group of Labour politicians, including Ramsay MacDonald, willing to work with them. Consequently, MacDonald remained prime minister but was expelled from the Labour Party; all of the Labour cabinet ministers—including Webb—who opposed the National Government were replaced, and Labour became the opposition.[3] The British administration in Palestine, too, experienced an overhaul. Harry Luke, the chief secretary and acting high commissioner when the riots broke out, was transferred out of Palestine after Kisch and other Jewish Agency leaders fought for his removal.[4] Of even greater significance, High Commissioner John Chancellor—whose assessment of the 1929 riots and reputation for antisemitism had earned him Zionist enmity—planned to step down in September, with Arthur Wauchope arriving in Jerusalem to replace him later that fall. From London to Jerusalem, the British leadership that had overseen Palestine's past two turbulent years was no more.

Norman Bentwich had observed this dramatic change of guard as an outsider. What the Bentwiches had thought would be a short leave in England in September 1930 had turned into a year-long purgatory for Norman. In talks with the Colonial Office, Norman was told that "feeling in Palestine ran so high that there would be outbreaks of violence" were he to resume his post. The government's position was that a Jew (and a Zionist one at that) represented far too inflammatory an appointment in such tense times. Refusing to resign—stepping down would be tantamount to "admitting that no Jew could again hold high office under the British Mandate"—Norman reluctantly agreed to keep quiet about the whole situation until a resolution could be reached. "Occasional work" thrown his way by the Colonial Office was poor consolation.[5] At long last, in late August 1931, nearly a year after he had left Palestine, Norman received the final word from Sidney Webb: he would be officially retired from his position as attorney general.

The year 1931 became the first since 1916 during which Norman remained entirely away from Palestine. He longed for the "half anchored and half-hearted" peripatetic life that had kept him moving between his two worlds—Britain and Palestine—for so long. The year had also been disheartening for reasons beyond the personal and professional. Unlike many Zionists, Norman believed that the wrongs spelled out in the Passfield White Paper had only been made worse by the policy acrobatics of the MacDonald letter, "the friction between Jews and Arabs . . . aggravated by the vacillating Government."[6] Now he found himself, restless but rooted, in a new home on the edge of Hampstead Heath in London. While Helen became an active member of the British Labour Party, Norman returned to Lincoln's Inn as a barrister and kept abreast of developments in Palestine by reading the local papers.[7] An early September article in the *Palestine Bulletin*—an interview with Arlosoroff about his recent appointment to the Political Department—buoyed the lawyer's spirits.

Norman decided to write to Arlosoroff to tell him "how admirable . . . in substance and in form" he had found the interview, in which Arlosoroff had declared his commitment to Zionist-British cooperation. "I think that I agree with every word of it and certainly I share its spirit," Norman declared. "I sincerely hope that you will be able to bring about that understanding between the three sides of the triangle, so to say: in case I come back to Eretz Israel—as I hope I may do sometime—I shall do what I can to assist. . . . My heart is always in the country and in some way I hope to serve it again," he concluded.[8] On the ground in Palestine, Arlosoroff soon discovered that the practical work of cooperation and progress was far more challenging.

COOPERATION AND STRUGGLE

Roy G. B. Spicer was struggling to pronounce the name "Greenfelder." The new inspector-general of the Palestine Police was among the mandatory officials visited by Arlosoroff and Kisch during the latter's final week of work in August 1931. Though he had previously written so much about the importance of protecting the Zionist-British partnership, Arlosoroff now witnessed firsthand the routine meetings, negotiations, and daily grind that went into maintaining the complex relationship. As he sat with the new police chief, Arlosoroff mused to himself that British, Jewish, and Arab societies existed side by side in Palestine but were separated by virtually "impenetrable partitions." Spicer, whose son was sick, only knew an English physician in Jerusalem who had no expertise in childhood illness. "We took this opportunity to name Dr. Greenfelder," recorded Arlosoroff in his diary. Spicer struck him as "a man of energy" who was dedicated to his work, but Arlosoroff somehow doubted the Englishman would take his son to see the Jewish pediatrician.[9]

Arlosoroff quickly realized just how much work lay ahead of him as he shadowed Kisch. Cultural differences, inexperience, commitment to the status quo, resentment, and prejudice all presented stumbling blocks to Zionist-British cooperation. Mark Young, for instance, who replaced Luke as chief secretary and would serve as acting high commissioner between the Chancellor and Wauchope administrations, acted with chilly reserve on first meeting Arlosoroff, surveying him from head to toe while Kisch spoke. His cold scrutiny struck Arlosoroff as stereotypically English, reminiscent of an amusing book he had just read entitled *The English: Are They Human?*[10] Arlosoroff's meetings with High Commissioner Chancellor, who was set to leave Palestine in a matter of weeks, reminded him that bitter feeling on both sides ran deep. At their first encounter, after a "rather long speech" in which Chancellor lectured Arlosoroff and Kisch about the terms of the mandate, the conversation moved to the topic of intercommunal relations in Palestine. "He turned to us with a call to strive for rapprochement between the two parts of the population," wrote Arlosoroff. Though "he knows the Jews blame him," Chancellor found the accusations "baseless." Echoing the Shaw Report, he emphasized—"as always"—that prewar Jewish colonies were better models for coexistence with the Arabs than present-day Zionist settlements.[11] At a second meeting with the high commissioner, Arlosoroff made a formal declaration of his commitment to the Zionist-British partnership. "For the past eleven years," he said, "I tried to promote a political strategy of cooperation and mutual trust with the mandatory government. Even in recent years, full of bitterness and misunderstanding, I did not change my opinion. I will act in this spirit when I defend the rights of the Jewish national home, even if I need to disagree with the government from time to time."[12] After discussing questions of land transfer and settlement policy in Palestine, Arlosoroff had the impression that Chancellor wanted "to appear... like a person who sympathized with our aspirations and dealt with them in fairness, but the anger and bitterness in his heart erupted every instant and rendered his good intentions worthless."[13] When Arlosoroff again stressed Jewish "loyalty to the British Commonwealth," Chancellor interrupted him, saying, "For the time being, it is still the British Empire."[14] Palestine, Chancellor made implicitly clear, was not a self-governing dominion.

Arlosoroff's dispiriting, if predictable interactions with Chancellor did not deter him from his commitment to improving the Zionist-British relationship. On August 27, 1931, six days before Chancellor traveled to Haifa to sail from Palestine for the last time, Arlosoroff gave an extensive interview—the one that Norman read with such enthusiasm—in which he articulated his broad vision of partnership for the Yishuv and Britain. Arlosoroff began by acknowledging the "momentous change" in leadership that had taken place, on both the Jewish and British sides.[15] "There has... been a change of guard and in my opinion the hour has come for an attempt to open a new chapter and reconstruct relations which were destroyed in the storm and stress of the last few years," Arlosoroff declared.[16] He also recognized that his own appointment represented something quite new for Zionist leadership, part of the broader Labor Zionist rise to dominance within the Zionist movement that the 1931 elections signaled. "The change from an officer of the British Army whose Zionism was only discovered and developed in the course of his work on the Executive, to a man coming straight from the ranks of Palestine Labour, among whom he has grown up, is indeed abrupt," he wrote, contrasting himself to Kisch.[17]

But the shift from a British Army man to an Eastern European-born Labor Zionist insider did not herald the end of Zionist-British cooperation. On the contrary, Arlosoroff argued that defending the Zionist-British partnership—working to improve it, regaining mutual trust, and promoting long-lasting ties—was key to his work of representing the Yishuv. "During the eleven years of my public activities in Palestine, cooperation with the British Government and relations of mutual confidence were politically my foremost aspirations," he said. "I will even go so far as to say that to my mind the tie which binds us and Palestine to Great Britain and the British is not merely a mechanical one," he continued, "and is not solely dependent upon the articles of the Mandate and the advantages that can be [squeezed] out of them."[18]

But "loyalty and good-will" only went so far. "It is hardly necessary to add that such sentiments cannot and must not prevent us from insisting upon our rights and the fulfilment of our aspirations," he argued, invoking a vocabulary of liberty and self-determination. Indeed, strong precedent already existed for this in other parts of the British Empire: "Even colonial countries with populations that were purely British by race and speech have known in their histories long periods of defending their rights against the Colonial Office, of misunderstanding, ill-feeling and bitterness on both sides, and have not given up their demands. It may even be said that in every land which the influence of British civilisation had reached there has awakened in the inhabitants this very desire to defend their rights and fearlessly to insist upon them."[19] In this statement, Arlosoroff echoed leaders in other reaches of the British Empire who argued that European Enlightenment ideals, which the British considered central to their own political and civic culture, were denied to inhabitants outside the metropole. British dominions, from Canada to New Zealand, had already achieved formal recognition of their autonomy and equal status to Britain in the Balfour Declaration of 1926. Advocates of Indian self-rule now pointed to this contradiction in their critique of imperial rule.

Arlosoroff maintained, however, that waging a struggle for rights and self-determination did not mean the end to the Zionist-British bond. "I should wish that we ... while refusing to yield any vital interests ... always conduct our struggle in the spirit of the intimate bond which binds us to the Mandatory Government and in the consciousness of the common task by which history has united us," he declared. "The rights which we are defending are rights which were conferred upon the Jewish people after ages during which they had no rights at all in the family of nations," Arlosoroff continued. Should those national rights be threatened, Jews had "no alternative but a stubborn and indefatigable defensive." But the struggle should be "only a dire necessity, not a programme ... and not a goal to strive for." "I shall not forget for one moment," he affirmed, "that our primary political aim is not this struggle, but cooperation, that we must overcome the deadlock which we have reached, and we must emerge from our isolation, that we must acquire friends everywhere throughout the world, and above all among those in whose hands the administration of Palestine is placed."[20]

Arlosoroff soon learned however that achieving cooperation and acquiring friends turned out to be far more difficult than making a platitudinous speech to the press. His days were a whirlwind of meetings with British officials, foreign dignitaries and diplomats, and local Jewish and Arab leaders. Discussions about immigration, the Yishuv's limited budget, education, employment, health services, and the impending World Islamic Congress, set to be held in Jerusalem that December, often proved contentious and frustrating. In a reply to Norman Bentwich, thanking him for reaching out after reading the press interview, Arlosoroff bemoaned the general unwillingness of British officials to collaborate and compromise with him. "I feel only in very rare cases a readiness to give more than the unavoidable minimum of cooperation. Your retirement from the service of the Palestine Government is of course a severe blow to me," he wrote. There remained in Palestine not a "single soul" who was Jewish among the senior British officials with whom Arlosoroff could work.[21] Ten years earlier—what "sounds like a legend today," Arlosoroff wrote—the posts of high commissioner, director of customs, and chief immigration officer, in addition to attorney general, had all been held by Jews.[22]

Arlosoroff also loathed the pomp, formality, and obsequious performance often required of his new post. For example, when Faisal of Iraq visited Palestine in late September 1931 to pay respects at his father's grave at the Al-Aqsa Mosque compound, Arlosoroff joined a coterie of leaders—"the usual crowd of dignitaries, clerks, clergy, and consuls"—to welcome the king as he disembarked his train in Jerusalem. Arlosoroff had been obliged to travel to the station on foot because it was the Jewish Sabbath (though he was not an observant Jew) and noted in his diary that he felt as if he were back in the "days of Pontius Pilate"—presumably a darkly humorous reference to the Via Dolorosa, the path Jesus walked to his crucifixion. At the station, Sydney Moody, the acting chief secretary of the Palestine government, remarked to Arlosoroff that "standing in the station and waiting for the train was a popular pastime in Jerusalem, but it was a very boring pastime." Arlosoroff thought Moody "really hit the nail on the head" in his depiction of a custom that served mostly as spectacle rather than practical diplomacy.[23]

Jerusalem represented a completely new social terrain for Arlosoroff, who had called Tel Aviv home since he immigrated to Palestine in 1924. Tel Aviv, the first modern Jewish city, offered an urbane milieu on the shores of the Mediterranean—coffeehouses, beach promenades, theater, a burgeoning Jewish literary scene, and a thriving urban Jewish secular culture.[24] Founded in 1909, Tel Aviv was built to provide Jewish residents with a clean, middle-class, European-style alternative to the neighboring and predominately Arab Jaffa, where, according to Tel Aviv's mayor, Meir Dizengoff, "the dirt and the trachoma and the lack of light" would inhibit the realization of Jewish modernity and progress.[25] Arlosoroff relished his final days in Tel Aviv in early September, finding the loaded crates and packed suitcases in his apartment "a sad site."[26] Jerusalem, like Jaffa, lacked the airy European modernity of Tel Aviv. The city was dusty and grimy; many of its streets were serpentine and unsuited for modern methods of transportation; and its diverse population—Muslim Arabs, Christian Arabs, ultra-Orthodox Jews, Armenians, secular Zionists, and British officials, among others—lived in close, and often tense, proximity. A conversation with a Reuters reporter convinced Arlosoroff what a waste it was that Jerusalem's diversity had not been instrumentalized in the name of both intercommunal peace and the city's cultural capital. The reporter lamented that Jerusalem boasted not a single decent club; the few tennis courts that existed, in his assessment, were not very good. "I told him seriously that the problem of the clubs was very interesting to me," Arlosoroff recorded in his diary. "The capital really needs a place where educated Englishmen, Jews, and Arabs can meet in a social atmosphere," he wrote.[27]

The lack of British-style clubs aside, Arlosoroff soon discovered that there existed a whole world of convivial gatherings—concerts, private dinners, luncheons, receptions, and parties—that brought together a range of Jerusalem elites in settings that fostered genuine interaction rather than sheer spectacle. His impression during his meeting with Spicer in August—that Jewish, Arab, and British societies existed side by side but with "impenetrable partitions" between them—shifted as his move from Tel Aviv and his position as head of the Political Department allowed him to enter a new social scene in Jerusalem, one that had been very familiar to the Bentwiches.[28] On October 8, for instance, Arlosoroff and his wife, Sima, went to a small luncheon at Government House, along with Judah and Beatrice Magnes and some British officials from Jerusalem. Later that month, Arlosoroff attended a concert given by the Jerusalem Music Society, which had been founded by Norman's sister, the cellist Thelma Yellin. The concerts were generally patronized by a mix of Jewish elites, British mandatory officials, American and European missionaries, and the occasional Arab elites. Arlosoroff understood the significance of these informal gatherings to his professional work of building ties between the Yishuv and the rest of Palestine. "In my opinion," he wrote of the concert, "this is part of the work of my department."[29]

At their social gatherings, Jerusalem elites often discussed political developments in metropolitan Britain with keen interest and excitement. At a celebration at the Czech consul on October 28, 1931, honoring the anniversary of the country's independence, Arlosoroff found the guests—Amin al-Husseini, the grand mufti of Jerusalem, among them—abuzz with gossip from the general election held in Britain the previous day. Though Ramsay MacDonald once again remained prime minister with the victory of the incumbent National Government, the prime minister's former party, Labour, suffered devastating losses in Parliament. "It seems to me that the English, as a general rule, take great pleasure in the crushing defeat of the Labour party," Arlosoroff observed. "On the other hand, their healthy political instinct almost immediately gives rise to the fear that there will be insufficient power to restrain the government when the opposition in parliament is so weak," he noted. Amid the political chatter, Arlosoroff had a brief chance to meet the mufti. After an awkward moment during which the two men stood looking at each other in the eye, Ruhi Abdel Hadi, the assistant secretary of the Palestine government, stepped in to introduce them. "We exchanged a few polite words," wrote Arlosoroff in his diary.[30] Though his meeting with the mufti was a first, Arlosoroff realized looking around at the party's attendees that he was seeing more and more "familiar faces" at these sorts of gatherings; after two months as head of the Political Department, Arlosoroff was also undoubtedly becoming a familiar face in Jerusalem's elite social scene.

UNEXPECTED ALLIANCES

Arlosoroff was surely thinking anxiously about the prospect of the upcoming World Islamic Congress during his encounter with the mufti.[31] Along with Shaukat Ali (1873–1938), the Indian Muslim leader of the Khilafat Movement, al-Husseini had called for an international conference of Muslims to convene in Jerusalem. Though political rivals of the mufti suspected that the congress was designed to boost the mufti's bid to revive and claim the title of caliph, the ostensible purpose of the gathering was to discuss the possibility of founding a Muslim university in Jerusalem. Many Zionists worried that the mufti, already an outspoken opponent of Zionism, would use the congress to foment resistance against the Yishuv's continued development. Some Palestinian Christians feared that the mufti's emphasis on Jerusalem as a Muslim city—likely to be strengthened should a Muslim university be established—could also threaten their security and position in Palestine, where they were already a minority. The newspaper *Mir'at al-Sharq* (Mirror of the East), for instance, which had been founded by a Palestinian Christian from Ramallah, voiced opposition to the congress; the paper was affiliated with *al-mu'arada* (the "opposition"), the broad affiliation of antimufti constituents led by the Nashashibis, the Husseini family rivals.[32]

In his talks with Acting High Commissioner Young, Arlosoroff inquired repeatedly as to whether the government would permit the congress to proceed, stressing that the mufti would likely also use the platform to encourage protest against Britain and the League of Nations. Arlosoroff wondered if the British might use their influence to pressure Shaukat Ali, who was a participant in the second Round Table Conference on India that was then ongoing in London. Young replied simply that he took "interest" in the idea, which Arlosoroff found "a rather poor contribution to political discussion."[33] At another meeting with Young, Arlosoroff voiced concern that the congress could be used to "exploit the question of the Western Wall to incite Jews."[34] He told Young again that it would be useful to know the government's firm position on the matter. Chancellor had previously expressed concern that the mufti was becoming too powerful among Palestinian Arabs; was Young not troubled by this development? Young finally conceded that the mandatory government did not plan to stop the congress. With regard to the mufti, he thought it unwise for government policy to be shaped by "concerns about a single person."[35]

Arlosoroff feared that the unwillingness of mandatory authorities to intervene in the program of the World Islamic Congress reflected a broader political calculation about the future of Pan-Islamic politics in the British Empire. On September 26, Gershon Agronsky organized a small tea where Arlosoroff discussed his ideas on the matter with Herbert Danby. An Anglican priest who served as canon of St. George's Cathedral in Jerusalem, Danby also worked as a (London) *Times* correspondent in Palestine.[36] "Here before us, it seems," Arlosoroff told Danby, "is part of a British political plan in the Middle East that intends to transfer the center of gravity of Islam to a country where British rule is strong." The partnership between al-Husseini and Ali presented the possibility that Pan-Islamists would focus their efforts increasingly on Jerusalem as the international center of Islam. Arlosoroff reasoned that the British thought it was safer to let a caliphate be reestablished in Jerusalem than somewhere outside the bounds of the empire or even in a place—such as India—where anticolonial movements represented a robust threat to British imperial hegemony. Danby doubted that these "political motivations"—"that is, a British plan to exploit pan-Islamic aims to benefit British policy in the Middle East"—existed in the first place. "He said that 'our little friends' (so he calls the Arabs) want to pull the strings that set big levers in motion, but that they will never succeed," reported Arlosoroff in his diary. He found Danby's analysis of the situation to be "uncomplicated and naive." "I do not accept this sort of interpretation," he wrote, "just as I do not accept the 'satanic' interpretations of British policy, that amuse . . . many of our people, the Jews."[37]

Gershon Agronsky, who often hosted cross-cultural gatherings at his home in the West Jerusalem neighborhood of Rehavia, had contemplated more than perhaps any other Zionist the ways Muslim political futures—especially in India—might shape relations on the ground in Palestine. After a trip to India on behalf of the Jewish Agency in the spring of 1930, Agronsky reported that "it would be the better part of wisdom for the Zionist Organization to consider without delay what measures can be taken that Zionism may turn its face, so to speak, to the East."[38] Like Arlosoroff, Agronsky believed that Palestine was part of a broader imperial dynamic; British imperial interests in India, for example, might shape British policy in Palestine. While Arlosoroff focused his attention on appealing to British authorities in his efforts to defend Zionist interests within this imperial dynamic, Agronsky identified a very different ally. He surmised that among the three potentially conflicting groups in India—Muslims, Hindus, and the British—many might assume the latter two to be obvious allies for the Zionists. On the one hand, an alliance with Hindu independence leaders might stop the movement from adopting an anti-Zionist stance. On the other hand, an alliance with the British might prevent the further reversal of commitments laid out in the Balfour Declaration, which could be made in an effort to appease Muslim Indians and gain their support against the Hindu leaders of the Indian independence movement. Agronsky proposed a third option: he determined that, instead of forging ties with the British or with Hindu Indians, the Zionist movement would be wisest to build alliances with moderate Muslim Indians.

Meyer Nissim (1882–1959), a prominent Baghdadi Jew and non-Zionist who in 1929 served a term as president of the Bombay Municipal Council (a position equivalent to mayor of the city), helped put Agronsky in touch with various local Muslim Indian leaders.[39] A meeting with the young barrister M. C. Chagla, who would go on to serve as chief justice of Bombay from 1948 to 1958, convinced Agronsky of the importance of moderate Muslim allies. Chagla, then only twenty-nine years old, was an "influential youth leader," according to Agronsky, as well as a disciple of Muhammad Ali Jinnah, the future founder of Pakistan. Jinnah, who in 1930 still believed in the possibility of a Muslim-Hindu alliance, had resigned from the Indian National Congress in 1920 largely in disagreement over Gandhi's alliance with the Khilafat movement, which Jinnah thought gave a political voice to religious zealotry. Chagla also opposed Khilafat, as well as Pan-Islamism more broadly. "A Hindu of his town and his class is nearer to him than a Moslem of another province and another class," wrote Agronsky of Chagla. "He believes in territorial evolution which would unite the Hindu and the Moslem." Moreover, Chagla, and other young followers of Jinnah, were "not concerned with the problem of the Arabs of Palestine merely because they happen to be Moslem." The young barrister and his friends, who were "Indians first and Moslems second," could potentially "come to understand our problem," Agronsky reasoned.[40]

While Agronsky advocated that Zionists begin looking eastward, Arlosoroff remained focused on the West. In early December 1931, days before the World Islamic Congress was set to open, Arlosoroff met again with Young to discuss the matter. "The whole conversation," he reported, "was tense." In the intervening months since Arlosoroff had last discussed the topic with Young, the organizers of the congress had narrowed their focus: they determined to minimize the issues of the caliphate and the Muslim university but bring the question of religious rights at the Western Wall and the Al-Aqsa Mosque to the forefront. Arlosoroff argued that the matter of religious access had already been settled by the League of Nations following the 1929 riots. The League's report had stated that Muslims maintained ownership of the Western Wall but that Jews had a right to pray there. Should not the Palestine Government insist on this as policy to the congress? Young responded that he doubted that the League's report would be a topic of discussion at the congress. Arlosoroff countered that if Young were right, an even more dangerous situation lay before them. He reasoned that if the congress did not mean to challenge the League's report, then its organizers intended to spread a much more alarming claim: that Jews wished to take over the entire Temple Mount. "This false propaganda has no trace of reality," Arlosoroff insisted to Young, to which the former replied that he wished he could be as sure as Arlosoroff that there was no truth in the charge. Citing Rabbi Kook's statement to the Shaw Commission, Arlosoroff explained that religious desire for the restoration of the Temple was similar to longing for the messiah—in essence, a hope that was "beyond the realm of mortal action." Young became embittered, accusing Arlosoroff of alleging that the British government, to save itself, wished to make the Jews the scapegoat of the congress. "I answered that I had not said that the government did so on purpose," Arlosoroff replied. But intentions aside, he told Young, "all I see are the results, which are perfectly clear."[41]

The way Arlosoroff navigated the prospect of the World Islamic Congress reflected several key aspects of his evolving politics—particularly his understanding of the relationship between the British Empire, Palestinian Arab politics, and Zionist ideas about the state—during the first few months of his tenure as head of the Political Department. First, he remained attuned to broader imperial realities, trends, and considerations. In the aftermath of the 1929 riots, Arlosoroff wrote that British policy in Palestine had been affected by concerns about Muslim opinion, particularly in India.[42] Arlosoroff employed a similar line of thought in his interpretation of British action—or rather, inaction—on the matter of the World Islamic Congress. Second, though this interpretation demonstrated Arlosoroff's intellectual immersion in British imperial political questions (a position that he understood as necessary because Britain was the imperial power with a stake in Jewish national futures), it did not reflect submissive loyalty or lack of critical engagement. On the contrary, just as he had pledged in the long interview he had given on his appointment as head of the Political Department, Arlosoroff expressed disagreement with British policy and tactics that he considered detrimental to Jewish "rights and the fulfilment of our aspirations."[43] Finally, Arlosoroff viewed Pan-Islamism, a transnational political movement that used religion rather than nationality to mobilize support, as a much greater threat to Zionism than a locally focused Palestinian Arab nationalism—an all the more striking assessment given that Arlosoroff, unlike many of his Labor Zionist colleagues, had resisted underestimating the power of Palestinian Arab nationalism. In short, Arlosoroff could not conceive of a political future in Palestine that could accommodate both Pan-Islamism and Zionism, even though he accepted the reality of an enduring Palestinian national movement.

Though he insisted on a political solution that accounted for the reality of both Jewish and Palestinian Arab nationalist aspirations, Arlosoroff found binational and autonomist futures problematic (in contrast to some Labor Zionists, as well as Norman Bentwich). At the time of the 1929 riots, Arlosoroff argued that a binational parliament in which Jews and Arabs had equal representation virtually guaranteed political deadlock, while autonomism, which was designed to protect minorities, would only recreate diaspora-like conditions of Jewish minority status in Palestine. Arlosoroff, instead, proposed a political model with regional councils and a national legislative council made up of eleven Arabs, six Jews, and representatives of the mandatory government. This scheme, he argued, would prevent deadlock, and at the same time—as it was a *temporary* plan—would not enshrine Jewish minority status.[44] Arlosoroff's plan depended on a Palestinian Arab political movement that would be willing not only to partner with the Jewish minority but would also be satisfied to realize national aspirations within a local Palestinian context—not a transnational Pan-Islamic one.

Arlosoroff grew progressively frustrated with his official meetings with mandatory authorities, increasingly worried about religious incitement between Muslims and Jews, and ever more convinced that an interim political solution needed to be reached immediately—the necessity of this final point becoming more pressing given developments in Germany. An interim program might give Jews in Palestine the levers of state-like power to address the Yishuv's pressing needs: direct land development and regulate immigration. At an evening spent with Arthur Ruppin and Hugo Bergmann at the home of David Werner Senator, Arlosoroff insisted on the importance of addressing immediate objectives to remedy the political impasse at which the Yishuv now found itself.[45] "We cannot conduct our political work on the basis of a sixty-year plan," he implored. "We are in need of a realistic formulation of intermediate goals . . . like milestones in our progress towards our grand goal. In the meantime, these intermediate goals must be the focus of all our political thought and all our will," he wrote.[46]

The World Islamic Congress opened on December 7 and as Arlosoroff had feared, the delegates focused substantially on the Jewish threat to Islam in Palestine. Arlosoroff had hoped that the recently arrived high commissioner, Arthur Wauchope (whom he had yet to meet personally), would grasp the "danger of fanning religious incitement" and would act to remove the topic of religious access at the Western Wall from the congress's agenda.[47] But his efforts were to no avail. Though Arlosoroff heard that Wauchope was "not pleased with the whole thing," the new high commissioner ultimately declined to intervene, and the congress went forth as planned.[48] Frustrated by his failure to change the course of events, Arlosoroff spent the evening away from Jerusalem, attending a production of *Twelfth Night* by Habima Theater in Tel Aviv.[49] Before the start of the performance, when the two national anthems were set to be played, Wauchope and some colleagues entered the theater and came to take their seats in the row in front of Arlosoroff. When the Zionist national anthem "Hatikvah" was played, the high commissioner and his companions sat, but they then rose in deference during "God Save the King." The mostly Jewish crowd at the theater bristled at the offense, and Arlosoroff worried that if Wauchope ever publicly repeated the faux pas, he would ensure Jewish resentment in Palestine. But Arlosoroff gave Wauchope the benefit of the doubt—perhaps the stakes had not been explained to him—and during the intermission, took the opportunity to chat with the high commissioner for the first time, sharing with him the history of Habima. "Wauchope knew nothing about all this, and he showed great interest."[50]

Soon after their encounter at the theater, Wauchope invited Arlosoroff for a private lunch at Government House on December 14, 1931. The two discussed a range of topics—Jewish life in Soviet Russia, the difference between Jewish and English humor, and the parallels between the Shakespearean character of Falstaff and the persona of the actor Charlie Chaplin. But they mostly avoided issues of politics and policy in Palestine. Finally, at a meeting on Christmas Eve, Arlosoroff confronted Wauchope with a frank assessment of the impasse that had been reached between the Yishuv and British authorities. Arlosoroff intended to use the meeting to discuss a land issue in the northern town of Wadi al-Hawarith. The land had been sold by its Lebanese Maronite owner to the Jewish National Fund (JNF) in April 1929. After the sale, the Nablus District Court ordered the Palestinian Arab tenant farmers living on the property to leave; when the farmers refused, British authorities removed them by force to an area north of the town. Jewish farmers moved in soon thereafter.[51] But when heavy winter rains flooded the northern encampment in 1931, the Arab residents moved back to Wadi al-Hawarith. Though police tractors were brought in to try to remove their tents, some of the Arabs lay in front of the vehicles in protest, effecting a tense standstill. The JNF demanded authorities enforce the court's decision, while several Palestinian newspapers, including *Filastin*, began extensively covering the plight of the Arabs of Wadi al-Hawarith.[52] British authorities equivocated.[53]

Arlosoroff had planned to advocate on behalf of the JNF on the issue of Wadi al-Hawarith, as well as discuss some other matters regarding development policy and public works. "But when I came to the commissioner," he reported later, "I spontaneously decided to abandon my entire agenda and began with a general and serious conversation about our situation." Wauchope responded by assuring Arlosoroff that he understood his position on the land issue and would have Young, who had resumed his role as chief secretary of the mandatory government, draft a letter addressing the matter. Arlosoroff told the high commissioner that he would wait to see the letter but wondered what good it or any other small policy development would do so long as there was "no fundamental agreement on the broader problems of Palestine." What he said next was a soliloquy of political analysis laying bare the past, present, and future of a Zionist-British partnership on the cusp of ruin. Arlosoroff began by speaking of what had once been:

> The situation between the British administration and world Jewry in general, and the Yishuv in Palestine in particular, is getting worse. Twelve years ago, Jews throughout the world clung to their loyalty for Great Britain. We are a scattered people between Vladivostok and San Francisco, between Stockholm and Cape Town. In our scattered state, we are weak, and consequently, we lack the proper weight of a people of sixteen million with our talents. But ... we are also powerful, and wherever there are Jews, there has been a stronghold of faith in the justice of Britain and in its fairness. This vast well of loyalty is wasted. [Your] Excellency is entitled to say: What is the value of talking about the British Empire if the Jews no longer have the same level of trust in Great Britain that they did before?[54]

At this point, the high commissioner interrupted Arlosoroff, declaring fervently, "It is of tremendous, tremendous value!" But Arlosoroff was undeterred by Wauchope's insistence, and continued with an assessment of the current situation:

> ... Dr. Weizmann had to go. He had to pay the price for his unshakable faith in a policy of an unreserved bond [with Britain].... I will continue to follow in the footsteps of Dr. Weizmann—as far as the general principles of our policy are concerned.... But if I were called upon at this moment to report to the Zionist Congress, based on my experience in these past five months, I would have to say, "I lost the game!" From the big things like the Muslim congress, to the minute details of administration—in almost everything I have encountered negative relations. I hardly see a ray of light.[55]

Wauchope insisted that he understood just how hard Arlosoroff had been working to improve the partnership; he had even written to the Colonial Office to say that he had found in Arlosoroff only "support and sympathy." Arlosoroff, however, did not cease his impassioned speech, continuing with a bleak outlook of an uncertain future:

> We have reached an impasse.... [Your] Excellency may ask: What if we do not succeed in working out a joint plan of action? I admit I do not know. I do not know to where Palestine Jewry will turn if Zionist policy abandons its British orientation.... I do not know what the world would have been like had Zionism not appeared on the stage and focused so many, many Jewish youth across the globe around the constructive idea of building a Jewish national home. All this is now in jeopardy, and I see no hope in the current state of relations between the Jews and the administration.[56]

Wauchope told Arlosoroff that he was "very disappointed" to hear this perspective. Did the Zionists not know that upon his appointment as high commissioner, Wauchope had declared his great respect for Jewish "hopes and aspirations" and that he had come to Palestine intending to help facilitate their realization? As far as the issue of Wadi al-Hawarith was concerned, did Arlosoroff wish for Wauchope to go against the recommendations of his advisers? "Could the police be ordered to remove these people from the ground?" he asked. Was it not true that "Jews were not interested in such conflicts and clashes"? Arlosoroff replied it was precisely so: peace was a political imperative for the Yishuv and mandatory authorities understood this. As a result, they depended on Jews not to stand up for themselves, counting on them eventually to "give up" their position, insisted Arlosoroff. He argued that the government should be capable of finding a place for "sixty or eighty families"—the Arabs of Wadi al-Hawarith—to live.[57]

On the one hand, Arlosoroff's position on Wadi al-Hawarith reflected a contravention of labor political ideals over an issue—the dispossession of tenant farmers—that was receiving growing attention among labor circles around the world.[58] As head of the Political Department, Arlosoroff was responsible for advocating on behalf of the JNF in the Wadi al-Hawarith dispute. He never acknowledged in his diary the contradiction between this position and central tenets of labor politics. His distancing from these ideals may be viewed in the context of his growing alienation from Britain. Arlosoroff had long viewed Britain as an international center of labor politics and British Labour as a vital beacon for Labor Zionists in Palestine. In contrast to left-wing anticolonial leaders across the empire who insisted that the ideals of socialism and nationalism were incompatible with the aims of imperialism, Arlosoroff had previously seen these three concepts as fundamental components of his Zionist vision. Now, as he came to believe that Zionism urgently needed to achieve state-like power—and that doing so within the framework of British imperialism seemed increasingly unlikely—Arlosoroff also retreated from some central principles of labor politics.

On the other hand, the fact that Arlosoroff spent most of his time with Wauchope focused not on Wadi al-Hawarith—the matter he had initially planned to discuss—but rather on the broader imbroglio of Jewish-British relations (of which Wadi al-Hawarith was for Arlosoroff but a part) reflected his assessment of Zionist priorities on the eve of 1932. Though Arlosoroff understood the power of Palestinian Arab nationalism better than most of his Labor Zionist colleagues—indeed, he had recognized its existence when that fact was still generally contested among Zionists—the question of Jewish-Arab relations in Palestine was subsumed in what was, in his assessment, the bigger, more consequential issue of Jewish-British relations.

As the year 1931 drew to a close, Arlosoroff found himself in a dramatically different political frame of mind than when he had first been appointed head of the Political Department. Frustrated with the state of Yishuv-British relations, he began to stress the necessity of Zionist political action that would happen independently—perhaps even in breach—of its British mandatory context, a position he would articulate to full effect the following spring in his famous letter to Chaim Weizmann.

RETURN TO JERUSALEM

Meanwhile, back in London, Norman Bentwich reluctantly readjusted to the rhythms of metropolitan life. Though his work as a barrister kept him occupied, he longed to return to Palestine. "I felt bound to the country which had been my goal for twenty years," he wrote.[59] Helen Bentwich felt differently, however, and the prospect of returning to an environment plagued by strife that had been so hostile to her husband pained her. "I went to the doctor again, & she said I was still anemic. I imagine I am making myself ill because

I so dislike the idea of going back to Palestine," she told her mother.⁶⁰ Helen's now active involvement in the Labour Party also contributed to her desire to remain in Britain.⁶¹ "Her activity complicated the question of my return to Palestine in a private capacity," wrote Norman.⁶²

An offer made in early 1932 presented the couple with an option for compromise. Norman received an invitation from the Hebrew University to join the faculty as a professor of law in the newly established Chair of the International Law of Peace, a position created by his friend and chancellor of the university, Judah Magnes. Norman accepted the offer with a caveat: "I should lecture and be resident during one only of the two terms of the year; and for the rest I should be free to study international relations wherever I pleased, and take part in international movements outside the country." For nearly two decades thereafter, Norman and Helen Bentwich spent half the year in Jerusalem and the other half in London. Helen, loath to be without purpose in Palestine, accepted a position as correspondent for the *Manchester Guardian* in the country.

With his return to Jerusalem imminent after almost a year and a half away, Norman thought anxiously about the future of Jewish-Arab relations. He worried he would be unable to effect positive change in his new position as a law professor given that he had been unable to make great strides in an official capacity with the mandatory government. In Palestine, Norman feared he would be "'wandering between two worlds, one dead, the other powerless to be born'; the Palestine of the administration which I had left, and the ideal Palestine in which Jews and Arabs would co-operate in peace. Jerusalem was the appropriate place, without a doubt, to lecture on the International Law of Peace; but to bring about peaceful international relations between its two nationalities was another story. I was reminded constantly of the Rabbinical maxim: 'It is not the doctrine but the deed which is essential'; and an English counterpart: 'Those who can, do, and those who cannot, teach.'"⁶³

The Bentwiches reached a blustery and frigid Jerusalem in early February 1932 and settled into a home in Abu Tor, a neighborhood with a mix of Jewish, Arab, and British residents.⁶⁴ Norman set out immediately to write his first lecture, but before he even delivered it, controversy erupted. "Our troubles have started, or rather, Norman's," Helen wrote to her mother. "He wants to give his lectures in English, as well as in Hebrew, feeling that International Lectures ought to help a larger audience than the Hebrew students. And the University people have the impudence to say he mustn't," she reported.[65] Norman experienced fierce opposition to his bilingual proposition, particularly from Menachem Ussishkin, the president of the Jewish National Fund who had been an early champion of Hebrew and had helped to found the Hebrew University. Helen believed that Norman would stand his ground and refuse reappointment were he not to get his way. "Much as I should like that, I think they are a rotten crowd to treat him like this," she wrote, "and Magnes is, as I always knew, a weak, poor-spirited creature, who gives way to them—Ussishkin & Co." Though she pilloried Magnes, about whom she had so often written affectionately, for capitulating to the Zionist establishment, Helen also pointed toward broader societal issues in the Yishuv. "It's all so rotten, Jews against Jews all the time, as well as everyone else against them," she wrote. "That's why I so hated coming back and will, I know, find it so uncongenial. All this 'separateness' of the Jews is so discordant with modern life," she bemoaned.[66]

The lecture itself, which Norman ultimately agreed to deliver solely in Hebrew, proved much more disastrous than its controversial prelude. "I cannot think why such a calm, peaceable, easy-going person like Norman should always be such a pivot for disharmony wherever he goes," Helen lamented following the incident.[67] A large crowd of roughly six hundred people gathered at the university on Mount Scopus on February 10, 1932, to hear the lecture. Arlosoroff, who was among the attendees, first began to worry that something was amiss soon after he entered the hall. Someone informed him that earlier that morning, three different leaflets protesting the event had been circulated by various student organizations. "Dr. Magnes had not told us that something was 'brewing,'" wrote Arlosoroff, regretting that "it was already too late to do anything."[68] Norman began the delivery of his lecture, entitled "Jerusalem, City of Peace," at which point someone in the crowd shouted, "Preach peace to the Mufti!"[69] A shower of stink bombs, boos, and protest leaflets followed.

"I heard the word Mufti, & thought it was another Arab going to shoot," wrote Helen, recalling a 1928 assassination attempt on Norman's life. "When I found it was only stink-bombs and not pistols, I was furious with Magnes, who, I gather had been warned [about] having no check on the audience at all."[70] The rioters, it turned out, were not Arabs but members of Brit HaBirionim, a clandestine, fascist wing of the Revisionist movement led by Abba Ahimeir.[71] Founded the previous year, Brit HaBirionim espoused "Revisionist Maximalism," which rejected centrist and left-wing Zionist ideas and, instead, fashioned itself in the image of the ancient Sicarii and advocated for a corporatist state modeled on Mussolini's fascist Italy.[72] The group protested the British presence in Palestine, opposed any cooperation with the Arabs, and condemned the Labor Zionist leadership as British collaborators. Though Norman tried to resume his lecture amid the tumult, the rioters continued shouting and throwing stink bombs. Eventually, and only after trying to contain the situation themselves, university authorities called in British police, who arrested twelve of the protesters. The entire episode—from the university's unpreparedness to the rioters' politics and tactics—infuriated Arlosoroff. "Anyone who did not see this spectacle with his own eyes would never know the extent of its disgrace and revulsion," he wrote. "The English do not care; the Arabs will rejoice; people on the outside will see this as a regular university scandal and be done!" he declared. Like Helen, Arlosoroff felt that Magnes and university officials had grossly mismanaged the situation. The instant the university chancellor had heard of potential unrest, Arlosoroff argued, he should have closed the lecture to the public and allowed only invited guests into the hall. The reluctance of university administrators to allow police onto the campus also incensed Arlosoroff. "As long as there are hooligans in the universities," he wrote, "there will also be policemen!"[73] He could not support the "ethics" of university leaders—whom he went so far as to call "antisemitic"—for treating the university as a "holy place," all the while willfully ignoring the "crimes taking place" inside. While the brunt of his anger was directed at Magnes and the university, Arlosoroff also condemned the Revisionist side, acknowledging that "the method of fighting controversial opinions with a pogrom is a terrible one."[74]

The incident threw into relief the increasingly divisive state of Yishuv politics—between left- and right-wing Zionists, between Revisionists and binationalists, and between binationalists and the mainstream Zionist establishment. Though the Yishuv, in fact, saw continued, stable development in the 1930s, its political and ideological rifts grew significantly more contentious following the 1929 riots. Prompting disillusionment for some supporters of binationalism, including Hans Kohn, the riots inspired renewed determination for others who advocated for a rapprochement between Jews and Arabs.⁷⁵ Judah Magnes, though he never officially joined the binationalist Brit Shalom, believed that the unrest demanded Jewish-Arab cooperation in social, political, and economic life. At the heart of the group was a coterie of intellectuals and university academics, including Hugo Bergmann, Gershom Scholem, and Martin Buber. "It had been obvious" to these individuals, Norman wrote, "that the principal political aim [of the Yishuv] should be not the maximum immigration but an understanding with the Arabs." Norman's appointment had thus been protested by Revisionist students because of his association with and general support for this binationalist circle. The Revisionists objected, too, to Norman's position on the university's purpose and design. "I deprecated the formation of a Law School because it seemed undesirable that we should indulge in a multiplication of Jewish lawyers in the National Home; and I stood for the development of research as against teaching of undergraduates, particularly in professional subjects." The Revisionists, in contrast, "demanded a normal university for the Jewish youth of Europe, to whom that boon was denied in their several countries." Writing in 1941, Norman conceded that "events were to justify them."⁷⁶

Arlosoroff's response reflected his own mounting frustration with the political situation in Palestine—not only the impasse he believed had been reached with the British but also the threat he perceived coming from Brit Shalom and supporters of binationalism. In his writings in the aftermath of the 1929 riots, as discussed in chapter 2, Arlosoroff argued that Brit Shalom had given rise to a politics far more nefarious than Revisionist Zionism. He wrote that "the psychological influence of the extreme pacifist agitators, especially among certain groups of intellectuals, has resulted in the creation of a spirit of disbelief in our own powers, however limited they may be."⁷⁷ The balance of Arlosoroff's moral outrage over the incident at the Hebrew University—the Revisionist protesters were "hooligans," but the Jewish university authorities were "antisemitic"—echoed this argument. This denunciation is all the more striking given that Arlosoroff had once so forcefully condemned his fellow Zionists for leveling blanket charges of antisemitism against British officials.⁷⁸ But his growing antagonism toward the binationalists also reflected a broader trend among Labor Zionist leaders following the 1929 riots. Though Berl Katznelson, for instance, had been friendly with many of the Brit Shalom intellectuals, after August 1929, he called them "uprooted people" without real connection to Jewish life. The newspaper *Davar*, which Katznelson edited, also started to censor pieces written by Brit Shalom supporters.[79]

In the days following the upset, Arlosoroff reflected on what had transpired in very different ways depending on his audience. At a February 12 meeting with Wauchope, Arlosoroff maintained that nothing of great significance had happened, likely in an effort to minimize internal Zionist dissension in front of the British high commissioner. "I said that of course it was regrettable," he recorded in his diary, "but that its importance should not be overstated." The following evening, at a relaxed and enjoyable party with student members of Mapai (many of whom had likely attended Norman's lecture), Arlosoroff had a different take. Far from seeing the incident as insignificant, Arlosoroff argued that a fundamental contradiction existed between Norman's vision for the university and Labor Zionist aspirations for the country.[80] That contradiction represented the disagreement not only between political Zionists and binationalists but also between political Zionists and cultural Zionists. Norman's position on the university was rooted in the ideas of Ahad Ha'am, who imagined Palestine as a cultural and spiritual, but not political, center of the Jewish world. Norman's vision was also founded on the concomitant assumption that Palestine would not become the demographic center of Jewish life. As a political Zionist, Arlosoroff understood his mission to be the political development of the Yishuv and an eventual Jewish majority in Palestine. The 1929 riots and his perception of the political stalemate that had been reached in the ensuing years convinced Arlosoroff that the Yishuv needed state-like power and national institutions—such as full-fledged universities—to achieve its goals. With the threat of Nazism growing in Europe, he judged that need ever more pressing.

THE PROBLEM OF TIME

"I was genuinely sorry that in our last talk you gave me the impression of being—I won't say discouraged, but sadly dissatisfied with the results of your work here during the past few months," Wauchope conveyed in a letter to

Arlosoroff soon after their turbulent meeting on Christmas Eve 1931. "I am sure you will remember Dr. Weizmann's warning and not expect difficulties to be solved with undue haste by the Palestine Government," he wrote, referring to Weizmann's policy of gradual, evolutionary Zionist development. "I possess, alas, no magician's wand," admitted Wauchope. What he did offer to Arlosoroff was "true sympathy" for Zionist ideals and "a real determination" to further the development of the country.[81]

The high commissioner's letter identified a key change in the Zionist political outlook in the 1930s. The 1920s had largely been a decade of international stability, with British imperial rule secure. The Yishuv, likewise, had seen slow, steady development and, for most of the decade, peace. The stock market crash of 1929, however, had plunged the world into crisis. The ensuing rise of Nazism in Germany and other fascist movements across Europe, coupled with a growing sense of the tenuousness of the Zionist-British partnership in the wake of the 1929 riots, ultimately convinced many Zionists that evolutionary Zionism could no longer pave the way for the Jewish national home.[82] The "time element," then, as Anita Shapira puts it, became key to Zionist policy, as the need for preparing Palestine as a haven for the Jewish masses of Europe emerged as a pressing reality. "Undue haste," to use Wauchope's words, no longer represented a risky approach—many Zionists now saw it as the only option.[83]

Arlosoroff, in his famous confidential letter to Chaim Weizmann in June 1932, became the first mainstream Zionist leader to propose a radical departure from the policy of evolutionary Zionism. As we will see, Arlosoroff laid out several possibilities for the future of the Yishuv, ultimately concluding that a revolution overthrowing mandatory authorities and establishing Jewish minority rule by force could be Zionism's only remaining option. That Arlosoroff—who for so long has been a leading champion of the Zionist-British partnership—was the first Zionist leader to articulate such a radically new position is evidence of just how dire he understood the situation to be.[84] Yet Arlosoroff did not in practice abandon relations with the British entirely. Instead, he traversed two seemingly contradictory political paths over the final year and a half of his life. In the first, he formulated a political vision for the Yishuv that, contrary to all his previous ideas about Zionist futures, would no longer take place within the framework of the British Empire. In the second, he developed a close personal friendship with High Commissioner Wauchope, became thoroughly entrenched in elite (largely British) circles in Jerusalem, and worked to build alliances with powerful Jews from across the British Empire.

In mid-February 1932, not long after Norman's ill-fated lecture at the Hebrew University, Arlosoroff had the opportunity to spend an afternoon with the high commissioner on a driving excursion across the coastal plain around Tel Aviv and Jaffa. Together with Sima and Wauchope's sister who was visiting Palestine, the party toured the suburbs of Givatayim and Ramat Gan, where Arlosoroff wished for the high commissioner to see "what Jewish families of the poorer petite bourgeoisie have achieved on only a few dunams of land, with a cow or two." Wauchope "seemed very strongly impressed," according to Arlosoroff, and "asked many questions, particularly about the lifestyle of the people in their countries of origin," where few had had experience working the land. "It is a point which I am constantly pressing upon him," wrote Arlosoroff, "so he will see the people in light of their past and understand correctly the transformation that has already taken place on the Jewish character under Palestine's effect."[85]

On the drive back to Jerusalem, Arlosoroff saw an opportunity to discuss frankly with Wauchope a topic about which he had lately thought a great deal: "the fundamentals of British policy in the Middle East and the wavering hyper-opportunist and hopelessly inadequate attitude of official circles." Arlosoroff likely referred to the positions espoused by the previous government under Chancellor, as well as Young's interim government, especially over issues such as the World Islamic Congress. He told Wauchope that Palestine seemed bound to become "just one link in the chain of Levantine States . . . which in due course would be merged into some Confederation with a definitely Asiatic and anti-western orientation." Here, Arlosoroff echoed arguments he had earlier made in his 1929 essay "The Ninth Dominion." At that time, however, Arlosoroff had argued that joining the British Commonwealth as a dominion would protect Palestine from the "naturally gravitating" inclination of the country's Arabs toward other nearby Arab states.[86] Now he warned Wauchope that the Yishuv might be the British Empire's only bulwark against an anti-imperial, Levantine pull. Whereas that inclination was "perhaps inevitable" in places such as Iraq, which would soon be granted independence, the same was not true for Palestine, where there was substantial Jewish settlement, Arlosoroff argued. Wauchope replied that "he generally agreed with this analysis."[87]

During a meeting with Wauchope the following month, Arlosoroff invoked another British imperial comparison—Canada—in a conversation about potential constitutional changes in Palestine. While he had previously proposed that Jews be placed in a *temporary* minority position on a future legislative council (to prevent deadlock with the Arabs), here Arlosoroff completely abandoned the possibility of Jewish minority status. There remained two potential options then: either Jews and Arabs could receive equal representation, or Jews could be granted a status "not compatible with their numerical strength" because of their disproportionally large stake in Palestine's economy. The first possibility, explained Arlosoroff, was based on binationalist visions for Palestine's future in which "the equality of two national entities... together will constitute the state of Palestine." One needed only look to Canada a century earlier, claimed Arlosoroff, to understand that this plan would fail. There, discontent over the Constitutional Act of 1791, which attempted constitutional parity through the creation of Anglo-Protestant Upper Canada (Ontario) and French Catholic Lower Canada (Quebec), ultimately led to the 1837 Lower Canada Rebellion and the unification of the two provinces. "The regime failed," Arlosoroff told Wauchope, "because it granted responsible self-rule, and therefore reached a point of constant stagnation between the two parts." The solution, then, was to give Jews, who "paid 40 percent of government revenues," an outsized, potentially majority status on a future legislative council.[88]

The evolution of Arlosoroff's political vision for Zionism found its most radical articulation in his June 1932 letter to Chaim Weizmann. By then, Arlosoroff could no longer foresee a future in which Jewish society provided a bulwark for British interests in the Middle East, or even one in which Jews received majority status on a legislative council organized by mandatory authorities. He could not envision these scenarios because he no longer could imagine a British future for the Yishuv. The startling and growing threat of Nazism in Germany, the seeming impossibility of productive Jewish-Arab relations, and the exasperating standstill of British policy in Palestine—despite his burgeoning working partnership with Wauchope—

all convinced Arlosoroff that Zionists were running out of time. His letter to Weizmann, regarded as a masterpiece of political analysis and evidence of the despair that had consumed Zionist leadership in the summer of 1932, depicted a grim reality facing the Yishuv. The evolutionary approach to Zionism—Weizmann its chief architect and proponent—had now become an "impossible" method. Zionism needed to settle "hundreds of thousands of Jews... within a relatively brief period of time" in order not to "reproduce Diaspora conditions in Palestine." But that prospect had become unfeasible. "I am forced to the conclusion that with the present methods and under the present regime," he wrote, "there is hardly a possibility of working out a solution for this problem of large-scale immigration and settlement." Had Arlosoroff envisioned another couple of decades of peace in the Middle East and around the globe, he would have been content, "without grumbling," to continue on the evolutionary path. But "the political situation in the world remains so unsettled and the fermentation in the Middle East is growing at such a pace," he reasoned, "that there is little hope for any such optimistic assumption." Arlosoroff asked Weizmann, "Can there be a doubt in anybody's mind that we are heading for a new great war?"[89]

Taking into account this growing worldwide unrest and anticipating a future British-Arab alliance, Arlosoroff argued that the deteriorating social and economic position of European Jewry demanded an immediate reckoning, a solution to the "real issue." He believed that four possible paths lay before the Zionist movement. The first was simply to "hold on" and hope for the best. This was "an extremely Jewish attitude," wrote Arlosoroff, and "a specifically Jewish form of heroism," but it was not, he believed, a *Zionist* attitude. Rather, surrendering to this holding pattern was tantamount to an abandonment of Zionist "political action." The second path was to forsake the Zionist dream altogether and to admit that it could not "be turned into a reality." Arlosoroff included members of Brit Shalom and the publishers of the Trotskyite newspaper *Ha-Or* among those who had already, in effect, decided on this course. They would ultimately "drift off to new shores"—be they pacifist or communist—"which have for them a stronger lure." The third path was to establish Jewish national sovereignty within a territorially limited canton. "There is no doubt in my mind that there is a sound core to all these [cantonization] schemes," wrote Arlosoroff. But the issue of Jerusalem, the challenge of limited territory, and the fragmented configuration of Jewish settlement in Palestine all made this plan problematic.⁹⁰

The fourth path, the most radical and drastic, reflected the apotheosis of Arlosoroff's ideas about state power. "The fourth possible conclusion would be," he wrote, "that Zionism cannot, in the given circumstances, be turned into a reality without a transition period of the organized revolutionary rule of the Jewish minority." This "nationalist minority government" would "usurp the state machinery, the administration and the military power in order to forestall the danger of [Zionists] being swamped by numbers and endangered by a rising." Arlosoroff suggested a possibility here, in other words, in which Zionists would overthrow British mandatory authorities and establish minority rule over Arabs in Palestine. He admitted to Weizmann that the plan "may at first sight appear impracticable, even more, fantastic" and that "it may seem to contradict the condition in which the British Mandate places us." It may even seem "dangerously near" certain Revisionist ideas. "All I feel, and with overwhelming force," Arlosoroff declared, "is that I should never accept the defeat of Zionism before an attempt was made which would be equal to the grim seriousness of our struggle for national life and to the sacredness of the trust which the Jewish people has laid in our hands."⁹¹

There is no reason to doubt the depth of Arlosoroff's worry or the seriousness with which he proposed this final possibility to Weizmann in the summer of 1932. He had long grappled with the importance of state power, and his propensity for realism rather than idealism meant that he took very seriously the rise of Nazism, the threat of world war, and any other "cruel contingency" the Zionist movement might face amid such great uncertainty.⁹² Yet the evolution—in fact, the climax—of Arlosoroff's political thinking that led him to a place where he felt compelled to propose revolution occurred while he was more deeply entrenched in Jerusalem's elite (and British-oriented) social scene than ever before; while he pursued alliances with Jews from across the British Empire; and while he developed with Wauchope a professional-turned-personal friendship marked by honesty and mutual respect.

After moving to Jerusalem, Arlosoroff became a part of the elite social scene that the Bentwiches had helped to build. After Norman and Helen returned to Jerusalem, the couple and Arlosoroff spent countless parties, concerts, and other heterosocial events together. And despite the growing chasm between Norman's binationalist-inclined politics and Arlosoroff's increasingly hostile attitude toward Brit Shalom, the two men, as well as Helen and often Sima, regularly dined together in small, intimate settings. These various gatherings, both large and small, generally included a mix of British authorities and Anglo-Jews, as well as Zionist leaders and local Arab elites. For example, in February 1932, Arlosoroff recorded in his diary that he "dined with Judge Frumkin[93] together with the Bentwiches, and a few of the Arab judges (El Khaldi,[94] Khayat,[95] and Jarallah[96])."[97] In March, Arlosoroff attended dinner at the Bentwich home and was joined by Dr. Strathearn (a British ophthalmologist) and Judge H. A. Webb (the government's legal assessor for claims of displacement), as well as the two men's wives.[98] Annie Landau, the headmistress of the Evelina de Rothschild School for Girls and an early friend of Helen Bentwich, whose home continued to serve as a center of elite sociability in Jerusalem, included Chaim and Sima Arlosoroff in several dinners and parties. In February 1932, Landau hosted a large party after Jascha Heifetz gave a concert, a rare underwhelming performance by the violin virtuoso that left "even a music enthusiast like" Wauchope (also in attendance) "unmoved," according to Arlosoroff.[99] In May and June 1932, Landau also invited the Arlosoroffs to dinners at her home. In May, the Arlosoroffs hosted a large reception at their Jerusalem home in honor of the Ukrainian Zionist leader Leo Motzkin. Guests included Norman Bentwich, Gershon Agronsky, Gad Frumkin, Max Nurock, and Arthur Ruppin. While Sima sometimes accompanied her husband to dinners and parties and occasionally served as hostess, Chaim Arlosoroff also attended many social functions alone and rarely documented Sima's voice in his diary when he wrote about gatherings during which she was present.

Just as Arlosoroff's quotidian and convivial activities in Jerusalem were shaped by an elite British imperial sociability, his work as a Zionist leader was also shaped by British imperial horizons. While questioning the fundamental tenability of the Yishuv's future in the British Empire, Arlosoroff decided not to shun ties with Britain but rather resolved to build relationships with influential (and often wealthy) Jewish elites from both the metropole and the empire in the hope that their intervention could improve Zionism's situation.

For instance, he wrote to Wellesley Aron, the Anglo-Jewish founder of the Jewish youth movement Habonim, about ways to further social contact between Jewish Agency officials and British authorities in Palestine. "I thought of establishing (unofficially) Citizens' Committees in each of the cities and colonies where British officials and troops are stationed with the purpose of working up systematically relations between the Jewish population and the British," he told Aron.[100] Here, Arlosoroff's approach—building relations with the rank and file of the British mandatory—echoed arguments he had made in his 1928 essay "British Clerks and the National Home."

In the spring of 1932, Arlosoroff became acquainted with Eva Isaacs, the daughter of Anglo-Jewish industrialist and Liberal-turned-Conservative politician Alfred Mond (1868–1930) and the daughter-in-law of Rufus Isaacs, 1st Marquess of Reading (1860–1935), the former viceroy of India.[101] Eva Isaacs first traveled to Palestine in 1928, accompanying her father, a close friend of Chaim Weizmann. On her return to England, Isaacs took up the study of Hebrew and became a dedicated and active Zionist. On her 1932 trip to Palestine, she developed a warm friendship with Arlosoroff. At one meeting in February—tea at the King David Hotel—Arlosoroff recorded in his diary that the two had had "a very pleasant talk on [his] favourite subject: British policy in the Middle East and the Jewish National Home." Isaacs also told Arlosoroff that Wauchope had "commented very favorably" to her on his developing relationship with the young Zionist leader.[102] The following month, Arlosoroff and Sima drove north to spend a Shabbat with Isaacs at the home her late father had built on the shores of the Sea of Galilee. On Saturday afternoon, Arlosoroff had "a serious conversation" with Isaacs about the help her father-in-law Lord Reading might provide to the Zionist movement, especially in times of such political uncertainty. "I pointed to the problem of the constitutional changes that might arise in the near future," Arlosoroff reported in his dairy. "In this matter, he could give us invaluable assistance. We still do not know what the actual form of the question will be for us. In any event, this will be a fundamental political problem that has a far-reaching impact on the future of the country," he wrote. Eva Isaacs "understood the object of [his] words and promised to help." Arlosoroff found her to be "very attentive and devoted" to the Zionist cause and a "brave soldier of the movement."[103]

Arlosoroff's friendship with Eva Isaacs led to other British imperial connections. For instance, she introduced him to Percival David, a Baghdadi Jewish financier from India, who was visiting Palestine. David, who over the course of his life amassed one of the most significant collections of Chinese ceramics and stamps, was quick to inform Arlosoroff that he was a "non-Zionist"; he opposed nationalism and supported cosmopolitanism. Arlosoroff had ideas about the utility of wealthy non-Zionists, who always seemed to want to endow a chair at the Hebrew University but not support the realization of a Jewish state.[104] "The question is—what will we do with all these chairs, if we have no place to put them?" he quipped. But Eva Isaacs had suggested to David that he use his money for a different purpose—to help develop Jewish-Arab relations. After discussing ideas, David settled on funding the planting of orchards for tribal leaders in the Transjordan, a scheme Arlosoroff hoped would help promote their favorable attitude toward Zionism.[105]

Arlosoroff's most significant British friendship proved to be with Arthur Wauchope. Since he had impassionedly lectured Wauchope on the state of Zionist-British relations on Christmas Eve the previous year, Arlosoroff had developed a relationship with the high commissioner marked by mutual respect and a forthrightness that belied Wauchope's high station. Wauchope, unlike his predecessor Chancellor, was openly sympathetic to Zionism and treated Arlosoroff as a wise and experienced colleague whose partnership was integral to Britain's mission in Palestine.

In May 1932, a month before Arlosoroff composed his famous letter to Weizmann, he and Wauchope exchanged a remarkable correspondence regarding Leon Pinsker's *Auto-Emancipation*.[106] Published anonymously in German in 1882 and considered the earliest articulation of political Zionism, *Auto-Emancipation* argued that neither humanism nor Jewish emancipation could solve the Jewish problem. Jews would continue to face antisemitism so long as they remained nationless aliens. The solution was a territorial Jewish nation, a place where Jews could promote on their own soil "national self-respect and self-confidence."[107] In May 1932, Arlosoroff found himself preparing a new edition of the short text, which had gone out of print. He thought that Wauchope might find it instructive and illuminating and decided to send the high commissioner a copy of the English edition from the

Hebrew University's library.[108] "This year it will be just half a century since this little booklet appeared," Arlosoroff told Wauchope. The exigencies of the day meant that even fifty years on, the text was still relevant. "What with the wave of Hitlerism in Central Europe, the crash of the Jewish middleclass structure in the United States, the 'Red' assimilation in Soviet Russia, and many other gloomy facts of these days, it remains appallingly up-to-date," Arlosoroff wrote.[109] He hinted here at many of the same concerns about the graveness of the Jewish situation that later he expressed in the letter to Weizmann.

Wauchope was "greatly obliged" for the loan of *Auto-Emancipation*, writing to Arlosoroff that "it is wonderful that so much could have been written fifty years ago, equally wonderful that so much could have been foreseen." Wauchope then remarked on the text in more detail, assessing which of Pinsker's recommendations had already been realized. "I am sure you agree there is great self-respect and great self-confidence among Jews both in Palestine and England of today," he wrote. He believed, too, that "a great and most successful step forward since the Balfour Declaration" had been taken. "How seldom in history, or in our own lives, do actualities achieved equal our high aspiration?" he wrote. "Affairs march so slowly and not quite as we wish," recognized Wauchope, but he believed the Zionist movement was progressing in the spirit envisioned in *Auto-Emancipation*. "'We must take the first step,'" he wrote, quoting Pinsker. "'Our descendants must follow us in measured and not over-hasty time.'"[110]

But Wauchope disagreed on one critical element of Pinsker's assessment of the Jewish condition. Pinsker believed that antisemitism was ineradicable so long as Jews were not a nation among nations. "Since the Jew is nowhere at home, nowhere regarded as a native, he remains an alien everywhere," Pinsker had written.[111] This condition was the root of antisemitism; legal, civic, and political emancipation could not solve the problem. Wauchope felt Pinsker was wrong not only when it came to "English feeling today" but also about the nature of antisemitism more broadly. "For instance . . . he says the prejudice against Jews is innate and ineradicable. I do not believe it to be innate: and where it exists today I believe it is less strong than fifty years ago certainly among educated people," wrote the high commissioner. Hitlerism, argued Wauchope, was not ineradicable; it was "ephemeral." Wauchope closed his letter deferentially, writing, "I am sure you will agree that I write in a spirit of friendliness and not controversy."[112]

Arlosoroff replied to Wauchope's note with a long, substantive letter, in which he took issue with the high commissioner's assessment of antisemitism, laid out in greater depth the seriousness of the worldwide Jewish condition, and explained that *time* had become a critical factor for Zionism. Regarding Wauchope's opinion on the decline of antisemitism, Arlosoroff wrote, "I am compelled to say that your belief seems to me to be based upon what one might call an optical error." Arlosoroff echoed Pinsker, explaining that "one root of this error is the current belief in human progress which may be well-justified in respect to external civilisation, social organization, legislation, standard of living and technical advancement, but is sadly ill-founded with regard to the deeper forces and instincts directing human life." Pinsker believed that antisemitism was innate and ineradicable, not because humans were "bad" but because "the Jews remain an element fundamentally alien to the instincts of the people in the midst of whom they dwell," clarified Arlosoroff. The only reason that antisemitism had not developed in Britain to the same extent that it had elsewhere was that turn-of-the-century immigration control there had kept the Jewish population "just short" of the critical mass that would inevitably provoke "a high tide of anti-Jewish sentiment."[113] Indeed, the established Anglo-Jewish community had been acutely aware of this dynamic since poorer Eastern European Jews started to immigrate to Britain in larger numbers beginning in the 1880s.

"The truth is that the anti-semitic movement of today is more powerful and incomparably better organised than it was fifty years ago," Arlosoroff argued. Antisemitism "today" had pseudo-scientific theory, extensive literature, and robust political parties, "with millions of voters." In contrast to Wauchope's claim that antisemitism had decreased particularly among educated people, Arlosoroff maintained that "it is [precisely] the universities that form the hotbed of militant anti-Jewish movements, backed by professors and students alike." Even in the United States—"fifty years ago a symbol of liberty"—social antisemitism meant that Jewish quotas had been implemented in many of the nation's top universities. "Thus, on the whole," wrote Arlosoroff, "I am afraid there is little reason for optimism."[114]

This bleak reality meant that time was not on Zionism's side. Arlosoroff made clear to Wauchope the great limitations that the "factor 'T'" now wielded over the Zionist movement:

> There is no doubt in my mind that as you rightly say, in the course of this half century the first step forward towards the national future of the Jewish people has been successfully taken. All of us know that our work must grow organically and that our liberty cannot be achieved by miracles or sleight of hand. But, on the other hand, there is no getting away from the fact that the world around us is not standing still to wait for us, and that our undertaking, which is not going on in a vacuum but at a definite point in time and space, in history and geography, cannot leave the factor "T" out of its equation. The world is moving: Jewish economic positions upon which our efforts in Palestine were based are either being destroyed (as in Soviet Russia) or crumbling away (as in the United States). The countries of the Middle East are in a state of ferment. The young generation of Palestinian Arabs is being brought up on teachings of hatred against everything Jewish. There seems to be a historical limit for the possibility of Zionism. We can never lose the sense of the limit and it is that which sometimes accounts for our reaction if we find that our rate of progress is inadequate or that obstacles are placed in our way.[115]

Arlosoroff, not surprisingly, stopped short of offering up the idea of revolution in his correspondence with Wauchope; perhaps, too, he had not yet reached the depth of worry that he would the following month. But both Arlosoroff's May letter to Wauchope and his June missive to Weizmann conveyed the same fundamental message: Zionism now faced a "historical limit," a true prospect of failure in the face of worldwide developments. It was in this one respect that Arlosoroff was compelled to disagree with *Auto-Emancipation*: Pinsker's recommendation for "measured and not over-hasty" Jewish national development was no longer tenable. This conclusion would push Arlosoroff to think seriously about Zionist futures that would no longer—perhaps *could* no longer—be bound up in the British Empire. Yet at the same time, Arlosoroff had become entrenched in a world in Jerusalem—through his friendship with the high commissioner, his social circle, and his contacts with British imperial Jewish elites—that had been shaped by Palestine's imperial horizons.

Arlosoroff's dire predictions turned out to be only half true: while Jewish futures in Europe grew increasingly bleak, Zionist fortunes in Palestine saw a dramatic reversal beginning in the fall of 1932 when Wauchope opened the gates of Palestine to Jewish immigration, thus ushering in the massive Fifth Aliyah.[116] Following Hitler's rise to power, the year 1933 saw the single largest wave of Jewish immigration to Palestine under British rule—more than thirty-seven thousand individuals, including many German and Polish Jews.[117] Fear that the Yishuv's economy would not be able to accommodate such an influx proved unfounded. While the world struggled through an economic depression, the Jewish economy in Palestine soared.

Arlosoroff did not live to see the grand sweep of this success. In June 1933, he traveled to Germany to help negotiate the Haavara (Transfer) Agreement with the Nazi government. The arrangement allowed German Jews fleeing Nazi persecution to immigrate to Palestine and to bring a portion of their assets with them in the form of German goods. This transfer of assets, vehemently protested by Revisionist Zionists, violated the anti-Nazi boycott of 1933. Two days after returning home to Palestine, Arlosoroff was murdered, shot point-blank on a beach in Tel Aviv while taking a walk with Sima, who was unharmed. The murder remains unsolved.

Imagined futures that had once seemed desirable changed dramatically in the early years of the 1930s. While Arlosoroff's political thinking in the 1920s had been marked by faith in the Zionist-British partnership and a curiosity—even excitement—over what that partnership might mean for Palestine's future, the 1930s saw the Zionist leader increasingly turn to a politics shaped by deep worry and dread. Arlosoroff's uncertainty and anxiety over what might realistically be done in the time that remained pushed him toward positions on political representation and the possession of capital that fell well outside accepted tenets of labor politics and social democratic ideals. And it compelled Arlosoroff to consider very seriously the possibility of Jewish futures in Palestine no longer taking place in the British Empire. As we will see in the next chapter, on India, uncertainty shaped Jewish politics in other reaches of the empire, too, and compelled a range of political positions not easily reconcilable.

FOUR

Between Empire and Nation

THOUSANDS OF MILES FROM PALESTINE, in the heart of the British Empire, August 1929 proved just as fateful for another Jewish community for an entirely different reason.[1] In that month, David Ezra (1871–1947), the most prominent Baghdadi Jewish businessman in Calcutta and a member of the famed Sassoon family, spearheaded a memorial campaign to have members of his community categorized as European in the Bengali electorate.[2] Signed by more than one hundred other elite Baghdadi Jews in Calcutta, the memorial argued that Baghdadi Jewish British subjects "living in the European style" in Bengal should be included in the European electorate based on a combination of their ethnic and racial background, European cultural practices, and unshakable loyalty to the British Empire.[3] Ezra launched the memorial when the Government of India Act of 1919—which had introduced new electoral laws and a bicameral legislative parliament (diarchy) to the British colony—was set to expire, ten years after its enactment.[4] The 1919 reforms, considered by Indian nationalists to have fallen far short of Britain's wartime pledge for expanded Indian self-government, had divided the Bengali electorate along communal lines into four distinct groups: European, Anglo-Indian, Mohammedan, and non-Mohammedan. The Jewish community fell into the non-Mohammedan category, the largest electoral group, comprising mostly Hindus.[5] By the summer of 1929, the seven British members of the Simon Commission, the group tasked with recommending new reforms for India, had returned to London after two extended trips to the subcontinent and were busy formulating plans for the next Government of India Act. The commission's visits to India had incited mass protests, boycotts, and calls for radical change, highlighting the challenge of negotiating individual and communal status within an unstable British colonial legal framework in an imperial landscape giving way to a national one.[6]

While David Ezra continued to push for European electoral categorization, stressing his community's "unswerving" commitment to British political interests, his wife, Rachel Ezra (1877–1952), privately conveyed a tentative hopefulness about the prospect of Indian self-rule.[7] "Just heard that Gandhi is sailing by this mail & he is on his way to Bombay.... We hope that there may be satisfactory results from his visit," she wrote in August 1931 in a letter to her nephew Solomon (Sulman) Sassoon.[8] From Bombay, Gandhi would sail for London to participate in the second Round Table Conference, where plans for legislative reform in India would be examined. When Gandhi had agreed to attend the second conference (he had boycotted the first), Rachel told Solomon about a Baghdadi friend who was becoming involved in Indian nationalist politics and had an upcoming interview with the Indian leader. "Meyer David is taking a real interest in the Peace Movement & he is to have an interview with Gandhi tomorrow!!" she wrote.[9] Both Rachel and David Ezra (even as he led the memorial campaign) cultivated affective and associational ties with a broad range of elites, including elite Hindus, Sikhs, and Parsis. They entertained each other at dinners and parties, joined the same social clubs, and served on the same institutional boards and civic committees. The Ezras' Jewishness—marked by their role as leaders of their community in Calcutta, their ardent observance of Jewish religion, and their participation in Jewish cultural institutions—shaped their daily lives and affective ties even more profoundly than did their embeddedness in elite Indian culture. Rachel and David Ezra grew to be enthusiastic Zionists, traveling to Palestine, nurturing a deeply instilled romantic notion of the Land of Israel, and directing Zionist organizations in Calcutta. In these convivial, quotidian, and communal settings, both Indian and Jewish, a range of political behaviors took shape that differed dramatically from the proimperial politics laid out in the memorial campaign.

This chapter offers a new account of elite Baghdadi Jewish politics that takes seriously both the memorial campaign and the Ezras' embeddedness in Indian and Jewish cultures and argues that elite Baghdadi politics in the late imperial period can be better understood in light of careful consideration of both. Previously, the claims made in the memorial campaign—chiefly that Baghdadi Jews were thoroughly European and unfailingly loyal to the British Empire—have shaped the way historians have understood the nature of Baghdadi politics in India. In these accounts, Baghdadi Jews' unquestionable allegiance to empire and their British-oriented European cultural practices distinguished them from other Jews and non-Europeans in India, who grappled (often publicly) with their identification as "Indian" and with the question of Indian nationalism.[10] This chapter, in contrast, insists on an examination of both the memorial campaign and the Ezras' relationships with Indian and Jewish cultures, but it does not argue that one constitutes a truer expression of the couple's politics.

Rather, the memorial campaign and the Ezras' embeddedness in Indian and Jewish cultures reflect two sides of an emerging late imperial elite Jewish politics shaped by a single political horizon: a growing uncertainty about Jewish futures in India amid the intensification of Indian nationalist sentiment and the expectation that the terms of British imperial rule on the subcontinent would change. For the Ezras, as the stakes of nationalism and imperialism grew higher throughout the 1920s and 1930s, the memorial campaign and the quotidian, convivial spaces of the couple's lives each generated distinctive, situational sets of political vocabularies, categories, and concerns. Uncertainty about Jewish political futures likewise compelled Chaim Arlosoroff—in a mirror image of the Ezras—to challenge the fundamental tenability of the Jewish-British partnership while simultaneously maintaining close ties to elite British social circles in Palestine. Yet despite the differences in their political ideas and expressions, the Ezras and Arlosoroff both ended up navigating the same complex entanglement of Jewish, British imperial, and anticolonial politics.

The first part of this chapter investigates the saga of the memorial campaign led by David Ezra, turning in the second half to an exploration of how the Ezras' daily lives and affective ties shaped their attitudes toward Indian nationalism and Zionism. Rachel Ezra, like her husband, was also a member of the wealthy Sassoon family.[11] The family patriarch, David Sassoon (1792–1864), born in Baghdad, founded the merchant house Sassoon & Company in Bombay in 1832. Trading in cotton and silk, and monopolizing the legal opium trade between British India and China, Sassoon & Company branched out across East Asia, opening satellite offices in Canton, Hong Kong, and Shanghai. Many Sassoon family members moved to Britain toward the end of the nineteenth century, following the transfer of company headquarters to London. Rachel Ezra, who had been born in Bombay, lived in London from 1901 until her marriage in 1912, when she joined her

FIGURE 4   Rachel Ezra in 1936. From the *Monthly Review* 59, no. 3 (March 1936): 313.

husband in Calcutta. Whereas the Sassoons had been the most prominent Baghdadi family in Bombay, the Ezras, who had made their fortune in trade and real estate, became leaders of the community in Calcutta. The marriage of Rachel and David Ezra represented the coming together of India's two most powerful Jewish families and solidified the establishment of the community's seat in Calcutta, despite the larger Baghdadi community in Bombay.[12] In this sense, the Ezras do not just provide a lens on elite Baghdadi Jewish politics in India; they were the torchbearers of those politics.

Like Helen and Norman Bentwich, the Ezras' marriage (which was also childless) represented a powerful Jewish partnership. Born into immense wealth, neither Rachel nor David pursued professional passions as Norman and Helen did. Like the Bentwiches, however, the Ezras both took on significant leadership roles in the Jewish and wider communities. In contrast to Helen, Rachel understood her leadership work not as the manifestation of deeply held political convictions but rather as a central duty of her high societal and communal position. She also occupied and embraced the role of hostess far more comfortably and enthusiastically than did Helen, who regularly bristled at this expected duty of a colonial wife. Yet Rachel Ezra, despite the claims of the memorial campaign, hardly behaved like a typical European wife in India. Just as Helen contravened expected norms of colonial femininity through her social work, so, too, did Rachel through her Jewish and Zionist leadership and her ideas about Indian nationalism.

THE MEMORIAL CAMPAIGN

The Baghdadi Jewish community in India had made efforts to align itself publicly with Britain since the Indian Rebellion of 1857. At that time, the Sassoon family patriarch, David Sassoon, had pledged his community's support for the British Empire.[13] He had been made a British subject in 1853, a status inherited by his descendants and granted to some other members of the Baghdadi community. The Baghdadi population increased steadily throughout the nineteenth and early twentieth centuries, bolstered by continued immigration from Iraq. By the 1930s, the total number of Baghdadi Jews in India, concentrated primarily in Bombay and Calcutta, had reached roughly five thousand, a quarter of whom were British subjects.[14]

Until 1885, Baghdadi Jews in India had been categorized by British authorities as European, a classification applied in criminal and educational matters. The revocation of that status in 1885 inspired small-scale efforts to have Baghdadi schools and pupils reclassified as European but did not gravely concern the community.[15] One Baghdadi Jew later reflected that, apart from education, the community's reclassification, "limited in scope," had a negligible impact and "did not create any invidious official distinction."[16] Baghdadi perception of the importance of official European classification—and indeed, its actual currency in British India—changed in the wake of World War I. In June 1919, against the backdrop of growing nationalist ferment, David Ezra sent a memorial on behalf of his community to the government of Bengal requesting exemption from the Indian Arms Act of 1878. The act, which prohibited Indians from bearing arms, made certain exceptions for non-Indian minority groups, including Europeans, Armenians, and Americans. Ezra argued that British subjects of the Baghdadi Jewish community in India constituted such a minority and deserved their own community exemption. They were loyal to the British Empire, practiced a European lifestyle, and were—because of their alleged Sephardi origins—just as racially entitled to the exemption as Armenians.[17] In reality, although many Baghdadi Jews followed a Sephardi religious rite, they were not historically from Spain or Portugal.[18] The Home Department rejected the request, citing an earlier decision to deny claims made on a racial basis.[19]

Six months later, in December 1919, Britain's Parliament passed the Government of India Act, introducing new measures of self-government and expanding the franchise among elites in India. The act mandated distinct electoral representation for different constituencies—including Europeans, Anglo-Indians, Muslims, Sikhs, and Indian Christians—reserving designated seats for them in the Indian legislature. But Jews in India, Baghdadi or otherwise, neither qualified for any of the special constituencies nor constituted a population large enough to warrant its own. As mentioned earlier, in Bengal, including its capital of Calcutta, the franchise was divided into four electoral constituencies: European, Anglo-Indian, Mohammedan, and non-Mohammedan. The European group, though small, wielded disproportionate influence in the legislature. This was by design—Bengal was the center of British business interests in India—and the result of the breakup and political fragmentation of the majority of the population between Muslims and non-Muslims.[20] Jews, barred by the parameters of the European, Anglo-Indian, and Mohammedan constituencies, were placed in the fourth, primarily Hindu, non-Mohammedan group.[21]

In 1929, on the expiration of the Government of India Act of 1919, David Ezra launched another memorial campaign with a new line of argumentation that differed from his memorial ten years earlier. Directed to the government of Bengal, the memorial argued that Baghdadi Jewish British subjects in Bengal, instead of being recognized as a special minority, should qualify as European in the electorate.[22] Ezra and other elite Baghdadi Jews, whose power had previously derived from their wealth and importance to the British imperial economy, believed that their influence would wane if they remained in a Hindu-majority electoral constituency. That constituency would likely expand—along with Indian self-rule—with the next set of reforms. The memorial, cosigned by 114 other prominent Baghdadi Jews in Calcutta, asserted that "all natural born British subjects of the Jewish Community living in the European style and domiciled in Bengal" should be included in the European electorate.[23] As the memorial ten years earlier had explained, the so-called Sephardi Jews of India—in other words, the Baghdadi Jews—were distinct from other "native" Jewish communities in the country, namely the Bene Israel, who resembled their Marathi neighbors in language, dress, and other quotidian practices.[24] The Sephardi Baghdadi Jews, whose ancestors had "migrated during the Spanish Inquisition among other places to pre-war Asiatic Turkey," according to the memorial, had roots in the Iberian Peninsula—that is, in Europe.[25] The memorial thus distinguished between native and foreign Jews in India, emphasizing their historical, ethnic, and social differences. The document further specified that the request for European classification was intended for those in the Baghdadi community who were "natural born British subjects" and who had "been educated and live in the British style"—not the other segment of the Baghdadi community that was "mostly foreign born, who with their families [had] retained their foreign habits and not yet adopted British standards of living."[26] In this way, the memorial relied on two different notions of a native-foreign dichotomy, hinging in one instance on ethnicity and place of origin and in the other on acculturation, social practices, and (implicitly) class. In other words, Baghdadi Jews who deserved to be included in the European electorate were originally foreign to India, with roots in Europe, but had lived in British India long enough to shed any social practices and customs adopted during their community's very long sojourn in "Asiatic Turkey."

The memorial also invoked loyalty and economic utility arguments, long the twin justifications of Jewish tolerance, to bolster its case. The segment of the Baghdadi community living in Bengal in the "British style" had "always kept aloof from all political agitation in this country because of its unswerving loyalty to the British Crown, its keen appreciation of the blessings of an enlightened and liberal Government, and its respect for law and constituted authority." Furthermore, Baghdadi Jews, though small in number, "[represented] considerable interests in Landholdings, Commerce, Trades and Professions in India."[27]

The memorialists argued that relegation to the non-Mohammedan electoral group put them at an unfair disadvantage, one that Jews in Britain and other reaches of the empire did not suffer. Those Jews, though not necessarily European according to the definition used in India, were "subject to no Political, Communal or Social disabilities."[28] Many Jews—including Baghdadi Jews—had settled in Britain, achieving prominent positions in society and even serving in Parliament. For instance, the Ezras' cousin Philip Sassoon (1888–1939) had been elected as member of Parliament for Hythe in 1912, the youngest member of the House of Commons at the time.[29] He later served as parliamentary private secretary for David Lloyd George and as undersecretary of state for air.[30] Baghdadi Jews in India, in contrast, faced an "undeserved hardship" because "the franchise legally allowed to them [was] rendered sterile" by inclusion in the non-Mohammedan constituency. The Anglo-Indian electoral group was not an option for Baghdadi Jews by virtue of the "purity of [their] race." For all these reasons, the memorialists concluded, they deserved to be included in the European electorate in Bengal and requested that the definition of *European* be amended to include "all natural born British subjects of the Jewish Community living in the European style and domiciled in Bengal."[31]

Though the memorial text itself made limited use of race as an argument (specifically to contrast Baghdadi Jews' pure race with the mixed-race status of Anglo-Indians), the broader memorial campaign subsequently expanded on the idea of race, employing contemporary ethnological notions of the

"Jewish race" as a white race. In an August 1929 letter to Rufus Isaacs, 1st Marquess of Reading, who served as viceroy of India from 1921 to 1926 and was the only Jew to hold the position, David Ezra echoed the claims of the memorial by emphasizing the divergence of interests between Baghdadi Jews and the "mainly Swarajist" non-Mohammedan constituency—that is, the majority Hindu bloc that supported *swaraj*, Indian self-rule.[32] Whereas the memorial used Sephardi identification to make explicit claims of European origin, Ezra acknowledged in his letter to Isaacs that the Baghdadi community was not, in fact, of European descent and, instead, based his argument on race. "There is a strong feeling among the British section of the [Baghdadi] community," he wrote, "that their members should be politically classified by Government on a Racial basis and that their Race entitles them to be attached to the 'European' group rather than the Indian despite the fact that their descent is not 'European.'"[33] The accompanying mention of Indian nationalist politics implied a connection between race and anticolonial activism. Ezra sent a similar statement at the same time to John Simon and the other members of his eponymous commission (which had by then returned to London), emphasizing the racial aspect of his claim.

This argument about race, which the memorial campaign maintained until its end in 1935, was tenable in large part because it was made in an imperial world attuned to racialism. The stratified electoral system implemented in the Government of India Act of 1919 built on a long history of racial thought that both reinforced communalism and casteism and differentiated between the white races of the metropole; the governed, nonwhite races of the empire; and the mixed-race population in between. But an essential element of Ezra's argument in his letter to Isaacs—privileging race over descent—ran against developing trends in British colonial discourse. Architects of the 1919 act had used the word *descent*, rather than *race*, in their descriptions of Europeans and Anglo-Indians. Indeed, Ezra's previous memorial in 1919 had been rejected ostensibly because the British government wished to eschew racial thinking—or at least the overt use of race-based political categories. In contrast to the geographically less-specific notion of race, descent produced a narrower, more easily definable category that could be tied to a specific place of origin. British preference for the softer category of descent only increased amid the rise of Nazism in Germany (and fascism at home). The use of race as a political category by a Jewish community might seem anathema or at least ironic against the backdrop of the rise of Nazism. Mitchell Hart has suggested that "rather than ask how Jews could have become involved in such unpalatable and potentially dangerous ideas . . . we might ask: What did Jews stand to gain by engaging with racial thought?"[34] In the case of the Baghdadi Jews of Calcutta, a racial argument may have seemed more defensible—if also more politically risky—than the tenuous argument about Sephardi descent, particularly when presented to Isaacs, whose ancestry on his mother's side included a long line of Sephardi Jews in Britain. But beyond race and descent, the memorial also divided the Baghdadi community itself based on social practices, arguing that only the segment living "in the British style" deserved European categorization. In other words, David Ezra and the memorialists understood that to be European in the British Empire required something both intrinsic and performative, both a lineage and a cultural grammar.

While Ezra awaited a response to the memorial, which was passed off from one department and government to the next, he encouraged the Baghdadi community in Bombay—larger than the one in Calcutta—to "actively participate in this matter" and submit their own memorial.[35] In a September 1929 letter to a leader of the Bombay community, Ezra conceded that it was unfortunate that the memorial needed to distinguish between ostensibly foreign and British Baghdadi Jews; indeed, a larger portion of Baghdadi Jews in Bombay would have fallen into the former category. But, continued Ezra, "it is an accepted and established fact in the civilized world that the Jewish race is a white one," and therefore "British Jews of pure descent have a right to be included by Government in their political classification of a European no matter where they were born." Indeed, the European electorate "was obviously formed to represent the White races domiciled in India."[36]

Much to the chagrin of the Calcutta memorialists, the memorial eventually submitted by the Bombay community made no mention of race. Edward Judah, one of the Calcutta memorialists who had worked closely with Ezra on the campaign, explained in letters to Baghdadi leaders in Bombay that he regretted their lack of attention to the "very serious question of the racial classification" of Baghdadi Jews in India. "The Jewish Race being a white one, your community will, I feel sure, not sacrifice our heritage by failing to take the necessary action in pressing this point on Government," he wrote.[37] Although Ezra had invoked race in his communication with Rufus Isaacs and the Simon Commission, he and Judah both made an explicit assertion of Baghdadi Jewish *whiteness* in their communication with the community in Bombay. Jael Silliman has argued that "most Baghdadi Jews had British colonial ideas about race and placed themselves in the upper echelons of the racial pyramid that structured social life in the colonies."[38] Here, however, Ezra and Judah represented their community as a racial group not simply alongside whites in India; rather, they argued that Baghdadi Jews and whites were one and the same. The Calcutta memorialists' vision of Jewish whiteness, in fact, more aptly reflected an emerging paradigm from another part of the empire—South Africa. There, the politician Jan Smuts envisioned the British dominion as a "composite" nation for a diverse array of white races, including Jews.[39]

Edward Judah's reprimand of the Bombay community's neglect of the race issue went without response for more than four months. Finally, in May 1930, a representative from Bombay responded to Judah, proffering an entirely new position that deviated even more significantly from the Calcutta community's scheme and from the memorial previously submitted by the Bombay leaders. "I may say that we are [of the] opinion," wrote the Bombay representative, "that it is not advantageous for our community to be classified along with the Europeans and that it will be better to seek separate representation as the minority community."[40] This development posed a potentially grave problem for the Baghdadi Jews of Calcutta: what would it mean for their case if their counterparts in Bombay did not want to be considered European? Rumors began to circulate that the Baghdadi Jews of Bombay planned to include the Bene Israel in their proposed minority constituency scheme, a move that would further undermine the Calcutta community's racial claims. The rumor proved unfounded, but the Baghdadi community in Bombay maintained its position on forming its own minority constituency. "We quite agree that our Community is 'non-Indian', but whether we are entitled to be included in the European group . . . is another question," wrote a Bombay representative, who wondered further if European classification would even be "advantageous." He argued, for example, that it was unlikely that a European constituency would ever elect a Jew.[41]

Edward Judah maintained that he did not believe that Jews in India had the "requisite numerical strength" for their own constituency. The Calcutta community, he claimed, had long allied itself with the Europeans and would not "stultify itself by abandoning its policy and rights."[42] Baghdadi Jews would be able to overcome any discrimination, typical of "any other civilized country," that they faced in the European group. "I feel sure that the abandonment of [our] policy . . . would be giving up the substance for the shadow," warned Judah.[43]

The representatives of the communities in Calcutta and Bombay ultimately waged the debate over electoral categorization in vain. The memorials, from the perspective of British authorities, raised minor political concerns in comparison to the vast and controversial constitutional challenges facing British India. To address these issues and draft reforms, the British government held three Round Table Conferences in London. Conference participants included British statesmen, colonial officials, and representatives from British India and the princely states. In advance of the second conference in 1931, Gandhi had reached a compromise with the viceroy of India, Edward Wood (Lord Irwin), agreeing to suspend the civil disobedience movement in exchange for the release of all Indian political prisoners. Gandhi would also attend the second Round Table Conference as the representative of the Indian National Congress. In the face of these political changes, the Baghdadi memorials sat shelved at the India Office for several years. In May 1935, the British Parliament finally addressed the issue of Jewish electoral categorization in India, deciding that the preferential treatment of one minority group created a problematic precedent that opened up the possibility that other questionably European, ambiguously white communities (including Armenians, Syrians, and Parsis) would also have grounds to demand European electoral categorization. The Conservative MP William Ormsby-Gore, a steadfast supporter of Zionism and a friend of Chaim Weizmann, argued against the inclusion of Baghdadi Jews in the European electorate, citing policy in another reach of the British Empire: "All recent development has been to regard Jewry as one people still adhering to Abraham, Isaac, and Jacob as their ancestors, and holding fast to the Mosaic law. We respect that faith and regard them as one. In Palestine we made no distinction in Jews, no matter where they come from, and therefore, I suggest that it would be unwise from the Jewish point of view and from the point of view of this Committee to accept the Amendment."[44]

Even after Parliament's decision, Edward Judah continued to pursue the matter of Baghdadi electoral categorization through the India Office, which finally responded in June 1935. The definitions of *European* and *Anglo-Indian* had already been finalized and were based on descent rather than race; Baghdadi Jews would not be included in the European electorate.[45] Judah made a final, desperate appeal to the House of Lords, but even those who had previously sympathized with his efforts thought the matter best abandoned. Suggesting an entirely new motivation for rejecting the memorial, Rufus Isaacs confided to Judah that he feared a debate on Jewish race in Parliament might provoke antisemitism akin to its German incarnation.[46] When Parliament finally passed the Government of India Act of 1935 in August of that year, the Baghdadi community found itself, as it had since the establishment of electoral categories in 1919, in the non-Mohammedan group.

INDIAN FUTURES

While David Ezra and the Calcutta memorialists asserted their community's thoroughly European and British cultural practices, the civic, social, and cultural life of Baghdadi Jewish British subjects in India, in fact, set them apart from the British in India. Many signatories of the memorial particularly members of the wealthy Ezra and Sassoon families—were marked both by their ambiguous whiteness and Jewishness and by their incredible wealth. Elite status for many Britons differed between India and Britain; it was not unusual to be "a 'somebody' in the empire, but a 'nobody' in Britain."[47] Baghdadi Jews' wealth may not have ensured their whiteness or Europeanness, but it did position them in elite moneyed circles that orbited high above the worlds of many Britons, even the "somebodies"—the rank and file of the colonial community in India. Similarly, some Baghdadi Jews may also have been better at translating elite status between empire and metropole. Many had family members in Britain or had spent time there themselves embedded in an elite British society unreachable by the majority of the British in India (or, indeed, the majority in Britain). Rachel Ezra had spent the eleven years preceding her marriage in prewar London, part of the Sassoon family that had close ties with Edward VII. In the late nineteenth century, her uncles Albert, Arthur, and Reuben had spent weekends away at their Scottish shooting boxes, hunting with Edward, then Prince of Wales.[48] Thus, though wealth and elite status may have afforded the leaders of the Baghdadi community a place at the viceroy's table at dinner parties, it also set them apart from most Britons in India; so, too, did their ability to operate in elite social circles in Britain.

The civic and social lives of elite Baghdadi Jews in India did not, in fact, reflect a British model but more closely followed elite Indian patterns. In 1927, David Ezra was knighted by King George V. Fellow honorees from India that year included prominent Indian politicians and civic leaders.[49] David likewise held a number of leadership positions that were also occupied by Indian elites. He served as sheriff of Calcutta from 1925 to 1926, an honorary position appointed annually since 1774 to a prominent resident of the city. The position was held exclusively by British individuals until 1878, when Mancherjee Rustomjee (1816–91), an Indian Parsi who had previously served as the Iranian consul in Calcutta, was appointed.[50] Thereafter, both British and non-British elites in India, including David Ezra's father and brother, occupied the post. Ezra was also elected in 1935 as vice president and in 1938 as president of the Bengal Asiatic Society, founded in 1784 for the advancement of oriental research.[51] Though initially founded and populated by British orientalists, Indian scholars and researchers later participated and served in leadership positions. In 1938, Ezra served as vice president of the King Emperor's Anti-tuberculosis Fund for India, jointly holding the position with other elite Indians.[52]

An elite circle of Indian professionals, intellectuals, and philanthropists in Calcutta followed similar patterns of leadership. For instance, Sir Upendranath Brahmachari, an Indian doctor and medical researcher, served as president of the Bengal Asiatic Society from 1928 to 1929 and was knighted in 1934. Sir Rajendra Nath Mookerjee, a prominent Bengali industrialist, was knighted in 1911 and also served as sheriff of Calcutta in that same year.[53] David Ezra and Mookerjee worked together to develop the Indian Academy of Fine Arts in 1933. The Ezras established friendships and alliances with elite Indians, mixing in cross-cultural social circles that included Hindus, Parsis, Sikhs, Armenians, and Britons, both civilians and colonial officials. "We dined with Sir Rajendra Nath and Lady Mookerjee," recorded Rachel

Ezra in her diary in 1926.⁵⁴ At a meal with the industrialist and his wife, the Ezras met Victor Bulwer-Lytton, the governor of Bengal, and his wife, Pamela Chichele-Plowden. Rachel's diaries also detail her organization of countless teas, lunches, and dinners that included prominent Indians among the attendees. Mrinalini Banerjee, the wife of prominent Brahmo mathematician Amiya Charan Banerjee; Mrs. J. C. Chatterji, whose husband directed the Kashmir Research Department and was a scholar of ancient Indian history; and Mrs. Percy Brown, whose husband was a specialist in medieval Indian architecture, all attended a women's luncheon held by Rachel in March 1926.⁵⁵ Though these women were defined both at the time and for posterity through their husbands, they played a central role in the formation of elite social circles through both their homosocial and heterosocial activities. Among the guests at another event hosted by Rachel Ezra that same year were Jagatjit Singh, the Sikh maharaja of the princely state of Kapurthala, whose controversial marriage to Anita Delgrada, a Spanish dancer, was frowned upon by British colonial officials in India.⁵⁶ Meyer David, the Ezras' Baghdadi friend who would become involved in Indian nationalist politics, was also present. Though Meyer David supported dominion status and other measures of increased self-government for India, other members of this elite social circle in Calcutta exhibited varied relationships to Indian nationalism. Many Indian elites derived their power and prestige from institutions and organizations initially established by the British in India, and they understood that their social position both depended on the maintenance of those structures and could be threatened by an expression of nationalist support. At the same time, their work developing important national, cultural, and civic institutions contributed to Indian nation building but without an overtly nationalist agenda.

The relaxed cross-cultural encounters among elites hosted by the Ezras and others in their social circle did not always replicate themselves more generally in elite British colonial society. Like other non-Europeans in India, Baghdadi Jews were excluded from certain social settings. For example, in 1907, David Ezra was barred from the Bengal Club, a European gentlemen's club open to whites only. Club members failed to realize that Ezra, who possessed vast real estate holdings in the city, owned the property on which the club stood. Excluded from the club, he proceeded to order the property vacated. When the club returned with an offer of membership, Ezra still refused to join but allowed the members to continue to rent his property. He then helped to found the Calcutta Club, which, though open to all races, only accepted wealthy societal elites as members.[57] In this manner, although Ezra and other non-British elites in India found themselves discriminated against based on race by certain segments of European society in India, they worked to structure a social space for themselves with the resources—wealth and status—they did possess. These elite Indian spaces, from which many of the colonial rank and file were excluded owing to their lack of wealth, represent a deviation from the public image projected in the Calcutta memorial of a Baghdadi community thoroughly entrenched in European life in India. Furthermore, though David Ezra asserted the centrality of white racial status to Baghdadi Jewish identity in the memorial, his experience in social settings such as clubs was often more determined by his nonwhiteness, as well as by his exceptional wealth.

The Ezras' affective ties and convivial interactions thus gave shape to a social and cultural scene that allowed for a more complex—even warmer—relationship to Indian nationalism than the memorial depicted. When Rachel Ezra enthusiastically reported on Gandhi's activities and developments in Indian nationalism in her letters to her nephew Solomon, she demonstrated an awareness and concern for social and political questions facing Indian society.[58] Days before the second Round Table Conference was set to begin in September 1931, she again wrote to Solomon. "I cannot describe to you what a great deal of unemployment there is in Calcutta now mostly among the Eurasians," she wrote. "Sir Henry Gidney is returning to London to represent them again," she noted, referring to the leader of the Anglo-Indian community.[59]

Two years later, during another visit to London to represent his community, Gidney came to the aid of Calcutta Jews when he interceded on their behalf in the matter of educational reforms, arguing that Jewish children should receive the same educational protections and grants afforded to Europeans and Anglo-Indians in India.[60] While the Baghdadi Jewish concern over educational privileges mirrored in some ways the electoral concerns articulated in the memorial campaign, the alliance with Gidney, an Anglo-Indian, complicates any clear-cut comparison. The memorial had, in fact, distanced Baghdadi Jews from Anglo-Indians, arguing that the former could not be categorized alongside the latter because of the "purity of [their] race."[61]

The Ezras themselves, like many elite Indians, did not become public or active participants in Indian nationalism, but one of their close Baghdadi friends did. Meyer David, a member of a prominent Baghdadi family from Bombay, was notable among Baghdadi Jews in India for taking an active political interest in Indian independence. He promoted the idea of dominion status as a means for India to achieve self-governance.[62] In March 1931, as Rachel Ezra reported approvingly in a letter to her nephew, Meyer David met with Gandhi and discussed his idea to establish a Welfare of India League (also referred to as the Good Will Movement and the Progressive League). A joint European-Indian venture, the league aimed to promote positive relations between the communities.

Members of the league included Meyer Nissim, the former president of the Bombay Municipal Council who had helped Gershon Agronsky during his 1930 visit to India, and Albert Raymond, another prominent Baghdadi resident of Bombay; Dr. E. Moses, the only Bene Israel Jew to join the league; and prominent Indians, including Purshottamdas Thakurdas, Chunilal V. Mehta, and G. D. Birla. The previous year, Birla had organized a committee within the Federation of Indian Chambers of Commerce and Industry (FICCI) to promote swadeshi, the idea championed by Gandhi that India could achieve political independence by working toward economic self-sufficiency.[63] The Welfare of India League played a critical role in negotiating a compromise after Gandhi was arrested in 1932 and began his hunger strike in protest of British authorities' decision to assign the Dalits (the "untouchable" caste) separate electoral representation. This compromise, known as the Poona Pact, removed separate electoral representation for the Dalits but provided them with special privileges within the general Hindu electorate.[64]

Meyer David also addressed Dalit social welfare—considered critical by Gandhi in his vision of an independent India—in other contexts. In 1932, David proposed a scheme to start a scholarship fund for Dalit students. He envisioned that higher-caste Hindus would financially support Dalit students; the amount of five hundred rupees could cover the higher education of one Dalit student for five years, while half of that could cover high-school education. The idea won Gandhi's approval in addition to that of the All-India Depressed Classes Association, which represented Dalits.[65] David himself contributed the first donation of twenty-five hundred rupees anonymously.[66] The David Scheme, as it came to be known, continued for a few years but ultimately folded when funds could not be successfully solicited from other donors.[67]

The Ezras' friendship with Meyer David, who worked openly on behalf of Indian nationalist causes, complicates the unequivocally negative disposition toward Indian nationalism put forth by David Ezra in the memorial campaign. The couple's involvement in Indian cultural institutions and their friendships with elite Indians also point to an aspect of their politics that differed significantly from the positions they showcased in their dealings with the imperial state. The Ezras' negotiation of these disparate contexts compelled very different political vocabularies, attitudes, and behaviors. Yet their broad concern for Baghdadi Jewish political futures in an India grappling with the shifting terms of imperialism and the growth of nationalism animated their experience in both settings.

JEWISH HORIZONS

The centrality of Jewish culture, religion, and society to the experience of the Ezras and their broader community also stands in stark contrast to the thoroughly Europeanized image presented in the memorial campaign. The Ezras' Jewishness—expressed through their role as leaders of their community, their devout religious observance, and their commitment to Jewish communal and cultural organizations—represented the most vital, salient force in their lives.

Rachel Ezra became involved in both Bengali and nationwide organizations by leading their Jewish branches or equivalents. Much like the Indian elites in her social circle who contributed to Indian nation building through the development of cultural and civic institutions, Rachel participated in aspects of Indian and Jewish nation building through her Jewishness. She directed Jewish branches of secular organizations, including the Council for Women and the Girl Guides Association.[68] She also played a part in the development of autonomous Jewish organizations. She served as the first president of the Judean Club, a Calcutta Jewish community center founded in

1929. In addition to hosting weekly lectures, the club functioned as a social space for young Baghdadi Jews and held dances and parties. The Ezras also served as their community's liaisons to British authorities, another important aspect of their role as Jewish leaders. In these situations—for example, when they dined with the viceroy and other colonial officials—the Ezras seemingly appeared most integrated into elite British colonial society. But the Ezras were often the only Jews—sometimes, with the exception of a maharaja or two, the only non-Britons—to attend these official dinners, where they found themselves invited as representatives of the Jewish community and as vastly wealthy imperial subjects. In this sense, while Norman and Helen Bentwich found themselves increasingly pushed out of mandatory society in Palestine by virtue of their Jewishness, the Ezras were granted inclusion in the elite British colonial scene in India because of that same identity.

The Ezras' home—invariably referred to as a mansion or palace—outdid many elite Indian residencies in its opulence and grandeur. The home's location, at 3 Kyd Street in the mostly British White Town neighborhood in Calcutta, physically separated the Ezras from the majority of the Baghdadi community. Most other Baghdadi Jews resided in Grey Town, the neighborhood sandwiched between White Town and the Indian-majority Black Town, a spatial and cultural nexus that Pradip Sinha has called "zones of interpenetration."[69] Grey Town, known for its immigrant, cosmopolitan, and diasporic communities, counted Baghdadi Jews, Portuguese, Armenians, Parsis, and Greeks among its residents.[70]

Despite British surroundings, Jewishness permeated the landscape of 3 Kyd Street. The Ezras' home functioned as a Jewish communal space, on par with the city's three synagogues. The Ezras often hosted religious services, weddings, and Jewish charitable events at their mansion and made the property's mikvah (Jewish ritual bath) available for communal use.[71] David Ezra, an animal lover and amateur zoologist, had amassed India's largest zoo on the mansion's grounds. Elephants, tigers, lions, a tortoise "whose carapace must have borne the weight, over the years, of hundreds of Jewish children,"[72] and a flock of mynah birds that Ezra purportedly trained to sing "God Save the King" lived on the property.[73] When Tel Aviv's zoo was founded in 1939, Ezra contributed many animals, including tortoises, parrots, and black swans.[74] Though Rachel and David Ezra sometimes included Jewish friends at the dinner parties they hosted for Calcutta elites, the couple often organized separate meals or events comprising solely Jewish friends. These gatherings of Baghdadi Jews spanned both secular and Jewish activities. For instance, in May 1926, Rachel Ezra hosted Jewish friends, both men and women, for a mah-jongg party.[75] Later that fall, she hosted Baghdadi community members for a celebration of the festival of Sukkot.[76]

The Ezras, like previous generations of their family in India, expressed their Jewishness through their leadership in the community, their dedication to Jewish culture, and their practice of Jewish religion—all manifestations of an identity that differed greatly from the image of the Europeanized community of the memorial. Increasingly, during the interwar period, they also took on Jewish leadership roles that were transnational in focus. This aspect of their Jewish leadership—concerned with issues of Jewish nation building, the refugee crisis in Europe, and Zionism—connected them to an international diaspora and distinguished them both from previous generations of their own family and from local patterns of elite leadership in India. For instance, David Ezra served as chairman of the Calcutta Committee for the World Jewish Congress (WJC), the international Jewish organization that first convened in 1936. Though not specifically Zionist, the WJC was dedicated to fostering a worldwide Jewish "national project," uniting Jews across nation-state borders in the development of Jewish social and cultural life.[77] David Ezra also headed the Jewish Relief Association (JRA), founded in response to the influx of Jewish refugees from Europe to India beginning in the 1930s. Most significantly, beginning in the 1910s, the Ezras encountered Zionism for the first time. Though their relationship to Jewish nationalism was not immediately enthusiastic, it grew to play a central role in their identity as Jews. Zionism presented a potential conflict for Baghdadi Jews who wished to remain politically aloof, a trait that the memorial campaign argued was integral to Baghdadi character.[78]

The geopolitical situation before World War I—specifically Ottoman control of Palestine—may also have contributed to the initial hesitancy of Baghdadi Jewish leaders like the Ezras to take up the call of Jewish nationalism. In the wake of the Young Turk Revolution of 1908, but before the Balfour Declaration and the British conquest of Palestine, some Zionist leaders, including David Ben-Gurion and Moshe Shertok, had sought to use an Ottoman political-legal framework to build and sustain a Jewish national home.[79] Moreover, some Sephardi Jews in the Ottoman Empire did not conceive of their Zionism (marked foremost by a commitment to cultural Hebraism instead of the territorial and political aspirations of European political Zionists) as contradictory to their Ottomanism. Rather, they saw the two as mutually beneficial.[80] Baghdadi Jews living under British control in India before 1917 may have been hesitant to support a political movement with ties to the Ottoman Empire—where their families had originated—because it was becoming increasingly antagonistic to Britain. Rachel Ezra noted in her diary in 1913 that "the 2nd meeting of the Zionist question took place. [David] did not wish me to attend."[81] It is unclear from her diary if Rachel Ezra, whose devout upbringing had imparted to her a strong religious longing for the Land of Israel, might have otherwise attended the meeting in Calcutta, were it not for her husband. In 1917, following the British conquest of Jerusalem, Rachel Ezra's brother wrote to her, saying, "We are extremely pleased to hear that the British have taken Jerusalem. . . . May God establish our kingdom there according to our orthodox Jewish hope as we express it in all our prayers every day."[82]

Attitudes toward (and, indeed, interest in) Zionism began to change toward the end of World War I, once Palestine came under British control. In April 1920, just weeks before the San Remo Conference assigned Britain the mandate for Palestine, David and Rachel Ezra made their first visit to the country, spending Passover in Jerusalem.[83] The next month, Baghdadi Jews in Bombay founded India's first Zionist association.[84] Meyer Nissim, one of the wealthiest Jews in the city, contributed funds. Shortly thereafter, a series of Zionist emissaries visited India. The first, Israel Cohen, then secretary of the Zionist Organization in London, arrived in the spring of 1921. His visit was part of a larger mission of inquiry to gauge the amenability of Jewish communities in the East to Zionism.

Despite these developments, Baghdadi Jewish reticence about Zionism persisted into the 1920s, particularly in Calcutta. When Israel Cohen visited the city, still without its own Zionist association, he was disappointed by the community's reluctance to involve itself in Zionist politics. In preparation for a speech at the Magen David synagogue (led by David Ezra), Cohen conferred with leaders from the city's other two synagogues. "One gentleman," he later wrote, "agreed to be present only upon condition that my address was not followed by the establishment of a Zionist Society." Cohen's speech was well attended but elicited donations far short of his expectations. The next day, he visited the Ezras' home, intending to gain their support: "I was ushered up the stairs of a sumptuous mansion to a large room on the first floor, in which the Mincha prayer was being offered up by a number of men, some in Baghdadi costume, whilst through the open doorway of an adjoining apartment came a cacophonous chorus from an animated aviary—a score of parrots, parakeets and other birds doing their best to drown the Hebrew supplications."[85]

After the service, Rachel Ezra invited Cohen to stay for tea. She led him to a large back garden, where he noticed "some strange pets disporting themselves," including monkeys, storks, and peacocks, all looked after by "a staff of barefooted native servants." Amid "this unwonted distraction," Cohen "related to [his] hosts some incidents of the suffering of the Jews in Eastern Europe and invoked their aid in the establishment of the Jewish National Home."[86] Cohen did not subsequently record the rest of this meeting but noted that the wealthier members of the Baghdadi community (presumably including the Ezras) were mostly absent from the next lecture he gave at the Magen David synagogue. There, he made clear that he had come to India with "visions not merely of lakhs but of crores of rupees, but that so far [his] dreams had been denied fulfillment."[87] Cohen's account of his trip is steeped in Orientalist ideas about the East: he is poised to expect extravagant donations from wealthy Baghdadi Jews yet unsurprised by their apathy; he is simultaneously amazed at the opulence and excess of their lifestyle, baffled by their eccentricity, and touched by their religious devotion. Still, despite his disappointment with fundraising, Cohen did inaugurate a Zionist association in Calcutta before his departure, and David Ezra was made president. Rachel Ezra succeeded her husband as president when he died in 1947.[88]

As Zionist associations emerged in India, so, too, did their auxiliary institutions. In 1921, the Bombay Zionist Association founded its official organ, *Zion's Messenger*, a large monthly newspaper edited by Florence E. Haskell, which ran until 1927. The newspaper reported on developments in Palestine, gave summaries of Zionist speeches, detailed visits of prominent (mostly British) individuals to Palestine, summarized Jewish news from other reaches of the British Empire, and relayed local Zionist developments—and setbacks. In October 1923, the paper reported that proposed Hebrew classes in Bombay were canceled owing to lack of "sufficient support." With regard to the Zionist Literary Committee, the paper noted that "there is nothing to say, somehow or other the Committee fell asleep and the Secretary literally faded away."[89]

Although the newspaper reported on Jewish religious holidays and quoted passages from the Torah, its focus was primarily political, addressing developments in Palestine and disagreements within and about Zionism. For instance, in January 1924, *Zion's Messenger* joined the chorus of outrage at Israel Zangwill following his declaration that "political Zionism is dead" in a speech to the American Jewish Congress.[90] "What he said is most unpalatable, so much so that he has created a storm of protest in the Jewish world of journalism," read the report.[91]

As Zionist activity in India increased (albeit at a plodding pace) and took on an explicitly political tone, the Ezras' involvement also grew. Their engagement paired a religious love of the Land of Israel with an evolving concern about Jewish political and national development in Palestine. In April 1924, David and Rachel Ezra, along with Rachel's brother, sister-in-law, and mother, traveled to Palestine for a second time, again for the Passover holiday. "I woke at 5 am to see the sunrise on Gaza. Our 1st sight of Eretz Israel! Thank God we have come here," wrote Rachel Ezra in her diary. The next morning, Saturday, the Ezras attended Shabbat services in Jerusalem with Herbert Samuel, the high commissioner.[92] Samuel was called up for the third aliyah, the blessing over the Torah. David Ezra was honored with the fourth aliyah. After services, Samuel accompanied the Ezras to their hotel for lunch, during which they listened to "some Zionist speeches."[93] On Sunday, Rachel attended tea with Samuel's wife, Beatrice Franklin Samuel. The next day, both Ezras had tea with the high commissioner at Government House. They continued to spend time with the Samuels throughout the rest of their visit.[94]

These activities—visiting with the openly Zionist high commissioner, attending synagogue, and listening to Zionist speeches—did not contradict the Ezras' loyalty to the British Empire. They understood their Zionism as working in conjunction with British imperialism. This political outlook reflected a time during the interwar period when Zionists envisioned a range of political futures for the Yishuv, including membership in the British Commonwealth of Nations as a dominion. Others imagined binational, federative, and autonomist state models. Assuming and even celebrating that the Yishuv might remain part of the British Empire was common among Jews living in the British Empire. As we saw in chapter 2, this was also true for prominent Zionist leaders in Palestine in the 1920s, including Arlosoroff and Jabotinsky.

Yet it was precisely in the 1930s, when Zionist leaders turned away from this possibility and became increasingly critical of Britain and its policies regarding Jewish immigration to Palestine, that Rachel and David Ezra redoubled their efforts on behalf of Zionism. In 1938, the Ezras supported the creation of a Calcutta branch of the Zionist youth movement Habonim, looking to the South African branch of the organization as a model.[95] The new Calcutta branch connected Baghdadi Jews not only to South Africa but to other parts of the British Empire, where Habonim groups had also already been established. Habonim's Anglo-Jewish founder Wellesley Aron (with whom Arlosoroff had corresponded) modeled the youth group on the British scouting movement, which likely appealed to Rachel Ezra because of her involvement in Girl Guides. Aron had founded Habonim (Hebrew for "the builders") in an attempt to counter Jewish assimilation in Britain. While the youth movement forged ties with kibbutzim in Palestine, its leadership across the empire and in North America differed over its primary goal—either to foster a Jewish national spirit and thus fight assimilation or to prepare members for life in Palestine.[96] Throughout the 1930s and into the 1940s in India, Habonim served the former purpose. Baghdadi Jews in this period resembled their counterparts in South Africa and America in this respect, "[identifying] with the notion of return to Zion without regarding it as directly applicable to themselves," as Gideon Shimoni has put it.[97] The first case of Baghdadi immigration to Palestine from India did not occur until 1945.[98] Zionist activity in India never achieved the institutional intensity it did in Europe or Palestine. Most notably, Zionists in India never divided into competing Zionist political parties. But developments such as the founding of Habonim indicate that by the 1930s, participating in Zionism increasingly became about cultural and political activity and not solely about religious conviction for the Ezras. The duality of their commitment—both political and religious—set the Ezras apart from Labor and Revisionist Zionists, both largely secular; so, too, did their sustained vision of Zionism as compatible with British imperialism. The Ezras' own conception of Zionism, then—in contrast to other elements of their Jewish identity, their embeddedness in elite Indian culture, and their attitude toward Indian nationalism—did not directly challenge the political claims of the memorial campaign. Still, their affiliation with Zionism was never without political risk. As British public opinion became increasingly antagonistic toward Jewish nationalism, the Ezras maintained their devotion.

Although the Ezras and other Baghdadi Jews did not see Zionism—insofar as it offered Jews a new physical home in Palestine—as pertinent to their own lives, they became increasingly aware after 1933 of the role it could play for the flood of refugees fleeing Nazi Germany. The influx of Ashkenazi refugees from Europe, many of whom hoped eventually to reach Palestine, introduced a new dynamic within the broader Jewish community in India. The refugees were mostly professionals—doctors, businessmen, teachers, technicians—and their families. The issue of refugee absorption became a central preoccupation of Jews in India, particularly the small community of European Jews who had already trickled into the country before Hitler's rise to power. They founded the Jewish Relief Association in 1934 and appointed David Ezra as president, which bolstered the organization's standing in India. Soon, the Indian government began granting a visa to any European Jewish refugee sponsored by the JRA. Though Baghdadi Jews donated generously to the JRA, European Jews in India ran most of the organization's operations. At the outbreak of World War II, the Indian government had admitted approximately a thousand refugees whom the JRA helped to settle throughout India. For the majority of refugees who were granted visas to India, electoral classification remained a nonissue. The Home Department of the Indian government determined that all refugees would remain aliens without franchise until they were made subjects. Many left India before attaining citizenship. Those who did remain and became citizens were allowed to join the European electorate (in contrast to Ormsby-Gore's vision that all Jews would be categorized in the same way). The new presence of Ashkenazi Jews in India disrupted the established Jewish hierarchy that had previously privileged Baghdadi Jews. Some refugees considered themselves superior to India's Jewish communities—Baghdadi, Cochini, and Bene Israel alike.[99] Some formed friendships with elite Indians.[100] Ultimately, however, the refugees' presence in India had little effect on the social position of the Ezras and other elite Baghdadi Jews.[101]

Though there is no evidence that the Ezras ever invoked explicit parallels between Jewish and Indian political futures, the two issues found common company in the couple's home in 1941. In that year, a Hindu priest working as an envoy of Gandhi visited the Ezras at least twice. He was struck by the many refugees from Europe passing through the couple's home—testimony, he believed, to the Ezras' warmth, hospitality, and charitable nature. "Sir Ezra and his wife donate not only to the needs of Jews, but their hand is also open to Indian institutions, and hospitals, convalescent homes, and schools are strengthened by their contributions in Calcutta and beyond." David Ezra, he opined, should "serve as a model to the Indian people, and especially to the wealthy tycoons who spend their time having fun and wish to ignore the needs of the poor." Rachel Ezra possessed "unequaled kindness."[102] On one occasion, the Ezras threw a party in celebration of the festival of Sukkot and organized a meal to be held in their sukkah. According to the Hindu priest, the Ezras demonstrated cultural sensitivity to both their Hindu and their Ashkenazi guests, who included forty refugees, many of whom wished ultimately to reach Palestine.[103] Hindu guests were served their meals on fresh banana leaves—a gesture to South Asian custom.[104] Although the Ezras' Indian servants attended to all the guests, "Lady Ezra went from table to table, concerned that [her guests] enjoyed all the delicacies and encouraged everyone with a word of comfort."[105] David Ezra and the Jewish guests "wore handsome skullcaps and recited different prayers during the eating and drinking."[106]

On another occasion, the same envoy of Gandhi arrived at the Ezras' home to find a group of refugees having a meal. "Suddenly," he recounted, "I saw one of the Indian servants pulling a cow by its horns into the magnificent hall." He continued: "I did not understand this bizarre manifestation and asked Sir Ezra what it was. He said with a smile that guests had come to him, the first group of refugees from Europe, and there were among them very devout ones who did not want to eat the cheese that was served to them, lest it was not kosher. Lady Rachel, recognizing the reason for their refusal, ordered an Indian servant to bring the cow from the dairy barn to prove to the refugees that the cheese was not bought in the market, but that it was homemade."[107]

The motifs of these gatherings—a lavish meal served by a large cast of servants, the Jewish refugees hoping to reach Palestine, the Ezras' attention to Hindu and Jewish dietary practices, the observance of Sukkot, the Jewish prayer, and Gandhi's envoy observing it all—serve as apt vignettes of the Ezras' entrenchment in both elite Indian and Jewish worlds, as well as their evolving relationships with Indian and Jewish national futures.

By 1935, David Ezra had officially abandoned efforts to have the Baghdadi community categorized as European in the Bengali electorate. The exigencies of World War II, however, presented Baghdadi Jews with a new way to attain European classification. In 1939, Colonel C. Warren-Boulton formed a Jewish platoon as part of the Calcutta and Presidency Battalion of the Indian Auxiliary Force (AFI), an all-European and Anglo-Indian volunteer branch of the Indian Army.[108] Baghdadi youths in Calcutta eagerly joined up. In 1940, however, Warren-Boulton's superiors in the AFI ordered him to cease Jewish enlistment—after all, the AFI was reserved for Europeans and Anglo-Indians.[109]

As he had more than a decade earlier, David Ezra mounted another campaign, this time to allow members of his community to serve in the AFI. Unlike the prolonged drama of the memorial, this effort was resolved quickly. Ezra and the AFI reached an agreement: a Jewish soldier could join the AFI if synagogue authorities—in other words, lay leaders, including Ezra—vouched for the individual's European descent.[110] As the war raged and it was in Britain's interest to enlist as many soldiers as possible, Baghdadi Jews finally achieved official European categorization, albeit without any electoral implications.

Between two great wars, the Ezras attempted to navigate the complex web of imperial politics, campaigning for inclusion in the European electorate. They insisted on their European identification through race, loyalty, utility, and cultural practice. They distanced themselves from Indian nationalism, declaring it incompatible with their identities as Jews and good imperial subjects. Yet the Ezras' associational ties—their friendships with Hindus, Sikhs, Parsis, and other Jews, which took form in convivial spaces and through quotidian activities—reveal a very different type of politics. Shaped by a social embeddedness in elite Indian and Jewish worlds, this politics featured a tentatively hopeful attitude toward Indian nationalism and a deep commitment to Zionism, even as British attitudes toward Jewish nationalism and Zionist attitudes toward Britain were becoming increasingly hostile. As we have seen, these two sites of political formation—the official dealings with the imperial state, on the one hand, and the convivial spaces and affective ties of quotidian life, on the other—served as structures that produced multiple, incongruous political attitudes and practices. Yet these distinct political outlooks were both shaped out of the same understanding of India's future—namely, that the terms of British imperial rule would change and that Indian nationalism would become an increasingly powerful force on the world stage. As we will see in the next chapter, Jewish leaders in South Africa, Palestine, and Britain shared this final view. In the 1930s, in anticipation of this new potential national horizon, they resolved to build ties between Zionists and leaders of the Indian independence movement.

FIVE

Legacies of Empire and Imagining the Postcolonial

IT WAS 1936, AND HERMANN Kallenbach had not seen Gandhi in more than two decades. The pair had spent years as intimate companions during the Indian leader's twenty-one-year-long tenure in South Africa.[1] Kallenbach, a Jewish architect and avid bodybuilder, had made Gandhi's mission of satyagraha his own.[2] Inspired by Tolstoyan ideals of bodily discipline, including vegetarianism and sexual abstinence, Gandhi and Kallenbach (who remained a lifelong bachelor) twice lived together. From 1908 to 1909, they stayed in Kallenbach's home in Johannesburg, known as the "Kraal," which the architect had designed himself.[3] The following year, the pair shared a tent on land owned by Kallenbach on Mountain View, a suburb of Johannesburg. When Gandhi left South Africa in 1914, bound for London with plans to return thereafter to India, Kallenbach accompanied him. But arriving in London days after Britain declared war on Germany, the two faced an untimely and unexpected separation. Though Kallenbach had lived in South Africa since 1896, he was German by nationality.[4] He spent the next two years interned on the Isle of Man as an enemy alien, while Gandhi—along with Kallenbach's luggage—journeyed on to India. After the war,

Kallenbach returned to South Africa and resumed his architecture practice. Though they corresponded occasionally, Kallenbach and Gandhi had yet to reunite. Now, with a letter in hand from Moshe Shertok, who had succeeded his late colleague Chaim Arlosoroff as head of the Political Department of the Jewish Agency in Palestine, Kallenbach faced the prospect of seeing his long lost "soul-friend" once again. "Upon the advice of some of our South African friends here I have decided to approach you with a . . . far-reaching request," explained Shertok. "I realise how startling it must appear to a man in your position to be so suddenly faced with a proposal of breaking his ordinary business routine to go off to a distant country on an errand of which he may never have dreamt," he wrote.[5] The errand Shertok proposed for Kallenbach was a mission to India with the aim of winning Gandhi over to the Zionist movement. Shertok felt certain, as we will see, that Kallenbach was the only person capable of the undertaking.

"In South Africa," Gandhi once told a reporter, "I was surrounded by Jews."[6] Two years after being called to the bar in London in 1891, Gandhi traveled to the Colony of Natal to work for Dada Abdulla and Sons, a Muslim Indian trading firm with branches in southern and eastern Africa. Intending to stay for only a year, Gandhi ultimately chose to remain in South Africa after his employment with Dada Abdulla had concluded in order to fight the discrimination faced by Indians and to lead a campaign for their civil rights.[7] During Gandhi's twenty-one years in the country, the majority of his closest European friends and allies were Jewish, among them several Tolstoyans and theosophists.[8] Henry Polak (1882–1959), a British-born journalist and theosophist who, like Kallenbach, was influenced by the writings of Tolstoy, met Gandhi in a vegetarian restaurant in Johannesburg in 1904.[9] Polak became an editor of Gandhi's newspaper, the *Indian Opinion*, and moved to the Phoenix Settlement, Gandhi's commune in Natal. Credited with introducing Gandhi to John Ruskin's *Unto This Last*, Polak also shared with the Indian leader excerpts from the writings of Max Nordau that had been published in the *Jewish Chronicle* (which he had delivered from London).[10] Polak became Gandhi's "right hand man" in South Africa. He was left in charge of Indian communal affairs when Gandhi traveled to Britain in 1906, and Polak himself also traveled twice to India on Gandhi's behalf to lobby the government to end the flow of indentured laborers to

South Africa. Both Polak and Kallenbach participated actively in Gandhi's satyagraha campaign. In 1910, Kallenbach purchased an eleven-hundred-acre farm—which he named Tolstoy Farm—outside of Johannesburg in order to provide a home for the families of imprisoned satyagrahis. In the wake of the satyagraha march of October 1913, Gandhi, Polak, and Kallenbach were all arrested and jailed.[11] In addition to Kallenbach and Polak, other Jews in Gandhi's circle in South Africa included Sonja Schlesin, who worked as his secretary;[12] L. W. Ritch, another theosophist Jew who worked as a law clerk for Gandhi;[13] and Morris and Ruth Alexander, leaders of the Cape Town Jewish community at whose home Gandhi stayed on his final night in South Africa.[14]

Beginning in the 1930s, as leaders of the Zionist movement in Palestine and Britain became increasingly convinced that imperial and anticolonial politics in India mattered significantly to the Yishuv, a group of South African Jews—most notably Kallenbach and Polak—emerged as uniquely equipped to navigate this issue. Their prewar ties to Gandhi and the Indian community in South Africa and their broader consideration of Indian political questions came to play an important role in the development of interwar Zionist political strategy. They worked to facilitate meetings between Zionist and Indian leaders, traveled to India in an effort to win support for the Zionist movement, and continued to promote the Indian cause at home in South Africa and across the Indian diaspora.

It is perhaps an unlikely story that individuals such as Hermann Kallenbach and Henry Polak—a bodybuilder-architect and a theosophist newspaper editor, neither active members of the organized Jewish community—came to serve as ambassadors between Jewish nationalism and the most significant anticolonial independence movement of the interwar period. Indeed, the group of Jews who forged ties with Gandhi during his time in South Africa were an unusual cohort and by no means uniform in their political beliefs, religious practices, relationships to the South African and broader Jewish communities, or attitudes toward Zionism (though almost all were members of the liberal professions). They included anti-imperialists and pro-Commonwealth Unionists, observant and nonpracticing Jews, and Zionists and non-Zionists. And despite their mutual conviction that Jews and Indians shared common challenges and aspirations, these South African Jews at

FIGURE 5 Left to right: Mohandas Gandhi, Sonia Schlesin, and Hermann Kallenbach in Natal in 1913. Courtesy of GandhiServe India.

times passionately disagreed over how those challenges should be tackled. They also maintained a wide range of critical opinions about the record of the broader South African Jewish community when it came to matters of race and discrimination, particularly regarding Indians. Kallenbach and Polak, for instance, publicly butted heads in the *Jewish Chronicle* in 1934 over the question of South African Jews' treatment of South African Indians.[15] Though Polak permanently left South Africa in 1916 out of concern over endemic racism, neither he nor Kallenbach spoke out publicly in support of the rights of Black South Africans. Their silence mirrored Gandhi's own refusal to include Black Africans in the satyagraha campaign.[16]

Despite their differences, Kallenbach—who by the 1930s had come to support Zionism—and Polak—who remained a non-Zionist—both came to the aid of the Zionist movement when its leaders resolved to pursue ties with Indian nationalists. Gideon Shimoni has noted that Gandhi's lacking understanding of Judaism, influenced by "Christian-induced misrepresentation," led to his repeated identification of Jews with "Old Testament" justice and later shaped his evaluation of Jewish responses to Nazism.[17] This mind-set was never corrected during Gandhi's time in South Africa because the Jews closest to him were not "equipped authentically to interpret Judaism." Rather, Gandhi's Jewish friends, Shimoni argues, embodied Isaac Deutscher's "non-Jewish Jew."[18] But more than solely explaining Gandhi's complex relationship to Judaism and Jewishness, as Shimoni frames it, the fact that Gandhi's Jewish associates had diverse and nonnormative relationships with the Jewish community, Jewish religion, and Jewish nationalism also testifies to the complexity and capaciousness of interwar Zionism. In a period when the Zionist movement had to navigate the forces of imperialism and anticolonial nationalisms, Jews with diverse experiences and convictions—including non-Zionist ones—ended up confronting the same Jewish national questions.

Although these Jews' engagement with Zionism did not reflect the way the majority of South African Jews related to Jewish nationalism, there are certain important continuities, distinct to the South African Jewish context.[19] By the Balfour Declaration in 1917, the vast majority of South African Jews—both the old Anglo establishment and newer immigrants from Lithuania and their descendants—had come to support the Zionist movement.[20] This distinguished South African Jews from other English-speaking diaspora communities (especially Britain and the United States), where the established elite generally provided the most vocal opposition to Jewish nationalism.[21] Though most South African Jews adopted British cultural practices and norms, South Africa's multiracial and multinational society allowed for the development of national (white) identities outside the framework of Britishness.[22] The presence of Afrikaner nationalism made Jewish identification with Zionism—even Revisionist Zionism, the branch of the movement that ultimately became most critical of British rule in Palestine—more permissible. Jewish support for Indian political issues and Indian nationalism must also be understood within the context of South Africa's racially and nationally segmented society.[23] In short, South Africa functioned not only as an incubator for Jewish relationships to Indians but also for Jewish relationships to national movements that offered everything from a supplemental identity to Britishness to a powerful critique of British imperialism.

This chapter explores how leaders of the Zionist movement came to view anticolonial politics in the British Empire as critical to the future of the Yishuv. It charts the story of how a small group of South African Jews—by virtue of imperial legacies wrought out of indentured servitude, colonial economies, and racial and religious discrimination—became uniquely positioned to navigate this new political frontier. Weaving together the stories of Kallenbach and Polak, this chapter also examines the efforts of Immanuel Olsvanger (1888–1961) to build ties between the Zionist movement and leaders of Indian nationalism. A Polish-born scholar of Sanskrit who translated and published widely, Olsvanger arrived in South Africa six years after Gandhi left. He remained there from 1920 to 1928, working as a delegate of Keren Hayesod (the institution dedicated to raising funds for the Zionist movement) and as an official in the South African Zionist Federation. While in South Africa, Olsvanger befriended Kallenbach and also met the Indian National Congress leader and poet Sarojini Naidu during her 1924 visit to the country.[24] When Olsvanger traveled to India in 1936 on behalf of the Zionist movement, Naidu would help to introduce him to other Indian political leaders.

FIRST CONTACT

When Gandhi departed South Africa in 1914, with Hermann Kallenbach by his side, Henry Polak decided that he, too, would leave the country. He and his wife, Millie—a Christian feminist whom he had first met in London—resolved to return permanently to Britain so that their children would not be raised in South Africa's "atmosphere of race and colour prejudice."[25] Though, at Gandhi's behest, he ended up remaining until 1916, Polak eventually returned to London, where he founded the Indian Overseas Association, an organization dedicated to advocating for the rights of Indians across the diaspora.[26] Polak believed that his Jewish identity demanded that he make the Indian cause his own. "I went to South Africa... and the more I became acquainted with the facts, the more I felt that I was facing, not a new problem, but one with which I was already unpleasantly familiar," he told the *Jewish Chronicle* in a 1913 interview:

> "Indians must be segregated and reside in locations. They must not be allowed to own fixed property. They must be deprived of the political and municipal franchises. Their trading rights must be limited. They must be restrained within provincial boundaries. Their means of locomotion must be curtailed. They must be forbidden to go to certain schools and higher education must be closed to them, as also careers in the Civil Service. Their methods of living are insanitary. Their competition is unfair. They underlive and undersell. They are a menace to the public welfare. They are an inferior race. They ought to be prevented from coming to South Africa, and those who are already in the country must be driven out by fair means or foul." This and much more was the burden of the white population's demand, to which effect had already been given, more or less, by statute and regulation. And I immediately realised that this was the Jewish problem all over again. Not a single argument that was advanced against Indians, but had already been urged against Jews in one or other European country. My sympathies have always been with the bottom dog, and I at once felt the need to throw all my energies into the struggle on behalf of the Indian community, for I felt that I was really fighting for the maintenance of Jewish rights and privileges and the preservation of our racial honour.[27]

Polak noted that while a handful of other South African Jews shared his determination (he mentioned Kallenbach, Ritch, and Morris Alexander by name), the majority had, by his account, betrayed the ethical spirit of Judaism. "I had hoped to find Jews in South Africa solidly opposed to a persecution of British Indian subjects of the Crown," he explained, "but I discovered, to my sorrow and shame, that, like so many others who have themselves recently emerged from suffering and persecution . . . many of them were amongst the most active of the persecutors." Polak thought that to forget that the persecution of Indians could so easily turn into the persecution of Jews was a grave miscalculation; to fail to take a stand against racial persecution was "un-Jewish."[28] Ten years later, in a 1923 letter to the *Jewish Chronicle*, Polak reasserted this position, maintaining the parallels between Jewish and Indian persecution and lamenting the sorry record of South African Jews to stand up against the injustice. Mentioning Kallenbach, Ritch, and Alexander once again as exceptions, Polak contended that Jewish traders in the Transvaal, whose chief competitors were Indian, were particularly guilty of condoning anti-Indian measures.[29]

Polak's charges did not go unchallenged. Percy Cowen, secretary of the South African Jewish Board of Deputies, responded in the *Jewish Chronicle* with a letter denying the "unfounded" accusations. "There may be a certain number of individual Jews sharing the views of one or other party in the present controversy over the Asiatic question," he wrote, "but to say that South African Jews, or a section of them, are taking sides as a body in this matter is absolutely untrue." As evidence, Cowen (like Polak) held up Morris Alexander, then MP and leader of the South African Jewish Board of Deputies Cape Town Committee, who "had always been indefatigable in his opposition" to anti-Indian discrimination.[30]

Despite Polak's record of fierce condemnation of South African Jewry and lack of involvement in Zionist politics, Selig Brodetsky (1888–1954), the head of the Political Department of the Zionist Organization in London, decided to ask him for help in the fall of 1931, when Gandhi was in Britain for the second Round Table Conference. Born in Russia, Brodetsky had come to London with his family as a child. As a young man, he studied at Cambridge and was part of the same Zionist circle as Norman Bentwich.

Later appointed a lecturer in mathematics at the University of Leeds, Brodetsky simultaneously served as head of the Political Department in London beginning in 1928, an arrangement he compared to working "two full-time jobs."[31] Like his counterpart Chaim Arlosoroff in Jerusalem, Brodetsky had become concerned about the influence of Pan-Islamism. Both men worried that Shaukat Ali and Amin al-Husseini, the coconveners of the upcoming World Islamic Congress set to open in Jerusalem in December 1931, would aim to make Palestine into an international Islamic issue that might, in turn, sway British imperial policy. India, the heart of the British Empire and home to the largest Muslim population in the world, suddenly became very important to the Zionist movement. While Arlosoroff labored—without success—to convince British authorities in Palestine to halt the Congress, and Gershon Agronsky a year earlier had advocated building ties between Zionists and moderate Indian Muslims to stem the tide of Pan-Islamism, Brodetsky sought out a third option: meet with Gandhi himself.

The need to meet became even more pressing after October 2, when the *Jewish Chronicle* ran an interview with Gandhi in which the Indian leader articulated a controversial vision of "spiritual" Zionism. Gandhi began by reminding the interviewer that he had made very close Jewish friends in South Africa. While he admitted never to have made a "proper study of Jewish religion," Gandhi had participated in certain Jewish customs in Johannesburg, including attending a Passover seder. "I heartily enjoyed, what do you call them now . . . ?" Gandhi asked. "Matzos," the interviewer replied, to which Gandhi returned, "Yes, matzos. . . . I think matzos are very nice and crisp." He had "great sympathy" toward Jews, he explained, first and foremost for "selfish motives" since he had so many Jewish friends. He also admired Jewish communal cohesion (to which, arguably, neither Kallenbach nor Polak actively contributed during Gandhi's time in South Africa).[32] But then Gandhi explained his understanding of what Zionism should be—a purely spiritual movement detached from the idea of a national territory:

> Zionism in its spiritual sense is a lofty aspiration. . . . By spiritual sense I mean [Jews] should want to realise the Jerusalem that is within. Zionism meaning re-occupation of Palestine has no attraction for me. I can understand the longing of a Jew to return to Palestine, and he can do

so if he can without the help of bayonets whether his own or those of Britan [sic]. In that event he would go to Palestine peacefully and in perfect friendliness with the Arabs. The real Zionism of which I have given you my meaning is the thing to strive for, long for and die for. Zion lies in one's heart. It is the abode of God. The real Jerusalem is the spiritual Jerusalem. Thus he can realise Zionism in any part of the world.[33]

Gandhi's statement provoked outrage from Zionists on both sides of the Atlantic. His ideal of Zionism was wholly incompatible not only with political Zionism but also with Ahad Ha'amian spiritual and cultural Zionism, which still depended on the physical space of Palestine. The *Jewish Chronicle* ran its own condemnation, which argued that—given his presence in Britain to advocate for the national rights of his people—Gandhi had tremendous nerve asserting that "we [Jews] must not think of our rehabilitation . . . on national lines."[34] In New York, at a dinner held by the Friends of Gandhi, the American Zionist rabbi Stephen Wise lamented Gandhi's categorization of Jews' return to Palestine as "re-occupation . . . with all of the sinister military meaning which 'occupation' and 're-occupation' convey." British bayonets had only appeared on the scene, maintained Wise, when "Arab bayonets perpetrated the massacre" of August 1929.[35]

This controversy astir, Brodetsky asked Polak to arrange a meeting for him with Gandhi. Nahum Sokolow, head of the Zionist Organization since Weizmann's ousting the previous year, would also attend. Around the time Brodetsky reached out to Polak, another reminder of the latter's association with Gandhi again appeared in the Jewish press. Henry Polak's wife, Millie, a close confidant of Gandhi in her own right, had recently published a biography entitled *Mr. Gandhi: The Man*; it was reviewed in the *Jewish Chronicle* in the same edition as Gandhi's controversial interview. "However strange or peculiar [Gandhi's] philosophy may appear to the Western world, he truly represents the mind of the awakening East," read the review. "Jews, with their special interest in Palestine, have a particular concern for the reconcilement of the Orient and the Occident," it explained.[36]

Polak arranged the meeting with the assistance of his sister Maud Polak, who, after serving as Gandhi's secretary during his 1909 trip to London, had once again been enlisted to aid him during the Round Table Conference.[37]

When Selig Brodetsky and Nahum Sokolow arrived at Gandhi's offices in Knightsbridge on October 15, 1931, Maud welcomed them. They found Gandhi seated on the floor with two artists—a sculptor fashioning a bust and a young girl with a pencil and pad in hand—busily capturing his likeness. After rising to greet his guests, Gandhi resumed his seat on the floor. Brodetsky and Sokolow, both ensconced in chairs, launched into a "brief account" of the achievements and goals of the Zionist movement and told Gandhi that they could understand well the "communal difficulties" facing India. "Similar troubles on a different scale existed in Palestine, where two civilisations were living side by side, each trying to develop in its own way," Brodetsky explained. This parallel established, the two Zionist representatives turned to the topic at hand. "We stated that it was a matter of great concern to us that Palestine should be kept as peaceful as possible," wrote Brodetsky. The efforts of Shaukat Ali "to draw Palestine into the ambit of the Indian Communal problems" might spell disaster for the Yishuv. They worried that Gandhi, who had first lent his support for Khilafat in 1920 in an effort to preserve a united India, might consent to make Palestine a political issue in his country. "We expressed the hope that we could rest assured that no attempt to bring the problem of Palestine into the discussions of the Round Table Conference . . . would meet with his approval," reported Brodetsky.[38]

Brodetsky's strategy of meeting directly with Gandhi appeared promising. Explaining that he already had some knowledge of the Zionist movement and sympathized with its aims (neither he nor the Zionist leaders made mention of his recent *Jewish Chronicle* interview), Gandhi pledged to Brodetsky and Sokolow that "so far as he was concerned, he would refuse to have anything to do with" pulling Palestine into Indian politics. Assurances provided, the three men turned to more innocuous conversation. Gandhi offered up that since he was living in the neighborhood of Bow, he often passed through London's Jewish East End on his way home from Knightsbridge. He "had, indeed, found it convenient to get his food—mostly fruit—from a Jewish shop, where he found he could get it better and cheaper than elsewhere."[39]

The Anglo-Jewish press reported positively on Brodetsky and Sokolow's work. "Delegates to the Indian Round Table Conference tell me that they have been very much impressed by the Zionist case submitted to them in recent conversations they have had with Mr. Sokolow and Dr. Brodetsky," a reporter for the *Jewish Chronicle* related. "The Zionist leaders have," the reporter wrote, "made a distinct impression" on Gandhi.[40] For several years, little effort was made by the Zionist movement to build on that impression.

A MISSION TO THE EAST

Although Polak never identified as a Zionist, Hermann Kallenbach began to sympathize with the movement as early as 1911 following a trip to Germany to visit his family.[41] While in Königsberg, he encountered a young Zionist named Louis Lewin, who impressed on him the similarities between the experiences of Zionist pioneers in the incipient kibbutz movement and the Indians who lived on Kallenbach's Tolstoy Farm outside Johannesburg. Lewin, who immigrated to Palestine the following year, wrote to Kallenbach, suggesting that he, too, should come "to see how to build a Homeland."[42] Kallenbach seems to have seriously considered the possibility, but Gandhi dissuaded him. "The remedy is not in Palestine," Gandhi wrote. "You would go to Palestine and there (at the bottom of the idea) have an independent and simple life, such as you have come to appreciate. It won't do. You have to see happiness in unhappiness and feel that life is made up of worldly miseries which rightly understood hammer us into shape," he insisted.[43] After many months, Kallenbach finally responded to Lewin, laying out his personal vision for the Jewish homeland. "I do not want to contribute to [making] a modern state out of Palestine, with armies, ships, police, industries and an army of dissatisfied workers," he wrote, maintaining that "to turn Palestine into another industrial State . . . is insanity." Ultimately, Kallenbach declined Lewin's invitation of immigration, writing that, while he had "been born as a Jew and will die as a Jew," his character was neither yet "firm" enough nor his heart "clear" enough to be able to contribute rightfully to the Zionist cause.[44] In response to Kallenbach's letter, Lewin enlisted the help of Arthur Ruppin, then working for the Zionist Organization in Jaffa. Ruppin contacted Kallenbach to try to disabuse him of his utopian expectations, explaining that he had gone "to Palestine not because of ideal reasons, but because of sober consideration."[45]

Sober considerations were ultimately to change Kallenbach's ideas about

Zionism. When Kallenbach finally returned to South Africa in 1920, the possibilities of Zionism had been transformed by the Balfour Declaration and the assignment of the Palestine mandate to Britain. For many South African Jews—indeed, for Jews across the British Empire—the merging of British and Zionist political futures was cause for celebration and convinced many finally to support Jewish nationalism.[46] Yet, it is implausible that Kallenbach, immersed as he was in critiques of empire and colonialism, saw the mandate as a boon to Zionism. Rather, it was the rise of antisemitism in Germany, where his family still resided, as well as the concomitant growth of antisemitism in South Africa, that prompted Kallenbach to become an active Zionist.[47] In 1925, when Hitler published the first volume of *Mein Kampf* and the Nazi Party began gaining traction in Germany, Kallenbach joined the executive committee of Keren Hayesod. Far from the utopian vision Kallenbach had expressed more than a decade earlier, work for the Keren Hayesod focused chiefly on the mundane: raising money. It was through this growing Zionist involvement that Kallenbach met Immanuel Olsvanger, the Keren Hayesod delegate for South Africa who would play a central role in Zionist efforts to build ties with leaders of the Indian independence movement. Olsvanger was also the one to put forth Kallenbach's name to Moshe Shertok.

When Kallenbach received Shertok's letter on July 15, 1936, asking him to undertake a mission to India on behalf of the Zionist movement, the situation in Palestine had shifted dramatically. That April, after more than three years of substantial growth, development, and relative quiet and stability for the Yishuv, the Arab Revolt commenced. Though the revolt began much like the 1929 riots—with a swell of haphazard attacks against the Jewish community—random violence soon turned to organized protest against British mandatory authorities and the Yishuv. The Arab Higher Committee was established by the mufti, Amin al-Husseini, and made formal political demands to the British: stop Jewish immigration and land purchases and implement representational government with a Palestinian Arab majority. The committee also called for a countrywide general strike, which lasted until October 1936. In May 1936, the British Government announced that it would form a commission—what became the Peel Commission—to investigate the unrest. Not only were the leaders of the Yishuv faced with the undeniable reality of a mature, organized Palestinian national movement, but they also had to reckon with the broader international implications of the revolt across the British imperial and Islamic worlds. The All-India Muslim League proclaimed its support for the strikers in Palestine and warned that British policy there greatly angered Indian Muslims. The Muslim press in India—and even some Hindu newspapers—began providing intense coverage of developments in Palestine and forcefully condemned British mandatory policy and the Jewish national home.

Moshe Shertok, in his capacity as head of the Political Department of the Jewish Agency, decided that the Zionist movement could not afford to ignore these developments in India. At the end of 1920, two years after the conclusion of his service in the Ottoman army recounted in the opening of this book, Shertok decided to continue his studies at the London School of Economics.[48] There, he developed close ties with his professor Harold Laski, who had been Jawaharlal Nehru's most important intellectual interlocutor throughout his time in Britain. During Shertok's studies, which he completed in 1925, he was introduced to Labour critiques of imperialism and studied alongside other elites from the empire who, after their education, returned to their home countries as anticolonial activists.[49] Shertok understood well the power of the Indian independence movement—what it could mean for Zionism as an ally and what it could mean as a foe.

Shertok first turned to Immanuel Olsvanger, whose academic scholarship on Sanskrit, he reasoned, made him an ideal candidate to reach out to Indian leaders. Olsvanger also had a proven record of cultivating cross-cultural relationships. He had spent 1935 in Palestine working on an "experiment" of "forming a mixed group of Jewish and Arab intellectuals for social intercourse and joint literary ventures."[50] The informal, relaxed setting of Olsvanger's literary salon, intended ultimately to produce more positive political relations between Jews and Arabs in Palestine, recalls Arlosoroff's idea for cross-cultural clubs, "where educated Englishmen, Jews, and Arabs [could] meet in a social atmosphere."[51] Arlosoroff's plan remained hypothetical, but Olsvanger's scheme met with measured success. He founded a Jerusalem club, and solicited interest in opening a Haifa branch, but the entire project was postponed following the Arab Revolt. Now, amid the ongoing unrest and strike, Shertok requested that Olsvanger apply his skills—both interpersonal and scholarly—on a mission to India. Olsvanger agreed and asked Shertok: had he heard of Hermann Kallenbach?

Shertok had not and was thrilled to know that there existed a Jew who both had come to identify as a Zionist and had been such an intimate friend of Gandhi. He wrote at once to Kallenbach, laying out in an extensive letter his understanding of the current state of Yishuv-India relations. "The problem of establishing contacts with the Indian world and of gaining the sympathy and understanding for our work and aspiration among leaders of the Indian renaissance has long occupied our attention," Shertok wrote, likely referring to the efforts of Agronsky and Brodetsky. "It is clear that our political future as of a nation returning to its home in Asia must ultimately depend in large measure on the amount of good-will and solidarity which we shall succeed in evolving on the part of the great Asiatic civilisations," he continued. While Shertok at first framed Jewish affinities to India in terms of a shared "eastern" heritage—rather than a common British imperial reality—he acknowledged that challenges to the Zionist-Indian relationship stemmed from imperial dynamics. While certain Muslim Indian leaders had long shown hostility to Zionism and the Yishuv, viewing Jews in Palestine as colonial interlopers, Hindu Indians began, now, to share this perspective. "The general tendency among Hindu politicians," Shertok wrote, "appears to be to regard us Jews in Palestine as intruders coming from the west." Reaching out to India thus had become "a matter of urgency." Immediate action was needed to stop misconceptions before they had "hardened and gained currency." Olsvanger, Shertok explained to Kallenbach, was prepared to travel to India for two to three months to embark upon this mission, the sensitive nature of which required delicate and strategic handling. "What we have in mind is not any form of political campaign . . . but a very cautious and discreet method of procedure—mainly individual talks with people that matter," he told Kallenbach. Olsvanger had Shertok's complete confidence. Not only would he be able to present the "Zionist case on a high cultural level," but—as evidenced through his partnerships with Palestinian Arabs—he could also "[endear] himself to persons with an oriental mentality" and had an extensive scholarly knowledge of Indian culture.[52]

But Kallenbach possessed something that Olsvanger did not: a personal relationship with Gandhi. For that reason, Shertok wished for Kallenbach not only to participate in the mission with Olsvanger but to lead it. He knew that this request might well seem like "an errand of which [Kallenbach] may never have dreamt." But the situation was desperate:

> Our movement is passing through dangerous times—its whole future is now at stake ... South African Zionism as a whole and every one of its leaders individually have behind them a splendid record of Zionist service in terms of internal unity, discipline, devotion and financial exertion. But all these are ordinary ways of serving Zion. There are but few people whom circumstances have placed in a position enabling them to render service of an extraordinary character. I am advised and believe that you are at the present moment such a person. The fact that there are Indians in South Africa and that there are Jews there who at a certain time identified themselves so closely with the Indian cause was, historically speaking, a mere accident. But circumstances arise when such historical accidents assume deep import and may truly be regarded as the work of Providence. ... What you have no doubt regarded as a part of your purely private past ... can now be of invaluable service to our national movement—it can, so to speak, be "nationalized," and with eminently useful effect.[53]

While Polak had written publicly about the connections between his Jewish identity and his support for the Indian cause, Kallenbach had not explicitly articulated a connection between those two central aspects of his life. Now, more than just connecting the two, Shertok proposed "nationalizing" Kallenbach's friendship with Gandhi. He would call on that relationship in the service of the Zionist movement.

Ten days later, on the eve of his departure from South Africa for a business trip to London, Kallenbach replied to Shertok, agreeing to the mission. "Our people are going through most anxious times and none of us should refuse the call for service," he wrote, confirming, "I am coming." Kallenbach had not previously heard "that some Hindu leaders [were] favouring the political aspirations" of the Palestinian Arabs over the Jews in Palestine. "Doubtless the position justifies your anxiety and your action," he told Shertok. Kallenbach also applauded the choice of his friend Olsvanger to help with the mission, writing, "I know him well and his keen interest for Eastern people and customs." As Kallenbach had pressing business in London, he instructed Shertok to allow Olsvanger to go ahead to India. After concluding his business, Kallenbach planned to travel first to Palestine and from there to India, where he intended to join Olsvanger in October 1936.[54] Having never set foot in either country, Kallenbach was thus poised to make two long-awaited pilgrimages.

Obliged to undertake the beginning of the mission alone, Olsvanger embarked from Palestine, reaching Bombay on August 12, 1936. In accordance with Shertok's plan, Olsvanger proceeded to meet with Indian political leaders to discuss the aim of Zionism and the development of the Yishuv. The first meeting Olsvanger documented in his diary of the trip, however, was not with a Hindu politician but with Meyer Nissim, one of the leaders of the Baghdadi Jewish community in Bombay. In addition to serving as president of the Bombay Municipal Council from 1929 to 1930 (equivalent to mayor of the city), Nissim was a member of Meyer David's Welfare of India League, which supported Indian self-rule and promoted positive European-Indian relations. In 1930, Nissim had helped put Agronsky in touch with Muslim leaders during the latter's trip to India. Echoing Agronsky's observation at the time that Nissim remained "aloof from the work-a-day Zionists," Olsvanger observed that Nissim "wants to be seen as a European. He knows everything about Palestine, has all the sympathies but doesn't want to be involved with it officially, . . . He is afraid that a closer cooperation between the Jews in India could lead to them being declared non-European."[55] Of course, Nissim and all Baghdadi Jews in Bombay, just like their counterparts in Calcutta, had officially been placed in the "non-Mohammedan" (Hindu majority) electoral category the previous year in the Government of India Act of 1935. While Rachel and David Ezra in Calcutta had by the 1930s become open in their Zionist commitments, viewing them as problematic neither to their British imperial loyalties nor to their relationship to Indian nationalists, Nissim likely was more concerned about how he would be perceived by the broader non-Jewish community in Bombay. His election as president of the Municipal Council had depended on securing the European vote, and his continued position on the council was repeatedly challenged by European candidates.[56] The optics of Olsvanger's visit—aimed at building ties between Zionists and Indian nationalists—likely concerned Nissim.

Olsvanger turned next to Sarojini Naidu, whom he had first met in South Africa in 1924. Instrumental in founding the Women's Indian Association, Naidu served as president—the first Indian woman to do so—of the Indian National Congress from 1925 to 1926.[57] A supporter of Gandhi who had been jailed with him after the 1930 Salt March and had participated with him in the second Round Table Conference in London the following year, Naidu offered to put Olsvanger in touch with India's leading politicians. "Sarojini phoned just now, at 8 p.m., that I should see her tomorrow to go together to [Nehru]," Olsvanger reported in his diary. "From the first moment on she treated me as her friend and felt obliged to show me all the hospitality possible," he wrote.[58] Naidu had long-established ties to the Jewish community in India and an interest in Jewish history and culture. In 1916, she delivered a well-attended and well-received lecture at the Bene Israel Friends' Society in Bombay. Examining the contributions and achievements of the Jewish people throughout history, Naidu extoled the works of Spinoza and Heine, and she lauded the Jewish community for their pride in their nationality and commitment to religion in the face of persecution. It is unclear if anyone in attendance pointed out the unintended irony of the two chosen heroes— one shunned for heresy, the other a convert to Christianity.[59] Naidu's admiration for Jewish culture inspired her warm attitude toward Zionism. When Olsvanger explained the goal of his trip to India, he reported that Naidu "thought it as something self-evident." "Well, of course, I don't see why the Jews should not colonise Palestine," she apparently responded.[60]

While some of Olsvanger's subsequent contacts—both Hindu and Muslim—expressed open attitudes toward Zionism, his discussions with India's two most prominent politicians—Nehru and Gandhi—proved far less promising. Olsvanger first met Nehru on August 20, 1936, at the Bombay home of the latter's youngest sister, Krishna Hutheesing, and her husband, Gunottam Hutheesing, who came from a prominent Jain family from Ahmedabad. Olsvanger noted that the home, a mansion on Bombay's upscale Carmichael Road, was a "rich house, just as [Nehru] is very rich." Naidu, who arranged the meeting, was also present. "He doesn't know anything about Zionism. [He] has seen Palestine once as he flew over the country," Olsvanger reported on Nehru. "[He] maintains, though, to know

Zionism and its connection with the 'affairs of the world' very well," he wrote. By "affairs of the world," explained Olsvanger, Nehru meant British imperialism.

Henry Polak, who happened to be in India at the time, told Olsvanger that he believed members of the Indian National Congress, including Nehru, opposed Zionism not because of their concern for Hindu-Muslim unity but because of "ignorance of the problem." Olsvanger wrote that while Polak "wasn't a Zionist . . . he would be ready to be in contact with London and Jerusalem and to do everything here that we should feel is correct and possible." Polak's contacts in London, Olsvanger noted, included Norman Bentwich and Selig Brodetsky, mainstays of British Zionism.[61] Olsvanger commented that whereas Polak's influence in India had once been substantial, it had waned in recent years as Indian public opinion grew increasingly wary of the European "so-called 'friends of India.'"[62] As we will see, although Polak and Gandhi remained close, they disagreed increasingly in the 1930s over Gandhi's program of noncooperation with the British, especially in light of Hitler's rise to power.

Olsvanger finally met with Gandhi, who had been sick when he first arrived, on September 19, 1936. Throughout his diary (both before and after meeting Gandhi), Olsvanger refers to Gandhi only as "*laemmel*," Yiddish for "little lamb" but with a connotation of weakness and naïveté. Olsvanger's plain dislike for the Indian leader is apparent throughout his diary, in which he recounts damaging (and dubious) tales about Gandhi's hypocrisy.[63] Their first meeting seemed only to confirm these preconceived opinions for Olsvanger. Mahadev Desai, Gandhi's secretary, met Olsvanger at the Wardha Railway Station, and the two traveled by car—"which I had to pay for," Olsvanger noted—to nearby Sevagram, the location of Gandhi's ashram. There, still weak and recovering from his illness, Gandhi sat on his bed, surrounded by fifteen of his disciples. "I got a place at the edge of the bed," wrote Olsvanger. "I talked to him for about 20 minutes. I disliked the whole environment. . . . I told the Rebbe everything in detail. The Rebbe was silent and the students listened," he wrote with disdain. Gandhi reported that he had been delighted to receive a cable from Kallenbach about his upcoming trip to India. Olsvanger told Gandhi that Kallenbach had become very involved in Zionism in South Africa. "I know!" responded

Gandhi, "but then he has so many poor relatives."[64] Olsvanger was exasperated. "That's how he understands Zionism," he wrote in his diary. The aspect of national and cultural reconstruction integral to the Zionist movement was lost on Gandhi, Olsvanger thought. Instead, the Indian leader viewed Jewish nationalism solely as a materialist movement. Shimoni notes that it is possible Gandhi did not mean anything "derisive" by his statement but was instead commenting on the financial devastation faced by Kallenbach's family in Germany following the Nazis' rise to power.[65] Olsvanger seemed to ignore that it was precisely these increasingly exigent circumstances—the "social death" of German Jews, as well as Polish Jews' growing sense that their future was untenable—that animated much of the Zionist sense of urgency in the late 1930s. In any event, Olsvanger decided to pursue the topic with Gandhi no further until Kallenbach arrived.

Olsvanger met again with Nehru on September 22, 1936, this time at the Nehru family home in Allahabad. "Nehru's only argument—Imperialism," wrote Olsvanger in sum of the leader's worldview. "Nehru said he was opposed to any imperialism whether British or Hitlerite," reported Olsvanger, who countered that "in Palestine one says that Hitler supports the Arabs." According to the Zionist emissary, Nehru responded that "we have sympathy for the national movement of the Arabs in Palestine because this movement opposes British imperialism. Our sympathies cannot be diminished by the fact that the nationalist Arab movement coincides with Hitler's interests."[66] Olsvanger wondered why the Arab nationalist movement lost nothing in Nehru's esteem for this association. "You could say with the same justification: we are sympathetic to the nationalist movement of the Jews and that this movement coincides with the interests of England doesn't change our sympathy," he put to Nehru. Olsvanger thought that Nehru seemed "a bit embarrassed" at this feat of reasoning. "I understand the Jewish problem," Nehru offered, "but it can only be solved when in the big fight between Fascism and Socialism, the latter succeeds." To this, Olsvanger responded: "Fight between Fascism and Socialism? In your eyes, is Hitler fighting on the side of Socialism? This fight could last for generations and we should wait patiently till then. You know whom I feel like here as a representative of the Jews? You tell me: 'Dear friend, you are very nice but you have to die. I'm very sorry about it, but I can't help it. Drink your cup of tea and be so kind as to die.'"⁶⁷ The absurdity of Olsvanger's remark had the intended effect. Nehru laughed and declared emphatically, "Naturally we condemn the riots and atrocities!" He continued with a reframing of the conflict in Palestine: "We are trying at present to explain to the Muslims here that the fight in [Palestine] is not one between Jews and Arabs, but between both and British Imperialism; and that they should not protest against Jews but against the British Government which hinders the development of peaceful relations."⁶⁸

While Olsvanger left buoyed, feeling that progress with Nehru had been made, his good spirits were dashed the following day when he read a morning paper. On September 18, four days before Olsvanger's meeting with Nehru, the All-India Muslim League had declared that September 27 would be observed as "Palestine Day" in solidarity with the Palestinian Arab national struggle. The morning press on September 23 included a statement from Nehru in support of Palestine Day, appealing to all of India to join in the observance. Olsvanger sent Nehru a letter demanding to know how he could issue such a statement—without any mention of the Jewish national struggle—in the wake of their meeting. Olsvanger went so far as to accuse Nehru of "siding with the enemies of freedom" in Palestine. In a letter of response, Nehru clarified that the statement had, in fact, been made the day before their discussion. Even so, he felt that neither man was "likely to convert each other completely" to his point of view. "With all deference to you my knowledge of the world situation is not insignificant," wrote Nehru, referring once again to British imperialism. "I hold that it is impossible to understand any problem, whether that of India or Palestine, without reference to that larger situation and I hold that the Arab movement is essentially a nationalist movement," he explained, continuing:

> It astonishes me for you to tell me that I am siding with the enemies of freedom in Palestine. . . . I mentioned the large additions to British troops that are being sent to Palestine. I suppose, according to you, these British troops are the friends of freedom in Palestine. I hold differently. As I dictate this letter my office is being searched by a crowd of police men under the orders of the local magistrate. This is a gentle reminder to me of how imperialism functions in this country. I cannot tolerate this imperialism in India or Palestine and the question I ask every one is whether he stands for this imperialism or against it.⁶⁹

Olsvanger could not convince Nehru of his position because the two, as Nehru put it, approached the "question" of British imperialism from "different view-points." For Olsvanger, British imperialism, which he neither outwardly praised nor condemned, represented the only moral option when the alternative was Nazism. His argument, then, rested on a vision of Jewish and Arab nationalism (or, rather, certain leaders of Arab nationalism, particularly the mufti) as a struggle between good and evil. Other Zionists at the time, however, made their claims to Indian leaders using different reasoning. For instance, Elias M. Epstein, the British-born editor of the English-language weekly the *Palestine Review*, appealed in broader humanist terms and denied the connection between Zionism and British imperialism.[70] In a letter written on Palestine Day in India to Yusuf Meherally, the secretary of the Socialist Party of the Indian National Congress, Epstein argued:

> The Jews are in Palestine not [on] behalf or because of British interests, but because they see in the creation of a Jewish National Home in this land, the only means of perpetuating their existence as an entity, and at the same time contributing their share to the progress of mankind. . . . I think therefore it is rather inconsistent to extend your sympathy to people who may be hostile to the Jewish National Home, because the Mandate of the League of Nations endorsing the Zionist movement has been handed to Great Britain. You may be critical of British imperialism, but that is no reason for withholding your support of a struggling race, still a minority in Palestine, the ideals of which are in the interests of mankind.[71]

Epstein's appeal, even were it to have been effective, came too late. The Indian National Congress observed Palestine Day on September 27. Demonstrations, including a mass meeting in Allahabad, were held across the country. At the Allahabad demonstration, Nehru gave a speech in which he insisted that the conflict between Jews and Arabs in Palestine was not a religious one but rather a struggle between imperialism and a national movement fighting for freedom.[72]

Though Kallenbach had intended to join Olsvanger in India in October, work continued to delay him in London. In November, Olsvanger left India on his own, returning to Palestine days before the Peel Commission arrived to begin its investigation.

HOMECOMINGS

Shertok, who maintained contact with Olsvanger throughout his time in India, was anything but otherwise unoccupied in Palestine. The Arab Revolt continued unabated through the summer of 1936 until additional British troops, deployed in August, succeeded in quelling the unrest by the fall. Shertok, as chief liaison between the Yishuv and British authorities, worked with High Commissioner Wauchope to organize Jewish mobile defense units that cooperated with the British police and military.[73] With the revolt contained and the general strike called off by the Arab Higher Committee in October, the British government made final plans for the Peel Commission's arrival in Palestine. Weizmann (who had been reelected as president of the Zionist Organization in 1935 following the death of Nahum Sokolow), Shertok, Ben-Gurion, and other Zionist officials testified before the commission in late November and, along with Arab leaders (who formally boycotted the commission), adamantly opposed the notion of cantonization for Palestine, a plan supported by the Colonial Office. Facing this deadlock, members of the Peel Commission began privately discussing the idea of partition—that is, dividing Palestine into two states, one Jewish and one Palestinian Arab. When Zionist leadership learned of the partition scheme in February 1937, they were bitterly divided over the prospect. Weizmann, Ben-Gurion, and Shertok ultimately came to support the partition idea, while other Zionists—most notably Berl Katznelson on the left and Jabotinsky on the right—opposed it. Norman Bentwich also opposed the idea, fearing it would extinguish any hope for Jewish-Arab cooperation. While the Zionist Organization officially rejected the Peel Commission's formal recommendation of partition during the Twentieth Zionist Congress in Zurich in August 1937, delegates also endorsed a "dual formula" approach: Zionist officials would publicly reject the terms of the partition, while working behind the scenes to ensure that the best plan possible for the Yishuv would be secured were partition to be implemented.[74]

In mid-February 1937, Shertok traveled to London to discuss partition plans with British officials and to campaign for continued land settlement and immigration—which had been more than halved by the British in 1936 in the context of the revolt. While successfully negotiating with the British at this time became imperative for the Zionist movement, the prospect of independence through partition made forging ties with other nations vying for autonomy all the more important. The sweeping success of the Indian National Congress in the Indian Provincial elections, held in January and February of that year, further evidenced the force of the Indian independence movement. Thus, even though Olsvanger's mission had ended without promising developments, and talks over the partition plan consumed the Zionist leadership, Shertok resolved that it was still critical to send Kallenbach to India.

On March 11, 1937, Shertok, Kallenbach, and Olsvanger all convened in London over lunch at the Royal Automotive Club to discuss Kallenbach's upcoming trip. Kallenbach told Shertok that receiving his initial letter in July the previous year had "thrilled" him, giving him "deep gratification and arousing his excitement." While Olsvanger had left India feeling that Nehru's influence had far overtaken that of Gandhi, Kallenbach "was certain that Gandhi was still the real leader" and that another trip was therefore still worthwhile for the Zionist movement. The three men determined that Kallenbach would first travel to Palestine for "training" in advance of his mission to India. "He is particularly interested in kibbutz life, which in his opinion may influence Gandhi more than anything else," Shertok noted in his diary.[75]

Not surprisingly, the kibbutz movement made a deep impression on Kallenbach during his 1937 trip to Palestine, reminding him of his days with Gandhi on Tolstoy Farm. Shertok and his wife, Tzippora, also showed Kallenbach around Jerusalem and Tel Aviv. Moved by what he saw, Kallenbach wrote in a letter to his family that "we need to give everything to Palestine: money, work, propaganda. Learn Hebrew. I am also learning." After signing his letter "Hermann," Kallenbach crossed it out, and wrote his Hebrew name "Chaim" in its place.[76] In a note to Shertok, Kallenbach wrote, "The days I spent [in Palestine] are not to be forgotten."[77]

Sailing from Port Said, Kallenbach reached India on May 20, 1937, finding it a "vast, strange, and so exceptional interesting country." Gandhi's son Ramdas met Kallenbach in Bombay and delivered a letter from his father.

"So after much waiting you have at last come," it read; "Welcome. Unless you have anything to do in Bombay, come by the first train." Gandhi was staying at the home of his secretary Mahadev Desai in Tithal, a coastal village north of Bombay. Arriving at the house in the early morning hours as Gandhi and his disciples were in morning prayer, Kallenbach and Desai silently took a seat on the floor to wait. When the prayers had concluded, Kallenbach rose (with a "little difficulty having lost the habit") to be embraced by Gandhi. "Your hair has turned gray like mine," the Indian leader said to his long-lost friend. Kallenbach was then sixty-six years old, Gandhi a year older.[78]

"I felt and still feel—the 23 years of separation non-existent," reported Kallenbach to Shertok regarding his reunion with Gandhi. "Just as in South Africa we eat together and sleep next to each other," he continued. Days began at 4:00 a.m., followed by morning prayer and a walk to the sea. Evenings echoed mornings, with another walk to the coast and prayer. Nights were spent on the floor with blankets. Two vegetarian meals were taken each day. Kallenbach felt that India was an entirely different world from the West. Perhaps, he suggested in a letter to Shertok, the problem between Jews and Arabs in Palestine was that Jews had "so fully associated themselves" with the West, they could no longer identify with "eastern habits and culture."[79] The solution was for Jews in Palestine to return to an original, authentic, "eastern" way of life. This observation recalled Shertok's July 1936 letter to Kallenbach, in which he framed the Yishuv as a "nation returning to its home in Asia."[80]

Against the backdrop of this rediscovered daily rhythm, Kallenbach worked to gain Gandhi's support for the Zionist movement. Olsvanger had given up on winning Gandhi over to Zionism when the latter had expressed his understanding that Kallenbach's Zionist convictions stemmed from having impoverished relatives. Now Kallenbach worked to illuminate for Gandhi the spiritual dimensions of the Zionist movement, while still emphasizing the critical aspect of the physical land of Palestine. He even intimated his desire to immigrate to Palestine, which Gandhi now supported. In a note detailing his thoughts on Kallenbach's potential future life in Palestine, Gandhi prescribed "all-around simplicity." He suggested daily spiritual readings, including the Bhagavad Gita, as well as vigorous study of Zionist literature. He recommended a diet of vegetables, fruits, and dairy;

early rising; and "walks covering 10 miles daily" whenever possible.[81] Gandhi desired that Kallenbach reproduce in Palestine the way of life to which Gandhi had first committed in South Africa and now continued in India.

When Kallenbach left India in late July, Gandhi furnished him with a short, single-page statement on Zionism in which he articulated a different vision from his 1931 interview given to the *Jewish Chronicle*. Then, Gandhi had disparaged the entire Zionist endeavor in Palestine, arguing that true Zionism was "in one's heart" and could be realized anywhere in the world.[82] Now, he recognized the theoretical possibility of a righteous and spiritual Zionism that included a Jewish territory in Palestine, but he objected to the means by which he saw that development occurring. "The introduction of the Jew in Palestine under the protection of British or other arms is wholly inconsistent with spirituality," Gandhi wrote. "Neither the mandate nor the Balfour Declaration can therefore be used in support of sustaining Jewish immigration into Palestine in the teeth of Arab opposition," he continued. Gandhi granted that "no exception can possibly be taken to the natural desire of the Jews to found a home in Palestine," but he argued that any Jewish settlement must "wait for its fulfilment till Arab opinion is ripe for it" and thereafter "depend upon the goodwill of the Arab population."[83] When Gandhi read the Peel Commission report, published in July, he reiterated his position in a letter to Kallenbach. "I am more than ever convinced that the only proper and dignified solution is the one I have suggested, now more so than before," he wrote, continuing, "My solution admits of no half measures. If the Jews will rely wholly on the Arab goodwill, they must once [and] for all renounce British protection."[84] Gandhi told Kallenbach that he would be willing to mediate talks between the Jews and Arabs in Palestine, so long as the British were not involved. Neither Gandhi's statement nor his offer to mediate were to be made public

Kallenbach, who was deeply impressed by the achievements of the kibbutz movement, nevertheless came to be an active supporter of Zionism because of the rise of antisemitism. He appreciated the *practical* role that Palestine played as a refuge for German Jews fleeing Nazi rule, Jews who had found the doors of the United States, Canada, Britain, and South Africa closed. Kallenbach does not seem to have pressed this point to Gandhi. When Kallenbach requested that a monograph on Zionism be prepared for

Gandhi by the Political Department, the ensuing text focused primarily on the "spiritual background" of Zionism, as well as on the achievements of Jewish settlement work in Palestine and the benefits it offered to the Arab population (further evidenced, according to the text, by the increase in Arab immigration into Palestine from neighboring countries). A small section (three pages out of twenty-five) examined "the position of the Jews in the Diaspora," covering the development of Jewish life in Europe since the French Revolution and citing Leon Pinsker's *Auto-Emancipation*. But only a few short lines in the monograph addressed the current situation in Germany.[85] Hence, neither Kallenbach nor the Political Department placed primary emphasis on the threat of Nazism in their efforts to win Gandhi's support for Zionism. They relied instead on underscoring the spiritual component of Zionist work in Palestine and argued that Jewish development had brought positive change for all the land's inhabitants.

On his departure from India in July 1937, Kallenbach promised Gandhi he would return that December. But work and family obligations forced him to delay his trip for more than a year. In the interim, relations between the Yishuv and India would reach a new low.

CONFRONTATION

When Kallenbach did not return to India in December 1937 as planned, Gandhi was filled with the "deepest disappointment" for his friend's "wholly unexpected" absence.[86] During their prolonged separation, Kallenbach urged Gandhi to make a public statement in support of Zionism, but the latter remained silent. Meanwhile, the situations in Palestine and Europe became increasingly dire. In Palestine, following the failure of the Peel Commission to reach a workable solution to the conflict, the Arab Revolt recommenced in the fall of 1937 when Arab gunmen assassinated Lewis Yelland Andrews, the British district commissioner for Galilee. The high commissioner, newly invested with the power to outlaw and disband organizations considered to be contributing to the insurrection, deposed the mufti as president of the Supreme Muslim Council and disbanded the Arab Higher Committee. At the same time, part of the Irgun, the Revisionist paramilitary group, officially rejected the policy of *havlagah* (restraint) observed by the Haganah and began staging attacks against Palestinian Arabs. In Europe, Nazi Germany annexed Austria in March 1938, and, with the Munich Agreement of September, took the Sudetenland, the areas of Czechoslovakia populated by ethnic Germans. The year 1938 also brought a new wave of anti-Jewish legislation, following the Nuremberg Laws of 1935. And for two days, beginning on November 9, Jewish communities were brutalized across Germany, Austria, and the Sudetenland. Rioters destroyed hundreds of synagogues, thousands of businesses, and murdered approximately one hundred Jews. The viciousness and scale of the destruction unprecedented, Kristallnacht marked a turning point in the persecution of Jews in Nazi Europe.

Ten days after the violence, Gandhi finally broke his silence with a wide-ranging statement on Palestine and the situation in Europe, published in his newspaper, *Harijan*.[87] His words stunned the Zionist movement and Jews around the world. "It is not without hesitation that I venture to offer my views on this very difficult question," he prefaced. "My sympathies are all with the Jews. I have known them intimately in South Africa. Some of them became life long companions," he shared. His Jewish bona fides established, Gandhi declared that his sympathies nevertheless would not "blind [him] to the requirements of justice." "The cry for the national home for the Jews does not make much appeal to me," he wrote:

> Why should [the Jews] not, like other peoples of the earth, make that country their home where they are born and where they earn their livelihood? Palestine belongs to the Arabs in the same sense that England belongs to the English or France to the French. It is wrong and inhuman to impose the Jews on the Arabs. What is going on in Palestine today cannot be justified by any moral code of conduct. The mandates have no sanction but that of the last war. Surely it would be a crime against humanity to reduce the proud Arabs so that Palestine can be restored to the Jews partly or wholly as their national home.[88]

Gandhi's depiction of the "proud Arabs" was coupled with a decree that "according to the accepted canons of right and wrong, nothing can be said against the Arab resistance." And while he wished Arabs had rejected violence, Gandhi argued that the Jews, "who claim to be the chosen race," could "[vindicate] their position on earth"—both in Germany and Palestine—by choosing nonviolence. Moreover, instead of building a national home in

Palestine, "the nobler course would be to insist on a just treatment of the Jews wherever they are born and bred," wrote Gandhi. "The Jews born in France are French in precisely the same sense that Christians born in France are French," he reasoned. As he had in his 1931 interview with the *Jewish Chronicle*, Gandhi also reiterated his belief that "the Palestine of the Biblical conception is not a geographical tract. It is in [Jews'] hearts."[89] Gandhi's argument about Palestine, then, rested on three principles. First, he maintained that Palestine belonged solely to the Arabs. Entertaining the idea of partition for Palestine would open up the same possibility for India, which he fundamentally opposed.[90] Second, Gandhi insisted that the true concept of the Land of Israel in Judaism was, in fact, not a physical land at all. And finally, he argued that Jewish distinctiveness stemmed from religious—not national—identity. The idea of a distinctive nationality, the pretense of which fueled the desire for the Jewish national home, placed diaspora Jews in peril. Gandhi wondered, "If the Jews have no home but Palestine, will they relish the idea of being forced to leave the other parts of the world in which they are settled? Or do they want a double home where they can remain at will?" He argued that "this cry for the National Home affords a colourable justification for the German expulsion of the Jews."[91]

Turning to the Jewish situation in Nazi Europe, Gandhi conceded that given the extent of the persecution—which "seems to have no parallel in history"—if ever there were a justifiable war, it would be one against Germany. "Germany is showing to the world how efficiently violence can be worked when it is not hampered by any hypocrisy or weakness masquerading as humanitarianism," he wrote, likening Nazism to an unbridled, unshrouded imperialism. "But I do not believe in any war," explained Gandhi. Thus, he would not entertain the "pros and cons" of the idea. Without war as an option—and without Palestine as a refuge—Jews had one path left if they were to "preserve their self-respect, and not feel helpless or forlorn":

> If I were a Jew and were born in Germany and earned my livelihood there, I would claim Germany as my home even as the tallest gentile German may, and challenge him to shoot me or cast me in the dungeon; I would refuse to be expelled or to submit to discriminating treatment. And for doing this, I should not wait for the fellow Jews to join me in

civil resistance, but would have confidence that in the end the rest are bound to follow my example.... The calculated violence of Hitler may even result in the general massacre of the Jews.... But if the Jewish mind could be prepared for voluntary suffering, even the massacre I have imagined could be turned into a day of thanksgiving and joy that [God] had wrought deliverance of the race even at the hands of the tyrant. For the God-fearing, death has no terror.[92]

Though he had initially stated that Jewish persecution in Germany was unparalleled in history, Gandhi then offered an "exact parallel" in the example of Indians in South Africa. "There the Indians occupied precisely the same place that the Jews occupy in Germany," he wrote. "The Indians, a mere handful, resorted to satyagraha without any backing from the world outside.... World opinion and the Indian Government came to their aid after eight years of fighting," he explained. Jews, Gandhi reasoned, who have "organised world opinion behind them," were even better positioned to launch their own satyagraha campaign in Germany. "And what has today become a degrading man-hunt," he wrote, "can be turned into a calm and determined stand offered by unarmed men and women." Gandhi felt sure that this demonstration would "convert" non-Jewish Germans "to an appreciation of human dignity." And for that, Gandhi argued, Jews "will have rendered service to fellow Germans and proved their title to be the real German as against those who are today dragging, however unknowingly, the German name into the mire."[93]

The following month Gandhi reiterated his position in a talk delivered to Christian missionaries in Tambaram, in southern India. He criticized Jews for not being "truly non-violent" because they "called down upon the Germans the curses of mankind, and ... wanted America and England to fight Germany on their behalf." Gandhi claimed that "if even one Jew acted [with nonviolence], he would salve his self-respect and leave an example which, if it became infectious, would save the whole of Jewry and leave a rich heritage to mankind besides."[94] Jewish leaders were astounded and appalled by Gandhi's statements, which received widespread attention in the Indian and Arab presses. In Palestine, former members of Brit Shalom, many of whom deeply admired Gandhi, were especially devastated by the Indian leader's words.

In the spring of 1939, the same intellectual circle, including Judah Magnes, Martin Buber, Gershom Scholem, Hugo Bergmann, and Ernst Simon, reconvened as Ha-'Ol, a group dedicated to discussing ethical and religious questions facing the Jewish world, especially as they concerned Jewish-Arab relations.[95] Magnes and Buber each wrote letters in response to Gandhi and published them together in a Ha-'Ol pamphlet.[96] They wrote from a place of respect and esteem for Gandhi, deciding to reach out only after introspection. "I have been very slow in writing this . . . to you," explained Buber in his letter. "Day and night I took myself to task, searching whether I had not in any one point overstepped the measure of self-preservation allotted and even prescribed by God to a human community, and whether I had not fallen into the grievous error of collective egoism," he continued.[97] Magnes wrote, "Your statement is a challenge, particularly to those of us who have imagined ourselves your disciples."[98]

Buber and Magnes objected to the "exact parallel" Gandhi drew between the Jewish condition in Europe and that of Indians in South Africa. Buber argued that in the wake of Kristallnacht and the subsequent mass arrests and internment of Jews in concentration camps, the persecution could not be compared. Furthermore, the nature of the Jewish and Indian diasporas differed fundamentally. "It is obvious that when you think back to your time in South Africa it is a matter of course for you that then as now you always had this great Mother India," wrote Buber. "That fact was and still is so taken for granted that apparently you are entirely unaware of the fundamental differences existing between nations having such a mother . . . and a nation that is orphaned," he continued. To Gandhi's assertion that Jews needed to "accustom themselves to the idea of being forced to leave the other parts of the world" where they lived as long as they looked to Palestine as their homeland, Buber posed a rhetorical question to the Indian leader: "Did you also say to the Indians in South Africa that if India is their home, they must accustom themselves to the idea of being compelled to return to India?"[99]

Buber and Magnes also maintained that satyagraha in South Africa had been applied in such a way that would prove impossible in Germany at present. "The word 'Satyagraha' signifies testimony," wrote Buber. "Testimony without acknowledgment, ineffective, unobserved martyrdom, a martyrdom cast to the winds—that is the fate of innumerable Jews in Germany," he explained.[100] "It is usually in the dead of the night they are spirited away," Magnes wrote. "It makes not even a ripple on the surface of German life," he declared:

> Contrast this with a single hunger strike in an American or English prison, and the public commotion that this arouses. Contrast this with one of your fasts, or with your salt march to the sea, or a visit to the Viceroy, when the whole world is permitted to hang upon your words and be witness to your acts. Has not this been possible largely because, despite all the excesses of its imperialism, England is after all a democracy with a Parliament and a considerable measure of free speech? I wonder if even you would find the way to public opinion in totalitarian Germany, where life is snuffed out like a candle, and no one sees or knows that the light is out.[101]

Magnes, though long a committed pacifist, struggled in particular with Gandhi's prescription for noncooperation. In his biography of Magnes, Norman Bentwich wrote that "hitherto [Magnes] had counted himself a disciple of Gandhi; but his faith in the principle of non-violence was strained to the breaking point when the Jews of Germany and Austria were the helpless victims of Nazi brutality."[102] Magnes implored Gandhi to consider what it would mean to participate—or *not* to participate—in talks with Germany to allow Jewish refugees to leave the country. "If one does not subscribe, no Jews will be able to escape from this prison of torture called Germany," he wrote. But "if one does subscribe one will be cooperating with that Government, and be dealing in Jewish flesh and blood." Invoking the Jewish principle of *pikuah nefesh* (saving a life), Magnes asked Gandhi: "Not to save a living soul? And yet to cooperate with the powers of evil and darkness? Have you an answer?"[103]

Magnes also asked Gandhi to rescind his refusal to consider the "pros and cons" of a war against Nazi Germany. "My pacifism, as I imagine the pacifism of many others, is passing through a pitiless crisis," he wrote.[104] If Britain, America, or France were "dragged into a war," what should such a pacifist do? "I know I would pray with all my heart for the defeat of the Hitler inhumanity; and am I then to stand aside and let others do the fighting?" he asked.¹⁰⁵ Choosing a side on which to fight was a "choice of evils—a choice between the capitalism, the imperialism, the militarism of the Western democracies, and between the Hitler religion." But could Gandhi doubt which was "the lesser [evil] of these two?" Magnes maintained that while there was no such thing as a "righteous" war, there was such a thing as *"necessary* war"—"not *for* something good, but, because no other choice is left us," he wrote.¹⁰⁶

Finally, Buber and Magnes challenged Gandhi on his characterization of the Jewish-British relationship in Palestine and on his insistence that Palestine "belonged" solely to the Arabs. "We began to settle in the land anew, 35 years before the 'shadow of the British gun' was cast upon it," wrote Buber. "We did not seek out this shadow; it appeared and remained here to guard British interests and not ours," he continued.¹⁰⁷ It was wrong, maintained Buber, for Gandhi to condemn Jews for allowing "British bayonets to defend them against the bomb-throwers" and to mention only as an afterthought that he wished "the Arabs had chosen the way of non-violence."¹⁰⁸ As for ownership of the land, Buber and Magnes cited Palestine's long history of conquest—including by the Arabs. "The Jews, who became a people in Palestine and whose great classic, the basis of whose life, the Bible, was produced there, have never throughout all the centuries forgotten the land and ceased to yearn for it," wrote Magnes.¹⁰⁹ This point aside, Magnes, as well as Buber, maintained that peace between Jews and Arabs was vital to them and had been a central aim of their work. "By a genuine peace we inferred and still infer that both peoples should together develop the Land without the one imposing his will on the other," Buber wrote of his work with Brit Shalom. "We considered and still consider it our duty to understand and to honour the claim which is opposed to ours and to endeavor to reconcile both claims," he affirmed.¹¹⁰ Magnes explained how the policy of *havlagah*, much like satyagraha, had been practiced by most members of the Yishuv during the past years of unrest. He now asked Gandhi to help the Jews in Palestine "to convert the Arab heart," to win a lasting peace.¹¹¹ Alas, Buber and Magnes's letters likely never reached Gandhi. No response was issued in *Harijan* (as was often his practice), nor did Gandhi ever acknowledge the letters in his correspondence with Kallenbach.¹¹² It is possible that Pyarelal

Nayyar, one of Gandhi's secretaries, intercepted them; he later admitted to keeping some materials on Zionism from reaching the Indian leader.[113]

Other Jewish leaders, however, succeeded in engaging Gandhi. A. E. Shohet, the Jewish Agency representative in Bombay and a member of the Baghdadi Jewish community, published a rebuke in the *Jewish Advocate* in December 1938, in which he presented many of the same criticisms that Buber and Magnes would raise.[114] To compare Indians in South Africa to Jews in Germany was to ignore "inexorable facts," Shohet argued, citing the intensity of the violence in Germany and the differences between the Indian and Jewish diasporas and their respective homelands. "But it is when he takes up the question of Palestine that Mahatma Gandhi is stone-blind to the truth and reality of the situation," Shohet wrote. "[He] takes up the Jewish paradox and flings it in our face as though it were of our own making," Shohet continued. He accused Gandhi of unfair bias. "Why does [Gandhi] call upon Jews to adopt 'the nobler course' and 'vindicate their position on earth'?" he wrote. Why did he "judge [Jews] by a skyey, spiritual standard when he [judged] Arabs by the 'accepted' cannons [sic]?" Shohet argued that Gandhi's "pre-occupation with Britain" unfairly colored his assessment of the Jewish situation. "We would urge him to shed away all prejudices and look at the Jewish question in light of the Jewish achievements in Palestine and the needs and agonies of the Jewish people," he wrote.[115]

While Gandhi did not reply to Shohet in the pages of *Harijan*, Shohet was able to meet with Gandhi twice in 1939 with the help of Kallenbach, who determined he could no longer delay his return to India in the wake of Gandhi's statement. Kallenbach departed from South Africa just weeks before the St James's Palace Conference (discussed in the next chapter). The conference, set to open in London, had been called to examine the end of the mandate and to determine Palestine's fate. In a cable sent to Gandhi before his departure, Kallenbach implored his old friend to "appeal this conference not to debar my people from their only remaining permanent refuge home."[116] Soon after he arrived, Kallenbach contracted malaria and found himself confined to bed for most of the trip. While he was too ill to attend himself, he arranged a meeting between Shohet and Gandhi in February. Shohet reiterated the points of his *Jewish Advocate* article but left feeling resigned that the Jews could "not expect anything from Gandhi at all." In a report to the Political Department in Jerusalem, Shohet wrote that Gandhi "views the Palestinian question as a purely Moslem question. He is susceptible to the Moslem propaganda here. The Mandatory in his eyes is the same imperialistic power that pulls all the strings here; it is suspect." Holding fast to this assessment, Gandhi nevertheless suggested that Shohet and other Zionist representatives maintain contact and provide him with reading materials. "For my part," wrote Shohet, "I am going to treat very seriously his suggestion."[117]

The Political Department, too, took the suggestion seriously and decided to send Joseph Nedivi, the Tel Aviv municipal clerk who had planned to visit the Jewish community in Bombay, to join Shohet for another meeting with Gandhi. Kallenbach arranged the meeting for March 21, 1938, and this time was well enough to attend. Speaking "enthusiastically and eloquently," according to Shohet, Nedivi chose to insist forthrightly on the need for Jewish self-defense in Palestine rather than stress the ways that Jews had long embraced nonviolence. "Mr. Nedivi said that he might agree to be thrown into the Mediterranean himself to test the efficacy of non-violence with the Arabs," wrote Shohet in a letter to the Political Department, "but he could not allow this to happen to his daughter." Gandhi replied that Nedivi did not need to respond to the arguments of the *Harijan* article. "What was written was done and finished," Gandhi said, asking what he could "do more and in what way he could help." Nedivi responded that he wanted Gandhi's help to "bring Indian public opinion" to the side of the Yishuv. Shohet added to the plea: "We are an Eastern people . . . and we want to return to our ancient home in the East. India constitutes one-fifth of mankind and being [an] Eastern nation we need its opinion and its sympathy in our favour."[118] Gandhi responded that "he knew what [Shohet] was suggesting, but . . . it would not serve any useful purpose to us if he were to condemn the way in which propaganda was carried on among the Muslims of India."[119] Gandhi's reply confirmed for Shohet his initial impression—that the internal unity of India between Hindus and Muslims mattered first and foremost to Gandhi and that he would approach the Palestine question with that consideration.

Despite Kallenbach's intervention, Gandhi continued to hold fast to his November statement in *Harijan*. Ultimately, it was Henry Polak who finally elicited a reconsideration from the Indian leader. Polak's work with the Indian Overseas Association in London, dedicated to lobbying on behalf of Indian interests in the diaspora, often required close contact and cooperation with the British government. While some in the Colonial and Indian offices viewed Polak as a "persistent agitator," others considered him a "trusted advisor."[120] Indeed, Polak served on the imperial advisory committee of the British Labour Party during the 1920s and 1930s.[121] These experiences made him increasingly critical of Gandhi's tactics, particularly his policy of noncooperation.[122] When he read Gandhi's claim that Jews were not "truly non-violent" because "they called down upon the Germans the curses of mankind, and ... wanted America and England to fight Germany on their behalf," Polak felt compelled to write to his friend. "I can hardly doubt that you have been misreported, for there is nothing that could possibly justify such a statement," he wrote, "but as the paragraph much distressed me, I should be glad to receive from you a word of reassurance."[123] In a response in *Harijan* entitled "No Apology," Gandhi affirmed the veracity of his statement and pointed to Kallenbach's feelings about the Nazis as evidence:

> I happen to have a Jewish friend living with me. He has an intellectual belief in non-violence. But he says he cannot pray for Hitler. He is so full of anger over the German atrocities that he cannot speak of them with restraint. I do not quarrel with him over his anger. He wants to be non-violent, but the sufferings of fellow Jews are too much for him to bear. What is true of him is true of thousands of Jews who have no thought even of "loving the enemy." With them as with millions "revenge is sweet, to forgive is divine."[124]

The response infuriated Polak, who countered, "You shock me ... to use a favourite expression of your own, I asked for bread, and you have given me a stone."[125] He challenged Gandhi to corroborate his claim about Jewish demands for vengeance or else retract it. Polak sent Kallenbach a copy of the letter, explaining he felt justified in his rebuke of Gandhi since Polak himself had so openly and fiercely criticized the Jewish community when he believed it to have been complicit in injustice.[126]

Gandhi took Polak's impassioned challenge seriously and instructed his secretaries Pyarelal and Mahadev Desai to "produce support" for his claim. "It is not always an easy task to find support for impressions one carries when speaking or writing," Gandhi noted. Meanwhile, he received similar rebukes from Herbert Samuel and Philip Hartog.[127] Hartog, whose response was reproduced by Gandhi in *Harijan*, wrote that he had seen hundreds of German Jewish refugees since 1933 and had "never heard one of them express publicly or privately the desire for a war of vengeance against Germany." Such a war, explained Hartog, would "bring further misery to the hundreds of thousands of Jews still in Germany as well as untold suffering to millions of other innocent men and women."[128] After "[great] diligence," Pyarelal and Mahadev's search failed; they were unable "to lay hand on any conclusive writing." In an official retraction published in *Harijan* on May 27, 1939, Gandhi wrote, "I cannot lay my hands on anything on the strength of which I made the challenged observation. . . . I must withdraw it without any reservation. I only hope that my observation has not harmed any single Jew. I know that I incurred the wrath of many German friends for what I said in all good faith."[129] Far from a statement of support for the Jewish National Home, the retraction nevertheless disavowed a central aspect of Gandhi's thought that his Jewish critics found particularly insidious and cruel: that Jewish nonviolence in the face of German brutality could somehow serve as atonement for collective Jewish sin—for the sin committed against Germany by seeking out another homeland and for the sin committed against Palestinian Arabs by forging ties with the British Empire.

The Zionist movement's overtures to India in the 1930s presented variously as the strategic geopolitics of an emerging nation; as a people reconnecting to the eastern world of their genesis; and as two nations, poised to emerge from the shackles of imperialism, building new connections founded on that shared history. Yet with unrest in Palestine and a world war on the horizon, it was through these encounters with India that leaders and representatives of the Yishuv were forced to articulate—and even defend—their ties to Britain and British imperialism. The 1920s saw the efflorescence of Zionist engagement with Britain—and its culture, history, and politics—shaped largely out of the assumption that Britain's connection to Palestine would be an enduring one, though it was unclear in what precise form. By contrast, the 1930s saw the transformation of Zionist ideas about empire. Zionists no longer assumed that the empire would prevail in the face of ever more powerful anticolonial political movements. Although the Zionist movement had always understood itself to be a movement for national liberation, in the wake of British handling of the 1929 riots, Zionists increasingly framed British mandatory policy as directly opposing Jewish national aspirations. In this context, leaders of the Yishuv determined that healthy ties with India would prove essential to the future of the Jewish national home. A cohort of South African Jews emerged as uniquely qualified to serve as the mediators and advocates of this new relationship. Kallenbach and Polak—one a converted Zionist, the other a resolved non-Zionist—were both immersed in critiques of colonialism and believed in the promise of national independence. Yet it was through their interventions, and through the meetings and connections they facilitated, that the Zionist movement was forced to reckon with its relationship to Britain and ultimately—in the face of Nazism and impending war—to defend its alliance with the British Empire.

SIX

Realism, Refugees, and the British Horizons of War

"THE DEMOCRACIES HAD LITTLE CONSCIENCE but less faith.... The more difficult the task, the smaller their will to deal with it radically," Norman Bentwich wrote of the outcome of the Évian Conference, held in July 1938.[1] Initiated by President Roosevelt, the conference convened in the French spa town of Évian-les-Bains, on the shores of Lake Geneva, and aimed to address the mounting refugee crisis in Europe. Representatives from thirty-two countries gathered and heard testimony from dozens of independent organizations (most of them Jewish) but failed to come to any substantive agreement that would provide refuge to the growing number of Jews trying to flee Nazi persecution. Though the Jewish Agency and Zionist groups sent representatives, conference organizers resolved to exclude discussion of Palestine as a potential refuge, a decision Norman called "stultifying."[2]

Norman attended the conference as a representative of the Council for German Jewry, an organization launched in Britain in 1936 with the goal of assisting one hundred thousand Jewish emigrants from Germany in their settlement in "all parts of the world."[3] Herbert Samuel, the first high commissioner of Palestine and Helen Bentwich's uncle, joined as the council's first chairman. Samuel in turn enlisted Norman as director for emigration and training. Refugee and immigration work was not new to Norman; from 1933 to 1935, he had served as deputy high commissioner for the League of Nations High Commission for Refugees, working to coordinate the legal status and settlement of Jewish refugees, primarily in France and the Netherlands. But judging the "palpable decline" and ineffectiveness of the League in refugee relief—its efforts had become "more a symbol than a pivot of international interest"—Norman focused his energy elsewhere.[4] Since joining the Council for German Jewry, his work had taken him to Nazi Germany and Poland.[5] A week after the Anschluss, despite warnings from the British Foreign Office, Norman also went to Vienna to establish contacts with what remained of the Jewish leadership there. When he tried to return to the city weeks later, this time coming from Palestine, he was thrown off the night train from Trieste when it reached the Austrian border. German officers inspecting the train discovered that Norman's British passport had been issued in Jerusalem and identified him as a Jew. Forced to retreat back to Trieste and return to London, Norman was finally able to return to Vienna months later after British Foreign Office intervention.[6]

Following the failure at Évian, Norman's travels on behalf of refugees began to take him beyond Europe, specifically to farther reaches of the British Empire that he believed represented the best last hope for refuge. As this chapter will explore, in August 1938, he and Helen traveled to Australia, spending a month and a half there. Norman then journeyed to South Africa, accompanied by an old friend and colleague from Palestine, Wyndham Deedes, who was also involved in refugee relief efforts. In Johannesburg, the pair heard reports of Kristallnacht. When Norman returned to London at the end of November, he found that the "pace of the work of salvage" could not "counter the increase of the pace of persecution" faced by Jews under Nazi rule. "The altogetherness of everything overwhelmed us, and the forced march of time overtook our puny efforts," he wrote.[7] Both he and Helen shifted their focus to bringing as many Jewish refugees as possible to Britain itself; Norman focused on men of working age, while Helen led efforts to rescue children. She became one of the chief architects of the Kindertransport.

The effort to find a British imperial solution to the Jewish refugee crisis was for Norman a matter of political realism. The rate of Jewish immigration to Palestine had declined significantly since 1936, curtailed by the British in response to the Arab Revolt. This meant that while Palestine remained one of the few possible destinations for Jews fleeing Nazi persecution, far fewer Jews could actually obtain immigration certificates. The White Paper of 1939 confirmed and formalized this policy, limiting Jewish immigration and land purchases. Norman belonged to the cohort of Jews, among them both binationalist Zionists like himself and non-Zionists, who were willing to explore limiting Jewish immigration to Palestine *temporarily* as a gesture of goodwill amid the Arab Revolt. This same group, including Judah Magnes, had opposed the Peel Commission's recommendation of partition—and the Jewish Agency leadership's ultimate accordance on the matter—on the grounds that the creation of two separate states would irrevocably preclude the possibility of Jewish-Arab rapprochement. Just as Norman's "heresies about partition" had positioned him outside the bounds of Zionist orthodoxy, so, too, did his approach to the refugee crisis.[8] Norman believed that the only logical answer—with Palestine increasingly closed off and a revolt ongoing—was to seek alternative destinations for refugees. These "territorialist" solutions pursued by Norman in his work for the Council for German Jewry, as well as by other Jewish refugee and relief organizations, including the American Jewish Joint Distribution Committee, were often vigorously opposed by mainstream Zionist leaders.[9] The latter worried that territorialist solutions would come at the expense of Jewish immigration to Palestine, a major concern both leading up to the Évian Conference and in its wake. In a speech he made in December 1938, Ben-Gurion declared territorialism to be a greater threat than ever before, including "in the days of Uganda," recalling the 1903 scheme to create a Jewish homeland in British East Africa. What had once been a "fleeting episode" now represented a major threat, one coming from the world's great powers. "The British government has become territorialist, America is prone to territorialism. Everyone knows that the great disaster will not be alleviated by the loss of hundreds or thousands of refugees to England, Holland, Switzerland and other countries," Ben-Gurion declared.[10] Weizmann, for all his political differences with Ben-Gurion, was "more than a little troubled" by territorialist plans. Writing after Kristallnacht to the Belgian Jewish leader Herbert Speyer, Weizmann expressed his worry about one of the territorialist schemes proposed at Évian: Jewish refugee settlement in British Guiana.[11] The country was "entirely undeveloped" and would not be ready to absorb "substantial numbers" of refugees for many years. "These various other schemes for settlement in 'new'—undeveloped—countries are merely useless distractions of energy and funds from the one real prospect of prompt and permanent help, which is Palestine," Weizmann wrote.[12]

Like Ben-Gurion and Weizmann, Moshe Shertok, too, was avowedly "Palestinocentric" (to use his biographer Gabriel Sheffer's term) in his focus on the refugee crisis and in his Jewish worldview more broadly. But he had much more in common with Norman Bentwich than either might well have recognized. Unlike some of his more activist colleagues, including Ben-Gurion, Shertok insisted not only in the period leading up to the war but throughout the entire war itself that it was essential for the Zionist movement to maintain a close working relationship with the British government. As the highest ranking Zionist official in Palestine for much of the war (during Ben-Gurion's long absences), Shertok worked determinedly to create a Jewish brigade in the British Army, a dream finally realized in 1944. And as it became clear that the Allies would win the war and Zionist leaders began formulating policy for a postwar period, Shertok predicted that Britain above all other world powers, including America and the Soviet Union, would remain the most important center of gravity for the Yishuv; for that practical reason, Zionists needed to maintain productive relations with the country.

In other words, despite profound disagreements over questions of partition, polity, and the refugee crisis, Moshe Shertok and Norman Bentwich, as well as Helen Bentwich, shared important assumptions about and approaches to securing Jewish futures amid utter catastrophe. Both believed that Britain and the British Empire offered the most realistic, practical solutions to the crisis facing world Jewry. Critically, while Shertok and the Bentwiches approached their causes with remarkable indefatigability, all three felt deep anger, disillusionment, and cynicism toward the British government for its policy decisions (including inaction) leading up to and during the war.

Of course, it was Shertok who in 1936 had sent emissaries to India, recognizing the magnitude of the Indian independence movement (and by implication, the increasingly tenuous grasp Britain had on its prized colony) and the importance of counting leaders like Gandhi and Nehru as allies rather than foes. Shertok's efforts to safeguard Yishuv-British relations appear then at first glance to contradict the logic of his overtures to India. As the previous chapter argues, the circumstances of an impending war, with such clear-cut stakes and alliances, forced Jews—both Zionist and non-Zionist—to defend their relationship with the British Empire. In this way, Shertok's outreach to India and his commitment to protecting the Yishuv's relationship with Britain in fact reflected two sides of the same coin—both were motivated by a sober political realism, by an effort to navigate the unpredictable terrain of rising anticolonial movements on the one hand and rising fascism on the other. But Shertok's varied activities and commitments also reflected a coherent vision. The negativity and skepticism he felt toward Britain, even while insisting on the importance of maintaining a working relationship with the government, was often expressed using a vocabulary typical of a movement for national independence and liberation. As we will see, Shertok imagined Jews as British *allies* rather than subjects, and he loathed that Britain took Jewish loyalty for granted. In this sense, his outreach to both India and Britain reflected the anticipation of a postwar and potentially postcolonial world-to-come, but one in which Britain would still remain a central power.

This mindset—a vision of Jews in Palestine as British *allies*, as well as agents of their own political fates—reflected not just an aspiration, but shifting facts on the ground. Though the late 1930s heralded disaster for the Jewish people, it was not in fact a period when the Yishuv was weaker than it had been in the past. The Yishuv's economy continued to grow during the 1930s, withstanding the global depression and bolstered by the influx of capital from German Jewish immigrants. And though the Haganah's activities in the 1930s were at times circumscribed by the British, Jewish military might in Palestine ultimately grew as well, enhanced (and legalized) by the creation of British-trained Jewish police units during the Arab Revolt. In 1939, amid talks on the constitutional future of Palestine, Shertok would acknowledge the effect of this growing power, remarking, "Our power in Israel will not be enough to force Britain to establish a regime that we want, but it may be enough to prevent the establishment of a regime that we will fight against."[13] Zionists in Palestine thus confronted profound Jewish vulnerability and precarity in Europe while simultaneously making political calculations vis-à-vis the British and Arabs in Palestine that assumed a level of their own power and capability that they had not possessed in years past.

In following the paths of Moshe Shertok and other Jewish Agency officials, on the one hand, and the Bentwiches and other prominent Anglo-Jews involved in refugee work, on the other, this chapter also explores the ways in which Zionist and non-Zionist politics and tactics converged during the war years. It picks up the story begun in chapter 1 that examined how Jews with a range of orientations toward Zionism ended up working together in the wake of the August 1929 riots in Palestine. Norman's objection to partition effectively exiled him from mainstream Zionist society and while he considered himself to be a Zionist, his politics were, in fact, much closer to the non-Zionist camp in this period.[14] In November 1938, however, when Britain announced its abandonment of the partition scheme, deeming its earlier policy recommendation impracticable, the situation changed. With partition apparently removed as a point of contention and war seeming ever more likely, Zionists and non-Zionists were able to cooperate both to present a unified front to the world and for practicality's sake.

Two broad narratives have typically defined the story of Zionism and the Yishuv in the years leading up to and during World War II. The first is encapsulated in Ben-Gurion's famous axiom: that the Zionists would fight the war as if there were no white paper and fight the white paper as if there were no war. In its broad arc, this was true. For Zionists and Jews all over the world, there was patently no other option but to support the Allied war effort. As we saw in the previous chapter, this was the case even for seasoned pacifists like Judah Magnes. And at the same time, Zionist leaders across the political spectrum maintained vigorous opposition to the white paper's policy, continuing their efforts to resist and mitigate its impact through a range of tactics spanning from behind-the-scenes negotiations to illegal immigration to terrorism. The second and related narrative charts the Zionist turn from Britain to the United States as the new focus of the movement's diplomatic and philanthropic efforts, as hopes for Britain's continued stewardship and faith in its global preeminence dimmed.

Although this chapter does not reject these accounts, it argues that key Zionist leaders, chief among them Moshe Shertok, continued to invest deeply—though often with immense frustration—in British solutions not solely to the war effort but to the Yishuv's future *beyond* the war. In other words, for Shertok, winning the war did not mean an end to the Zionist-British partnership. Despite America's growing power in the Middle East, he maintained that Britain would remain the most important and relevant power for the Yishuv.

Finally, this chapter also builds on recent scholarship investigating twentieth-century Jewish political thought and action in the context of little hope and narrowing options, on the one hand, and the simultaneous convergence of political tactics and ideas across the Jewish political spectrum, on the other.[15] In particular, the chapter examines in detail Moshe Shertok's experience at the St James's Palace Conference in February and March 1939. Organized by the British to examine the question of Palestine's future constitutional arrangements, the prospect of ending the mandate, and the matter of Jewish immigration, the conference included a series of separate Jewish-British and Arab-British negotiations, as well as two tripartite meetings.[16] Often relegated to little more than a sentence or two in histories covering the mandate era, the entire conference is generally framed as a failure—significant only insofar as it was a prelude to the release of the white paper of 1939.[17] By contrast, this chapter examines the conference in depth and argues that Shertok's political thinking and maneuvering at the conference—a strategy of preserving what was left of an increasingly limited range of options coupled with a steadfast insistence on maintaining relations with Britain despite profound policy disagreement—set the terms for his political outlook for years to come. Shertok also found himself, much to his surprise, working in concert with non-Zionists, their mutual goals shaped by the exigencies of the time.

"THE END OF EVERYTHING WE'VE EVER LIVED OR STOOD FOR"

In late August 1938, after a twenty-three-day voyage, the Bentwiches reached Australia, where Norman was to attend the Commonwealth Relations Conference, an "unofficial" meeting organized by the independent Institutes of International Affairs, which had convened once previously in Toronto in 1933. Norman, in his role with the Council for German Jewry, also planned to use his time in Australia to meet with government officials and refugee organizations in an effort to "persuade them to enlarge the possibilities of immigration" after the disappointing outcome of the Évian conference.[18] Helen's calendar was likewise filled with speaking engagements, Jewish communal events, and meetings with Australian politicians.

Norman and Helen sailed on the P&O cruise line from Marseilles on a route that included stops in Aden and Bombay. Though the refugee crisis in Europe was at the forefront of his mind, Norman also saw trouble brewing in these more eastern stations of Jewish life. Alighting in Aden on Tisha B'Av, a Jewish fast day, Norman and Helen met with members of the Jewish community, many of whom had fled the region's hinterlands to find refuge in the port of Aden, under direct British control. Norman lamented that this "large Jewish community in an important British outpost" had been "almost utterly neglected by British Jewry."[19] He also reported "apprehension" among Aden's Jews over deteriorating relations with the local Arab population, attributed to the situation in Palestine. In Bombay, where the Bentwiches' ship was met by a group of Jewish refugees from Germany, Norman observed the jarring contrast between the poorer Bene Israel community, many of whom worked in the city's mills, and the Baghdadi elite, including members of the Sassoon family. The city's built environment—from the "splendour and luxury of the clubs and villas on Malabar Hill, [to] the industrial slums"—mirrored this stark class inequity on a larger scale. "A few hours' drive in Bombay was an instigation to Communism," wrote Norman of the brief visit.[20]

On arriving in Australia, the Bentwiches spent several days in Perth and Adelaide before flying to Sydney, where the conference opened on September 3, 1938. Many delegates were professors and other experts on international relations, law, and trade, drawn from Britain and from each of the self-governing dominions, including Ireland. A delegation from India also joined, "in anticipation of self-government."[21] While many delegates had served or would go on to serve in government, each attended the conference as a private individual. The trade unionist Ernest Bevin, who would later earn the enmity of the Zionist movement as British Foreign Secretary after World War II, called the conference "a very peculiar one." "It was the first I had ever attended," he quipped, "at which nobody had to come to a conclusion about anything."[22] In other words, while the pressing and contentious topics of foreign policy, defense, trade, and immigration were discussed, the "unofficial" status of the conference meant that no mandates or resolutions were passed. Speaking of the original 1933 conference in Toronto, the historian and international affairs expert Arnold Toynbee explained that the intention was rather to produce a "friendly as well as frank" discussion, though not one "without effect."[23]

But the spirit of intellectual exchange and imperial amity was dampened, as Norman put it, by "the clouds in Europe . . . rolling up fast in the thunderstorm over Czechoslovakia."[24] Six days before the conference began, Hitler mobilized 750,000 troops along the border with Czechoslovakia. On September 13, in Australia, the day before the country learned of Chamberlain's intentions to meet with Hitler, Helen pondered that in this remote stretch of the British Empire, with the specter of Czechoslovakia "unutterably far away," denial of the situation came all too easily. "I have to *think* here, & use my *intellect*, to reach a point of view which instinct & feeling would give me at home," she wrote. "I feel convinced there *will* be no war. But that Hitler will play his game of keeping us in suspence for months, & then make a behind-the-scenes bargain, & a public gesture for peace, & we'll agree to him having a hunk of Czechoslovakia before the People know what has happened."[25]

Helen's prediction of appeasement and annexation proved accurate in all but the timeline. Only two days later, while the Commonwealth Relations Conference convened, Chamberlain flew to Germany to meet with Hitler in an effort to maintain the policy of appeasement. Norman reflected that the fast-shifting situation in Europe rendered much of what had been planned for the conference moot. "The studies so carefully prepared about foreign policy of the Commonwealth and common economic measures were suddenly deprived of their seriousness," he wrote, concluding grimly, "We were riding on the rim of the abyss."[26]

Discussions on immigration—both the question of Jewish refugee emigration from Nazi Europe and immigration to the Commonwealth countries from British India—dismayed the Bentwiches. Immigration to Australia, including Jewish emigration from Europe, had slowed to a trickle since the stock market crash in 1929. And long before domestic economic woes brought on by the depression, the White Australia policy, the discriminatory laws designed to bar non-European immigrants from the continent, effectively banned emigration from British India alongside other Asian countries. In South Africa, which also had a delegation attending the conference, the government promoted Indian repatriation and imposed restrictive laws that barred most emigration from the entire Asian continent.

The Indian delegation to the conference, led by H. N. Kunzru, voiced resolute opposition to the policies barring Indian immigration to the Commonwealth. Kunzru, a moderate liberal nationalist who had studied at the London School of Economics, had met the Bentwiches on the ship to Australia.[27] In his 1941 memoir, Norman recalled Kunzru as an "invincible dialectician" who skillfully voiced the "burning grievance" over "the inequality of Indians in the [Commonwealth] family." While Norman agreed that this "utter discrimination . . . could not be defended on any ethical or equitable ground," he differed with Kunzru and his fellow delegates on other matters. Members of the Indian delegation (which included another Hindu and two Muslims) voiced many of the same criticisms of Zionism and Jewish presence in Palestine that Moshe Shertok had first sought to counter in India two years earlier. "In their eyes," Norman wrote, "the Jews coming to Palestine represent another Western aggression on the Orient."[28] Reflecting on the discussions around immigration that she observed at the conference, Helen wrote in her diary that many delegates were "pretty offensive in their remarks about 'coloured people', & don't at all condone to unity of the British Empire & the Commonwealth." But unlike Norman, she registered no concern over Kunzru's stance on Zionism and, in fact, *compared* him to Zionists. "Kunzru is great," she wrote, "but in some ways too much of an idealist & 'movement-man' for a Conference of this nature." He was "rather like the too-ardent Zionists over the Refugee problem," she declared, referring to those in the movement—including the bulk of the Yishuv's Labor Zionist leadership—who insisted that *Palestine*, rather than any other territory, serve as the solution to the Jewish refugee crisis.[29]

Helen may have been inclined to identify Zionists with an overzealous disposition—echoing her grumblings of nearly two decades earlier—but on the question of refugees, she, too, felt profound outrage. Following a Jewish communal event in Perth, where both Bentwiches gave speeches, Helen bemoaned in her diary what she saw as "smugness & lack of understanding of [the] real Jewish world-problem."[30] Beyond the Jewish community, Helen likewise observed widespread resistance among the politicians she met to the prospect of increasing immigration and "a sort of dog-in-manger attitude to the rest of the world."[31] While the Bentwiches might have expected to find like-minded thinkers in the Australian Labor Party, the opposite proved true. In a meeting in Perth with the Western Australian premier John Willcock and other members of his Labor government to discuss the prospect of refugee group settlement, Norman reported little enthusiasm for the idea. Though he thought the western part of the continent "[cried] out for wholesale immigration," Norman encountered a "steadfastly Conservative" and "isolationist" outlook among the Labor leaders. Norman found it telling that the Australian Fairbridge Farm School, an immigrant youth settlement in the western town of Pinjarra, had trained only a few hundred English children, whereas the Youth Aliyah organization had settled eight thousand children in Palestine since 1933.[32]

On the other side of the country, in Canberra, the Bentwiches encountered similar attitudes toward refugees and immigration. Helen referred to the Australian capital as "the planned city of the future, without the planned population to fill it." Founded in 1913 as a compromise in the contest between the cities of Sydney and Melbourne over where to establish the capital, Canberra had a population of only approximately ten thousand—a fraction of Australia's other major urban centers. In a conversation held in the capital with the senator for Queensland Joe Collings, who had immigrated to Australia from Brighton in his youth with his unemployed father and large family, Helen was quick to point out the politician's hypocrisy. "I emphasized that his present policy would have kept out him & his father," she wrote in her diary. Collings agreed but argued that socialism just needed to be "accomplished"—a three-year project by his account—and then Australia would be self-sufficient and could accommodate more immigrants. Helen found his views "all very reactionary & deplorable."[33]

As the Bentwiches' visit to Australia stretched through September, each report from Europe amplified their frustration over the refugee question and their anger over Chamberlain's negotiations with Hitler. While appeasement remained popular with much of the British public, Labour leaders in Britain increasingly spoke out against Chamberlain's policy and began advocating for rearmament. The Australian Labor Party, for the most part, did not follow this metropolitan example. Following a meeting on September 22 with John Curtin, leader of the Labor opposition who would go on to serve as prime minister from 1941 to 1945, Helen condemned the politician's attitudes as "limited, insular, self-sufficient, & utterly false." Curtain argued that "Chamberlain was doing the only right thing" and—as Helen bitterly summed up his attitude—that "peace at any price was better than war," and while "platonically Labour here is sorry for the Czech workers, they are not worth fighting for." More broadly, Helen identified a shifting attitude toward Britain and the empire as a whole, one that ran counter to interwar discourse on dominionization (including in Palestine) that stressed the political and economic value of imperial belonging. According to Helen, Australian Labor's connection to Britain was based on "race & kinship"—not on a commitment to empire-wide economic, legal, military, and diplomatic cooperation. "They have nothing fundamentally in common with the international outlook of the British Labour Party—but more in common with the die-hard Tories who want a white Australia policy," wrote Helen.[34]

On the same day Helen met with Curtin, Chamberlain attended his second meeting with Hitler in Bad Godesberg. When no solution to the Czechoslovakian crisis was reached—Hitler demanded the evacuation of ethnic Czechs from German-majority territory, which the Czechoslovakian government rejected—it seemed war was imminent. Czechoslovakia mobilized its army on September 23. France followed suit with a partial mobilization the next day. The prospect of war made Helen think anxiously back to 1916, when, just a year into her marriage, she had left Norman in Cairo, not to see him again for three years. This time around, Helen longed to return to her work with the London County Council, to which she had been elected the previous year, but knew Norman wanted to be back in Palestine. "Feel naturally depressed all the time about this war business. . . . I'm very depressed about the thought of the separation, too," she wrote, continuing, "I feel less able to stand up to it now than 20 years ago. It all seems so much the end of everything we've ever lived or stood for."[35]

War, however, was forestalled. Australia's evening papers on Friday, September 30, trumpeted the news of the agreement that had been reached in the early hours of that morning in Munich between Germany, Britain, France, and Italy. "Well, Chamberlain has sold the pass, & there is Peace with Honour. The dirty bastard.... Fascism will creep in. God damn Chamberlain!" Helen penned in the wake of the news.[36] "We unmade and remade plans for the return journey, having decided that first war was not to be averted, and then with shame realizing that it had been averted ignobly," wrote Norman.[37]

No immediate hostilities meant the Bentwiches could continue their travel as planned; the annexation of the Sudetenland by the Nazis meant that their work on behalf of refugees was all the more pressing. The couple left Australia in a westbound flying boat in the second week of October, making stops across Asia and the Middle East, including a landing on the Sea of Galilee on October 20. As their flying boat circled over the northern half of Palestine, the Bentwiches took in the familiar landscape below. To the west, in Zichron Ya'akov, they could see Carmel Court, the Bentwich family's grand estate nestled amid pine and olive trees. To the east, Pinhas Rutenberg's hydroelectric powerhouse—"a little white speck" from such a great height—glinted in the sun on the banks of the Jordan River.[38] The country appeared "so calm & peaceful."[39]

But distance masked a smoldering reality. In the wake of the Peel Commission's formal recommendation of partition in July 1937, the Arab Revolt—suppressed by the British since the fall of 1936—experienced a resurgence marked by violent armed resistance. Beginning in the Galilee and the Triangle and later spreading to the countryside around Hebron and Jerusalem, the uprising reached its height in the summer and fall of 1938. Rebels—primarily Palestinian peasants and tenant farmers but also members of the urban middle and working classes—seized control of several urban spaces, including the Old City of Jerusalem. In Tiberias, where the Bentwiches spent their brief layover in Palestine, Palestinian rioters had attacked a Jewish neighborhood, killing nineteen Jews, including eleven children, earlier that month. The Irgun had likewise increased its attacks on Palestinians during the summer of 1938, including bombings in Haifa in July that killed more than sixty Palestinians and a bombing attack in Jaffa in August that killed twenty-four Palestinians.

After the Bentwiches' flying boat landed and taxied to Tiberias, Norman attempted without success to phone his brother Joseph in Jerusalem. Though British troops—reinforced by new arrivals no longer on standby for war in Europe—had reestablished control in the Old City days earlier, civilian communication lines were still disrupted. There was, as Helen wrote in her diary, a "regular war" happening.[40] Following lunch, the Bentwiches reboarded their flying boat for the final leg of their journey together, landing in Alexandria later that afternoon. That evening, the Bentwiches met their old friend Wyndham Deedes, who had flown in from England. Together, Deedes and Norman planned to continue onward to South Africa on behalf of the Council for German Jewry, while Helen would return alone to London. The following month, in the wake of Kristallnacht, she would help spearhead what would become the Kindertransport.

THE ST JAMES'S PALACE CONFERENCE

When his wake-up call rang at eight o'clock on the morning of February 7, 1939, Moshe Shertok could not bear to rouse himself from his hotel bed in London.[41] The St James's Palace Conference was set to begin in mere hours, and the past week had been filled with long days and late nights of intense, final preparation. Delegations arriving from abroad were greeted, interviews with the press were given, "informal" meetings were held, and conference speeches were crafted, debated, and revised—and revised again. The Jewish delegation included not only Zionists from Britain, Palestine, America, and other reaches of the Jewish world but also non-Zionists of various backgrounds, ranging from the Agudat Yisrael leader Moshe Blau to the prominent Anglo-Jewish oil magnate Walter Samuel, 2nd Viscount Bearsted. Notably absent were the Revisionist Zionists, who had seceded from the Zionist Organization in 1935 and who viewed the conference as a foregone conclusion in favor of the Arabs, ridiculing the idea that anything might be gained at this stage through talks. Writing in the Revisionist paper *Ha-Mashkif*, the journalist Yosef Netz remarked that "on the Jewish side there is astounding unity among all the delegations, from Agudat Yisrael to Hashomer Hatzair. For the burial of Zionism, all of them were united."[42]

On the matter of unity, Moshe Shertok would likely have begged to differ. In the months and days leading up to the conference, those in the upper ranks of the Zionist Organization and Jewish Agency continued to disagree over strategy and goals. Even participation in the conference itself proved controversial—not only among Revisionists—especially after the British refused to admit ten thousand Jewish children to Palestine in the wake of Kristallnacht.[43] Ben-Gurion, in particular, had come to favor approaches—including noncooperation, illegal immigration, and even potentially a revolt against the British in Palestine—that might ultimately compel the government to reverse its restrictive immigration policies.[44] Even among those with a less-activist stance, opinions on the most effective tactics to use with the British varied considerably. The American rabbi and Zionist leader Stephen Wise, for instance, announced on arriving in London that he had figured out a "surefire solution" for making the Zionist case: the Jewish delegation would simply remind the British that they were legally bound by the terms of the Balfour Declaration and the Mandate. "It was hard to believe that he really thought that this winning argument would panic the government," wrote Shertok in his diary. The head of the Political Department explained to Wise that "legal reasoning alone" was insufficient to solve what was, in fact, a *political* problem.[45]

In contrast to Ben-Gurion, Shertok (and ultimately most other members of the Jewish Agency) approached the conference convinced that noncooperation with the British might in the short term assuage the Zionists' "wounded feelings" but would ultimately "harm [their] true interests."[46] But Shertok was far from hopeful about the outcome of the conference. His attitude was, in fact, simultaneously marked by a clearheaded political realism and a firm skepticism. As we will see, Shertok's insistence on cooperation with the British during the conference was informed by his understanding that Jewish Agency officials and Yishuv leaders would have to communicate with the British regardless of their participation in the conference or its outcome. As the war progressed, Shertok's dogged efforts to create a Jewish brigade in the British Army were motivated by real security concerns as Rommel's forces advanced in North Africa; later, when an Allied victory was in sight, Shertok saw the creation of a Jewish brigade in the British Army that could fight on the European front and save the remnants of European Jewry as a Zionist imperative. But critically, these efforts—to keep lines of communication open, to create a Jewish brigade—were accompanied for Shertok by profound skepticism and a conviction that British policy ran contrary to

Zionist aims and that trying to change the fundamental underpinnings of that policy was a futile cause.

After sleeping for another hour, Shertok finally managed to drag himself out of bed. Pandemonium quickly ensued. The telephone started ringing: Ben-Gurion, calling from his own hotel room, wanted to know if Yitzhak Ben-Zvi and Benzion Mossinson had arrived.[47] Shertok had no idea; he would check with the office of the London Executive of the Jewish Agency. Moments later, as if summoned, the office called. Arthur Lourie, secretary of the Jewish Agency's Political Department in London, wanted to know the same thing: Had Shertok seen the two Zionist leaders? Their connecting flight from Rome was supposed to have arrived, but the office had no knowledge of the men's whereabouts. Ben-Zvi, chairman of the Va'ad Leumi (the Jewish National Council) since 1931, was one of three Zionists, along with Weizmann and Wise, scheduled to speak that day at the conference. And he was the only one set to deliver his address in Hebrew, an act of symbolic importance. "Who would speak in Hebrew if Ben-Zvi were late?" worried Shertok.[48]

The phone rang once again: Ben-Gurion had found the wayward Zionists; they had arrived at the hotel. Tending to a very different matter of symbolic importance, Shertok immediately went to check on the two men and their attire. The bespectacled Ben-Zvi had dressed well enough but had neglected to wear a tie—Shertok produced one for him. Mossinson, who sported an impressive Herzlesque beard, emerged from Shertok's sartorial scrutiny with "more success"; not only had he worn a tie, but a fashionable one.[49] Shertok himself had spent the previous evening with Arthur Lourie obtaining a rental suit since his own formalwear—then somewhere in transit between Palestine and Britain—had yet to materialize.[50] Shertok's anxiety over conference appearance, specifically when it came to the more casually inclined delegates from Palestine, was not unfounded. Berl Katznelson, for example, insisted on wearing his own worn black suit rather than the traditional long-tailed morning coats that British etiquette demanded for such occasions. That choice, however, reflected more than a cultural sensibility. "The outcome which the Government is preparing for us does not justify my dressing more elegantly in its honor," Katznelson wrote in a letter to his partner Leah Miron.[51] The London-based doctor Ben-Zion Kunin, who saw to the medical needs of the Jewish delegates during their time in the city, managed to convince Katznelson at the very least to pair the old suit with a stiff-collared white shirt. "So I can show my face in society," Katznelson quipped.[52]

The entire question of dress at the conference—from Shertok's desire to enforce the boundaries of British sartorial respectability to Katznelson's insistence on transgressing them—reflected a long-standing tension for Zionists that likewise concerned nationalist movements across the British Empire. To what extent should these movements express their political and cultural ideals through "an idiom of British and imperial citizenship"?[53] That question could play out in the realm of political alliances and ideological content—as had been the case with Arlosoroff's overtures to British Labourites in the late 1920s—but it also, and no less consequentially, could inform cultural cues and expectations around dress and decorum more broadly. British-educated imperial elites, like Shertok, possessed a deep familiarity with British culture and its material trappings. Shertok understood well the stakes of respectability in this moment—that, despite grim expectations for the talks, the way the Jewish delegation presented itself to the British and was, in turn, depicted by the press, could have real consequences. Yet Shertok's knowledge of British cultural norms did not reflect affinity or unbridled admiration. On the contrary, his savoir-faire when it came to British culture was matched by a resigned frustration over the need to observe its norms. That attitude mirrored Shertok's broader conviction that continued cooperation with the British—even in the likely event of a poor conference outcome—was the only option.

Once Shertok was confident that his fellow delegates were satisfactorily outfitted in a manner befitting a British imperial round table conference, he departed the hotel for the Jewish Agency's London office at 77 Great Russell Street, located a block from the British Museum in the heart of Bloomsbury.[54] There, he found Weizmann's personal secretary, Doris May, looking "awake and fresh" despite having worked until 4:30 in the morning. May presented Shertok with the final version of Weizmann's speech, and Shertok, in turn, dictated an English translation of Ben-Zvi's address for May. Then, after changing into his rented formal attire—including the requisite top hat—Shertok, accompanied by Arthur Lourie, made the short mile and a half drive to St James's Palace for the opening day of the conference.[55]

The first day, during which the British met separately with the Jewish and Arab delegations, consisted of press photos and formal opening remarks rather than substantive negotiations. Though Colonial Secretary Malcolm MacDonald (1901–81)—son of the former prime minister Ramsay MacDonald—would lead all subsequent meetings, Chamberlain served as chair of the conference's first gathering. Shertok found the prime minister's speech "typical" in its "English simplicity, as if he were conversing innocently"; by contrast, Weizmann—"our great Jew," wrote Shertok in his diary—"spoke his words quietly and with inner confidence . . . a proud, restrained, and firm stand." When Ben-Zvi rose and delivered his address in Hebrew, Shertok imagined "all the generations of kings of England," whose portraits adorned the walls of the conference hall, "amazed at the meaning of the strange language." Wise spoke next. Shertok had been skeptical when reading a draft of the rabbi's speech, worried about the "stiff American style and the exaggerated and cumbersome formulas." But in the actual delivery, Wise's "voice made up for everything."[56]

FIGURE 6 The Jewish delegation at the St. James' Palace Conference in London in February 1939. Moshe Shertok is seated in the front row (second from right). Courtesy of the Moshe Sharett Heritage Society.

Shertok was least charitable to the Jewish delegation's final speaker, Gerald Isaacs, 2nd Marquess of Reading, whom Weizmann added to the roster of presenters at the last minute, much to Shertok's chagrin.[57] Along with Lord Bearsted, Isaacs was one of two members of the Jewish delegation who was also a British peer (in his diary, Shertok referred to the two men collectively as "the lords"). Gerald Isaacs was the son of the late Rufus Isaacs, who had been Viceroy of India during the 1920s and had taken a keen interest in Jewish development in Palestine, serving as board chairman of Pinchas Rutenberg's Palestine Electric Corporation. The younger Isaacs's wife, Eva Isaacs, was likewise deeply interested in the advancement of the Jewish national home. As we saw in chapter 2, she had befriended and earned the admiration of Chaim Arlosoroff during a trip to Palestine in 1932. The two had discussed the help Eva Isaacs's father-in-law could provide the Zionist movement in light of the "constitutional changes that might arise in the near future," and Arlosoroff had called her a "brave soldier of the movement."[58] Gerald Isaacs, who had inherited the marquessate in 1935 on his father's death, also interested himself in developments in Palestine, though officially from the standpoint of a non-Zionist, a position typical of the Anglo-Jewish elite by the 1930s.[59] At the Twentieth Zionist Congress in the summer of 1937, for example, Isaacs was appointed as one of six non-Zionists to a newly formed London-based Jewish Agency Political Advisory Committee, a group launched as part of broader conciliatory efforts—in which Norman Bentwich played a key role—to avoid a non-Zionist exodus from the Jewish Agency and to come to a consensus on the question of partition and its implications for Jewish-Arab cooperation.[60] But Isaacs had earned the enmity of Zionist leaders in November 1937 when he, along with other prominent non-Zionist Anglo-Jews, had sent a memorandum to the Foreign Office formally opposing the prospect of partition and Jewish statehood. Like Norman Bentwich, Isaacs had concluded that partition and statehood would preclude the possibility of Jewish-Arab rapprochement.[61] Weizmann at the time had excoriated the memorandum's authors as "assimilationist Jews," who wanted to "try for peace with the Arabs while they are killing us."[62] In the intervening period leading up to the 1939 conference, as the Jewish situation in Europe continued to deteriorate, Isaacs became a leader of refugee work in Britain, operating in the same organizational circles as the Bentwiches. When it came time to put together the Jewish delegation for the St James's Palace Conference, with the prospect of partition ostensibly abandoned by the British, Jewish Agency leaders determined that presenting a united Jewish front—however acrimonious behind-the-scenes disagreements were—was essential. Of course, the benefit of counting among their ranks the only Jewish marquess in Britain also had tremendous strategic value.

Nevertheless, Shertok still bristled as Isaacs gave his opening remarks for which he had been allotted just one minute—"and he did not exceed it," noted Shertok. "But in one minute he managed to emphasize three times that he and his friends are not of one mind with us [the Zionists], yet even so, they are ready to help with a solution that is 'just for the Jews, fair for the Arabs and befitting the British Empire,'" wrote Shertok. He saw the non-Zionist's statement as a "completely unnecessary performance" that detracted from the sense of unity and expression of resistance that the first three speeches had aimed to cultivate.[63] Yet as the conference dragged on and the prospect of avoiding a damaging outcome seemed more and more remote to members of the Jewish delegation, Shertok would come to revise his initially negative outlook on Isaacs.

With the first meeting concluded, Shertok maintained that the Jewish delegation had no choice but to continue with talks, despite his skepticism over the outcome of the conference and his frustration with the pomp and circumstance the occasion demanded. That evening, Shertok asked Ben-Zvi, who had initially objected to Jewish participation in the conference, if he still believed that it would have been better to have boycotted the meeting. Ben-Zvi conceded that the only thing to do at this point was to continue the talks, but he still insisted that a boycott should have been implemented months ago. Envisioning that scenario, Shertok imagined that the British press—he had just carefully reviewed the evening papers' coverage of the opening day—might have published the headline "Jews Sulk in Their Homes." In his assessment, boycotting the talks, months ago or now, was an ineffective way for the Zionists to manage their relationship with the British, who still would have met unilaterally with the Arabs had the Jews announced a boycott. A boycott also would not have caused the British government to reverse its decision against admitting ten thousand Jewish refugee children to Palestine, Shertok reasoned. In other words, alongside his cynicism and frustration, Shertok believed that Zionists had much more to lose by ceasing communication with the British than by continuing it.

Over the next several weeks, members of the Jewish delegation met more than a dozen times with the British and twice in tripartite meetings with both the British and Arabs. These meetings covered a range of contentious topics, chief among them the question of Palestine's political future and the issue of continued Jewish immigration: What kind of polity would Palestine be? A single, independent state? A federation? Would there be parity in the government? Would Jews be a minority in a Palestinian Arab state? And who would get to determine how many Jews could immigrate to Palestine? Amid all of these questions loomed two major considerations: the ever-expanding Jewish refugee crisis in Europe and Britain's ability to fight a potential war that would likely require the support (or at the very least, the neutrality) of Arabs and Muslims from across the Empire.

Thus, the delicate balance of British imperial amity and loyalty, specifically amid the potential for war, emerged as a central theme in the negotiations. Shertok and other members of the Jewish delegation approached the negotiations at St James's Palace with an awareness that the Zionist movement and the Yishuv were part of a broader imperial dynamic. This, of course, was not a new realization; for example, Frederick Kisch, the first head of the Jewish Agency's Political Department, had criticized the impulse he perceived among some Zionists to antagonize the British: "I am very far from satisfied with the attitude of the Government and many of its acts, but I am a realist enough to appreciate that no Government can treat Palestine as if it were an island of interest only to Jews. The growth of Arab nationalism, the Pan-Islamic movement..., the variable Indian situation... are among a few of the factors which any great Power or group of Powers dealing with the destiny of the Jewish National Home will necessarily take into consideration."[64] Kisch's successor, Chaim Arlosoroff, as we have seen, likewise recognized this broader imperial calculus, identifying it as the reason, for example, that British authorities refused to stop the World Islamic Congress from convening in Jerusalem in December 1931. Shertok, like his predecessors, recognized this pattern of thought among British leaders, but he considered its current application a miscalculation in two somewhat contradictory ways.

First, Shertok believed that the British were now placing *too* much emphasis on the role that Palestine and its Jewish community played in the political decision-making of the Arab and Muslim world; that is, the British grossly overestimated how central the Yishuv and its fate were in determining the loyalty and cooperation of Arab countries and Muslims across the empire. At the meeting between the Jewish delegation and the British on February 14, Malcolm MacDonald explained that the security of the empire depended on Arab countries, where the British relied on access to the Suez Canal, important airways, the naval base in Alexandria, and, of course, oil. "The spite that [Arab countries] have in their hearts towards Britain on account of the Land of Israel might spell calamity on the day of reckoning," he argued. What was more, MacDonald told the Jewish delegation, anger over the Yishuv extended well beyond the immediate neighborhood, spanning "westward across North African countries and eastward across India." The Land of Israel was, in short, the empire's "Achilles heel."[65]

Shertok thought that this interpretation failed on three accounts: it inflated the geographic scope of the impact of the Palestine situation; it falsely placed the Yishuv at the center of imperial balance; and it exaggerated the danger that continued growth of the Yishuv posed to imperial amity. These conclusions somewhat belied Shertok's own outreach efforts in India in the preceding years. Then, he had recognized that Palestine could become a powerful rallying cry thousands of miles away and sought to counter anti-Zionist sentiment among Indian independence leaders. But the global situation had changed, and Shertok reasoned that decisions about whether to oppose the British Empire now held quite different consequences. Weizmann and Ben-Gurion agreed. "Egypt knows it must be loyal to Britain or it will fall into the clutches of the enemy," Weizmann declared at the meeting, adding that "the same is true for Iraq." Ben-Gurion likewise stressed the "optical error" in MacDonald's logic. "Certainly Arab countries are pressuring Britain regarding the Land of Israel," he said, "but that does not determine their position in the event of war."[66] At a later meeting, Ben-Gurion similarly argued that framing Arab countries at once as "endangering the position of the British Empire" and "in fear of the Jews of the Land of Israel" seemed like a contradiction. "Can that be true? These huge countries, which are threatening the security of the British Empire, will they themselves fear the Jewish Yishuv in Palestine?" he asked.⁶⁷

At the February 14 meeting, MacDonald countered these claims with reasoning Shertok would have found familiar. "Objective interest" might dictate Arab states' ties to Britain, MacDonald claimed, but the Arab *public* did not always abide by that logic, instead turning to "popular slogans" where the Palestine issue featured prominently. Shertok responded that support for the British Empire and anger toward the Yishuv might exist side by side, noting that in the weeks leading up to the Munich Agreement, the Egyptian press was simultaneously "full of oaths of allegiance to Britain" and attacks on the Yishuv.⁶⁸

Second, and alongside his argument that the British exaggerated the centrality of the Yishuv in determining Arab and Muslim political loyalties, Shertok simultaneously believed that the British *underestimated* the Yishuv's actual and potential power, especially its military capability. Ruminating on MacDonald's assessment of imperial loyalty in the event of war, Shertok thought that it was as if "we ourselves, as a positive factor of security, do not exist." He argued that if there were concerns about Arab loyalty, the British should consider "the military support that the Jewish Land of Israel could provide . . . even as a reserve for Arab support and perhaps as an alternative." Shertok outlined some of the tactical advantages of this plan: Palestine's ideal position between the Red Sea and Persian Gulf, its relative proximity to Italy's airfields, its "great industrial possibilities," and "last but not least, the great reserves of dedication and self-sacrifice" in the Jewish community. "If there is anything certain in this mad and changing world, on which it is possible to base policy, it is the loyalty of Jews—not the loyalty of subjects, but of allies," he declared.⁶⁹

This final statement, in distinguishing between subject and ally, reflected a departure from earlier interwar political visions that saw the Yishuv remaining part of the British Empire perhaps, as Arlosoroff had once imagined, as a dominion. Zionist hopes for the Yishuv's future had, after all, changed considerably by the early spring of 1939. By that point, the Zionist leadership of the Jewish Agency had already quietly accepted, then campaigned for ardently, and then ostensibly lost the prospect of national independence under the Peel Commission's partition plan. Negotiations over Palestine's future polity (or polities) during the St James's Palace Conference operated under the assumption of some kind of continued relationship with Britain but not necessarily in the imperial mold. Critically, for Shertok, the framing of Jews as British allies did not just mean a rejection of imperial models of subjecthood or the compelled loyalty of the ruled; it also entailed a continued working relationship with Britain. In this vision, the Yishuv remained wrapped up in the workings of the British Empire, even as political hopes shifted from autonomy to sovereignty, from subject to ally.

Responding to Shertok, MacDonald assured him that the British government "did not discount the reserve of human power and the technical industrial prowess of the Yishuv." What was more, the government was also "sure of the [Yishuv's] loyalty." But that certainty, MacDonald admitted openly, meant that Britain could make decisions that Zionists might oppose because "the Jews have no other choice" but to support Britain. MacDonald continued to speak frankly, explaining that were the government forced to choose between Jews and Arabs, it would choose the Arabs "without any hesitation . . . because as important as the support of the Jews is, it cannot make up for the loss of support of the Arabs." But fortunately, concluded MacDonald, Britain was not yet "faced with such a choice."[70]

If the Jewish delegation found this candid statement surprising not so much in its content but in the admission itself, the next declaration from the British side proved even more distressing. The British foreign secretary Edward Wood, 1st Earl of Halifax, had thus far remained quiet but finally spoke as the meeting came to a close. Shertok observed that the earl possessed a style of speech that seemed to indicate a "lofty idealism" but that such an impression quickly faded as soon as he took in what the man was actually saying. "He ended by calling us to resolve the matter of conflict between moral rights and the needs of the government by voluntarily giving up, out of generosity, our rights," wrote Shertok of Halifax. He continued: "it could be interpreted that since the fate of the Jewish people depends on Britain's victory over Hitlerism, it is the duty of the Jews toward themselves to help in [the country's] victory by unloading any unnecessary burden from it."[71]

That "unnecessary burden" was understood by all present to mean continued Jewish immigration to Palestine. The Jewish delegation—which had no intention of voluntarily offering such a concession as Halifax suggested—

was braced for the possibility that the British would decide to continue limiting Jewish immigration to Palestine after the conference. But it came as a complete surprise when the British indicated that Palestinian Arabs might be given a veto on further Jewish immigration after a certain period. "When we entered negotiations, I was certain that I was prepared for the worst possibility," wrote Shertok. "I realized I was wrong. It did not occur to me that a proposal for a complete Arab veto on aliyah might occur. We are fated to remain a minority," he lamented.[72]

That prospect, which the Jewish delegation rejected as a basis for negotiation, was bound up not only in the immigration question but the polity question. During the conference, the British floated the idea of several different constitutional and political arrangements, including federation and parity, arguing that provisions could be made that would protect the Jews even if their numbers made them a minority. "A numerical minority does not necessarily mean a minority in terms of status," MacDonald stated, attempting to reassure the Jewish delegation at their meeting on February 15. There were options, he explained, for "parity in the constitution, or increased representation of the minority, as is the case for Muslims in India." But what was more, MacDonald continued, "a Jewish minority in an Arab country is one matter, but let's say that there is no Arab state, then that's a completely different matter." And even if an independent state were to come to pass, "it is possible that the polity would be built on parity," he said. These more palatable options, MacDonald argued, would only be possible if a compromise—through suspending or limiting Jewish immigration in the present—were to be reached.[73]

Jewish delegates thought seriously about the prospect of these various political options, even though they would later deride Britain's ultimate decision that it would grant independence to Palestine within ten years (thus by default creating a Palestinian Arab majority state with Jews as a minority) as having been a foregone conclusion all along. But during negotiations, MacDonald and other British leaders continued to insist not only that parity, federation, and other arrangements were legitimate potential options but that it was impossible to know what would happen down the line, in five or ten years after an interim period. MacDonald even went so far as to suggest that "after a certain period of time, the issue of partition would surely fade and then the Jewish minority would be able to gain independence."[74]

More immediately, it was similarly impossible to know where the world would be in just six months. At a private meeting at Downing Street on February 16 among Chamberlain, Weizmann, Wise, and Ben-Gurion, the prime minister intimated that he felt Britain's position had strengthened following the Munich Agreement and that it was only becoming "stronger and stronger." The Jewish delegation should resist, he argued, thinking about "a solution for the distant future" when so much was likely to change in the next several months.[75]

Over the next week and a half, through a combination of formal negotiations at St James's Palace and private meetings and dinners, Shertok and members of the Jewish delegation came to learn of yet another British intention for Palestine that likewise disturbed their already cynical expectations for the conference: that the British indeed planned to grant independence to Palestine, thus creating a Palestinian Arab majority state. On the evening of February 20, Shertok, Weizmann, and Ben-Gurion dined at the home of Rab Butler, the undersecretary of state for foreign affairs, who informed his guests that Britain was considering eliminating the mandate and replacing it with some form of independence. Butler explained that this new political plan might be "in appearance independence" but "British control in fact"—an arrangement that would have mirrored the indirect rule still exerted on ostensibly independent nations including Egypt and Iraq.[76] The following night, Shertok attended dinner at Arthur Wauchope's home, where he spoke one-on-one with the former high commissioner, who intimated something similar. Wauchope had "the impression that it would be difficult for the British government to get out of the demand for independence.... Something like this would have to be given—otherwise the Arab governments would be forced to return empty handed."[77]

If intelligence gleaned from private and personal connections made some form of independence appear increasingly likely, announcements from the British foreclosed on certain constitutional arrangements within a future independent state. The Jewish delegation learned on February 20, for example, that parity was "off the agenda"; the Arab delegation had categorically rejected it. "One mirage with which they had intended to purchase our consent to minority status has already vanished," wrote Shertok.[78] In a meeting with MacDonald on Friday, February 24, Shertok and Weizmann learned that the British Cabinet Committee on Palestine had resolved to hold a Round Table Conference in the mold of India later in the year, whereupon they would draft a constitution for an independent Palestine. In the interim period before independence, governing institutions would be formed, with the British administering the country alongside Jewish and Palestinian representatives, chosen in numbers proportionate to their populations. The Jewish delegation opposed this arrangement, even for an interim period, because it risked enshrining their status as a minority. At the formal meeting at St James's Palace that evening, Weizmann expressed remorse that Britain intended to relinquish the mandate. Were Britain to pursue independence for Palestine, he said, there could be no "solution based on minority status for the Jews."[79] Weizmann cited the persecution of Jews in Yemen and the increasingly tenuous position of Jews in Egypt as telltale warnings.

The meeting that evening concluded past midnight; it was already the early hours of Saturday. Shertok—after pointing the Sabbath-observant Rabbi Blau in the direction of the East End, the latter setting off on foot—returned to the Jewish Agency office to send a telegram to Jerusalem detailing Britain's new plan. Then, despite the hour, Mapai members of the Jewish delegation gathered to discuss their options. Ben-Gurion declared that the only way forward now was to demand the establishment of a Jewish state; Berl Katznelson disagreed, arguing that pushing for the state would only bring about internal damage to the Zionist movement. "Be that as it may, what we fear has come to pass for us," Shertok later reflected in his diary. But the situation was not a foregone conclusion, he thought; in fact, Britain's plan, created an opening for the Yishuv to resist:

> Before the negotiations began, we were sure that on the question of independence the government would say an absolute no to the Arabs. And low and behold there is such a great shift on this point that in fact we are already facing the horror, but the government has entered a bind in this matter and knows it. Our power in Israel will not be enough to

force Britain to establish a regime that we want, but it may be enough to prevent the establishment of a regime that we will fight against. The very attempt of the government to follow this path gives us a powerful lever in our hands. Just as a law was decided that the mandate could not be possible and then the same law was decided regarding partition and the establishment of the states, so too will it be established regarding the independence of Palestine in its current state—it will transpire that this regime cannot be fulfilled either.[80]

In this moment of profound uncertainty, Shertok struggled, on the one hand, to believe that the British really would grant independence to Palestine. He reasoned that this new plan—like partition before it—would likely be reversed. But, on the other hand, he still seriously considered what the Yishuv's options would be were Britain to proceed with the plan for independence. His insight—that the Yishuv did not possess enough power to force the British to establish the regime Zionists wanted, but likely did have enough power to *prevent* an undesired regime—reflected at once a sense of expanded Jewish economic and military might in Palestine and a sober assessment of the realistic limits of that power. At the same time, Shertok's vision of a potential future conflict did not reflect an enthusiastic embrace of force as a tool, what would come to be known (in reference to Ben-Gurion's philosophy) as "fighting Zionism." Over the course of the remaining days at the conference, Shertok expressed both an increasing acceptance that Jews in Palestine might need to resort to force *and* anxiety over the implications of such a development. When Ben-Gurion recalled a conversation during which he wondered if the British would have the nerve to shoot at Jews in Palestine, Shertok countered with the question he found more troublesome: what would happen if the *Jews* were forced to shoot at the *British*? "What then?" he demanded.[81] In other words, Shertok was coming to terms all at once with the fact the Yishuv had a greater ability to wield force than it had in the past, that a conflict with the British (or the Arabs) might be inevitable, and that such a conflict might permanently alienate the Yishuv from Britain.

Shertok and members of the Jewish delegation in London raced to make final edits to a formal letter of rejection of the British plan, violence and unrest surged in Palestine. News of celebrations among Palestinians over the announcement of Britain's intention to grant independence was followed by reports of multiple Irgun bombing attacks, including in markets in Haifa and Jerusalem, that killed thirty-three Palestinians. Pronouncements from Zionist leaders still in Palestine echoed the promise of resistance were Britain to implement its plan. The Va'ad Leumi issued a statement declaring that "the Yishuv will stand united against any attempt to impose on it the status of a minority and fetter its growth and free development in its Homeland.... There will be no Jewish ghetto in the Land of Israel."[82] The mayor of Tel Aviv, Israel Rokach, similarly vowed in a statement to the colonial secretary that "Tel Aviv, with the whole Jewish people in Palestine and abroad, will do everything in its power to frustrate such an attempt.... Under no circumstances shall we submit in this dark hour to the imposition of minority status."[83]

While the Jewish delegates made clear their opposition to the independence plan, delivering a formal refusal to the government on the afternoon of February 27, they struggled for days to formulate an alternative proposal. Finally, after a week of debate, the Jewish delegation resolved to propose the continuation of the mandate with economic absorptive capacity and continued land development—in other words, the status quo before restrictions were put in place following the Arab Revolt. If asked what they would propose in place of the mandate, the delegation would say Jewish independence in accordance with the Peel Commission's proposals—that is, a Jewish state in a portion of Palestine.

The question of the mandate and its future and the Jewish delegation's conclusion on the matter reveal a political outlook among Jewish leaders across the Zionist and non-Zionist spectrum that was still deeply bound up—if in extremely fraught ways—in the British Empire. Proposing the continuation of the mandate was in one sense a compromise. While Ben-Gurion continued to trumpet an independent Jewish state as the best option, other members of the Jewish delegation, including both Zionists and non-Zionists, were uncomfortable with the idea of Jewish independence either entirely or at the present juncture; others maintained that the Jewish delegation did not have the authority to make such a proposal at the conference. The mandate option also reflected broader strategic considerations—a path of realism rather than idealism. Preserving the mandate meant maintaining the status quo in Palestine in a world otherwise in flux. It could allow for the continued building of the Jewish national home, through immigration and land development, unimpeded by Arab majority rule.

Critically, however, this stance toward the continuation of the mandate and toward Britain as a whole occurred as the Yishuv more broadly was becoming increasingly anti-British, even as the Zionist movement's primary leadership—Weizmann, Shertok, and even Ben-Gurion until relatively late in the conference—attempted to maintain productive relations with the government. Throughout the Arab Revolt, the Hebrew-language press, including Labor's mouthpiece *Davar*, regularly published scathing editorials, accusing mandatory authorities and the British government of taking an indifferent—or even insidious—attitude toward the loss of Jewish life. Both Shertok and Ben-Gurion had criticized this tendency to demonize the government, viewing it as inaccurate and damaging.[84] Shertok had argued in a speech at the Mapai Central Committee in June 1936 that any mistakes made by the British in Palestine had also been made in other stretches of the empire where Jews were not a factor. "It is impossible to say that the action of the government would have taken a different form if the events had struck the English rather than the Jews," he had argued then.[85]

As the conference stretched on into March, and the Jewish delegation came to see it as increasingly likely that Britain would grant Palestine independence and severely restrict Jewish immigration and land settlement, Shertok's understanding of the situation coalesced around two major points. First, he resisted placing the blame for the anticipated direction of British policy solely or primarily on MacDonald, considering it instead reflective of a much more entrenched, expansive government policy. By contrast, some other members of the Jewish delegation, as well as those in the broader Zionist orbit in London, viewed MacDonald's actions as treacherous and placed all the blame on him—"as if it were his personal betrayal that caused all the trouble," wrote Shertok.[86] He found this view naive—an "easy" though false reading of the state of things. MacDonald was in fact only a "tool" carrying out a "calculated government position." In other words, the issue was much broader and more deeply rooted than just one government official who promoted policies that ran contrary to Zionist aspirations. Shertok's position represented a departure from previous patterns of Zionist diplomacy that relied heavily on the cultivation of close, personal ties with sympathetic British politicians. It had been after all, Zionist-led intersession to contacts in Parliament that had prompted Prime Minister Ramsay MacDonald, Malcolm MacDonald's father, to reverse the 1930 white paper issued by then-colonial secretary Sidney Webb.[87] Many on the Jewish delegation—even Ben-Gurion—anticipated that a similar saving hand might intervene this time. On more than one occasion during the conference, Ben-Gurion left meetings with the prime minister feeling buoyed, hopeful that the prime minister might intervene and propose a more amenable solution.[88] Shertok, by contrast, thought that such deeply fixed policy commitments could not be undone by a single politician—even the prime minister.

Second, Shertok grew increasingly convinced that the developing situation in Europe would ultimately have little impact on British policy in Palestine. Members of the Jewish delegation were repeatedly told by British officials and other political contacts that just *waiting* might improve their situation. Chamberlain had previously predicted that the British position in Europe would improve following the Munich Agreement and implored the Jewish delegation to resist thinking about long-term outlooks in Palestine, implying that Britain might in the immediate future be in a more favorable situation and thus able to make different policy choices. Less than a month later, during a brief visit to Paris, Weizmann was advised by the American ambassador to France, William Christian Bullitt, that "things are going to change dramatically in Europe within a month." Bullitt urged Weizmann to "strive to postpone the decision [of the conference], even for a month." But Shertok disagreed with this advice. "I don't know what will change in Europe in the course of a month," he wrote, "but in any case it seems to me that we are greatly exaggerating the direct connection between any shock in Europe and Britain's position regarding us in Palestine." Shertok recognized that Britain's "orientation" toward the Arabs was shaped by broader imperial and global politics; indeed, earlier in the conference, he had argued against the logic of this position and its concomitant framing of the Yishuv as a less consequential political and military factor. "But [that orientation] has already reached such a level of consolidation and has become such a decided law regarding the essential affairs of the empire that there is no hope that it will change under the effect of imminent transformations in Europe, even in the event that they do occur," he wrote.⁸⁹ Just as Shertok was convinced that British policy on Palestine reflected an entrenched government program, not just the whims of one man, he likewise considered that policy to be so firm and deeply rooted that even a war was unlikely to shift its course.

While Shertok grew increasingly resigned and frustrated about British policy, his attitude toward the non-Zionist participants on the delegation, especially the Lords Reading and Bearsted, warmed as his commitment to practical measures overtook ideological objection. "With all the difficulty and the danger so far, the lords have not failed us—on the contrary, they've added to our strength," he wrote.⁹⁰ Regarding Reading in particular, Shertok praised his "sharp mind" and noted that he was a "decent man, who despite being a typical non-Zionist has behaved with us this whole time with total loyalty." As for Bearsted, Shertok commended the viscount's "patience and his serious attitude."⁹¹ "It is necessary to do everything to preserve the alliance with them until the end," he insisted.⁹²

On the evening of March 14, the day before what would be the Jewish delegation's final meeting with the British, Shertok went to the Weizmann home. The house at 16 Addison Crescent in Holland Park, where the Weizmanns had lived in London since 1919, had been partially disassembled two years earlier, when Vera Weizmann had moved some of its furniture to the new home she and her husband had built in Rehovot.⁹³ That night, a dejected and despondent Weizmann recounted his meeting earlier that day with Chamberlain. Weizmann had informed the prime minister that the impending government announcement spelled the "end of a chapter" in Zionist-British relations. "This is the end of cooperation between me and you," Weizmann declared. Chamberlain, who "expressed his sorrow," said that he understood and that he did not blame Weizmann. The prime minister lamented that "his heart is for the Jews" and invoked the memory of his late father, Joseph Chamberlain, who in his meetings with Herzl decades earlier to discuss the prospect of Jewish settlement in British East Africa had been one of the first statesmen to treat Zionism as a legitimate political force. Weizmann told Chamberlain that it was a tragedy that the prime minister was being "used as a tool to put an end to a twenty year enterprise." Vera Weizmann cried as her husband conveyed the story. "The feeling in the house was as if a void had been cast upon it," wrote Shertok.⁹⁴

The British press that evening carried news of the creation of the Slovak State, a client state of Nazi Germany. The next morning, German troops invaded and occupied what remained of Czech lands, where approximately 118,000 Jews still lived. The Munich Agreement had been broken. That same day, the Jewish delegation learned in more precise detail what the government planned to propose and what would ultimately be formalized as a white paper: Palestine was to become an independent state over time, governing councils were to be established, and Jewish immigration was to be limited to a total of seventy-five thousand over the course of the next five years.

There were no surprises that evening at St James's Palace. MacDonald announced the British proposal to members of the Jewish delegation; the Jewish delegation in turn presented its formal rejection. That night, after Ben-Gurion sent a telegram to America and Shertok one to South Africa, updating Zionist groups in both locations on the day's developments, Shertok wrote in his diary, "I believe our visit tonight to St James's was the last."[95]

FROM IMPERIAL TO METROPOLITAN SOLUTIONS

Norman Bentwich and Wyndham Deedes traveled by flying boat from Egypt to South Africa in late October 1938. Their southward journey there and their return journey included stops in Kenya, Uganda, and Mozambique. In each location, the pair called on local Jewish leaders and government officials, imploring them to support the refugee cause. Crossing Kenya, Norman thought about what might have been possible had the British East Africa scheme proposed by Joseph Chamberlain come to fruition all those years ago. "It would have been a precious 'Asyl' to-day," he reflected.[96] Echoes of this African territorialist dream were heard repeatedly during the trip. Max Nurock, the former assistant secretary of the Palestine government and close friend of the Bentwiches who had become assistant chief secretary in Uganda in 1937, encouraged Norman to explore the possibility of refugee settlement in the protectorate. During an excursion to Southern Rhodesia, Norman met with the community of Sephardic Jews from Rhodes who ("under some strange influence of names") had immigrated from the Mediterranean island to southern Africa in the early 1900s. The community was now engaged in a desperate effort to bring over relatives still in Rhodes, which had come under Italian control in 1912. Among these Jews,

Norman found an "insistent yearning for a Jewish territory... a home for a people constantly and agonizingly rendered homeless." Some supported the idea of a Jewish territory in Angola, while others proposed Madagascar or Northern Rhodesia. "The how and the where seemed of little importance," observed Norman.[97]

In South Africa, by contrast, the hope for refugee settlement was slim. As a result of the 1937 Aliens Act, passed in response to the influx of Jewish immigrants fleeing Germany the previous year, immigration had come to a near standstill.[98] Anti-Jewish sentiment in the country and Nazi Party sympathy, particularly among the Afrikaner population, was also on the rise.[99] Thus, Norman focused much of his energy in South Africa on raising money for the refugee cause among members of the Jewish community, distinguished as having donated more to Zionist causes per capita than any other Jewish community in the world. On their tour of the country, Norman and Deedes were also able to "catch a glimpse" of Black townships, including the "wretched" Pimville, part of the broader township area in Johannesburg that later came to be known as Soweto. "The glimpse we saw appalled us because of the callousness and ruthlessness of the segregation," he wrote. Norman felt there was "all too close a likeness" between White South African attitudes toward Black South Africans, and the Nazi attitude toward Jews. "But few Jews would see it," wrote Norman.[100]

When Norman finally returned to London in late November, Helen greeted him with the news that the British government had approved plans to bring Jewish refugee children to Britain. With little hope for large-scale refuge out in the empire, and the British government's refusal to allow an influx of Jewish children (or refugee adults) to Palestine, metropolitan Britain became the only remaining option. Immediately after Kristallnacht, while Norman was still in southern Africa, Helen helped spearhead a new large-scale effort to rescue Jewish children living under Nazi rule. There is debate over who specifically conceived the Kindertransport idea, with some accounts crediting Helen (to whom the idea is attributed in the minutes of an executive committee meeting of the Council for German Jewry). Other accounts credit the social worker Salomon Adler-Rudel or the German Jewish leader and businessman Wilfred Israel, who played a central role in facilitating the Kindertransport from Berlin.[101] The idea of child rescue was also not new in Britain. Smaller-scale operations were already in place, including the Inter-Aid Committee for Children from Germany and Austria, founded by Wyndham Deedes and Gladys Skelton, the Australian-born (and non-Jewish) poet and playwright who wrote under the penname John Presland. Concurrent efforts were established to bring nearly four thousand children from the Basque region to Britain during the Spanish Civil War.

What is clear is that Helen was instrumental in initiating the Kindertransport and in leading the subsequent operation to house and care for the nearly ten thousand children who would make the journey. To achieve this large-scale undertaking, Helen mobilized overlapping networks of contacts, including Zionist and non-Zionist Anglo-Jewish elites involved in philanthropic pursuits, Jews and non-Jews committed to social welfare work, and—critically—friends and contacts from her years in Palestine. Together with Dennis Cohen, an Anglo-Jewish publisher who had known the Bentwiches during his time in Palestine's Immigration Department under Herbert Samuel, Helen drafted an initial plan to bring one thousand Jewish children to Britain immediately. Helen and Cohen enlisted Samuel to present the idea to Samuel Hoare, the Home Office secretary. Hoare agreed to the proposal so long as private organizations and individuals (most of them Jewish) could guarantee the children's "maintenance." Soon after, Parliament agreed to suspend lengthy visa requirements for the children. Though child-focus rescue organizations, including the Inter-Aid Committee, already existed, leaders of the refugee movement in Britain decided that a new organization, under the aegis and with the financial support of the Council for German Jewry, should be formed given the enlarged scale of the scheme. Thus, Helen and Dennis Cohen, along with Rebecca Sieff and Inter-Aid's Gladys Skelton, founded the Movement for the Care of Children from Germany, later known as the Refugee Children's Movement.[102] Rebecca Sieff (née Marks), the daughter of the Manchester Jewish family that founded the British department store Marks & Spencer, was one of the founders of the Women's International Zionist Organization. Her sister Elaine Laski (later Blond) codirected the movement's voluntary committee with Lola Hahn Warburg, niece of the German-born American banker and non-Zionist Felix Warburg.[103] Herbert Samuel and Wyndham Deedes were appointed the movement's presidents. Norman, only two days after returning to London from Africa, traveled to the Netherlands to coordinate rescue plans. The first transport, carrying two hundred children from a Jewish orphanage in Berlin, arrived in Harwich on December 2, 1938.

Though the Movement for the Care of Children from Germany had been established to streamline refugee relief for children, in reality, lack of coordination, inefficiency, and redundancy often hindered efforts, particularly with regard to the transition from care at camps near the coast, where the children were initially housed on arrival, to other accommodations including private homes. In an appeal to order and efficiency that echoed her attitude (and frustration) during her social work efforts in Palestine in the 1920s, Helen implored those interested in housing children to coordinate with the movement. In an article for the *Jewish Chronicle* entitled "Warning against Unorganized Effort," Helen explained that coordinating would "save a great deal of duplication" and "prevent all fear of overlapping." She likewise mentioned the importance of streamlining donations, encouraging would-be philanthropists to give to the Central British Fund for German Jewry, the umbrella organization responsible for fundraising for refugee relief, rather than to smaller subsidiaries.[104] Helen also warned the public against showing up at Dovercourt Camp (one of the temporary transit camps) or removing a child "without a written authority" from Helen herself.[105]

A report issued on Christmas Day 1938, written by a group of children who had been housed on arrival at Lowestoft camp, another transit camp seventy miles up the coast from Dovercourt, likewise commented on this early chaos. The children encountered "quite adverse conditions" sleeping in frigid, damp bathing huts built for summer use; "there was little organization and order"; and "the food situation ... was uneven but also impaired by lack of organization, distribution, and discipline." From Lowestoft, the children were sent to the coastal resort town of Broadstairs, a journey that took them through London, including an "exciting" bus trip between Liverpool Street and Victoria stations. On the first night in Broadstairs, the children were housed in St Mary's Convalescent Home, run by Anglican nuns. From there, most moved in small groups into private homes. There was now plenty of hot water, but the bedrooms were cold. Some homes had better living standards than others. Still, the conditions were a considerable improvement from Lowestoft, and relations with locals were generally positive. "We are repeatedly touched by the incredible kindness of people of all classes, which, as it is Christmas now, is also shown to us in the form of many gifts of many kinds," the children relayed in their report. "Our mood is excellent. Indeed, during the day we often completely forget about German matters and even about our own uncertain future prospects," they concluded.[106]

While the children sent to Broadstairs described a relatively warm reception marked by the generosity of British Christians, there was great concern among leaders of the Movement for the Care of Children from Germany that sending *too* many Jewish children to any single location could spark a backlash of antisemitism. "We are anxious to spread out children as far over the British Isles as possible," relayed Helen. "We do not want too great numbers of them in any one place," she explained.[107] Even before the children's arrival, selection strategies were employed by the movement, as well as Jewish agencies on the continent, in an attempt to ensure that rescued children could be easily integrated. Criteria included age, gender, health, and personality. In practice, this meant that children who were deemed "difficult," for instance, or who had a chronic illness or disability, might ultimately be excluded from rescue.[108] In a June 1939 communication to the welfare office of the Jewish Community of Vienna (*Israelitische Kultusgemeinde Wien*), the movement explained that "children who are difficult to raise, who cause problems here, endanger the chances for accommodating completely normal children who have not yet been placed."[109] This chilling, clinical policy decision reflected an often cruel reality. In contrast to the reported experience of the children in Broadstairs, many young refugees, in fact, faced difficult situations with their foster families, who expected their placements to be "well-bred" and to "fit in with their life."[110]

While Helen focused on refugee children, Norman worked in a parallel effort to bring young Jewish men to Britain; the couple were both, as Helen put it in a personal letter to Judah Magnes, "up to our eyes in refugee work."[111] Many of the refugees Norman sought to aid had been imprisoned (or were at risk of being imprisoned) in concentration camps and could only secure their safety by leaving Germany. In early 1939, the Council for German Jewry procured a former military camp in the town of Sandwich on the coast of Kent to house arriving refugees. The Home Office agreed, as it had done for children, to ease visa requirements. In another parallel to the Kindertransport, the effort to bring over young Jewish men involved members of the Anglo-Jewish elite who possessed a range of positions on Zionism, including the non-Zionist industrialist Robert Waley-Cohen and the World Zionist Organization executive Harry Sacher, director of Marks & Spencer and an old friend of the Bentwiches from their Palestine days (and Rebecca Sieff and Elaine Laski's brother-in-law). By May 1939, one thousand refugees were living at Kitchener Camp, as the men's camp came to be known. By the outbreak of the war, the population reached thirty-five hundred—larger than the host town of Sandwich. The camp possessed a "very lively society" all created and run by the refugees themselves—an orchestra, dance band, and cinema; a weekly newspaper; and courses and lectures given by the various academics and scholars living in the camp.[112] Local teachers also offered English language instruction. Hebrew was offered to those planning to immigrate to Palestine, as was Spanish for those planning to go to Latin America.[113]

Both the Kindertransport and adult rescue efforts had been sanctioned by the British government with the agreement that Britain would, for the vast majority of refugees, be only a temporary refuge, a place of transit before moving on to Palestine, the Americas, or elsewhere. Among the Kindertransport children, for example, fifteen hundred emigrated from Britain between 1939 and 1940. The Anglo-Jewish leadership involved in the rescue efforts largely supported this policy. For the Zionists among them, Palestine represented the ideal destination for persecuted Jews, especially the youth. For others, Zionist and non-Zionist alike, the impulse to help the persecuted Jewish masses was twinned with a fear—one deeply engrained in the Anglo-Jewish consciousness over generations—that bringing foreign Jews to British shores would be an overwhelming financial burden on the community, would spark antisemitic backlash, and would threaten the existing community's hard-won political security.

When Britain declared war on Germany on September 3, 1939, the question of the refugees' "uncertain future prospects" (as the Broadstairs children had put it) became considerably more complicated. Emigration generally proved much harder. Refugee children who had been placed in homes and hostels in London and in other urban centers vulnerable to aerial bombings had to be evacuated alongside British children in Operation Pied

Piper, which Helen helped to carry out through her work on the London County Council. In the chaos of those early days, as Helen saw to the evacuation of London's children (both citizen and refugee), she wrote of feeling "a sense of terrible urgency" and "despair that we hadn't started sooner." News of the ongoing collapse of Polish defenses under Nazi invasion and Luftwaffe bombardment made everything all the more "horribly grim." Helen wondered what would happen were the Allies to lose the war. "It's a ghastly thought—it'll mean the end of all the things we believe in, such as freedom, democracy, brotherly friendship with other nations—& the end of the British Empire," she wrote. "What will happen to us? If only we could keep our freedom, a little England with democracy & socialism vital in it might not be so bad," she considered in desperation.[114] Grasping at a potential future with the empire defeated, Helen's anxious thinking mirrored her and Norman's own forced turn away from *imperial* solutions to the refugee crisis, as *metropolitan* Britain emerged as the only possible option of asylum—even one that was intended to be temporary.

For adult refugees, the war turned them into enemy aliens. An initial plan from the government to convert Kitchener Camp into a place of internment was scrapped; instead, the camp's thirty-five hundred inhabitants were put to practical use, shoring up Kent's costal defense. Six alien tribunals, appointed by the government to investigate the status of enemy aliens and the legitimacy of refugee claims, spent weeks in Sandwich interviewing each Kitchener man individually. The tribunals ultimately deemed all but two men as legitimate "'refugees from Nazi persecution' whose loyalty could be relied on."[115] A visit from the Archbishop of Canterbury during this period, rallying the men to the war effort, prompted many to express a desire to enlist. When the War Office finally approved such a scheme, under which refugees could join up in special "alien companies" of the Royal Pioneer Corps, more than half of the Kitchener men enrolled at once. The camp itself was transformed into the first training center for the alien companies, with the refugee men working in various noncombat capacities, including cooking and tailoring, as well as in intelligence work monitoring German broadcasts. Gerald Isaacs (Lord Reading), who had succeeded Herbert Samuel as chair of the Council for German Jewry, resigned his position in order to become commanding officer of the new camp. In early 1940, the first five alien companies to receive their training at Kitchener landed in France to assist forces in Normandy and Brittany. Following the German invasion of France in May, and the eventual evacuation of British troops, the previously unarmed alien companies were given weaponry and guidance on how to load and fire not only rifles but machine guns. All five companies returned safely to Britain. Despite praise from British military officials and politicians for their service, there was considerable stigma around serving in the Pioneer Corps, and many refugees protested their exclusion from combat units. Members of the Pioneer Corps were disparaged as "laborers" and included various social outsiders and outcasts, including gay men, former psychiatric patients, and those with criminal records, all of whom were deemed unfit for combat roles.[116]

The "midsummer nightmare" of 1940 created still new challenges for refugee work. During the early months of the war, when the western front had been quiescent, Norman and other leaders of the refugee movement had been able to keep in touch with partner organizations in France, as well as Belgium and the Netherlands—"precarious bridges with the oppressed in the countries of oppression." But with the Battle of France, "the doors on the Continent were finally bolted and barred," with the exception of some small Spanish and Portuguese "portals."[117] For those refugees already in Britain, a new wave of "wild suspicion and panic apprehension" made their position all the more precarious. "In the dire peril of the country it was easy to work up a feeling that every alien, whatever certificate the authorities had given, was a potential agent of the enemy," wrote Norman, who blamed the panic partly on the press and partly on military authorities.[118]

As a result, refugee men, as well as older Kindertransport boys, who did not or could not enlist generally faced internment. The "civilian remnant" from Kitchener Camp was arrested and removed, along with many other refugees in other parts of the country, to the Isle of Man. About one thousand Kindertransport children—mostly boys between the ages of sixteen and eighteen—were likewise interned there. Many other refugees were interned in makeshift camps in other reaches of the country. Norman visited one such "camp"—a racecourse in the home counties. Men lived in the stables, with ten each to a stall, and were prohibited from using the racecourse itself. Norman noted that the sentries who patrolled the barbed-wire enclosed course "troubled their charges as little as possible." Rather "the hardship was the denial of freedom, the bitterness of confinement in a country where they had been granted refuge, and for which they had a deep attachment..., and the perpetual suspense and fear of expulsion."[119] This apprehension was not unfounded. Several thousand refugees, including some of the older Kindertransport children, were deported to Canada and Australia and imprisoned once again—a horrible irony given the attitude adopted by the dominions toward the refugee question in the years leading up to the war. One of the ships carrying interned refugees, the SS *Arandora Star*, was torpedoed on its way to Canada resulting in the death of nearly half of the passengers on board. Though leaders of the refugee movement, as well as church officials and liberal-minded politicians, including Josiah Wedgwood, quickly launched efforts to free interned refugees, the entire process took nearly a year.[120]

THE JEWISH BRIGADE AND THE FUTURE OF BRITAIN IN PALESTINE

Between the conclusion of the St James's Palace Conference in March 1939 and the official release of the white paper that May, Shertok had remained in London with the exception of a short trip to Warsaw to survey the condition of Polish Jewry. He continued to lobby the British government to grant more Jewish immigration permits to Palestine, hoping for a last-minute revision of certain minutiae of white paper policy. Ben-Gurion, who saw any further negotiation with the British government as an implicit acceptance of its policy stance on Palestine, vehemently opposed this effort. But Shertok felt that negotiating remaining details—for example, whether the British would factor in Jews who *left* Palestine in calculating the total number of permitted new immigrants—would certainly not save European Jewry *en masse* but could potentially spare thousands of lives. He viewed these negotiations as a critical element in the fight for aliyah and, moreover, a tactic with precedent. "Indeed we have been in practical negotiations with the government constantly on immigration issues even during the period of the political maximum, which is still ongoing, in spite of our opposition to this regime and our principled war against it," Shertok reflected.[121] In other words, despite Zionist opposition to British policy, continued negotiations were critical—all the more so given the perilous situation in Europe. Every successfully negotiated detail could mean lives saved.

Alongside his continued efforts to increase immigration rates, Shertok also pressed for the creation of Jewish units in the British military. On the eve of the war, after returning to London following the Zionist Congress in Geneva, Shertok met with British military leaders and War Office officials in an attempt to persuade them to create Jewish units stationed in Palestine, as well as ones that could serve abroad. Though Shertok's British contacts expressed interest in the idea in theory, they raised concerns about the feasibility of finding suitable officers and obtaining enough weaponry, alongside the issue of further damaging relations with Palestinian Arabs by arming Jewish forces. General Edmund Ironside, then the inspector general of British Overseas Forces, told Shertok that "the Jews should not be impatient or pressure the government too much" on the matter. "It was the fate of the empire that hung in the balance," the general told Shertok, adding that "he was certain [Shertok] would agree with him that the fate of the Jews depends on the fate of the empire."[122]

Though he returned to Palestine briefly at the start of the war, Shertok spent most of the remainder of 1939 and the first few months of 1940 in London, resuming his push for Jewish units and attempting to finesse any possible changes to white paper policy. By the time Shertok returned to Palestine in April 1940, Britain had agreed to allow Jews from Palestine to enlist alongside Palestinian Arabs in mixed companies in the Pioneer Corps; those troops were deployed to France, serving alongside the Jewish refugee "alien companies" from Britain. Jews from Palestine were also permitted to enlist in the Royal East Kent Regiment (known as the "Buffs") and, later, in the newly formed Palestine Regiment, both infantry regiments tasked mainly with guard duty. British authorities also required parity in enlistment between Jews and Arabs in Palestine. The policy was designed to quell Palestinian Arab concerns about the threat of Jewish military power but quickly faced the practical issue that far fewer Palestinians desired to enlist in the British military. Despite these limitations and despite widespread anti-British sentiment among the Yishuv public, made worse by the SS *Patria* and *Struma* disasters, Jews in Palestine enlisted in the British military in high numbers; ultimately more than thirty thousand volunteered. The Italian bombing of coastal Palestine beginning in July 1940 and the looming threat of Rommel's forces in North Africa motivated many Jews to join up out of a desire to protect the Yishuv. By late 1942, as knowledge of the mass murder of European Jewry reached Palestine, motivation for serving shifted; increasingly, Jewish soldiers from Palestine desired to fight on the front in Europe and to carry out revenge against the Nazis.[123] But they still were not permitted to do so under a Jewish banner.

When Chamberlain resigned a month later and Churchill replaced him as prime minister, Shertok hoped that the latter, who had long expressed pro-Zionist convictions, would be more amenable to the creation of an exclusively Jewish formation. While Churchill himself supported the idea, the rest of his government continued to refuse such a plan, fearing not only the potential wartime ramifications from the Arab (and broader Muslim) perspective but, increasingly, the *postwar* implications of creating a combat-ready Jewish formation. For example, George Lloyd, who replaced Malcolm MacDonald as colonial secretary in Churchill's new cabinet, objected to the creation of a Jewish formation, arguing that Zionists were motivated by ulterior political aspirations. The creation of a Jewish formation, according to Lloyd, would constitute the "recognition of the Jewish people as a nation" and might earn the Yishuv "a standing in the War Councils of the Allies and ultimately in the discussion of terms of peace." Lloyd argued that Zionist leaders knew well that such recognition and privileged standing might help in the "the conversion of Palestine into a Jewish State as a reward for Jewish military assistance."[124] British leaders also expressed more explicit concern that an armed Jewish formation might turn *against* Britain after the war, logic that became all the more compelling once the Irgun resumed its attacks against British targets in February 1944.

For Shertok, the creation of a "Jewish fighting force" or "Jewish army" was indeed about Jewish nationhood. In 1942, he wrote that the right to a Jewish army was "rooted in the fact that there is a Jewish people in the world who are the object of aggression by the enemy."[125] The chief goal of Zionism, especially at this juncture as Shertok saw it, was "to save the body of the Jewish people."[126] A Jewish army would play a central role in effecting this national imperative.

Traveling to Britain in February 1944, Shertok presented the idea for a Jewish army in front of Zionist leaders in London. Given that the war in Europe was "now entering upon its last chapter," a Jewish army should be sent to Europe to participate in the final battles of liberation, Shertok argued. He reasoned that previous objections to a Jewish army in the Middle East—that its presence might anger and worry Arabs—"could not be applied to the European theatre." What was more, there was no need to train new troops for such an army; they could simply be drawn from the existing Palestine Regiment. But the rationale was more than practical, according to Shertok; it was a matter of principle. Having lost millions of their own people, Jews "had an account to settle with the enemy ... a moral debt was owed to them."[127] The following month, Weizmann took the plan to Churchill and James Grigg, the British war secretary, arguing that "the least we can ask is that a force of free, fighting, Jews be enabled to uphold the honour of their people, avenge its martyrs, and help to liberate the survivors."[128]

While many British leaders anticipated that a Jewish army would both validate Jewish nationality and all but guarantee a postwar anti-British Jewish insurgency, Shertok's corresponding attitudes toward Britain were not so straightforward. During the summer of 1944, while the British cabinet considered the proposal for a Jewish army, Shertok published a careful, sober analysis, reminiscent of Arlosoroff's "Ninth Dominion" essay, in which he considered the geopolitical landscape of the anticipated postwar era and its implication for Zionism and the Yishuv. Entitled "Main Factors in Zionist Politics," the essay examined Zionist political futures in relation to four entities, each with their own spheres of influence: the Arab world, the United States, the Soviet Union, and—mostly critically—Britain.

Shertok began the essay by placing Palestine and the Yishuv in the broader context of the Middle East, where "the independence, in fact as well as theory," of the surrounding countries made Palestine—the only remaining Class A Mandate without self-government—an outlier. "It is clear that as neighboring countries become independent, Palestinian Arabs will become more anxious for independence," wrote Shertok. More than just a harbinger of what would likely transpire in Palestine, developments in the Arab world also signified an unforeseen and powerful commentary on polity and the nature of sovereignty. While various theorists and onlookers had hypothesized that "Arab countries were developing toward a Federation," there was actually "no sign of any approach to such a solution." Rather, Arab countries appeared "anxious to preserve their sovereignty, not only against the Great Western Powers, but against each other." What arose in place of a federation, then, was a "process of rapprochement through the creation of mutual bonds [among Arab countries], not through the abandonment of sovereignty." As for the Yishuv's place in the Arab world, Shertok insisted that Zionists must "continue [their] efforts to make contact." But he was skeptical that it would lead to productive relations. "The maximum that the Arabs are prepared to offer is very far from the minimum upon which we are forced to stand," he wrote.[129]

With his thoughts on the Arab world established, Shertok turned to the three Great Powers, weighing the relative benefits of focusing the "center of gravity" of Zionist political efforts on the United States, the Soviet Union, or Britain. "The Jewish people constitute a world problem which seriously concerns the Great Powers and commits the whole civilized world to a grave responsibility," he wrote. The United States, Shertok explained, had become increasingly important to the Zionist cause, both because of the large Jewish population there that enjoyed the freedoms of democracy and because of "the rapid growth of a realization of America's responsibility for peaceful conditions in the postwar world." But critically, Shertok argued, American support could not supplant Zionist relations with Britain. "Our prospects of help from America will be increased to the extent that our support in England grows stronger—and not *vice versa*," he reasoned.[130]

The Soviet Union, with new avenues of contact made possible by the war, represented in theory another potential focus of Zionist political efforts. But the fact that Jews lived with strictly curtailed freedoms and Zionist emissaries could not easily enter the country posed a serious challenge. "Did it ever occur to anyone to consider it important that British Jewry is permitted to maintain a Zionist Organization and . . . that American Jewry has similar rights? Have we ever understood the value of being granted visas and space in airplanes during a war, even though it was clearly understood that these were granted to persons who intended to combat the current policy of the government which extended them?" Shertok posed rhetorically.[131]

"Reality brings us back to Great Britain as the pivot of our political efforts at this time," Shertok thus reasoned. But the nature of the Jewish problem—an "international one," not solely a "British one"—must necessarily define both the approach to a solution and the character of Zionist-British relations in a postwar world:

> Not alone does the Jewish people face a historic turning point as a result of the slaughter in Europe, but the war has brought the whole world to a crossways. These circumstances, in their relation to the problems of Palestine and the whole Middle East, have made it possible as well as necessary for the Zionist movement to fight for a more radical and immediate solution of our problem. If this analysis is correct, there arises the serious question, whether our policy is adequate to the situation. We must decide above all this question: Have we now a chance for a new political campaign, unprecedented in the power which can be marshalled behind it and the prospects which lie before it? If so, it is clear that a demand for the continuation of the mandate is totally inadequate. If there is room for argument among us, it can only be on this basic question: whether we now have the opportunity to abandon our defensive position, for, if this can be done, we must be clear what we wish to achieve. . . . Do we wish to achieve a situation in which vital decisions about our future will be in the hands of others? Or is it our aim that such matters be in our own hands, so that we may be given a real opportunity to save as many Jews as possible in the shortest possible time?[132]

In other words, Shertok tied the possibility of saving the surviving Jewish remnant in Europe with a new vision of Jewish sovereignty in Palestine in relation to Britain, one that echoed his assessment of the emerging mutual relations among Arab countries. Though he did not outline the precise contours of this new political arrangement, he argued that the grave reality of the Jewish situation called for radical solutions and a rejection of the status quo—that is, the continuation of the mandate, what the Jewish delegation to the 1939 St James's Palace Conference had proposed. Still, in establishing this vision of sovereignty, Shertok insisted that Zionists could not simply cut ties with Britain, despite what more activist and anti-British wings of the movement desired. "What we see about us, if we are clearsighted, forces us back to Great Britain," he wrote. Zionists needed to counter the image that they were "foes of England"—a charge sometimes leveled from the outside but one also felt within the movement. "We cannot permit ourselves to forget that we are engaged in a political struggle and that such a struggle is different in kind from a military campaign," explained Shertok. Whereas a military campaign aimed to "vanquish the opponent," a political campaign aimed not to sever all ties but rather to foster "closer relations." But here Shertok added an essential caveat: those improved relations would only be possible "in light of our strength and in consideration of our honor." Indeed, this new relationship would not be dependent on the "question of loyalty or moral obligation" but would instead be grounded on the right to oppose policy and reach out to other allies, including the United States or even the Soviet Union. "As long as we are engaged in this political effort, we shall not neglect any opportunity of attacking in the forum of public opinion, the policy officially accepted, or of leading the [British] government to question their own policy and particularly their willingness and ability to follow it to its logical end," wrote Shertok of white paper policy.

Shertok had been willing to advocate for the continuation of the mandate back in 1939, with a world on the brink of catastrophe. Then, it had appeared to be the safest possibility among limited, less-than-ideal options. Then, too, Shertok had believed that events in Europe would have little impact on such deeply entrenched British policy. But by 1944, with millions of Jews already murdered but an Allied victory seeming ever more likely, Shertok's calculations shifted considerably. Factoring in what sort of rescue efforts Jews themselves might be able to carry out were they to have their own army, as well as the role that changes in international opinion might play in forcing Britain to amend its policy on Palestine, Shertok concluded that now was the time for "grand conceptions, bold conclusions, and radical solutions."[133] Although in 1939 he had already framed Jews as "allies" of Britain rather than "subjects," by 1944 he made a more explicit argument for sovereignty, for putting "matters . . . in our own hands." Though this position moved him closer to his more activist colleagues, including Ben-Gurion, Shertok still insisted on maintaining close, cooperative relations with Britain—even while opposing white paper policy—in the anticipated postwar period. And though he wrote of "radical solutions," Shertok's insistence on working with Britain was—as it had been in 1939—rooted in a clearheaded realism. "Even after we shall have achieved great things, we will have much to do in this part of the world with Great Britain, and we will still need good and mature judgment," he concluded.[134]

In September 1944, the month following the publication of Shertok's essay, the British government finally approved the plan to create a Jewish brigade in the British Army, a combat military formation that would fly a Jewish flag. The brigade, whose soldiers would be drawn from the existing Palestine Regiment, would be a "formation complete in structure and able to take the field as a self-contained unit."[135] The affirmative decision was at last rendered in part owing to persistent Jewish pressure (particularly from Shertok and Weizmann), in part owing to Churchill's support, and in part owing to developments in Europe, specifically the deportation and mass murder of Hungarian Jewry that summer, which went unimpeded by the Allies. The decision to raise a Jewish brigade then was seen by some in the British government as a "compensatory" measure.[136] In October 1944, after a period of training in Egypt, the newly formed Jewish Brigade was deployed to Italy to join the Eighth Army.

And so it was that Moshe Shertok found himself in April 1945, with cannon fire booming in the distance, standing before soldiers of the Jewish Brigade stationed near the front along the Senio River in Northern Italy. The night before Shertok's arrival, Jewish troops, who had been manning dugouts monitoring German soldiers across the line, returned to brigade headquarters "under cover of darkness" to await the Zionist leader's arrival.[137] The next day, in a "simple, quiet ceremony" in a meadow in front of a "shell-pocked" mansion, Shertok presented the flag—a blue and white standard with a Star of David that he had brought with him from Palestine—to the brigade's commander. Shertok's speech, delivered in Hebrew against the sound of crashing cannons "like the ruffle of war drums," linked together the liberation of Europe and of Jewish survivors with the national liberation of the Jewish people brought about by Zionism—connected together now by the potent symbol of a flag.[138] "This is a great moment in the history of the Palestine volunteering movement, in the life of the Jewish people, and in the lives of all engaged in this effort," Shertok began. "It has been given to us today to raise the flag of the Jewish people, the standard of Jewish liberation, on the very battlefront where the struggle for liberation of Europe ... is taking place," he continued. Shertok acknowledged that the soldiers, many of whom had joined up at the beginning of the war, had likely waited years to see "this flag flying overhead." Many might have "given a silent salute to this flag in [their hearts]." The flag, he declared, was "saturated with the blood" of millions of Jews who had been murdered. "We raise it as a torch for the surviving remnants of our people, a signal for them to join us in the struggle of liberation and the return to Zion," he concluded.[139]

After Germany surrendered just over a month later, on May 8, 1945, the Jewish Brigade was transferred to northeast Italy near the Austrian border. There, brigade soldiers organized welfare and educational services for Holocaust survivors. In contravention of British policy, troops also worked clandestinely to get survivors to Palestine on ships departing the Italian coast, part of the broader Bricha movement that helped Holocaust survivors escape Europe for Palestine. Along with emissaries from the Jewish Agency and with the support of the Joint, brigade soldiers also traveled to Austria and Czechoslovakia to find survivors and help bring them back to Italy to await transit to Palestine. The work was carried out at a furious pace, relying on ingenuity and luck to circumvent British authorities. Word quickly spread among survivors of the potential for transit through Italy, and during the summer of 1945, roughly fifteen thousand of them came to the country—still only a fraction of the total number of survivors in Europe. When British military intelligence finally caught on to the operations, the Jewish Brigade was transferred to Belgium.[140]

With the war over, Zionist leaders stood on a new precipice. Hundreds of thousands of survivors, many interned in DP camps, awaited immigration to Palestine while Britain refused to amend white paper policy. While there was resounding agreement among Zionists on admitting the surviving remnant to Palestine, old disagreements over statehood and polity and Jewish-Arab relations, which had simmered below the surface during the war, now resurfaced. The question of Britain—its future in Palestine and how and whether to subvert British policy—likewise created bitter divisions among Zionists. Norman Bentwich joined Judah Magnes's Ihud Party, founded on the binationalist principles of the former Brit Shalom movement. Shertok, who vehemently opposed binationalism, still aimed to preserve Yishuv-

British relations and sought to restrain violent responses to white paper policy. At the same time however, he approved of more covert methods of subversion—including sending Haganah members to Europe to bolster illegal immigration and using the Jewish Brigade to purchase, both legally and illegally, arms for the Haganah.

Shertok also openly began calling for Jewish statehood. At a large gathering at the Hebrew University a week after victory in Europe, he stood on a platform in front of a facsimile of the Jewish Brigade flash, flanked by Union Jack and Zionist flags. "In view of the staggering proportions of catastrophe, let us not belittle the miracle of deliverance," he declared before the crowd. "Let us remember the countries which stood on the brink of the precipice—one such country was England, another was Palestine," he said. But Britain now needed to unlock the "gates of Palestine" and "open them widely" to the survivors in Europe. "The world must know ... that Israel had decided to live differently," he said. "Israel claims its country back not to displace others but to resettle and develop; not to subjugate others but to deliver itself. We claim freedom of immigration and settlement, freedom to defend ourselves, to be the masters of our own destiny.... We claim equality, and statehood."[141]

SEVEN

The Eve of Empire

ON MARCH 18, 1947, SHERTOK stood before members of the Jewish Agency Executive at a meeting held in Jerusalem and reported on the state of relations between the Yishuv and the fifty-five member countries of the United Nations, the postwar successor of the League of Nations. As for India and the broader Asian continent, a delegation representing the Yishuv, Shertok related, had just been sent to New Delhi, where in five days the Asian Relations Conference was set to open. Called by Nehru and organized by the Indian Council of World Affairs, the conference would host delegations from across the Asian continent to discuss the common economic and social problems facing Asian nations as they transitioned from colonial states to independent ones. Shertok reported to his colleagues that the Jewish delegation from Palestine would be "limited in its action" in many respects; the conference, in the mold of the Commonwealth Relations Conference attended by Norman Bentwich in 1938, would provide a space to discuss ideas and problems but not to legislate. But the Jewish delegation had a different kind of mandate, though not one without political import, Shertok explained: it must "use the opportunity to make personal connections ... to see how the wind blows."[1]

Developments over the previous year—for Shertok, for Palestine, for the British Empire—heightened the stakes of this new mission. In March 1946, after visits to DP camps in Europe and a stop in Cairo, the twelve-member Anglo-American Committee of Inquiry arrived in Palestine. The joint group, proposed by Britain with the aim that the United States might share in the burden of responsibility for Palestine, spent three weeks in the country and then retreated to Lausanne to deliberate; Shertok followed. There, on the northern shore of Lake Geneva, he lobbied and waited, hoping that rumors that the committee might revive the partition plan were true. Instead, on May 1, the Anglo-American Committee recommended that Palestine should become "neither a Jewish state nor an Arab state" but rather a binational one based on parity. Any future constitutional arrangement would need to circumvent the issue of demography as it was "precisely the struggle for a numerical majority which [bedeviled] Arab-Jewish relations."[2] In a compromise pushed by its American cochair, the committee also recommended that one hundred thousand Jewish refugees be admitted to Palestine. Shertok gave a speech in London days later accepting the proposal on immigration but roundly rejecting the constitutional recommendations. Asking Jews to give up a state in exchange for immigration was "tantamount to expecting the Zionist movement to give up its very heart," he declared.[3]

Meanwhile, the situation in Palestine was rapidly deteriorating as the Jewish insurgency reached new heights. Since October 1945, with the war over but the 1939 white paper still in force, the Jewish Agency and the Haganah had resolved to cooperate with the right-wing paramilitary groups Irgun and Lehi in carrying out acts of sabotage against the British. Shertok, though opposed to the unrestrained violence promoted by some Revisionists, believed that the time had arrived to adopt a two-pronged approach: the careful deployment of force combined with continued political efforts directed at the British. A month into this united effort, Ernest Bevin, the foreign secretary under the new Labour government headed by Clement Atlee, angrily asked Weizmann and Shertok if the Jews had declared war on Britain. Shertok replied no but insisted that they would were Britain to maintain the white paper's policy.[4]

In the spring and summer of 1946, Jewish paramilitary groups carried out some of their most brazen attacks against the British yet. In April, just before the Anglo-American Committee released its report, Lehi operatives attacked a car park in Tel Aviv used by the 6th Airborne Division, killing seven British soldiers. In June, when Britain still had not acted on the Anglo-American Committee's recommendation to admit one hundred thousand refugees, the Haganah bombed ten of the eleven bridges connecting Palestine to neighboring countries in a large-scale coordinated attack. Later that month, the Irgun kidnapped six British soldiers and threatened to hang them if two of their own members were not released from British custody. On June 29, with official permission from the British cabinet, mandatory authorities in Palestine mounted Operation Agatha, a massive offensive that came to be known in Hebrew as the "Black Sabbath." British security forces, which had swelled to one hundred thousand men, surrounded Jewish settlements, raided the offices of the Jewish Agency and other Jewish organizations, and arrested thousands of members of the Yishuv. With Ben-Gurion in Paris and Weizmann in London at the time, Shertok was the highest ranking Zionist official to face arrest. He was interned at Latrun detention camp, where, through secret channels, he was able to maintain communication with the Jewish Agency. Golda Meyerson (later Meir) stepped in as acting head of the Political Department in Shertok's stead.

In the wake of the bombing of the King David Hotel weeks later—an attack carried out by the Irgun that claimed ninety-one lives—the Jewish Agency and the Haganah decided to end their partnership with the Revisionist paramilitary groups. But the turn away from the Irgun and Lehi did not lead to increased cooperation with the British. In September 1946, when talks opened in London, Jewish Agency leaders rejected the British invitation to join the parley; the British had refused to entertain the option of partition, instead insisting that a plan to turn Palestine into a federal trusteeship under British rule with semi-autonomous Palestinian Arab and Jewish regions (adapted from the Anglo-American Commitee's recommendations) would be the only basis for negotiation. Shertok, still imprisoned at Latrun, agreed with the decision to boycott. The Jewish Agency would incur "political humiliation on the outside and moral havoc on the inside" by conceding. "I stress all this precisely because I am held to be a notorious and sworn co-operator with no hope for redemption," Shertok explained in a secret letter sent to Mapai colleagues.[5]

Facing pressure from the United States and with the signal from Jewish Agency leaders that they might be amenable to negotiations under certain circumstances, the British released Shertok and the other senior Zionist leaders imprisoned with him at Latrun in early November 1946. After 130 days of detention, Shertok was able to participate both in the Twenty-Second Zionist Congress in Basel in December, the first to convene since the war, and in talks with the British that opened in London on January 29, 1947. Palestinian and Arab League representatives held parallel negotiations. While the Jewish delegation reiterated its opposition to a binational state or federal trusteeship, the British came back with an offer for precisely that: they proposed the continuation of the mandate for five years, followed by the establishment of a single binational state. Both the Arabs and Jews rejected the proposal. Britain, anticipating this turn of events, announced on February 18, 1947, that it had exhausted all options and would consequently refer the matter of Palestine to the UN.

Palestine, of course, was far from the only imperial question confounding the British in that moment. Just as the Anglo-American Committee of Inquiry was wrapping up its survey of Palestine in March 1946, a British Cabinet Mission arrived in India to investigate the transfer of power from British to Indian rule and to make constitutional recommendations. After failed tripartite talks between the British, the Indian National Congress, and the Muslim League, the Cabinet Mission decided to make a unilateral recommendation: a federal solution, designed to maintain a united India while still affording Muslims a measure of autonomy. Though an agreement based on the plan seemed possible at first, negotiations had collapsed by June, and the Cabinet Mission departed India in failure. Amid profound uncertainty over what would ultimately transpire for the country, intercommunal violence erupted. On February 20, two days after Britain declared it would refer the matter of Palestine to the UN, Prime Minister Atlee announced the British would leave India no later than June 1948. The arrival of Louis Mountbatten, India's final British viceroy, on March 22, 1947, was met with further large-scale riots and bloodshed. The following day, amid this tumultuous backdrop, the Asian Relations Conference opened in Delhi.

Thus, when Shertok stood before his colleagues in Jerusalem in March 1947—the Jewish delegation on its way to India—Yishuv-Indian and

Yishuv-Asian relations more broadly were at once imbued with the weight of an impending UN decision and with the fraught prospect of postcolonial independence. Though the mission echoed Political Department activities of a decade earlier, when Shertok had enlisted Hermann Kallenbach, Immanuel Olsvanger, and others to help win over Gandhi to the Zionist cause, these new circumstances made the purpose of the 1947 endeavor all the more pressing. The internal diversity of India and Palestine and the uncertainty over what would become of both countries—would each remain as a unitary state with a federal solution, or would they be partitioned?—produced a dizzying array of political variables. Determining the appropriate strategy, identifying the right allies, and emphasizing the right parallels between the two cases was a sensitive, unpredictable endeavor.[6]

While the stakes were higher for the Yishuv, expectations were also tempered. The excitement and optimism that had accompanied initial efforts to win Gandhi's support for Zionism in the 1930s were now long dashed. There were likewise no illusions that Nehru would suddenly throw his support behind the Yishuv. "We are facing a wall there," Shertok acknowledged. "There is a firmly established bias against us. We are seen as a sword that the West jabs in the East," he continued. Indian conceptions of the Yishuv—specifically identifying it with British imperial power—meant that Zionist outreach to the subcontinent and to a decolonizing Asia more broadly would necessarily look distinct from diplomatic efforts directed elsewhere. "Our point of departure for India is the fact that we exist in Asia, we are part of a regenerating Asia, a part of ancient Asia, whether we want it or not," Shertok told his colleagues in Jerusalem.[7]

The fanfare that accompanied the Asian Relations Conference was quickly subsumed in the conflagrations of the summer of 1947. As for posterity, historians who have examined the conference have typically framed it as part of the broader story of Israel-India relations or, alternatively, as an important episode in the saga of Zionist Asianism—that is, an effort from within the Zionist movement to reorient Jews and Jewish nationalism to a resurgent East.[8] But for Zionists, the conference also represented a reckoning with empire's denouement—with their complex, shifting relationship with Britain and with their uneasy standing in an emerging postcolonial world. As Palestine and India teetered on the precipice of independence, the Jewish delegation would find that as much as their impetus and imperative were shaped by the anticipation of their own *future*—the prospect of a UN vote on Palestine and the potential for an independent Jewish state—their relations with other Asian delegates at the conference, particularly those representing India, were still very much bound by their shared colonial *past*.

ARRIVAL IN DELHI

The initial invitation to the conference, extended by Sarojini Naidu on behalf of the Indian Council of World Affairs, was sent to the Hebrew University rather than the Va'ad Leumi or Jewish Agency, an indication of the sensitive matter of including a delegation from the Yishuv, as well as the intended "non-political" nature of the conference itself.[9] David Werner Senator, a member of Ihud (and previously Brit Shalom) who had served on the Jewish Agency Executive as a non-Zionist member, responded to the invitation in his capacity as administrator of the Hebrew University. Werner explained that the Va'ad Leumi, as "the body officially representing the Jewish Community in Palestine," was, in fact, better positioned than the University to put together a delegation; a representative from the University would thus only "form part of the group which [would] attend the conference."[10] In a subsequent communication with the Hebrew University, the secretary of the conference, Dr. A. Appadorai, clarified that the Indian organizers "[expected] the [Jewish] delegation to consist of as many University representatives as possible." Elaborating on his request, Appadorai relayed that Naidu had asked him "to stress the fact that all political controversies [would] be strictly eschewed from the deliberations" during the conference. "You will appreciate how detrimental it would be to the very purpose of this Conference if any internal political controversies of any country were allowed to vitiate the atmosphere," he wrote.[11]

After months of back-and-forth communication between leaders of the Hebrew University, the Va'ad Leumi, and the Organizing Committee of the Conference in India—and despite Appadorai's caution—a roster of ten delegates was selected that, in fact, included activists and Zionist insiders, in addition to scholars and academics. At the delegation's helm was Hugo Bergmann, the philosopher and Hebrew University professor who had cofounded Brit Shalom. The Sanskritist Immanuel Olsvanger, who had assisted the Jewish Agency alongside Kallenbach in its outreach efforts to India before World War II, likewise joined. The delegation also included Alfred Bonné (1899–1959), a German-born economist who had immigrated to Palestine in 1925 and was an expert on the economies of developing countries. Bergmann, Olsvanger, and Bonné all operated in similar intellectual and social milieus in Palestine, overlapping circles of former Brit Shalom members and academics committed to Jewish-Arab rapprochement. Beyond the academic delegates were David Hacohen (1898–1984), Bracha Habas (1900–1968), Ya'akov Shimoni (1914–96), and Ben-Zion Ilan (1913–75), all tied to the Labor Zionist establishment. Hacohen, the director of the public works company Solel Boneh and a high-ranking leader of the Haganah, had been detained at Latrun with Moshe Shertok, whom he had known since his youth. Both Shertok and Hacohen had graduated from the Herzliya Hebrew Gymnasium and had served in the Ottoman army during World War I. For three years after the war, they had shared a small flat in Kilburn while studying at the London School of Economics. Hacohen's spouse, Bracha Habas, a journalist and pedagogy expert, had immigrated to Palestine with her family as a child and later joined Ahdut ha-Avodah, developing its educational offerings for young workers. Shimoni had been a leader in the Hechalutz movement in Berlin before immigrating to Palestine in 1936. During the war, he ran the Arab Bureau of the Haganah's intelligence unit and later joined the Political Department's Arab Section. There, he and other officials adopted what Benny Morris has called a policy of "ambivalence," marked at once by a determination to build productive local and regional ties between Arabs and Jews and by furtive efforts to use Arab contacts to gather intelligence information.[12] Ben-Zion Ilan, a New York–born veteran of the Jewish Brigade and member of Kibbutz Afikim, attended the conference as an expert on collective farming.

The final two delegates from Palestine, the psychologist and educator May Bere Mereminsky (1894–1986) and the physician Anna Brachyahu (1887–1969), were active members of the women's movement in Palestine. The Canadian-born Mereminsky trained as a psychologist in the United States before immigrating to Palestine; she also had close ties to the Labor Zionist movement and from 1939 to 1941 served in America as an emissary of Moetzet Hapoalot (the Yishuv's Council of Women Workers), while her husband worked as the Histadrut's representative in New York.[13] Brachyahu was born in the Russian Empire and received her medical training in Edinburgh. Like David Hacohen, Brachyahu had old ties to Moshe Shertok. On Shertok's return to Palestine at the conclusion of World War I, following his service as an Ottoman soldier in Aleppo, he sought out Brachyahu, who had acquired English as a medical student in Scotland, to help him continue his studies of the language. When she protested that she did not know how to teach, Shertok reportedly quipped, "*How* to teach—I will tell you; you must know *what* to teach."[14] Along with Bracha Habas, who was likewise involved in the women's movement, Brachyahu and Mereminsky's presence at the conference fulfilled a specific request made by Naidu in her initial invitation: that "at least one woman" join the delegation in order to participate "in the discussion of the status of women and women's movements in Asia."[15] Finally, Fritz W. Pollack, who had moved from Palestine to Bombay in 1940, joined the nine delegates from Palestine on their arrival in India. Pollack had helped coordinate refugee relief efforts in India during the war and was active in Bombay Zionist circles; he went on to become Israel's trade commissioner in Southeast Asia. Before the final roster of delegates was con-

FIGURE 7   Moshe Shertok (second from left) and David Hacohen (second from right) in Latrun detention camp, 1946. Courtesy of the Moshe Sharett Heritage Society.

firmed, various alternates were proposed, including Norman Bentwich. Ultimately unable to attend—Helen was ill, and he returned to London from Jerusalem to be with her—Norman later wrote that he had "never ceased to regret" missing the Asian Relations Conference. He also remarked on the political tension of choosing delegates and at the time had to pledge to the Va'ad Leumi that he would not "intrude [his] heresies at the conference."[16]

The ostensibly nonpolitical nature of the conference posed challenges beyond the selection of Yishuv delegates. Two days before the conference opened, the Muslim League announced it would boycott the event. An editorial in Jinnah's newspaper, the *Dawn*, argued that the conference was "a thinly disguised attempt on the part of the Hindu Congress to boost itself politically as the prospective leader of the Asiatic peoples." The editorial further contended that the present moment—when there was so much internal strife and "the future shape of independent India [was] still to emerge from the welter of the present"—was hardly the time to host an international conference.[17] The Muslim League also encouraged other Muslim nations—in an act of solidarity with Indian Muslims—to join in the boycott of the conference. Though invitations were extended to Arab nations, including to Palestinian Arabs, all but Egypt ultimately declined to send a delegation to the conference. The Arab League, founded in March 1945 by the independent nations of Egypt, Iraq, Jordan, Lebanon, Syria, and Saudi Arabia, ultimately accepted an invitation to attend but with observer status. Whether Arab states were also motivated to boycott the conference because of the inclusion of the Yishuv would become a point of contention.

In late March, soon after their visas arrived, the nine delegates from Palestine made their way to India—a journey that took thirty hours, most of it by flying boat—and were joined on their arrival by Pollack. The next week and a half, during which the Yishuv representatives attended formal conference sessions and roundtables, and met privately with other delegates and local contacts, was marked by awe and amazement but also frustration and tension. Over the course of their visit, the Jewish delegates struggled to understand how to place themselves, and the Zionist movement and the Yishuv more broadly, in the framework of an emerging postcolonial Asia. They grappled with the extent to which the situation in India—its reckoning with British imperial rule, the possibility of partition there, and the division between religious and national groups on the subcontinent—paralleled their own condition in Palestine.

The "opening spectacle," hosted in a massive outdoor tent draped in colorful Indian fabrics and outfitted throughout with electric fans, included a procession of the delegations. Ushered in alphabetically by Nehru and Naidu, many of the delegations sported the national dress of their country. Habas, who along with her husband published a Hebrew-language memoir of their time in India after their return to Palestine, was particularly struck by the red robes of the Tibetan attendees. She lamented that the Jewish delegation from Palestine had no such distinguishing equivalent.[18] Yet their dress hardly served as a neutral backdrop. Habas and Hacohen both remarked that the Jewish delegation's European dress, as well as their lighter complexions, made them stand out, not their Judaism per se. But Hacohen also noted something that set the Jewish delegates apart from other Europeans attending the conference (mostly as observers and reporters): the "special Eastern ring" of the Hebrew language they spoke, which necessitated a "distinct definition" for the delegation—something *almost* Asian despite their European clothing and the "light color" of their skin.[19]

While he ruminated romantically on the Jewish delegation's Asian connections—a logic of self-soothing assurance, as well as self-Orientalism—Hacohen also reflected on the physicality and comportment of the Indians he encountered, stressing their difference from Europeans with a typical Orientalist gaze, while flattening their internal diversity. Whether it was "the great leader and hard-working journalist, the millionaire industrialist or the socialist thinker, the philosopher whose name is known worldwide, or the Jain ascetic," all appeared to Hacohen as "similar to each other in their clothing and in their manners, in the makeup of their faces and in the quiet of their restrained speech." At the same time, Hacohen also drew comparisons between the Indian leaders he encountered and Jewish notables, once again assimilating Asian and Jewish cultures. For example, he thought K. M. Panikkar, the prime minister of the princely state of Bikaner, who had a "thick, little beard," possessed an almost Weizmann-like countenance.[20]

While the Jewish delegation's visit to India was framed by the delegates themselves and by Zionist leaders in Palestine as emblematic of the Jewish "return to Asia," this argument was made just as often, if not more frequently, out of strategic, practical concerns rather than solely out of a sense of cultural affinity (whether real, imagined, or aspirational). Shertok's argument that the Zionist approach to India had to be distinct from its approach to Europe and America—that it needed to underscore, as he put it, that Jews "exist in Asia, we are a part of regenerating Asia, a part of ancient Asia, whether we want it or not"—was part of a broader geopolitical strategy that aimed to win the support of UN member countries. Similarly, David Hacohen, in a letter sent to Nehru during the conference, wrote, "We are an Asiatic people returning to our homeland and identifying completely with that part of the world." But Hacohen followed this prefatory statement with an appeal to make political decisions based on moral imperatives, reminding Nehru that Jews were still languishing in the "graveyards of their six million butchered brethren," stuck in DP camps in Germany. "I am sure the progressive social forces and statesmen of broad vision, profound thinkers and great revolutionaries, like you, will never allow to approach the Palestine problem and to decree the future of the Jewish people by considerations of power politics only," he wrote, implying that Nehru's position on Zionism stemmed from his desire to appease Muslim Indians.[21] Even for those Jews who were long-standing proponents of the Jewish-Asian cultural connection, the opportunities of the conference were patently political, despite its "non-political" banner. The writer Moshe Ya'akov Ben-Gavriel (born Eugen Hoeflich), who saw Zionism as part of a broader Pan-Asian movement, encouraged the organizers of the conference to convene a committee that might address the issue of Jewish–Palestinian Arab relations and arrive at "a just peace acceptable to both." Ben-Gavriel proposed that "an attempt at mediation between these two Asiatic peoples, coming from Asia and not from powers politically involved or interested in Palestine, would surely help to bring peace nearer."[22] Thus, the "return to Asia" idea, often a stand-in for outreach specifically to India, was, in fact, a strategy for a number of political ends, including promoting an effective diplomatic approach for an emerging Jewish state and fostering Jewish-Arab rapprochement. In other words, like the dominion idea of years past, the language around the Jewish return to Asia reflected a process of making the categories of empire—and its anticolonial horizons—legible to a range of Jewish political sensibilities. Also like the dominion idea, outreach to India and Asia may have been bolstered or supplemented by genuine affinity, but its central underpinning was practical and political.

For Hacohen, the anticolonial atmosphere of the Asian Relations Conference was as manifestly evident as the long history of colonial violence and exploitation in India, visible in everything from the built environment of the country's cities to the poverty of its people. "The history of the conquest of India is unlike any colonial conquest in the modern era in the extent of its exploitation, murder, hypocrisy, and the scope of its purpose," he wrote. As for the various institutions the British built up in India—including universities, courts, legislative bodies, and the Indian Army—"none of these were intended to educate a generation in whose hands the fate of the nation would be entrusted," Hacohen explained. Rather, they were "intended to raise a class of servants who would always depend on the uppermost English bureaucracy and its directive." Life in India was highly racially segregated, with exclusive social spaces reserved for Europeans only, no matter if "the guest were a Maharaja."[23] Statues and monuments of "English officials and statesmen whose names almost no one knows" dotted "every street corner," while poverty, on a level wholly unknown in Europe, afflicted the masses, whose opportunities for upward mobility, whether through agriculture or industry, were abysmal.[24] Viewing all of this, Hacohen explained, an observer could not help but

> understand how the hearts of Indians shudder when they see how monuments and memorials were erected with their money, scattered all across the country, to exalt and glorify the memory of those who carried out the murder and widespread subjugation of their ancestors.... Their hearts shudder at the sight of all these—and in that moment they will remember the Amritsar massacre at the end of the First World War, a site of horror and a bloody wound to this day.... Because of these sins alone the English have been condemned to be expelled from India permanently and in disgrace.[25]

What was more, Hacohen noted, complicity ran through every strata of British society. Even though the wealthiest of Britons may have benefited the most, "every thought of the [British] people—in school, in church, in

Parliament—was directed toward the recognition and assurance that their existence and their spirit depended on their control of the empire and the belief that this was the decree of history, an almost sacred and exalted mission from on high."[26]

Whereas Hacohen's condemnation of the colonial regime in India was forceful and unequivocal, he and his fellow delegates trod more carefully when it came to drawing parallels between the situations in India and Palestine. There was, of course, no shortage of possible similarities, with the countries' shared prospect of partition, resistance against the British, and intercommunal strife. While Hacohen thought that partition was the best option for Palestine, his discussions with Indian delegates convinced him that the plan would spell disaster for the subcontinent, bringing "panicked migrations," "fratricidal wars," and "unprecedented bloodshed." Hacohen concluded that a future Pakistan would be incapable of protecting the sizable Muslim minority that would remain in India after partition, able only to "retaliate against Hindus within its own borders."[27]

Hacohen also warned that while the Jewish insurgency against the British in Palestine might have earned the admiration of some Hindu Indians, it would be a "mistake to think that likewise with regard to the schism between us and the Arabs that there is—or could easily be created—a sort of closeness—one based on the foundation of the Hindu-Muslim conflict." The intercommunal conflict in India was something very different from the one in Palestine. "We must not forget," Hacohen clarified, "that the people living in India—whether Muslim or Hindu—are from one race, speak one language, live in a common village and are doomed to the same fate of hunger and poverty and ignorance."[28] He was also struck by what he perceived to be the lack of animosity among Hindu Indians toward Islam. When he asked his Hindu interlocutors if they harbored any anger toward Muslims for the conquests and forced conversions of the past, they balked at the suggestion—so dissimilar, Hacohen thought, from the long and tenacious Jewish collective memory of the Inquisition and the Khmelnitsky massacres. While Hacohen acknowledged that the last couple of years had seen unprecedented intercommunal violence in India, he believed it was wrong to assume that the conflict could be translated into support for an "anti-Muslim politics in another part of the world."[29]

If these parallels were inexact or problematic, they still conceptualized Jews as anticolonial resisters, just ones in a different country, with different internal dynamics that demanded their own solutions. But the Jewish delegation quickly discovered that other attendees at the Asian Relations Conference were often unwilling to view them as fellow anticolonial activists, seeing them instead, as Hacohen put it, as part of a "European invasion of an Asian country."[30]

THE "INCIDENT"

The aim to avoid "controversial and problematic issues" at the conference came at a cost, according to Shimoni, who authored the delegation's official report on its time in India. "The outcome has been that most of the real problems have either not been touched at all, or were touched on slightly and casually and immediately hushed up," he wrote. Such provocative topics included the fear of Indian and Chinese imperialism and the discrimination faced by Chinese immigrants in Burma, Malaya, and Indonesia. The aim to maintain a "non-political" atmosphere at the conference "lent an unreal and phraseological note to a good many of the beautiful speeches delivered," Shimoni noted. The commitment to avoiding controversy even affected the name by which the Jewish delegation was recognized. While the delegates wanted to be known as the "Jewish Palestine Delegation," they were at times referred to simply as the "Palestine Delegation," a designation they found inappropriate since they did not, in fact, represent all of Palestine—namely, Palestinian Arabs. Conversely, they were at times also referred to as the "Hebrew University Delegation," which likewise lacked accuracy. "The common ground for these two contradictory trends seems to me to be found in the endeavour not to mention and not to refer to *Jewish* Palestine, in order, thus, to avoid controversies," observed Shimoni.[31]

Indeed, the Jewish delegation's very presence at the conference, imbued as the gathering was with anticolonial political feeling, proved divisive. In Nehru's inaugural speech on the first day of the conference, he addressed the countries of Asia, even including "the Arab countries," which (with the exception of Egypt and the Arab League) had boycotted the conference. He did not, however, mention Palestine or the Jewish delegation specifically. The Jewish delegates disagreed among themselves whether the slight was intentional. "There were those among us who wished to be lenient [in our judgment] and said that it was self-evident that he included us among the 'Arab countries,' and there were the pedants who saw intent in the speech," reported Habas.[32] Shimoni, likely in the latter camp, thought Nehru was doing his best to avoid social interaction with the Jewish delegation in public.[33]

The following evening, at the second opening plenary session of the conference, speeches of salutation were given by various delegation leaders, including Bergmann, who stressed the Asian origins of the Jewish community. "Those are the greetings of the representatives of an old religion and an old Asian people which was driven from its Asian motherland 1,800 years ago by the force of the Roman sword, but has never ceased to be linked in thought and daily prayer with this holy land which is at the same time a holy land to Christianity and Islam," he told the conference. "We are happy and proud to take part as an old Asian people at this Conference and we strive to be a loyal member of this great family of nations," he declared. But despite their Asian origin, Bergmann explained, the Jews of Palestine still had much to learn from Asia, particularly when it came to its model of "multi-racial, multi-religious and multi-cultural" cooperation. "This lesson Europe was unable to teach us" during the Jews' long sojourn on that continent, Bergmann explained. "We have been everywhere a persecuted minority, and during the last war six millions of our brethren, the third part of our people—and the best part—babies, children, women and men, have been ruthlessly murdered in the gas chambers," he said. "This last lesson of Europe to us we shall never forget." He hoped Palestine would "not go the European way of 'solving' . . . problems by dispossessing populations" but would instead strive "to make room for more people . . . more cooperation, more reciprocal help."[34]

The Jewish delegation came to refer to what transpired next as the "incident." After Bergmann finished and a series of other delegates gave their remarks, Takieddin el-Solh (1908–88), the Arab League observer, rose to speak. The countries of the Arab League, el-Solh told the audience, had "always been known as the door to India." As a result of that position, they had suffered at the hands of colonial powers in the past. "We now share with you your freedom, as your freedom is necessary for our freedom," el-Solh explained: "We have always been determined to place these [Arab] states at the service of right and against oppression and colonisation. In the heart of these countries is Palestine. It is more oppressed than any other country. The nation is Hebrew-Semitic like any one of us and it has been oppressed everywhere except in our country. But it is trying to take advantage as a special minority under the defense of British bayonets. We object to that and we hope that you will stand by the side of right with us."[35] In other words, the Jews in Palestine, according to el-Solh, may have had their origins in the region—being a "Hebrew-Semitic" nation—and they may have faced great oppression everywhere else in the world, but their presence in Palestine, backed by British colonial violence, came at the expense of Palestinian Arabs.

After el-Solh finished, Nehru, who had not been present during Bergmann's speech, announced that he was going to allow Karima el-Said, a delegate from Egypt and a representative of the Egyptian Feminist Union, to give additional remarks, even though she had already delivered greetings earlier in the evening. "I understand that, in my absence, certain references were made to Palestine and she feels that, on behalf of the women of Egypt she should say something," Nehru said. "As you know, we have tried to avoid, for obvious reasons, raising and discussing controversial issues at this Conference. It is well known to all of you what the opinion in Asia is about most of these controversial issues. There is no doubt about it. Nevertheless, if this Conference enters into these questions, we will get involved in them," he told the crowd, turning over the platform to el-Said.[36]

El-Said began by objecting to "any settlement in Palestine except for the Arabs." Like el-Solh, el-Said did not actually reject the notion that Jews originated in the region. But they had still spent the last eighteen centuries in Europe—something Bergmann himself had acknowledged—while Arabs had spent the last fourteen centuries in Palestine. "The Americans have been in America for less than five centuries and still they consider that America is their home," el-Said reasoned. Her objection to Jews settling in Palestine was not on account of their Jewishness, she declared; rather, it was because they were European by virtue of their long sojourn on the continent. "We object to them as foreigners, as Europeans," she affirmed. "The Arabs must live in Palestine," she said, concluding, "Palestine cannot belong any more to its original inhabitants." Her rationale used familiar anticolonial tropes—resisting the European interloper—while it simultaneously elided the colonial experience of other groups, namely Native Americans, in order to make an argument about tenure and landownership.[37]

Bergmann attempted to respond to el-Solh and el-Said, but Nehru refused him the platform. In protest, Bergmann, followed by the nine other Jewish delegates, moved to leave the conference hall amid cries of "Let him speak!" from the audience. Several Indian delegates, including Sarojini Naidu's daughter, Padmaja Naidu, and H. N. Kunzru (whom the Bentwiches had met on their way to Australia in 1938), ran after the Jewish delegation, attempting to get them to return. "They expressed loudly and openly their opinion that we had been wronged and requested us to do them the favour of returning because by our walk-out the whole Conference would be upset," reported Shimoni. Ultimately, the delegation returned, with Bergmann returning to the dais "amid a storm of applause." He approached el-Solh, extended his hand, and the two shook, with a second eruption of clapping filling the hall.[38] Bergmann later called the gesture "an altogether impromptu, spontaneous act."[39]

In his closing remarks for the day, Nehru "expressed regret that Prof. Bergmann should have been hurt by him" and "stressed the great sympathy the Indian people [had] always felt for the Jews." Nevertheless, he explained, the Indian people believed that Palestine was "essentially an Arab country." He hoped that a solution might be reached between Jews and Arabs, something he felt certain would be easier to achieve if only the "third party"—in other words, the British—would withdraw.[40]

Two nights after the incident, Nehru invited the Jewish delegates to join him for dinner at his home, where, with the exception of Nehru's daughter Indira Gandhi and his sister Vijaya Lakshmi Pandit, they were the sole guests. Some of the delegates assumed the lack of other guests meant that Nehru "did not wish to give publicity" to the dinner. Indeed, it turned out that he had no plan to avoid discussing controversial matters in the relative privacy of the setting. On retiring to the veranda after the meal, Nehru asked the Jewish delegation pointedly, "What will happen in Palestine?"

The question—or rather the proper way to answer it—proved contentious enough among the Jewish delegates, diverse as their own hopes for Palestine and the Yishuv were, that it prompted an argument after they left. "Some of us were disappointed with the parts others had played," wrote Shimoni, though they all "tried hard to say the right thing." Nehru listened intently, and the questions he posed, according to Shimoni, revealed "a great deal of understanding." Still, despite this understanding and despite what even seemed to be Nehru's "sympathetic attitude towards the Jewish problem," Shimoni did not think the delegation succeeded in winning over the Indian leader. "He seemed to approach the problem not so much on the merits of our case but rather on political constellations," he wrote. "He surprised us by interrupting the discussion on the merits of our case by the brutal question, 'what is the force behind you, the force you can rely on?'" Shimoni recalled.[41]

Nehru's frankness was ultimately matched by the Jewish delegates—or, rather, by David Hacohen, who became the sole converser with Nehru as the night progressed and the discussion became more and more discouraging to the other delegates. Whereas in all other meetings, the Jewish delegates had been careful to mention partition as "*one* of the many possible" solutions in Palestine, that evening, Hacohen spoke candidly that he believed territorial separation to be the only possible option—an opinion not shared by Bergmann. After dinner, the delegation sent Nehru a letter, signed by Hacohen, to follow up on their conversation that evening. "We are in Palestine with a clean conscience," the letter stated. "We never came and never will be an outpost of foreign domination," it continued. The letter challenged the idea that if Jewish "claims were acceded to, a general conflagration would occur throughout the Middle-East." Certainly, challenges would occur, but they would be temporary and would not prove worse than the current situation. The missive expressed hope that Nehru and other progressive statesmen would "treat [the Palestine situation] courageously and unbiased according to their conscience and high morals."[42] Though the delegation confirmed with Nehru that he received the letter and read it, they did not receive a response.

The Jewish delegates processed the "incident" on two levels. First, they grappled with the immediate effects it had on their remaining time at the conference and on their efforts to cultivate relationships with other delegates and contacts. Shimoni thought that "regrettable as it was in itself," the incident ultimately brought about positive results. The attention "aroused a special interest in our affairs, bringing them into the limelight," he wrote. Though coverage in the Indian press was "completely and unreservedly anti-

Zionist," according to Shimoni, the delegation found the broader public, particularly the Hindu public, to be "in many cases, not unsympathetic." As a general rule, Shimoni believed that "the less a man was connected with official politics, the more he dared to express sympathy with our aims."[43] K. M. Panikkar, the Weizmannesque head of Bikaner State, gave similar advice. Though Panikkar had not made any special overture to the Jewish delegation during the conference, after the summit concluded, he invited Alfred Bonné and Hugo Bergmann to visit Bikaner State, whereupon he "revealed himself as an ardent friend" of Zionism.[44] Panikkar told them that top leaders such as Nehru and Gandhi were "fixed" in their policy outlook, which was "determined by political calculations" that were "necessarily pro-Arab." Panikkar believed that would remain the case so long as Nehru and Gandhi thought that they had to "appease Muslim opinion." In the interim, Panikkar advised, Zionists should focus their outreach efforts on lower-level leaders who would be "free to form, and even to voice, their own unbiased opinion." Panikkar was in a sense evidence of his own advice; a high-ranking Indian leader, he had not reached out until *after* the conference—and the accompanying media frenzy—had concluded.[45] Still, it was these various personal contacts—made in every venue from official receptions to informal hallway conversations—that the Jewish delegation believed were "the most important asset" gained from their time in the conference, aside from the "mere fact" of their participation. The incident at the second plenary session, and the attention, even sympathy, that it garnered, arguably put the Jewish delegation into contact with more delegates than they might have otherwise had occasion to meet.

But beyond its immediate, practical ramifications, the incident also forced the Jewish delegates to confront what it meant to have been so thoroughly identified with the colonizer. As upsetting, uncomfortable, or objectionable as the Jewish delegates found this characterization, it hardly came as a surprise; there was broad recognition in advance of the conference that the Zionist movement and the Yishuv were viewed as "a sword that the West jabs in the East," as Shertok had put it. A statement drafted before the conference and delivered by Shimoni for All India Radio, the national public radio service, anticipated this charge. "Our returning to Palestine and our developing the country has not done any harm to anybody, nobody has been dispossessed or expelled, we have come not as foreign conquerors or exploiters but as sons of the country returning home for building and developing the country for the benefit of all its inhabitants," he declared on the broadcast.[46]

One of the memoranda prepared by the Jewish delegation for the conference, entitled "The Jewish Movement of National Liberation," similarly anticipated the charge but attempted to maneuver around it more subtly. Written for the roundtable group meeting on "National Movements for Freedom," the text argued that "the Jewish liberation movement differs significantly from other freedom movements." Jews had indeed had their own encounter with imperial domination—nearly two millennia earlier with Rome. But the contemporary Jewish "struggle for national freedom [was] not directed against any individual Power, but against a state of things"—in contrast to most other movements, which tended to be "directed against an alien usurper exercising open or veiled control over the national territory." If there was no single antagonist—no single "alien usurper"—for the last many centuries of Jewish history, the backing of a great power likewise did not characterize the development of Jewish nationalism, according to the memorandum. The movement may have "received international recognition in the Palestine Mandate of 1922, yet its strength lies not in such external recognition, but in the spiritual needs and aspirations from which it sprang," the document explained. Jews were in Palestine returning to their "roots, to the land of their origin"; they were there "not to conquer or to dominate but to rebuild." The Zionist in this framing was thus not the colonizer. And if the Zionist did not appear to fit more familiar conceptions of the *colonized*, that was the result of the dispersion, dislocation, and upheaval of the Jewish historical experience. The memorandum also both glossed over Britain's role in sanctioning the development of the Yishuv (Britain was not mentioned by name once in the entire ten-page document) *and* elided the ongoing Jewish insurgency in Palestine, a more recognizable anticolonial manifestation of Jewish nationalism, but one also tied to violence—an abrogation of Gandhi's satyagraha. In other words, the controversial matter of Zionism's relationship to Britain—the answer to Nehru's pointed question "what is the force behind you, the force you can rely on?"—was avoided altogether.

If there was a general shared anticipation that the Jewish delegation might face charges of representing the colonial usurper—or, at the very least, of hiding behind that power—the delegates themselves responded to the accusation, and the broader fact of Asian support for the Arabs, in different ways. Habas's mood was one of dejection. She felt that what happened on the stage was "not only an affront" to the delegation but also a revelation of the inescapability of the situation in Palestine. "Its strings are wrapped around us with an unyielding hand here, too, despite the explicitly non-political nature of this gathering," she wrote.[47] Bergmann, in a letter he composed to Martin Buber before leaving India after the conclusion of the conference, acknowledged that Asian support for the Arab cause made sense. "The sympathies of all those nations are (understandably) with the Arabs," he wrote. He anticipated that despite their work at the conference, India, and likely China and Iran as well, would stand against the Yishuv in a UN vote; but he still found cause for hope, particularly in the realm of future exchange over economic and agricultural matters.[48] Of all the delegates, Shimoni issued the most scathing condemnation, targeting Nehru specifically in an editorial in *Davar* published after his return to Palestine. The Indian leader might be "one of the greatest statesmen of the present period," but "the attitude which he has openly adopted of late . . . towards the Jewish people, is hardly a testimony of high moral stature," contended Shimoni. By contrast, he argued, Nehru had had "nothing to say" when it came to the "Quislings and traitors" sitting on other delegations "against whom legitimate objection can be levelled." Shimoni also believed that determining policy toward Palestine based on internal Muslim-Hindu dynamics in India was a poor excuse. "If that reading is correct, is this the way men of spirit and moral stature act?" he asked. "[Nehru] must be aware that Palestine represents the only hope of our salvation within this hostile world which is thirsty for Jewish blood," he wrote.[49]

As we saw in the previous chapter, by 1939, the Zionist movement and the Yishuv had come to have a sense of staying power—despite the situation in Europe and despite strict British immigration policy in Palestine. That sense of power, despite the continued enforcement of the white paper and the uncertainty of what lay ahead, was only emboldened in the wake of the war. Jewish military might proved to be effective, disciplined, and a formidable opponent to British forces, and the Yishuv's economy—in contrast to

Britain's postwar austerity—was thriving. Yet the murder of six million Jews in the Holocaust and the stunning indifference of world powers to the survivors who remained trapped in the limbo of DP camps in Europe made the continued reality of Jewish persecution strikingly clear, despite the Yishuv's undeniable power. Postwar Zionist political arguments—including the arguments made by the Jewish delegates in Delhi—still hinged on the fact of Jewish suffering. Most of the delegates were also swift to insist that neither Jewish power—all the achievements that had been realized in Palestine—nor Jewish powerlessness—the pressing need for a home for Jewish survivors—had or would have a negative bearing on Palestinian Arab life. Shimoni, as we have seen, flatly denied that anyone had been dispossessed by Zionist settlement in Palestine. Bergmann acknowledged Palestinian dispossession as a possibility—but one that might occur in the future should the Yishuv fail to adopt certain lessons from Asia. This appeared to many Indian and Asian onlookers as a stunning blind spot, primarily because of their own experiences with colonialism, which mirrored that of the Palestinians more closely, but also because of the commitment many of these leaders had to socialism. The dispossession of Palestinian farmers that occurred when Jews purchased land from Arab landlords—often absentee ones—contravened fundamental principles of labor politics, for example. Still, that the Jewish delegates resented the accusation that Zionists hid behind British bayonets was perhaps unsurprising. The Arab Revolt of the previous decade—and the fact that the British had created and armed Jewish police units to help crush the rebellion—now seemed a distant memory compared to the ongoing reality of the Jewish insurgency (carried out by many of the same individuals who had served in those units). Palestine now resembled Ireland of the early 1920s in more ways than one. The pattern of reprisals—on both the Jewish and British sides—the kidnappings, and the targeted assassinations all echoed the Ireland of decades earlier. The Irgun and Lehi received training from the Irish Republican Army, while a significant number of Black and Tans veterans served among British forces in Palestine.[50] Members of the Jewish delegation remembered Operation Agatha of the previous summer well—the searches, the sieges, and, for Hacohen, the imprisonment, all at the hands of the British. If the delegates—all Labor Zionists or binationalists—objected to the terrorist tactics of the Revisionists, the embattled dynamic between the British and Jews in Palestine since the end of World War II was nevertheless wholly manifest.

Still, the Zionist turn away from the British Empire remained incomplete, even on the eve of its collapse. Just as the Jewish delegates realized that their political futures were delimited by a colonial past—whether they liked it or not—the Zionist political imagination likewise remained enmeshed in empire and the question of its future. For three decades, British rule in Palestine had meant that Jewish political futures were bound to the fate of the empire and that a vast imperial world agitating for political change—chief of all, India—became relevant to Jews in Palestine. As we have seen, navigating a changing empire produced a politics of uncertainty, of attempting to account for the many potential outcomes of empire and what each would mean for Jews and the Yishuv. Those politics necessarily encompassed strategies and outlooks that were seemingly paradoxical because the fates of empire were paradoxical. After the conclusion of the Asian Relations Conference, Hanns G. Reissner (1902–77), a German Jewish historian who had found refuge in India in 1939, penned a short article on his impressions of the seminal meeting that embodied this seemingly paradoxical view. "Zionist politicians have always looked to the West for support, and this onesidedness cannot be remedied within the twinkle of an eye," he wrote. Solidifying a renewed relationship with the East would require tremendous effort and time, but there was fortunately an existing model to achieve these aims, according to Reissner:

> Unless Prof. Weizmann had assimilated British thought and reactions he could probably not have hoped to win over to his cause the late Lord Balfour and his ministerial colleagues. Exactly the same patient study of Eastern thought and reactions seems a prerequisite for the vindication of the Jewish cause with the awakening East. . . . The present political impasse on Palestine seems to call for an all-out revision of the desirable attitude in between East and West. Centres of gravity shift, often far away from present centres of Jewish domicile or refuge. It is perhaps premature to envisage a future Eastern declaration of active sympathy in addition to the Balfour Declaration which has spent its dynamic force. But it is timely to admit to oneself that Palestine has got to face both West and East.[51]

While acknowledging that the British period in Zionist history was coming to a close, and imagining the dawn of a new Eastern-gazing Zionist era, Reissner still looked to the imperial past—to the most consequential Jewish political achievement to come from the Jewish-British partnership—as an essential model in the postcolonial world-to-come. He imagined a Yishuv bookended by the Balfour Declaration and an Eastern declaration—by both an imperial and postcolonial political promise.

Before leaving India, the Jewish delegation met with Gandhi at his Delhi residence, located in the city's Bhangi Colony, the neighborhood populated by members of the Dalit caste of "untouchables," whose traditional occupation was sweeping. For days, Gandhi had been trying to hold a prayer meeting that would include a recitation of verses from the Quran. After three days of objections coming from his audience, Gandhi finally found success on the fourth day, when no protest was raised. The Jewish delegation was there to witness a female prayer leader sing in Hindi, while also incorporating Quranic verses. After Gandhi's demonstration of Muslim-Hindu unity, the delegation met briefly with the Indian leader during which David Hacohen implored him to "raise his voice in favor of our persecuted people." Gandhi inquired about the current state of terrorism in Palestine and questioned what Zionist leaders were doing to fight that part of the Jewish insurgency. "He hinted that if somebody would insist that he, Gandhi, should say something about the Palestine question his words would necessarily be directed mainly against terrorism and therefore it would be better for our sake to leave him out of the picture," Shimoni noted. When the delegates countered that they thought terrorism would "subside by itself" if only the British permitted more immigration or offered a "friendly gesture," Gandhi likened the answer to "the dealings between the British Government and Hitler, when everyone said if only my demands are fulfilled, everything would be alright."[52] The comparison to the Munich Agreement was surely just as upsetting to the delegates as Gandhi's assertion in 1938 that the "cry for the [Jewish] National Home affords a colourable justification for the German expulsion of the Jews" had been to Buber, Magnes, and others.[53] But it was deemed less worthy of attention this time—likely because it was not unexpected and because it drew negative attention to an already sensitive situation. Shimoni covered the meeting only briefly in his internal report. Habas glossed over the encounter, leaving out Gandhi's comment about appeasement, in her and Hacohen's 1947 memoir of the trip. Though the meeting was mentioned in the Hebrew and Jewish presses, that particular detail of the conversation was excluded. The Jewish Agency and Va'ad Leumi likely never made it public.

TOWARD PARTITION

The Asian Relations Conference and its proposed plans—chiefly to create an Asian Relations Organization to foster inter-Asian cooperation—were quickly overshadowed by events in the spring and summer of 1947. In May, days after the Irgun carried out the infamous Acre prison break, the UN created the Special Committee on Palestine (UNSCOP). Made up of representatives from eleven countries (including India) and tasked with recommending a possible constitutional solution, UNSCOP began its fact-finding mission in Palestine on June 16, 1947. Members of the committee were still in the country a month later to witness the British interception of the SS *Exodus*, a packet steamship carrying more than forty-five hundred Holocaust survivors. The British boarded and fought the passengers—resulting in three Jewish casualties—and ultimately deported the rest back to Germany. The story of the ill-fated ship and its passengers—and the heartlessness of British rule—made headlines around the globe. The Irgun's kidnapping and murder of two British sergeants in retaliation for the capture and execution of three Revisionist operatives produced outrage and fury among the British at home and abroad. By August, Palestine had become an inferno. British police in Tel Aviv attacked and set fire to civilian homes and businesses. The Jewish community in Britain was likewise targeted; synagogues and Jewish shops were burned and defaced with antisemitic graffiti.[54]

While UNSCOP was preparing for its mission to Palestine, Viceroy Mountbatten—who had been tasked with finding a solution that would keep India united—surprised the world when he announced that India would, in fact, be partitioned into two independent dominions and that the British would withdraw by August 15, 1947—ten months earlier than Atlee had previously announced. On the eve of independence, while Mountbatten was safely ensconced in Viceroy's House, intercommunal violence erupted on a scale previously unseen even during all the months of unrest leading up to partition. Mass slaughter and rape ensued as Muslims and Hindus, as well as Sikhs, who found themselves on the wrong side of the British-drawn border, desperately tried to make their way to safety. Partition in India claimed the lives of one to two million and displaced more than fifteen million.

Just over two weeks later, UNSCOP submitted its report, recommending the end of the British mandate in Palestine. The majority of the committee's members—eight out of the eleven—proposed that Palestine be partitioned into two separate states: one Arab and one Jewish. It was this recommendation that was brought to the UN General Assembly for a vote in November 1947.

Conclusion

IN THE LAST WEEK OF February 1948, Norman Bentwich arrived in Aden. The last and only other time he had visited the small British colony had been a decade earlier, while on his way with Helen to Australia. Back in that frantic, desperate age, as the Bentwiches raced to find solutions to the surging Jewish refugee crisis in Europe, Norman had worried about deteriorating relations between Aden's Jewish community and the colony's Muslim population, deterioration he attributed to the situation in Palestine. Ten years later, he returned to Aden following a deadly riot targeting the Jewish community, carried out in response to the UN General Assembly's vote to endorse UNSCOP's partition plan for Palestine. Norman came to assist the Jewish community—which had lost eighty-two members and suffered extensive property damage in the riot—in its testimony before the British investigative commission formed in the wake of the violence. Soon after his arrival in Aden, Norman received a letter from his friend and colleague David Werner Senator, who wrote that "as a 'wanderer between two worlds' "—a reference to the title of Norman's 1941 memoir—"I can understand that this is precisely the sort of thing to appeal to you." But Senator implored his friend to return to Palestine—or even to London or New York—where he "might be more useful."[1] In reply, Norman admitted that he had, indeed, come to Aden because he found the situation in Palestine so hopeless. By February 1947, a civil war between Jews and Palestinians was under way with little British intervention; the mass flight and dispossession of Palestinian civilians had already begun; and the binational future Norman had longed for seemed definitively foreclosed. He also lamented what he saw as the "frenzied anti-British policy" of the Yishuv. "So rapidly are we rushing down the headlong slope to perdition," he wrote.[2]

In June 1948, a month after Zionist leaders declared independence as the state of Israel and armies of the surrounding Arab nations invaded, precipitating a wider regional war, Norman agreed to lobby the Colonial Office to allow for the immigration of Jews from Aden and Yemen to Israel. In the summer of 1949, he returned to Aden for a third time to witness the early airlifts that would ultimately bring the majority of Adeni and Yemini Jews to Israel. Though that immigration was part of the broader migration of Middle Eastern Jews that occurred following the founding of the state of Israel, the flight of the Jews of Aden, in particular, represented for Norman a new kind of exigency shaped by the upheavals of empire's end and also a profound reversal of the past. In the years leading up to World War II, Norman had sought out places of refuge in the British Empire for the imperiled Jews of Europe when immigration to Palestine had proved impossible; a decade later, he instead helped to facilitate Jewish emigration *from* a British colony to the newly created state of Israel. But he did so as he felt deep grief over the state of things there—the now "quixotic" goal of Jewish-Arab rapprochement and the creation of the "homeless mass" of more than seven hundred thousand Palestinians who, whether they had fled in fear or faced forcible expulsions by the Israeli military, now found themselves refugees.[3]

"I shall be, as I have been, a Jew errant, wandering between two worlds," Norman had predicted in his 1941 memoir. Norman, in fact, wandered between many worlds—between Zionist and non-Zionist, between British and Jewish, between colonial official and civilian, between war and peace, and between empire and nation. This abundance of worlds, and the struggles Norman experienced as he navigated their shifting frontiers, was a sign of the times. The period of British rule in Palestine was, globally, an age of coalescing and unraveling, of borders rewritten and contested, of the throes and pangs of an old order giving way to new terrain.

What Norman perhaps failed to see through his wanderings and his sense of alienation was how often his many "worlds" overlapped and intertwined in unexpected ways and, moreover, how often the competing pulls and contradictions he felt characterized the broader Jewish experience navigating an empire in flux. As Jews across the British Empire traversed the pulls of British imperialism, anticolonial nationalisms, and Zionism, they imagined Jewish political futures rooted in an enduring British Empire. They regarded British history, politics, and culture as models for the Yishuv. They even hoped that Palestine might become a dominion in the British Commonwealth of Nations. But they also gazed toward national horizons, contemplating the potential triumph of anticolonial independence movements and fostering ties with the torchbearers of those politics.

This consideration of the many possible fates of the British Empire produced varied and entangled worlds and worldviews—diverse political attitudes, strategies, and relationships that, as we have seen, at times appeared paradoxical and contradictory. Throughout the 1920s, Chaim Arlosoroff passionately advocated for close, productive Jewish-British ties in Palestine and thought seriously about the prospect of Palestine joining the British Commonwealth as a dominion. Yet it was precisely Arlosoroff's appreciation of state-like power—and what it would afford the Zionist movement—that led him to support the idea of dominion status. In other words, Arlosoroff understood that long-lasting imperial ties, on the one hand, and national self-determination (within the framework of the commonwealth), on the other, might be mutually achievable for the Yishuv. By the early 1930s, however, as progress in the Yishuv had reached a dire standstill, Arlosoroff became convinced that the Jewish-British partnership had grown untenable. Still, it was amid the crystallization of this conviction that Arlosoroff became most entrenched in elite British social circles in Jerusalem and formed a warm, open friendship with the British high commissioner Arthur Wauchope. In India, Rachel and David Ezra asserted the Baghdadi Jewish community's European cultural identity and insisted on their steadfast loyalty to the British Empire in their dealings with the imperial state. But their Jewish identity—their religious practice, communal leadership, and dedication to Zionism—remained the most salient force in their lives. They also forged relationships with elite Indians, contributed to Indian nation-building projects, and expressed tentative hopefulness about the prospect of Indian self-rule. Hermann Kallenbach and Henry Polak, through their relationship with Gandhi and their connection to Indians in South Africa, emerged as uniquely capable of guiding Zionist efforts to establish ties with Indian nationalists in the 1930s. While Kallenbach had come to support Zionism after witnessing the rise of antisemitism in Europe and South Africa, Polak remained a steadfast non-Zionist. And though both men were immersed in critiques of colonialism and supported Indian independence, the rise of Nazism in Europe compelled them to rethink—and even to defend—Jewish relationships to British imperialism. Moshe Shertok came to articulate a vision for Jewish independence in Palestine, while simultaneously carefully guarding the Zionist-British relationship and promoting Jewish relations with the emerging postcolonial world. These seeming contradictions were all shaped out of a single, broad horizon of uncertainty over Jewish political futures—futures that since 1917 had become bound up in the fate of an empire grappling with increasingly powerful anticolonial movements vying for independence.

Though Jews in all modern empires grappled variously with imperial policies and burgeoning nationalisms, Jews in the British Empire after 1917 faced the unique situation of living under the power that controlled the territory at the heart of Jewish political, cultural, and religious aspirations both in and beyond the empire. This reality shaped how British imperial Jews with diverse opinions on Jewish political questions thought about and engaged with the Zionist movement. Both Zionists in Palestine and non-Zionist Jews across the empire ended up confronting the entanglements of Jewish, British, and anticolonial politics. They ended up agreeing on the challenges facing Jews in Palestine as nationalisms near and far staked their claims against British imperialism—and at times, they even tackled those challenges in the same way. Non-Zionists such as Helen Bentwich—initially so hostile to the Zionist movement—and Henry Polak—a vocal critic of the South African Jewish community—both found themselves working on behalf of Zionist causes, throwing in their lot with a movement with which they never truly identified.

In recovering the sheer vastness of the interwar Jewish political imagination and in reconstructing the diverse and complex visions Jews had of their own political futures, historians have explored the countless paths not taken, the failed schemes, the dashed hopes, the unrealized dreams—the entire firmament of what could have been. It is true that Palestine never became a British dominion. But far from illuminating something that simply never came to pass, an examination of the dominion scheme—particularly Arlosoroff's consideration of it—reveals the central concerns about governing and sustaining a modern state that carried the Zionist movement through to the founding of Israel in 1948.

While the dominion scheme appealed to Zionists concerned with state power, it also attracted those pursuing nonstatist ideals. In a parallel to the Zionist and non-Zionist visions that converged in the British Empire amid the upheavals of the era, Jews with statist and nonstatist visions for Palestine (and vastly different Zionist politics) found agreement around the idea of dominion. From Norman Bentwich, who supported binationalism and Jewish-Arab cooperation and rejected the notion of separate political sovereignty for each community; to Arlosoroff whose moderate Labor Zionist politics became increasingly focused on achieving state-like power for the Yishuv; to the right-wing Revisionist Jabotinsky who saw in Britain an international power that could impose a Jewish-majority state—all regarded dominion as potentially the best option for Palestine. Uncertainty, then, as Jews navigated and negotiated the many possible fates of empire, made for strange bedfellows.

Investigating Jewish politics in the British Empire and through the lens of uncertainty forces us to rethink many of the organizing categories and tropes of modern Jewish history—and not only those of Zionist and non-Zionist (or statist and nonstatist Zionist visions). This is a story in which Eastern European Jews, Middle Eastern Jews, and Western European Jewish elites were all central players. It is a story that reframes the geographic space of the modern Jewish experience, pushing the more familiar triangulation of America, Europe, and Palestine/Israel toward southern and eastern vistas. Finally, this is a story in which the modern narratives of empire and colonization, of national deliverance and self-determination, lack a straightforward binary and oppositional character and, instead, are deeply imbricated.

Notes

Introduction

1. See Shertok's description of his work in Moshe Shertok to Meir Bogdanovski, mid-June 1918 in Moshe Sharett, *Nitra'eh ve-ulai lo: mikhtavim min ha-tsava ha-'Otomani, 1916–1918* (Tel Aviv: ha-'Amutah le-moreshet Moshe Sharett, 1998), 339–43. All translations are mine unless otherwise indicated. Already a native Yiddish-speaker, Shertok studied German at the Herzliya Hebrew Gymnasium. For more on Shertok, see Gabriel Sheffer, *Moshe Sharett: Biography of a Political Moderate* (Oxford: Clarendon, 1996).

2. Moshe Shertok to Tzippora Meirov, Jan. 27, 1918, in Sharett, *Nitra'eh ve-ulai lo*, 280.

3. The Zionist Commission, formed in March 1918, was headed by Chaim Weizmann (1874–1952) and included Israel Sieff (1889–1972), Leon Simon (1881–1965), and David Eder (1865–1936), who were all active in Anglo-Jewish Zionist circles. The commission arrived in Palestine in April 1918 to investigate conditions on the ground and make recommendations to the British government.

4. Moshe Shertok to Tzippora Meirov, July 13–14, 1918, in Sharett, *Nitra'eh ve-ulai lo*, 349.

5. Moshe Shertok to Tzippora Meirov, Dec. 15, 1918, in Moshe Sharett, *Yeme London: mikhteve Moshe Sharett mi-yeme ha-limudim* (Tel Aviv: ha-'Amutah le-moreshet Moshe Sharett, 2003), 1:25.

6. Kenneth Moss, *An Unchosen People: Jewish Political Reckoning in Interwar Poland* (Cambridge, MA: Harvard University Press, 2021), esp. chapter 6; Joshua M. Karlip, *The Tragedy of a Generation: The Rise and Fall of Jewish Nationalism in Eastern Europe* (Cambridge, MA: Harvard University Press, 2013); Emmanuel Melzer, *No Way Out: The Politics of Polish Jewry* (Cincinnati, OH: Hebrew Union College Press, 1997); Ezra Mendelsohn, *The Jews of East Central Europe between the World Wars* (Bloomington: Indiana University Press, 1983), esp. chapter 1.

7. On German Jewish immigration to Palestine, and how shifting conditions in both Germany and Palestine created successive periods of more intense immigration followed by slower movement, see Hagit Lavsky, *Before Catastrophe: The Distinctive Path of German Zionism* (Detroit, MI: Wayne State University Press, 1996), 249–53.

8. On the Damascus affair, see Jonathan Frankel, *The Damascus Affair: "Ritual Murder," Politics, and the Jews in 1840* (Cambridge: Cambridge University Press, 1997). On Montefiore, see Abigail Green, *Moses Montefiore: Jewish Liberator, Imperial Hero* (Cambridge, MA: Harvard University Press, 2012). On Crémieux, see Lisa Leff, "Trusting Adolphe Crémieux: Jews and Republicans in Nineteenth-Century France," in *On the Word of a Jew: Religion, Reliability, and the Dynamics of Trust*, ed. Nina Caputo and Mitchell B. Hart (Bloomington: Indiana University Press, 2019), 101–16.

9. Todd Endelman, *The Jews of Britain, 1656 to 2000* (Berkeley: University of California Press, 2002), 190–93.

10. Of course, Jewish engagement with Zionism and Palestine did not hinge solely on a political agenda but included a broad range of aspirations spanning cultural development, psychical regeneration, and religious messianism that sometimes explicitly rejected the notion that Palestine represented a political solution for Jews. This book, though it includes historical actors whose initial encounter with Zionism was through one of these "nonpolitical" visions, is chiefly concerned with the *political* questions vis-à-vis Zionism and Palestine that were provoked by the rapidly shifting circumstances of both the Jewish condition and the British Empire in the interwar and post–World War II period.

11. Ezra Mendelsohn, *On Modern Jewish Politics* (Oxford: Oxford University Press, 1993), 5.

12. See, e.g., Tony Michels, *A Fire in Their Hearts: Yiddish Socialists in New York* (Cambridge, MA: Harvard University Press, 2009); and Eran Kaplan, *The Jewish Radical Right: Revisionist Zionism and Its Ideological Legacy* (Madison: University of Wisconsin Press, 2005).

13. See, e.g., Julia Phillips Cohen, *Becoming Ottomans: Sephardi Jews and Imperial Citizenship in the Modern Era* (Oxford: Oxford University Press, 2014).

14. My conception of a politics of uncertainty is in dialogue with arguments in both Eastern European Jewish history and the history of the Yishuv that emphasize the responsive and event-driven nature of Jewish political thought, particularly in the context of exigency, in contrast to historiography that primarily emphasizes ideological predeterminations or acculturation in its analysis of Jewish politics. See Moss, *An Unchosen People*; Hasia Diner

and Gennady Estraikh, *1929: Mapping the Jewish World* (New York: New York University Press, 2013); Anita Shapira, *Land and Power: The Zionist Resort to Force* (Stanford, CA: Stanford University Press, 1999). On Zionism as an emotion, see Derek J. Penslar, *Zionism: An Emotional State* (New Brunswick, NJ: Rutgers University Press, 2023).

15. Dmitry Shumsky, *Beyond the Nation-State* (New Haven, CT: Yale University Press, 2018); Arie Dubnov, " 'Ha-medinah she-ba-derekh' o ha-imperiah makeh shenit: imperializem federativi ve-le'umiut yehudit be-ikbot milhemet ha-olam ha-rishonah," *Yisrael* 24 (2016): 5–36; Arie Dubnov and Hanan Harif, "Zionisms: Roads Not Taken on the Journey to the Jewish State," *Ma'arav*, April 29, 2012, http://maarav.org.il/english/2012/04/29/zionisms-roads-not-taken-on-the-journey-to-the-jewish-state-arie-dubnov-hanan-harif/. Dimitry Shumsky, *Ben Prag li-Yerushalayim: Tziyonut Prag ve-ra'ayon ha-medinah ha-du-le'umit be-Eretz-Yisrael* (Jerusalem: Leo Baeck Institute, 2010). Shumsky and Dubnov have argued that nonstatist visions were, in fact, central to interwar Zionist politics, while other scholarship on binationalism and nonstatist ideas has tended to stress their radical and exceptional quality. See Noam Pianko, *Zionism and the Roads Not Taken: Rawidowicz, Kaplan, Kohn* (Bloomington: Indiana University Press, 2010); David N. Myers, *Between Jew & Arab: The Lost Voice of Simon Rawidowicz* (Waltham, MA: Brandeis University Press, 2008); and Shalom Ratzabi, *Between Zionism and Judaism: The Radical Circle in Brith Shalom, 1925–1933* (Leiden: Brill, 2002).

16. On the Zionist struggle to obtain large-scale loans and loan guarantees throughout the 1920s, see Michael J. Cohen, *Britain's Moment in Palestine: Retrospect and Perspectives, 1917–1948* (London: Routledge, 2014), 182–92. Eliezer Kaplan, in his capacity as treasurer of the Jewish Agency, secured the Zionist movement's first major international loan, a sum of £500,000 from Lloyds Bank, in early 1935. "The Histadrut Reports," *Jewish Frontier* 2 no. 14 (Dec. 1935): 25; "Who's Who in Israel: Eliezer Kaplan," *Israel Digest*, July 12, 1949, 2. The latter cites the year as 1934; it is likely that negotiations took place in 1934, but the loan was not officially granted until early 1935.

17. Scholars of British colonialism and British India, in particular, have pioneered the work of looking beyond official spaces and contexts, as well as archives, to understand politics. In this literature, domestic spaces, clubs, teahouses, and garden parties prove just as central to the colonial and national projects as the Viceroy's House and the Indian National Congress. In this framing, the personal, associational, and quotidian emerge as critical sites in the reproduction of—as well as resistance to—colonial power. See Benjamin B. Cohen, *In the Club: Associational Life in South Asia* (Oxford: Oxford University Press, 2015); Durba Ghosh, *Sex and the Family in Colonial India: The Making of Empire* (Cambridge: Cambridge University Press, 2006); Elizabeth Buettner, *Empire Families: Britons and Late Imperial India* (Oxford: Oxford University Press, 2004); Antoinette Burton, *Dwelling in the Archive: Women Writing House, Home, and History in Late Colonial India* (Oxford: Oxford University Press, 2003); Mary A. Procida, *Married to the Empire: Gender, Politics and Imperialism in India, 1883–1947* (Manchester: Manchester University Press, 2002); and Mrinalini Sinha, "Britishness, Clubbability, and the Colonial Public Sphere: The Genealogy

of an Imperial Institution in Colonial India," *Journal of British Studies* 40, no. 4 (2001): 489–521. My approach to politics is also indebted to Leonore Davidoff and Catherine Hall, *Family Fortunes: Men and Women of the English Middle Class, 1780–1850* (London: Routledge, 2002), particularly for the way they conceive of the so-called public and private spheres as deeply imbricated.

18. I am grateful to an anonymous reviewer for Stanford University Press for putting this so aptly. On the relationship between gender and Jewish internationalism and nationalism, see Jaclyn Granick and Abigail Green, eds., "Gendering Jewish Inter/Nationalism," special issue, *Journal of Modern Jewish Studies* 21, no. 2 (2022).

19. Sarah Abrevaya Stein, *Plumes: Ostrich Feathers, Jews, and a Lost World of Global Commerce* (New Haven, CT: Yale University Press, 2010), 153; David Feldman, "Jews and the British Empire c. 1900," *History Workshop Journal* 63, no. 1 (2007): 70–89, esp. 70. Stein also notes that "it is striking that scholars of Jewish studies have not entered these conversations, particularly in light of how probingly we have explored the relationship between Jews and empires that more often than not are not considered . . . to have practiced imperialism— including the Russian, Ottoman, and Austro-Hungarian empires." Sarah Abrevaya Stein, "Protected Persons? The Baghdadi Jewish Diaspora, the British State, and the Persistence of Empire," *American Historical Review* 16, no. 1 (2011): 83. Recent work on Jews and modern empire includes Stephanie M. Chasin, *British Jews and Imperial Service: Nationalism, Pan-Islamism, and Zionism in Mandate Palestine and Colonial India* (London: I.B. Tauris, 2024); Ethan B. Katz, Lisa Moses Leff, and Maud S. Mandel, eds., *Colonialism and the Jews* (Bloomington: Indiana University Press, 2017); Joshua Schreier, *The Merchants of Oran: A Jewish Port at the Dawn of Empire* (Stanford, CA: Stanford University Press, 2017); Sarah Abrevaya Stein, *Extraterritorial Dreams: European Citizenship, Sephardi Jews, and the Ottoman Twentieth Century* (Chicago: University of Chicago Press, 2016); Devin E. Naar, *Jewish Salonica: Between the Ottoman Empire and Modern Greece* (Stanford, CA: Stanford University Press, 2016); Adam D. Mendelsohn, *The Rag Race: How Jews Sewed Their Way to Success in America and the British Empire* (New York: New York University Press, 2014); Cohen, *Becoming Ottomans*; Sarah Abrevaya Stein, *Saharan Jews and the Fate of French Algeria* (Chicago: University of Chicago Press, 2014); Abigail Jacobson, *From Empire to Empire: Jerusalem between Ottoman and British Rule* (Syracuse, NY: Syracuse University Press, 2011); Joshua Schreier, *Arabs of the Jewish Faith: The Civilizing Mission in Colonial Algeria* (New Brunswick, NJ: Rutgers University Press, 2010); Stein, *Plumes*; Eitan Bar-Yosef and Nadia Valman, eds., *"The Jew" in Late-Victorian and Edwardian Culture: Between the East End and East Africa* (London: Palgrave Macmillan, 2008); Ruth Fredman Cernea, *Almost Englishmen: Baghdadi Jews in British Burma* (Lanham, MD: Lexington Books, 2006); Assaf Likhovski, *Law and Identity in Mandate Palestine* (Chapel Hill: University of North Carolina Press, 2006). On the gap between Jewish and imperial historiographies, see Feldman, "Jews and the British Empire"; and Sarah Abrevaya Stein, "Modern Jewries and the Imperial Imagination," *AJS Perspectives* (Fall 2005): 14–16.

20. Feldman, "Jews and the British Empire," esp. 70. Todd Endelman has pointed out a

similar absence of Jews as historical actors in metropolitan British history: "Unaccustomed to viewing minorities as historical actors in the British context, committed to the tolerant, assimilative powers of English culture, and above all, wishing to avoid the appearance of being too concerned with Jews (and thus open to charges of intolerance), historians of Britain are content to ignore or minimize the Jewish presence in their work." Endelman, *The Jews of Britain*, 6.

21. Stein, "Protected Persons," 84.

22. See, e.g., Jaclyn Granick, *International Jewish Humanitarianism in the Age of the Great War* (Cambridge: Cambridge University Press, 2021); Nathan Kurz, *Jewish Internationalism and Human Rights after the Holocaust* (Cambridge: Cambridge University Press, 2021); James Loeffler and Moira Paz, eds., *The Law of Strangers: Jewish Lawyers and International Law in the Twentieth Century* (Cambridge: Cambridge University Press, 2019); James Loeffler, *Rooted Cosmopolitans: Jews and Human Rights in the Twentieth Century* (New Haven, CT: Yale University Press, 2018); Gil Rubin, "The End of Minority Rights: Jacob Robinson and the Jewish Question in World War II," *Simon Dubnow Institute Yearbook* 11 (2012): 55–71; and Carole Fink, *Defending the Rights of Others: The Great Powers, the Jews, and International Minority Protection, 1878–1938* (Cambridge: Cambridge University Press, 2004).

23. While not focused on the British Empire, an important exception to this is Granick, *International Jewish Humanitarianism in the Age of the Great War*, which argues that overseas American Jewish philanthropic and humanitarian efforts were part of an ascendant American empire during and in the wake of World War I.

24. See, e.g., Fredrik Meiton, *Electrical Palestine: Capital and Technology from Empire to Nation* (Berkeley: University of California Press, 2019); and Jacob Norris, *Land of Progress: Palestine in the Age of Colonial Development, 1905–1948* (Oxford: Oxford University Press, 2013).

25. Work framing Zionism as settler colonialism includes earlier scholarship from the generation of Israeli sociologists and historians sometimes identified as the "New Historians," as well as "Post-Zionist"; from historians of the Palestinian experience; and more recently from within Jewish history. Baruch Kimmerling, *Zionism and Territory: The Socioterritorial Dimensions of Zionist Politics* (Berkeley, CA: Institute of International Studies, 1983); Gershon Shafir, *Land, Labor and the Origins of the Israeli-Palestinian Conflict, 1882–1914* (Berkeley: University of California Press, 1996); Areej Sabbagh-Khoury, *Colonizing Palestine: The Zionist Left and the Making of the Palestinian Nakba* (Stanford, CA: Stanford University Press, 2023); Rashid Khalidi, *The Hundred Years' War on Palestine: A History of Settler Colonialism and Resistance, 1917–2017* (New York: Macmillan, 2020); Liora Halperin, *The Oldest Guard: Forging the Zionist Settler Past* (Stanford, CA: Stanford University Press, 2021).

26. For instance, on the influence of British colonial law in shaping Jewish identity under the mandate, see Likhovski, *Law and Identity in Mandate Palestine*. On the intellectual and institutional exchange between British and Jewish social workers in the development

of Yishuv social work practices, see Tammy Razi, *Yalde ha-hefker: he-hatzer ha-ahorit shel Tel Aviv ha-Mandatorit* (Tel Aviv: Am Oved, 2009). On Jewish encounters with the English language in Mandate Palestine, see Liora Halperin, *Babel in Zion: Jews, Nationalism, and Language Diversity in Palestine, 1920–1948* (New Haven, CT: Yale University Press, 2015), esp. 99–141. On the ways British rule textured Jewish wartime experience, see Hadas Fischer, "*Tokhnit 'to'elet': tzarkhanut milhamtit ha-monit be-hasut memshelet ha-mandat, 1942–1946*," *Zion* 79 (2014): 201–30. On the way imperial transition shaped how Jews and Arabs experienced urban space and navigated political and social alliances, see Abigail Jacobson, *From Empire to Empire: Jerusalem between Ottoman and British Rule* (Syracuse, NY: Syracuse University Press, 2011). On how colonial memory shaped post-1948 Israeli culture, see Eitan Bar-Yosef, "Bonding with the British: Colonial Nostalgia and the Idealization of Mandatory Palestine in Israeli Literature and Culture after 1967," *Jewish Social Studies* 22, no. 3 (2017): 1–37; and Eitan Bar-Yosef, "'The Horror' in Hebrew: *Heart of Darkness* in Israeli Culture," *Interventions: International Journal of Postcolonial Studies* 18, no. 3 (2016): 319–334. On the ways sensibilities around westernization, disease, and hygiene shaped the Zionist movement, see Dafna Hirsch, *Banu henah le-havi et ha-ma'arav: hanhalat higyenah ve-beniyat tarbut be-hevrah ha-Yehudit bi-tekufat ha-Mandat* (Sde Boker: Ben-Gurion Research Institute for the Study of Israel and Zionism, 2014); and Sandra M. Sufian, *Healing the Land and the Nation: Malaria and the Zionist Project in Palestine, 1920–1947* (Chicago: University of Chicago Press, 2008). On Jews, Palestine, and Orientalism, see Ivan Davidson Kalmar and Derek J. Penslar, *Orientalism and the Jews* (Waltham, MA: Brandeis University Press, 2005); Yaron Peleg, *Orientalism and the Hebrew Imagination* (Ithaca, NY: Cornell University Press, 2005); and Stefan Vogt, "The Postcolonial Buber: Orientalism, Subalternity, and Identity Politics in Martin Buber's Political Thought," *Jewish Social Studies* 22, no. 1 (Fall 2016): 161–86. On the intersections between postcolonial studies and the historiography of Zionism, see Stefan Vogt, Derek Penslar, and Arieh Saposnik, eds., *Unacknowledged Kinships: Postcolonial Studies and the Historiography of Zionism* (Waltham, MA: Brandeis University Press, 2023).

27. Yair Wallach, "The Racial Logic of Palestine's Partition," *Ethnic and Racial Studies* 48, no. 8 (2023): 1576–98; Matthew Hughes, *Britain's Pacification of Palestine: The British Army, the Colonial State, and the Arab Revolt, 1936–1939* (Cambridge: Cambridge University Press, 2019); Arie Dubnov and Laura Robson, eds., *Partitions: A Transnational History of Twentieth-Century Territorial Separatism* (Stanford, CA: Stanford University Press, 2019); Penny Sinanoglou, *Partitioning Palestine: British Policymaking at the End of Empire* (Chicago: University of Chicago Press, 2019); Susan Pedersen, *The Guardians: The League of Nations and the Crisis of Empire* (Oxford: Oxford University Press, 2015); Laura Robson, *Colonialism and Christianity in Mandate Palestine* (Austin: University of Texas Press, 2011); Lucy Chester, "Factors Impeding the Effectiveness of Partition in South Asia and the Palestine Mandate," in *Order, Conflict, and Violence*, ed. Stathis N. Kalyvas, Ian Shapiro, and Tarek Masoud (Cambridge: Cambridge University Press, 2008): 75–96. Rory Miller's edited collection contains essays by historians working both within and beyond Jewish

history; see Rory Miller, ed., *Britain, Palestine, and Empire: The Mandate Years* (London: Routledge, 2010).

28. Eitan Bar-Yosef and Nadia Valman adapt Homi Bhabha's concept of colonial mimicry—"almost the same, but not quite"—to Jews in Palestine and in other colonial contexts, including the proposed so-called Uganda Scheme to settle Jews in British East Africa. Eitan Bar-Yosef and Nadia Valman, "Introduction: Between the East End and East Africa: Rethinking Images of 'the Jew' in Late-Victorian and Edwardian Culture," in Bar-Yosef and Valman, *"The Jew" in Late-Victorian and Edwardian Culture*, 3, 6. On colonial mimicry, see Homi Bhabha, "Of Mimicry and Man: The Ambivalence of Colonial Discourse," *October* 28 (1984): 125–33.

Chapter 1

1. Helen Bentwich, *If I Forget Thee: Some Chapters of Autobiography, 1912–1920* (London: Paul Elek, 1979), 3.

2. Jennifer Glynn, ed., *Tidings from Zion: Helen Bentwich's Letters from Jerusalem, 1919–1931* (London: I.B. Tauris, 2000), 4; Bentwich, *If I Forget Thee*, 140–55.

3. Helen Bentwich to Caroline Franklin, Oct. 26, 1923, Women's Library at the London School of Economics (hereafter WL), 7HBE/2/7. The individuals Helen Bentwich named include Pinhas Rutenberg (1879–1942), the Russian engineer and Zionist who established the Palestine Electric Company; Joshua Gordon (1889–1941), a Labor Zionist and senior official in the Jewish Agency; Judah Magnes (1877–1948), the American Reform rabbi, pacifist, advocate of binationalism, and one of the founders of the Hebrew University; Yitzhak Ben-Zvi (1884–1963), the leading Labor Zionist who later served as President of Israel; Frederick Kisch (1888–1943), the Anglo-Jewish first head of the Political Department of the Jewish Agency, who married Helen's cousin Ruth Franklin; Max Nurock (1893–1978), an Irish-born Jew who worked for the Zionist Commission, as Herbert Samuel's private secretary, and later as Israel's ambassador to Australia (not to be confused with Mordechai "Max" Nurock [1879–1962], the Latvian-born Religious Zionist); and Harry Sacher (1881–1971), a friend from Norman's youth and the legal adviser to the Palestine Executive who later served as director of the British department store Marks & Spencer.

4. On the history of Chovevei Zion in England, and on Zionism in England more broadly, see Stuart A. Cohen, *English Zionists and British Jews: The Communal Politics of Anglo-Jewry, 1895–1920* (Princeton, NJ: Princeton University Press, 1982). See also Stephan E. C. Wendehorst, *British Jewry, Zionism, and the Jewish State, 1936–1956* (Oxford: Oxford University Press, 2012). On Herbert Bentwich, see Ofri Krischer and Arie Dubnov, "*hasagah le-vet Bentwich*," *Yisrael* 27–28 (2021): 271–312; and Norman Bentwich and Margery Bentwich, *Herbert Bentwich: The Pilgrim Father* (Jerusalem: Hotza'ah Ivrith, 1940).

5. Norman Bentwich to Judah Magnes, April 18, 1922, Central Archives for the History of the Jewish People (CAHJP), Judah Magnes Papers P3/58.

6. Norman Bentwich, *My 77 Years* (Philadelphia: Jewish Publication Society of America, 1961), 17. Those friends included Robert Sebag-Montefiore, Leon Simon, Jack Myers,

Harry Sacher, and Mortimer Epstein. The settlement movement was a reformist movement started in Britain that aimed to establish settlement homes in poor urban neighborhoods. These homes, in which reformist-minded middle- and upper-class volunteers lived, offered a range of welfare services. On the transnational manifestations of the movement, see John Gal, Stefan Köngeter, and Sarah Vicary, eds., *The Settlement House Movement Revisited: A Transnational History* (Bristol: Bristol University Press, 2020).

7. Norman Bentwich, *Wanderer between Two Worlds* (London: Kegan Paul, Trench, Trubner, 1941), 19. On the history of Toynbee Hall, see Standish Meacham, *Toynbee Hall and Social Reform* (New Haven, CT: Yale University Press, 1987).

8. See Steven J. Zipperstein, *Elusive Prophet: Ahad Ha'am and the Origins of Zionism* (Berkeley: University of California Press, 1993), esp. 277–315. The scholar Israel Friedlander, married to Norman Bentwich's sister Lilian, was also a "devoted disciple" of Ahad Ha'am and translated his Hebrew essays into German. Lilian Bentwich Friedlander, translated some of those into English. Israel Friedlander was murdered by Red cavalry units in Ukraine in 1920 while on a relief mission for the American Jewish Joint Distribution Committee. Bentwich, *My 77 Years*, 22.

9. Bentwich, *Wanderer between Two Worlds*, 34. On the history of the relationship between British Labour and Zionism, see Joseph Gorny, *The British Labour Movement and Zionism, 1917–1948* (Abingdon, UK: Routledge, 1983).

10. Bentwich, *Wanderer between Two Worlds*, 349.

11. Bentwich, *My 77 Years*, 67.

12. Helen Jones, "National, Community and Personal Priorities: British Women's Responses to Refugees from the Nazis, from the Mid-1930s to Early 1940s," *Women's History Review* 21, no. 1 (2012): 121–51.

13. In this respect, the Bentwiches resembled another Labour marriage—that of Sidney and Beatice Webb. Both (though Sidney in particularly) would earn the resentment of the Zionist movement following the issuing of the Passfield White Paper in 1930. For more on the Webbs, see Lisanne Radice, *Beatrice and Sidney Webb: Fabian Socialists* (London: Macmillan, 1984).

14. Norman Bentwich and Helen Bentwich, *Mandate Memories, 1918–1948* (London: Hogarth, 1965).

15. Bentwich, *If I Forget Thee*, 3.

16. Bentwich, 10–11.

17. For more on Lily Montague (1873–1963) and the West Central Jewish Girls' Club, see Judith R. Walkowitz, *Nights Out: Life in Cosmopolitan London* (New Haven, CT: Yale University Press, 2012), 186–87; Jean Spence, "Working for Jewish Girls: Lily Montagu, Girls' Clubs and Industrial Reform, 1890–1914," *Women's History Review* 13, no. 3 (2004): 491–510; Ellen M. Umansky, *Lily H. Montagu and the Advancement of Liberal Judaism: From Vision to Vocation* (Lewiston, NY: Edwin Mellen, 1983); and Eric Conrad, *Lily H. Montagu, Prophet of a Living Judaism* (New York: National Federation of Temple Sisterhoods, 1953).

18. Bentwich, *If I Forget Thee*, 8–9.

19. Bentwich, 30–32. For more on Helen Bentwich's work in education and social work before and after her time in Palestine, see Jane Martin, "Beyond Suffrage: Feminism, Education and the Politics of Class in the Inter-War Years," *British Journal of Sociology of Education* 29, no. 4 (2008): 411–23.

20. In this sense, her politics aligned with the Fabians, though she never identified explicitly as one.

21. Bentwich, *Wanderer between Two Worlds*, 203.

22. Scholars of nationalism outside of Jewish history have similarly shown the centrality of nonstatist ideas. See Rogers Brubaker, "Myths and Misconceptions in the Study of Nationalism," in *The State of the Nation: Ernest Gellner and the Theory of Nationalism*, ed. John Hall (Cambridge: Cambridge University Press, 1998), 233–65.

23. On the Central European origins of binationalism, see Steven E. Aschheim, *Beyond the Border; The German-Jewish Legacy Abroad* (Princeton, NJ: Princeton University Press, 2007), esp. chapter 1; and Ratzabi, *Between Zionism and Judaism*.

24. Norman Bentwich cited both Herzl and Ahad Ha'am as critical figures in bringing him closer to Zionism.

25. For more on this scheme, see chapter 2. For more on Jabotinsky, see Hillel Halkin, *Jabotinsky: A Life* (New Haven, CT: Yale University Press, 2014); Shmuel Katz, *Lone Wolf: A Biography of Vladimir (Ze'ev) Jabotinsky*, 2 vols. (New York: Barricade, 1996); Yaacov Shavit, *Jabotinsky and the Revisionist Movement: 1925–1948* (Abingdon, UK: Frank Cass, 1988); Joseph B. Schechtman, *Rebel and Statesman: The Vladimir Jabotinsky Story, the Early Years* (New York: T. Yoseloff, 1956); and Joseph B. Schechtman, *Fighter and Prophet: The Jabotinsky Story, the Last Years* (New York: A. S. Barnes, 1961).

26. For a discussion and refutation of this trend, see Endelman, *The Jews of Britain*, esp. 1–5. David Ruderman has also argued against this trend; see David Ruderman, *Jewish Enlightenment in an English Key: Anglo-Jewry's Construction of Modern Jewish Thought* (Princeton, NJ: Princeton University Press, 2002).

27. See Kristian Ulrichsen, *The First World War in the Middle East* (Oxford: Oxford University Press, 2014), 106–18.

28. Helen Bentwich to Caroline Franklin, Jan. 27, 1919, WL 7HBE 2/3.

29. Ronald Storrs, *The Memoirs of Ronald Storrs* (New York: G. P. Putnam's Sons, 1937), 307.

30. On the history of the Evelina de Rothschild School for Girls, see Laura S. Schor, *The Best School in Jerusalem: Annie Landau's School for Girls, 1900–1960* (Waltham, MA: Brandeis University Press, 2013).

31. Jack Mosseri (1884–1934), born to a wealthy Egyptian Jewish family, was an early supporter of political Zionism, a rare position among the Egyptian Jewish elite. He and Norman Bentwich had been close friends during the latter's time in Cairo. Elly Kadoorie (1867–1944), born to a Baghdadi Jewish family in India, worked for David Sassoon & Co. in Shanghai. He later became an active philanthropist, funding educational initiatives in the Middle East and Asia. He died in a Japanese prison camp in Shanghai during World War II.

32. Quoted in Schor, *The Best School in Jerusalem*, 84.

33. Helen Bentwich to Caroline Franklin, Jan. 27, 1919, WL 7HBE 2/3.

34. Schor, *The Best School in Jerusalem*, 81–87. See also Deborah Bernstein, "Gender, Nationalism and Colonial Policy: Prostitution in the Jewish Settlement of Mandate Palestine, 1918–1948," *Women's History Review* 21, no. 1 (2012): 81–100; Margalit Shilo, "Women as Victims of War: The British Conquest (1917) and the Blight of Prostitution in the Holy City," *Nashim*, no. 6 (2003): 72–81; Margalit Shilo, "*Zanutan shel banot Yerushalayim motza'e Milhemet ha-'Olam ha-Rishonah: mabat gavri ve-mabat nashi*," *Yerushalayim ve-Eretz-Yisrael* 1 (2003): 173–96; and Liat Kozma, *Global Women, Colonial Ports: Prostitution in the Interwar Middle East* (Albany: State University of New York Press, 2017).

35. Abigail Jacobson, "Negotiating Ottomanism in Times of War: Jerusalem during World War I through the Eyes of a Local Muslim Resident," *International Journal of Middle East Studies* 40, no. 1 (2008): 87n50.

36. The Contagious Diseases Acts were first suspended in 1883, then repealed in 1886. On the regulation of prostitution in the metropole and feminist responses to it, see Judith R. Walkowitz, *Prostitution and Victorian Society: Women, Class, and the State* (Cambridge: Cambridge University Press, 1980). On prostitution in the empire, see Philippa Levine, *Prostitution, Race & Politics: Policing Venereal Disease in the British Empire* (New York: Routledge, 2003).

37. See Shilo, "Women as Victims of War." Chaim Weizmann, leader of the Zionist movement during the interwar period, served as president of the Zionist Organization from 1921 to 1931 and again from 1935 to 1946. Born near Pinsk, Weizmann moved to Britain in 1904 to join the faculty of the chemistry department at the University of Manchester. During World War I, he developed a process that used bacterial fermentation to make acetone, a substance that was essential in the production of explosive propellants. The invention, which played a significant role in the war effort, placed him in touch with important British politicians. See Jehuda Reinharz and Motti Golani, *Chaim Weizmann: A Biography* (Waltham, MA: Brandeis University Press, 2024).

38. The American Colony was founded in 1881 by members of a Christian utopian society from Chicago.

39. Helen Bentwich to Caroline Franklin, June 3, 1919, WL 7HBE 2/3.

40. Helen Bentwich to Caroline Franklin, July 15, 1919, WL 7HBE 2/3.

41. Helen Bentwich to Caroline Franklin, April 12, 1919, WL 7HBE 2/3.

42. Helen Bentwich to Caroline Franklin, Dec. 5, 1924, WL 7HBE/2/8; Lucy Adlington, *Great War Fashion: Tales from the History Wardrobe* (Gloucestershire: History Press, 2013), 213.

43. Helen Bentwich, *If I Forget Thee*, 31.

44. Abigail Jacobson challenges the dichotomy between Ottoman and British rule that has shaped scholarship on Jerusalem, showing that social and political alliances that bridged ethnic and religious divides often persisted between the two. Jacobson, *From Empire to Empire*.

45. Alison Blunt, "Imperial Geographies of Home: British Domesticity in India, 1886–1925," *Transactions of the Institute of British Geographies* 24, no. 4 (1999): 421–40.
46. Sinha, "Britishness, Clubbability, and the Colonial Public Sphere," 518–19.
47. Helen Bentwich to Caroline Franklin, June 3, 1919, WL 7HBE 2/3.
48. Helen Bentwich to Caroline Franklin, Feb. 6, 1919, WL 7HBE 2/3.
49. Glynn, *Tidings from Zion*, 21; Helen Bentwich to Caroline Franklin, April 28, 1919, WL 7HBE 2/3.
50. Helen Bentwich to Caroline Franklin, April 28, 1919, WL 7HBE 2/3.
51. Bentwich, *If I Forget Thee*, 8.
52. See Dafna Hirsch, "'We Are Here to Bring the West, Not Only to Ourselves': Zionist Occidentalism and the Discourse of Hygiene in Mandate Palestine," *International Journal of Middle East Studies* 41, no. 4 (2009): 577–94; and Dafna Hirsch, "'Interpreters of Occident to the Awakening Orient': The Jewish Public Health Nurse in Mandate Palestine," *Comparative Studies in Society and History* 50, no. 1 (2008): 227–55.
53. Bentwich, *Wanderer between Two Worlds*, 95.
54. Helen Bentwich to Caroline Franklin, Jan. 27, 1919, WL 7HBE 2/3.
55. Helen Bentwich to Caroline Franklin, March 3, 1919, WL 7HBE 2/3. Helen likely managed in Yiddish because of her German lessons at school and her experience working in the East End of London. Modern Hebrew uses a pronunciation based on Sephardi rather than Ashkenazi Hebrew. Helen's mother would have been shocked about her daughter's ability to speak Yiddish because it was the language of the unassimilated, impoverished Jewish immigrant population of the East End.
56. Helen Bentwich to Caroline Franklin, Feb. 6, 1919, WL 7HBE 2/3.
57. Helen Bentwich to Caroline Franklin, March 20, 1919, WL 7HBE 2/3.
58. Helen Bentwich to Caroline Franklin, March 22, 1919, WL 7HBE 2/3.
59. Helen Bentwich to Caroline Franklin, April 12, 1919, WL 7HBE 2/3.
60. Helen Bentwich to Caroline Franklin, April 12, 1919, WL 4HBE 2/3.
61. Both Jabotinsky and Rutenberg had worked to set up the Jewish Legion of the British Army during World War I. For more on Rutenberg and the Palestine Electric Company, see Fredrik Meiton, *Electrical Palestine: Capital and Technology from Empire to Nation* (Oakland: University of California Press, 2019); Ronen Shamir, *Current Flow: The Electrification of Palestine* (Stanford, CA: Stanford University Press, 2013); and Eli Shaltiel, *Pinhas Rutenberg: 'aliyato u-nefilato shel "ish hazak" be-Eretz-Yisrael, 1879–1942*, 2 vols. (Tel Aviv: Am Oved, 1990).
62. Herbert Samuel would commute all the sentences once he took office.
63. Helen Bentwich to Caroline Franklin, April 30, 1920, WL 7HBE 2/4.
64. For a comparison of Mandate Palestine and Ireland in later periods, see Tom Bowden, *The Breakdown of Public Security: The Case of Ireland, 1916–1921, and Palestine, 1936–1939* (Beverly Hills, CA: Sage, 1977).
65. Bentwich, *If I Forget Thee*, 9.
66. Fred D. Schneider, "British Labour and Ireland, 1918–1921: The Retreat to Houndsditch," *Review of Politics* 40, no. 3 (July 1978): 368–91.

67. Helen Bentwich to Caroline Franklin, July 5, 1920, WL 7HBE 2/4.
68. Helen Bentwich to Caroline Franklin, July 5, 1920, WL 7HBE 2/4.
69. Helen Bentwich to Caroline Franklin, July 9, 1920, WL 7HBE 2/4.
70. Sinha, "Britishness, Clubbability, and the Colonial Public Sphere"; Benjamin B. Cohen, *In the Club: Associational Life in South Asia* (Oxford: Oxford University Press, 2015).
71. Helen Bentwich to Caroline Franklin, Oct. 6, 1920, WL 7HBE 2/4.
72. Helen Bentwich to Caroline Franklin, August 30, 1920, WL 7HBE 2/4.
73. Helen Bentwich to Caroline Franklin, Oct. 6, 1920, WL 7HBE 2/4.
74. Helen Bentwich to Caroline Franklin, Nov. 16, 1920, WL 7HBE 2/4.
75. Helen Bentwich to Caroline Franklin, June 26, 1921, WL 7HBE 2/4.
76. Helen Bentwich to Caroline Franklin, May 9. 1920, WL 7HBE 2/4.
77. Helen Bentwich to Caroline Franklin, Jan. 14, 1921, WL 7HBE 2/4.
78. Helen Bentwich to Caroline Franklin, Dec. 14, 1920, WL 7HBE 2/4.
79. Helen Bentwich to Caroline Franklin, Jan. 14, 1921, WL 7HBE 2/4.
80. Henrietta Szold (1860–1945), born in Baltimore, founded Hadassah, the Women's Zionist Organization of America, in 1912. Hadassah, with Szold at the helm, led the charge in establishing a health care system in Mandate Palestine. See Dvora Hacohen, *To Repair a Broken World: The Life of Henrietta Szold, Founder of Hadassah* (Cambridge, MA: Harvard University Press, 2021).
81. Bentwich and Bentwich, *Mandate Memories*, 65.
82. Helen Bentwich to Caroline Franklin, Jan. 14, 1921, WL 7HBE 2/4.
83. Bentwich and Bentwich, *Mandate Memories*, 65–66.
84. Helen Bentwich to Caroline Franklin, August 20, 1920, WL 7HBE 2/4.
85. For a discussion of the response to and contested blame for Friedlander and Cantor's murders, see Michael Beizer, "Who Murdered Professor Israel Friedlander and Rabbi Bernard Cantor: The Truth Rediscovered," *American Jewish Archives* 55, no. 1 (2003): 63–114.
86. For more on Thelma Bentwich Yellin, see Margery Bentwich, *Thelma Yellin: Pioneer Musician* (Jerusalem: Rubin Mass, 1964).
87. For more on Edwin Samuel, see Edwin Samuel, *A Lifetime in Jerusalem: The Memoirs of the Second Viscount Samuel* (Jerusalem: Israel Universities Press, 1970).
88. Ahdut ha-Avodah was a labor Zionist party founded in 1919 by David Ben-Gurion, Yitzhak Ben-Zvi, and Berl Katznelson. See Yonathan Shapiro, *Ahdut ha-'Avodah ha-historit* (Tel Aviv: Am Oved, 1975); and Yosef Gorny, *Ahdut ha-'Avodah, 1919–1930: ha-yesodot ha-ra'ayonim ve-ha-shitah ha-medinit* (Tel Aviv: Tel Aviv University Press, 1973).
89. Gudrun Krämer, *A History of Palestine: From the Ottoman Conquest to the Founding of the State of Israel* (Princeton, NJ: Princeton University Press, 2008), 210–15.
90. Helen Bentwich to Caroline Franklin, May 13, 1921, WL 7HBE 2/4.
91. Helen Bentwich to Caroline Franklin, May 21, 1921, WL 7HBE 2/4.
92. Helen Bentwich to Caroline Franklin, May 13, 1921, WL 7HBE 2/4.
93. Helen Bentwich to Caroline Franklin, May 21, 1921, WL 7HBE 2/4.
94. Krämer, *A History of Palestine*, 211.

95. Quoted in Sahar Huneidi, *A Broken Trust: Sir Herbert Samuel, Zionism and the Palestinians, 1920–1925* (London: I.B. Tauris, 2001), 131.

96. Huneidi, 132–33.

97. Helen Bentwich to Caroline Franklin, July 16, 1922, WL 7HBE/2/6.

98. Bentwich, *Wanderer between Two Worlds*, 129.

99. Frederick Kisch, *Palestine Diary* (London: Victor Gollancz, 1938), 18.

100. Kisch, 18. Kisch's reference to his "many associations in India" probably referred to Muslim friends and allies there.

101. Norman Bentwich wrote the only biography of Kisch; see Norman Bentwich, *Brigadier Frederick Kisch: Soldier and Zionist* (London: Vallentine Mitchell, 1966).

102. Helen Bentwich to Caroline Franklin, Nov. 26, 1922, WL 7HBE/2/6.

103. Helen Bentwich to Caroline Franklin, July 2, 1923, WL 7HBE/2/7.

104. For more on Judah Magnes, see David Barak-Gorodetsky, *Judah Magnes: The Prophetic Politics of a Religious Binationalist* (Lincoln: Jewish Publication Society and University of Nebraska Press, 2021); and Daniel P. Kotzin, *Judah L. Magnes: An American Jewish Nonconformist* (Syracuse, NY: Syracuse University Press, 2010). Norman Bentwich also wrote a biography of Magnes; see Norman Bentwich, *For Zion's Sake: A Biography of Judah Magnes* (Philadelphia: Jewish Publication Society of America, 1954).

105. Helen Bentwich to Caroline Franklin, Oct. 5, 1923, WL 7HBE 2/7.

106. Helen Bentwich to Caroline Franklin, Oct. 26, 1923, WL 7HBE/2/7.

107. Helen Bentwich to Caroline Franklin, Jan. 12, 1924, WL 7HBE/2/8.

108. Helen Bentwich to Caroline Franklin, Jan. 1, 1924, WL 7HBE/2/8.

109. Helen Bentwich to Caroline Franklin, Dec. 26, 1924, WL 7HBE/2/8.

110. Norman Bentwich, *England in Palestine* (London: Kegan Paul, Trench, Trubner, 1932), esp. 273–78. Assaf Likhovksi argues that these pro-Labour economic policies often put Norman Bentwich at odds with Conservative factions of the Colonial Office and the Mandatory authority in Palestine. Likhovski, *Law and Identity in Mandate Palestine*, 57.

111. Bentwich and Bentwich, *Mandate Memories*, 53.

112. Bentwich, *Wanderer between Two Worlds*, 34.

113. See Joseph Heller, *Mi-Berit Shalom le-Ihud: Yehuda Leib Magnes ve-ha-ma'avak li-medinah du-le'umit* (Jerusalem: Magnes Press, 2003).

114. On the history of the Hebrew University, see Adi Livny, "The Hebrew University in Mandatory Palestine: A Relational History (1918–1948)," PhD diss., Hebrew University of Jerusalem, 2021; Diana Dolev, *The Planning and Building of the Hebrew University, 1919–1948: Facing the Temple Mount* (Lanham, MD: Lexington Books, 2016); and Hagit Lavsky, ed., *Toldot ha-Universitah ha-'Ivrit bi-Yerushalayim: hitbasesut u-tzemihah* (Jerusalem: Magnes Press, 2005).

115. Helen Bentwich to Caroline Franklin, April 10, 1925, WL 7HBE/2/8.

116. Norman Bentwich, "I Remember," Middle East Centre Archive, St Antony's College, University of Oxford, GB165-0025, 2/1.

117. Helen Bentwich to Caroline Franklin, Dec. 12, 1925, WL 7HBE/2/8.

118. Helen Bentwich to Caroline Franklin, April 24, 1928, WL 7HBE/2/10.

119. Helen Bentwich to Caroline Franklin, Sept. 7, 1929, WL 7HBE 2/11.

120. Helen Bentwich to Caroline Franklin, Sept. 14, 1929, WL 7HBE 2/11. Later letters make clear that far greater numbers actually required food and shelter.

121. Albert Hyamson (1875–1954) shared Norman's commitment to a binational future for Palestine. See Albert Montefiore Hyamson, *Palestine: A Policy* (London: Methuen, 1942).

122. Helen Bentwich to Caroline Franklin, Sept. 14, 1929, WL 7HBE 2/11.

123. Helen Bentwich to Caroline Franklin, Sept. 21, 1929, WL 7HBE 2/11.

124. Helen Bentwich to Caroline Franklin, Oct. 5, 1929, WL 7HBE 2/11; *agudah* refers to Agudat Yisrael, the non-Zionist Orthodox organization founded in 1912.

125. See Anita Shapira, *Israel: A History* (Waltham, MA: Brandeis University Press, 2012), 96.

126. Helen Bentwich to Caroline Franklin, Oct. 5, 1929, WL 7HBE 2/11.

127. Helen Bentwich to Caroline Franklin, Oct. 5, 1929, WL 7HBE 2/11.

128. For more on the Zionist "defensive ethos" and the impact of the 1929 riots, see Shapira, *Land and Power*, esp. 173–94.

129. Adi Gordon, "'Nothing but a Disillusioned Love'? Hans Kohn's Break with the Zionist Movement," in *Against the Grain: Jewish Intellectuals in Hard Times*, ed. Ezra Mendelsohn, Stefani Hoffman, and Richard I. Cohen (New York: Berghahn, 2014), 117–42.

Chapter 2

1. The marriage, in 1927, was the second for both Sima Rubin Arlosoroff (1901–76) and Chaim Arlosoroff (1899–1933). Arlosoroff had a daughter, Shulamit (1919–97), with his first wife, Gerda Goldberg (1898–1986). Sima had a daughter, Nava (1925–2005), with her first husband, Moshe Moisei Balosher. Arlosoroff raised Nava after he married Sima. Arlosoroff and Sima also had a son, Shaul. For more on Arlosoroff, see Shai Horev, *Ideolog u-medina'i: hashkafat 'olamo u-mekomo ha-ideologi shel Hayim Arlozorov be-misgeret ha-manhigut ha-ideologit shel Tenu'at ha-'Avodah* (Haifa: Duhifat, 2015); Shlomo Avineri, *Arlosoroff* (New York: Grove Weidenfeld, 1989); Simha Kling, "Chaim Arlozorov," in *Fields of Offering: Studies in Honor of Raphael Patai*, ed. Victor D. Sanua (Cranbury: Associated University Presses, 1983), 243–63; Miriam Getter, *Hayim Arlozorov: Biografiah politit* (Tel Aviv: Hakibbutz Hameuchad, 1977); Yosef Shapiro, *Hayim Arlozorov* (Tel Aviv: Am Oved, 1975); Eliyahu Bilitzki, *Hayim Arlozorov* (Tel Aviv: Tarbut V'hinukh, 1966); and Margot Klausner, *Sufat Sivan: parashah aharonah be-haye Hayim Arlozorov* (Tel Aviv: Sifre Gadish, 1956).

2. Chaim Arlosoroff to Sima Arlosoroff, August 18, 1929, Central Zionist Archives in Jerusalem (hereafter CZA), A44/11. Arlosoroff wrote to Sima regularly and openly about his political work during his many travels on behalf of the Zionist movement during the second half of the 1920s. In this sense, she was a receptacle of his political ideas. It is challenging, however, from a historian's perspective (especially methodologically) to frame their marriage as a political partnership akin to the Bentwiches. The majority of Sima's letters to

her husband did not survive, nor did any diaries or other personal papers (with the exception of some letters following Chaim Arlosoroff's murder in 1933, which are held together with his personal papers at the Central Zionist Archives in Jerusalem).

3. The meeting in Geneva never happened. After the August 1929 riots, the Zionist Actions Committee meeting was moved up and transferred to London.

4. Chaim Arlosoroff to Sima Arlosoroff, August 17, 1929, CZA A44/11.

5. Chaim Arlosoroff to Sima Arlosoroff, August 18, 1929, CZA A44/11.

6. Chaim Arlosoroff to Sima Arlosoroff, August 18, 1929, CZA A44/11.

7. Shumsky, "Brith Shalom's Uniqueness Reconsidered," esp. 340; Arie Dubnov, "'Hamedinah she-ba-derekh'," *Yisrael* 24 (2016): 5–36; Dubnov and Harif, "Zionisms." On the links between binational and federative visions for Palestine, see Arie Dubnov, "Notes on the Zionist Passage to India, or: The Analogical Imagination and Its Boundaries," *Journal of Israeli History* 35, no. 2 (2016): 177–214, esp. 196; Gil Rubin, "From Federalism to Binationalism: Hannah Arendt's Shifting Zionism," *Contemporary European History* 24, no. 3 (2015): 393–414; Yosef Gorny, *From Binational Society to Jewish State: Federal Concepts in Zionist Political Thought, 1920–1990, and the Jewish People* (Leiden: Brill, 2006); and Susan Lee Hattis, *The Bi-national Idea in Zionism during Mandatory Times* (Haifa: Shikmona, 1970).

8. See Chaim Arlosoroff, "The Future of Zionist Policy (1932)," in *The Origins of Israel, 1882–1948: A Documentary History*, ed. Eran Kaplan and Derek J. Penslar (Madison: University of Wisconsin Press, 2011), 229–38.

9. See, e.g., Arlosoroff's speech at a Mapai meeting in Tel Aviv in January 1933. Chaim Arlosoroff, "Mediniyut mamlakhtit—be-terem medinah," in *Am, hevrah, u-medinah*, ed. Ascher Maniv (Tel Aviv: Yad Tabenkin, 1984), 119–29.

10. Arie Dubnov discusses how the idea of dominion for both Zionist and Indian political leaders was "the definitive federal-imperialist formula: full citizenship and self-rule without full independence.... Breaking away from the multinational empire was certainly not the preferred tactic in this unprecedented political climate." Dubnov, "Notes on the Zionist Passage to India," 196.

11. For more on the subsequent investigations and trial, see Committee for Assisting the Defence, *The Arlosoroff Murder Trial: Speeches and Relevant Documents* (Jerusalem: Hassolel Partnership, 1934). Shabtai Teveth's 1982 book *Retzah Arlozorov* reignited Israeli public interest in the crime; see Shabtai Teveth, *Retzah Arlozorov* (Jerusalem: Schocken, 1982).

12. See Jonathan Frankel, *Crisis, Revolution, and Russian Jews* (Cambridge: Cambridge University Press, 2009); and Stefani Hoffman and Ezra Mendelsohn, eds., *The Revolution of 1905 and Russia's Jews* (Philadelphia: University of Pennsylvania Press, 2008).

13. For more on the pogroms of October 1905, see Victoria Khiterer, "The October 1905 Pogroms and the Russian Authorities," *Nationalities Papers* 45, no. 5 (2015): 788–803; and John Doyle Klier and Shlomo Lambroza, eds., *Pogroms: Anti-Jewish Violence in Modern Russian History* (Cambridge: Cambridge University Press, 1992), esp. 191–289.

14. Avineri, *Arlosoroff*, 7.

15. For more on Landauer, see Paul Mendes-Flohr and Anya Mali, eds., *Gustav Landauer: Anarchist and Jew* (Berlin: De Gruyter Oldenbourg, 2015).

16. For more on Hapoel Hatzair in Germany, see Lavsky, *Before Catastrophe*; Baruch Ben-Avram, "Ha-Po'el Ha-Tza'ir ha-Germani—parashah shel kevutzat intelektualim 1917–1929," *Ha-Tziyonut* 7 (1981): 80–85. For more on Hapoel Hatzair generally, see Meir Chazan, *Metinut: ha-gishah ha-metunah be-ha-Po'el ha-Tza'ir u-ve-Mapai, 1905–1945* (Tel Aviv: Am Oved, 2009).

17. Lavsky, *Before Catastrophe*, 50–52.

18. Chaim Arlosoroff, "Peter Kropotkin," in *Kitve Hayim Arlozorov* (Tel Aviv: A. J. Stybel, 1934), 5:9–33.

19. Meir Chazan, "The Dispute between Aharonovitch and Arlosoroff over the Zionist Stance on the 'Arab Question,'" *Middle Eastern Studies* 43, no. 6 (2007): 983–96, esp. 986.

20. Arlosoroff, "Meora'ot Mai," in *Kitve Hayim Arlozorov*, 1:5–11.

21. Arlosoroff, "Ne'um ba-ve'idah ha-Tziyonit ha-shenatit be-Karlsbad," in *Kitve Hayim Arlozorov*, 6:35–36, 36.

22. Chazan, "Dispute between Aharonovitch and Arlosoroff," 987–90.

23. Chaim and Gerda Arlosoroff divorced soon after they arrived in Palestine. Gerda then married Zvi Luft and had another son and daughter. Though she—like Arlosoroff—pursued a doctorate in economics in Germany, she did not complete her degree and, instead, worked as a journalist in Palestine. She served as a correspondent for the German-language Zionist newspaper *Jüdische Rundschau* from 1924 to 1938. After the founding of the state of Israel, Gerda wrote for the *Jerusalem Post* and the *Economist*. See Luise Hirsch, *From the Shtetl to the Lecture Hall: Jewish Women and Cultural Exchange* (Lanham, MD: University Press of America, 2013), 249.

24. For more on the Permanent Mandates Commission of the League of Nations, see Pedersen, *The Guardians*.

25. Pedersen, *The Guardians*, 146–55.

26. Arlosoroff, "Homah shel zekhukhit," in *Kitve Hayim Arlozorov*, 1:29–42, 34–35. The title of the essay, "Wall of Glass," is possibly a reference to Jabotinsky's 1923 essay "The Iron Wall," which discussed Jewish-Arab relations in Palestine. Vladimir Jabotinsky, "On the Iron Wall (1923)," in Kaplan and Penslar, *The Origins of Israel*, 257–63.

27. James Vernon, *The Cambridge History of Britain: Modern Britain, 1750 to the Present* (Cambridge: Cambridge University Press, 2017), 260.

28. Arlosoroff, "*Homah shel zekhukhit*," 36.

29. Arlosoroff, 38

30. Arlosoroff, 33.

31. "Palestine Jews' Complaints," (London) *Times*, May 29, 1926, 11. Coincidentally, the author of the article was Gershon Agronsky, the *Times* correspondent in Palestine, whom Arlosoroff would later befriend.

32. Arlosoroff, "Yoman Geneva," May 30, 1926, June 1, 1926, in *Kitve Hayim Arlozorov*, 1:45–67, 45–48.

33. Arlosoroff also attended the International Labour Conference.

34. "French Overtures to Zionism," *The Letters and Papers of Chaim Weizmann*, ed. Barnet Litvinoff, ser. B, vol. 1, August 1898–July 1931 (New Brunswick, NJ: Transaction, 1983), 476.

35. Arlosoroff, "Yoman Geneva," June 12, 1926, in *Kitve Hayim Arlozorov*, 1:58–59.

36. Helen Bentwich, for instance, criticized the French for being "so aggressive with their subject peoples, & pig-headed about suppressing papers & speeches etc." early in the conflict in August 1925, even while recognizing that the French had employed tactics quite similar to those used by the British in Iraq in 1920. See Helen Bentwich to Caroline Franklin, August 8, 1925, WL 7HBE/2/8.

37. Pedersen, *The Guardians*, 149.

38. Arlosoroff's assessment of the failings of the League of Nations pushed him toward British imperial solutions. But he arrived at this conclusion in the same era in which other Jews, by contrast, continued to invest in the League and the new international politics it represented as the best opportunity to secure Jewish national rights in Palestine and Jewish minority rights in the diaspora. See Loeffler, *Rooted Cosmopolitans*, esp. chapters 1 and 2; and Natasha Wheatley, "Mandatory Interpretation: Legal Hermeneutics and the New International Order in Arab and Jewish Petitions to the League of Nations," *Past & Present* 227, no. 1 (2015): 205–48.

39. "Jewish Delegation Urged England's Assistance in Upbuilding National Home," *Sentinel*, June 18, 1926, 35.

40. Giveon Cornfield, with Max Seligman, *Zion Liberated: Jewish Nation Building under the British Mandate in Palestine* (Bloomington, IN: Xlibris, 2013), 44.

41. For more on Arlosoroff's trips to America, see Michael Brown, "A Tale of Two Bad Trips: Chaim Arlosoroff in America," in *Between History and Literature: Studies in Honor of Isaac Barzilay/Ben historyah le-sifrut: sefer yovel le-Yitzhak Barzilay*, ed. Stanley Nash (Tel Aviv: Hakibbutz Hameuchad, 1997), 7–35.

42. Inter-imperial Relations Committee, *Imperial Conference 1926: Report, Proceedings and Memoranda*, Nov. 1926. For more on dominionization, see John Darwin, "A Third British Empire? The Dominion Idea in Imperial Politics," in *The Oxford History of the British Empire*, vol. 4, *The Twentieth Century*, ed. Judith Brown and Wm Roger Louis (Oxford: Oxford University Press, 1999), 64–87.

43. Wedgwood was originally a member of the Liberal Party but joined Labour in 1919. For more on Wedgwood, see Paul Mulvey, *The Political Life of Josiah C. Wedgwood: Land, Liberty, and Empire, 1872–1943* (Woodbridge, UK: Boydell, 2010); and Joshua B. Stein, *Our Great Solicitor: Josiah C. Wedgwood and the Jews* (Selinsgrove, PA: Susquehanna University Press, 1992).

44. Helen Bentwich to Caroline Franklin, Oct. 30, 1926, WL 7HBE/2/4; Glynn, *Tidings from Zion*, 149.

45. Norman Rose, "The Seventh Dominion," *Historical Journal* 14, no. 2 (1971): 397–416, esp. 399.

46. Rose, "The Seventh Dominion." For more on the Zion Mule Corps, see Martin Sugarman, "The Zion Muleteers of Gallipoli, March 1915–May 1916," *Jewish Historical Studies* 36 (1999–2001): 113–39.

47. Clapham Junction is a major rail hub in London.

48. Josiah Wedgwood, "The Seventh Dominion," *Palestine Bulletin*, Feb. 16, 1927, 2. The February 18, 1927, issue of the paper contained a conclusion to Wedgwood's essay.

49. Josiah Wedgwood, *The Seventh Dominion* (London: Labour Publishing, 1928). For more on the Seventh Dominion scheme, see Rose, "The Seventh Dominion"; Norman Rose, *The Gentile Zionists: A Study in Anglo-Zionist Diplomacy, 1929–1939* (Abingdon, UK: Routledge, 1973), esp. chapter 7; Cecil Bloom, "Josiah Wedgwood and Palestine," *Jewish Historical Studies* 42 (2009): 147–72; and Joshua Stein, "Josiah Wedgwood and the Seventh Dominion Scheme," *Studies in Zionism* 11, no. 2 (1990), 141–55.

50. Leo Amery (1873–1955) served as secretary of state for the colonies from 1924 to 1929 in Stanley Baldwin's government and was a key drafter of the Balfour Declaration of 1917. Amery's mother, Elisabeth Johanna Saphir, had come from a Hungarian Jewish family.

51. For more on the relationship between British Labour and Zionism, see Gorny, *The British Labour Movement and Zionism*; Cecil Bloom, "The British Labour Party and Palestine, 1917–1948," *Jewish Historical Studies* 36 (1999–2001): 141–71; and David Feldman, "Zionism and the British Labour Party," in Katz, Leff, and Mandel, *Colonialism and the Jews*, 193–214.

52. Frederick Kisch to Chaim Weizmann, Jan. 20, 1927, CZA A209/156. The "second part" of the Balfour Declaration refers to Britain's commitment "that nothing shall be done which may prejudice the civil and religious rights of existing non-Jewish communities in Palestine," while the first part refers to the pledge to support the establishment of a Jewish national home in Palestine. See "The Balfour Declaration (November 2, 1917)," in *The Jew in the Modern World: A Documentary History*, 3rd ed., ed. Paul Mendes-Flohr and Jehuda Reinharz (Oxford: Oxford University Press, 2011), 660.

53. David Ben-Gurion and Moshe Pearlman, *Ben Gurion Looks Back in Talks with Moshe Pearlman* (New York: Simon and Schuster, 1965), 69.

54. Rumors circulated among the English elite that the Eton and Oxford educated Luke, born Harry Lukach to a Hungarian-American father and a Polish-Catholic mother, was, in fact, half-Jewish. Tom Segev disputes this claim. See Tom Segev, *One Palestine Complete: Jews and Arabs under the British Mandate* (New York: Metropolitan, 2000), 311.

55. Helen Bentwich to Caroline Franklin, May 21, 1921, WL 7HBE 2/4.

56. Arlosoroff, "Ha-pekidut ha-britit ve-ha-bayit ha-le'umi," in *Kitve Hayim Arlozorov*, 1:71–81, 81.

57. Arlosoroff, 72.

58. Arlosoroff, 71.

59. Arlosoroff, 72.

60. Arlosoroff, 72–73. Wyndham Deedes (1883–1956), who became a close friend of Helen and Norman Bentwich, served as chief secretary to High Commissioner Herbert

Samuel from 1920 to 1922. Brigadier General Gilbert Clayton (1875–1929) replaced Deedes as chief secretary, serving until 1925. James Edward Francis Campbell (1879–1953) received praise from Frederick Kisch, Edwin Samuel, and Norman Bentwich for fairmindedness. See Bentwich, *England in Palestine*, 240; Kisch, *Palestine Diary*, 134; and Samuel, *A Lifetime in Jerusalem*, 82.

61. Arlosoroff, "Ha-pekidut ha-britit ve-ha-bayit ha-le'umi," 1:71.

62. Wilfrid Scawen Blunt (1840–1922) was a British poet, critic of imperialism, and supporter of Egyptian nationalism. Annie Besant (1847–1933) was a British-born socialist and women's rights activist who was a member of the Indian National Congress and founded the Indian Home Rule movement in 1916.

63. Arlosoroff, "Ha-pekidut ha-britit ve-ha-bayit ha-le'umi," 72. Gertrude Bell (1868–1926) was a British writer, traveler, and colonial administrator who was instrumental in the establishment of the Hashemite dynasty in Iraq; St John Philby (1885–1960) was a British Arabist and colonial official who served as head of the Secret Service in Palestine from 1921 to 1924; Percy Cox (1864–1937) was one of the leading figures in British colonial administration in the interwar period and served as high commissioner of Iraq from 1920 to 1923; Ernest Richmond (1874–1955), before his tenure in Palestine, worked as an architect for the British Army in Egypt.

64. Helen Bentwich to Caroline Franklin, June 6, 1922, WL 7HBE 2/6.

65. Arlosoroff, "Ha-pekidut ha-britit ve-ha-bayit ha-le'umi," 74.

66. Arlosoroff, 75.

67. For perceptions of Jews among British politicians in the early twentieth century, particularly in terms of race and antisemitism, see James Renton, *The Zionist Masquerade: The Birth of the Anglo-Zionist Alliance, 1914–1918* (New York: Palgrave Macmillan, 2007), esp. chapter 1.

68. Arlosoroff, "Ha-pekidut ha-britit ve-ha-bayit ha-le'umi," 75–76.

69. Arlosoroff, 77.

70. Arlosoroff, 76.

71. Arlosoroff, 78.

72. Arlosoroff, 79.

73. Arlosoroff, 79–80. Also in 1928, the editorial board of the Hebrew-language newspaper *Davar* proposed a similar idea: an English-language supplement that could foster communication between the Zionist Labor movement and British officials in Palestine. The supplement was established the following year, with Moshe Shertok (who would later succeed Chaim Arlosoroff as head of the Political Department) serving as editor. See Gabriel Sheffer, *Moshe Sharett: Biography of a Political Moderate* (Oxford: Clarendon, 1996), 43.

74. Arlosoroff, "Ha-pekidut ha-britit ve-ha-bayit ha-le'umi," 80–81.

75. The idea of dominion as a means toward self-determination experienced popularity elsewhere in the British Empire, particularly in India. Gandhi, Nehru, and Jinnah all supported dominion status for India in the interwar period. See Lloyd I. Rudolph and Susanne Hoeber Rudolph, *Postmodern Gandhi and Other Essays: Gandhi in the World and at Home*

(Chicago: University of Chicago Press, 2006), 60–91. See also Dubnov, "Notes on the Zionist passage to India."

76. Ze'ev Jabotinsky to Josiah Wedgwood, Oct. 15, 1927, Jabotinsky Institute in Israel (hereafter JI), A1/2/17.

77. Rose, "The Seventh Dominion," 403. Rose argues that criticism of the mandatory government, coupled with faith in the goodwill of the metropolitan government, "represented the foremost view within the Zionist movement" in the late 1920s before the August 1929 riots.

78. Ze'ev Jabotinsky to Josiah Wedgwood, August 21, 1928, JI, A1/2/18/2.

79. Ernest Bennett (1865–1947) argued that Wedgwood—"more Zionist than the Zionists"—was unfairly critical of the British mandatory government in Palestine simply for paying heed to Arab national demands. "Why a Dominion," *Palestine Bulletin*, May 24, 1928, 2; "The Seventh Dominion," *Palestine Bulletin*, July 18, 1928, 2; "What Col. Wedgwood Said in Berlin," *Palestine Bulletin*, Oct. 29, 1928, 1.

80. "Ma rotzeh Wedgwood?" *Doar Hayom*, June 19, 1928, 1; see also "Shvil ha-zahav," *Doar Hayom*, July 9, 1928, 1.

81. This likely refers to the General Zionist Ya'akov Klivnov, who settled in Haifa after making aliyah in 1921, and the lawyer Ze'ev Finkelstein (later Shoham), who had previously worked for the immigration department of the Zionist Executive in London before moving with his family to Haifa, also in 1921. Finkelstein's wife was the agronomist Tzila Feinberg, a classmate of Moshe Shertok at Herzliya Hebrew High School. Her brother, Avshalom Feinberg, had been a leader of the Jewish spy network Nili during World War I.

82. "Haifa," *Davar*, April 24, 1928, 4.

83. Ze'ev Jabotinsky to Josiah Wedgwood, August 21, 1928, JI, A1/2/18/2.

84. Schechtman, *Fighter and Prophet*, 109.

85. Chaim Arlosoroff, "The Ninth Dominion: Shall Palestine Become an Integral Part of the British Empire?" *New Palestine*, April 5, 1929, 291–93, 308–9. A Hebrew translation of the article is included in Arlosoroff's collected writings. Arlosoroff, "Ha-dominiyon ha-teshi'i," in *Kitve Hayim Arlozorov*, 1:85–97. Arlosoroff called the essay "The Ninth Dominion," rather than the "seventh," because he believed that India and British East Africa would become dominions before Palestine. Arlosoroff's previous two essays dealing with the issue of Zionist-British relations ("Wall of Glass" and "British Clerks and the National Home") had both been published in Hebrew in *Hapoel Hatzair*. "The Ninth Dominion," however, was published in English in the *New Palestine*, the official organ of the Zionist Organization of America. Arlosoroff was in America, on another extended trip, at the time of the article's publication. See Brown, "A Tale of Two Bad Trips: Chaim Arlosoroff in America."

86. Arlosoroff, "The Ninth Dominion," 291.

87. Menachem Ussishkin (1863–1941) was president of the Jewish National Fund.

88. Arlosoroff, "The Ninth Dominion," 292–93.

89. Arlosoroff, 293.

90. Arlosoroff, 293. The comparison was not a perfect parallel. By referencing Canada's strong economic ties to its southern (English-speaking) neighbor, Arlosoroff likely intended to compare Anglo-Canadians and the United States to Palestinian Arabs and surrounding Arab countries. But he also presumably referred to the French-Canadian population that was resistant to "British allegiance" as a parallel to Palestinian Arabs, not Jews.

91. Arlosoroff, 293, 308.

92. Arlosoroff, 308. Whereas British dominions enjoyed representative government, British crown colonies were ruled by a governor.

93. The British naval base in Singapore was the centerpiece of Britain's interwar defense strategy, known as the Singapore strategy.

94. Arlosoroff, "The Ninth Dominion," 308.

95. Arlosoroff, 309.

96. Arlosoroff, 309.

97. Furthermore, while Wedgwood's arguments for why Palestine should become a British dominion addressed strategic and geopolitical factors, his central reasoning rested on conceptions of Jewish-British affinity. See Wedgwood, *The Seventh Dominion*, 2. For more on the relationship between British Labour and imperialism, see Partha Sarathi Gupta, *Imperialism and the British Labour Movement, 1914–1964* (New Delhi: Sage, 2002); Billy Frank, Craig Horner, David Stewart, eds., *The British Labour Movement and Imperialism* (Newcastle upon Tyne: Cambridge Scholars, 2010); and David Russell, "'The Jolly Old Empire': Labour, the Commonwealth and Europe, 1945–51," in *Britain, the Commonwealth and Europe*, ed. Alex May (London: Palgrave, 2001), 9–29.

98. Frederick Kisch to Chaim Weizmann, Jan. 20, 1927, CZA A209/156.

99. Segev, *One Palestine Complete*, 337.

100. Non-Zionists included in the new Jewish Agency supported Jewish cultural development in Palestine but opposed political development. See Gideon Shimoni, "From Anti-Zionism to Non-Zionism in Anglo-Jewry, 1917–1937," *Jewish Journal of Sociology* 28, no. 1 (1986): 19–47; and Gideon Shimoni, "The Non-Zionists in Anglo-Jewry, 1937–1948," *Jewish Journal of Sociology* 28, no. 2 (1986): 89–115.

101. The under-secretary of state for the colonies at the time was the Labour politician William Lunn (1872–1942).

102. Chaim Arlosoroff to Sima Arlosoroff, August 24, 1929, CZA A44/11.

103. Anita Shapira argues that while the 1929 riots were viewed by Zionists at the time (as well as by many historians in retrospect) as a massive turning point for Palestine, the historical view suggests otherwise. The 1930s, in fact, saw continued, stable development of the Yishuv, and the riots did not ultimately lead to major changes in British or Zionist policy. Shapira, *Land and Power*, 173.

104. Norman Rose, "The Seventh Dominion," 406.

105. The Shaw Commission, led by Sir Walter Shaw (1863–1937), who had served as a judge in various British colonial locales, was the first of two British groups tasked with inves-

tigating the August violence. The other three members of the commission included Labour MP Henry Snell (1865–1944), Conservative MP Henry Betterton (1872–1949), and Liberal MP Rhys Hopkin Morris (1888–1956).

106. Chaim Arlosoroff, *Jews, Arabs and Great Britain: A Study of Zionism in the Light of Recent Events* (Winnipeg: Israelite Press, 1930), 25–26. The essay, under the title "An Attempt to Sum Up," appeared originally in three installments in Hebrew: Chaim Arlosoroff, "Nisayon le-sikum," *Hapoel Hatzair*, Oct. 18, 1929, Nov. 1, 1929, Nov. 29, 1929.

107. Helen Bentwich to Caroline Franklin, Sept. 7, 1929, WL 7HBE/2/11.

108. Arlosoroff, *Jews, Arabs and Great Britain*, 34–35.

109. Arlosoroff, 37.

110. Arlosoroff, 39.

111. Arlosoroff, "The Ninth Dominion," 308.

112. Arlosoroff, *Jews, Arabs and Great Britain*, 38.

113. The Simon Commission (also known as the Indian Statutory Commission) was tasked with investigating constitutional reform in India. Led by John Simon and including six other British MPs, the commission arrived in India in February 1928.

114. Arlosoroff, *Jews, Arabs and Great Britain*, 40.

115. Helen Bentwich to Caroline Franklin, Oct. 5, 1929, WL 7HBE 2/11.

116. Chaim Arlosoroff, "Land, Immigration, and the Shaw Report," in *Documents and Essays on Jewish Labour Policy in Palestine* (Westport, CT: Greenwood Press, 1975), 175.

117. The citrus grower and writer Moshe Smilansky (1874–1953) provided testimony to the Shaw Commission. Smilansky was a chief critic from within the Zionist movement of the principle of Hebrew labor. For more on the citrus industry in Palestine, see Nahum Karlinsky, *California Dreaming: Ideology, Technology, and Society in the Citrus Industry in Palestine, 1890–1939* (Albany: State University of New York Press, 2005). On the Jewish and Arab economies in Palestine during the mandate, see Jacob Metzer and Oded Kaplan, *Meshek Yehudi u-meshek 'Aravi be-Eretz-Yisrael* (Jerusalem: Falk Institute for Economic Research, 1991).

118. Arlosoroff, "Land, Immigration, and the Shaw Report," 178–79. The Australian study was P. D. Philips and Gordon Leslie Wood, eds., *The Peopling of Australia* (Melbourne: Macmillan, 1928).

119. Reverse immigration represented a significant challenge for the Yishuv. In 1927, two thousand more Jews left Palestine than entered it.

120. Arlosoroff, "Le-she'elat ha-irgun ha-mishutaf," in *Kitve Hayim Arlozorov*, 3:135–68, 157–61. For further discussion, see Zachary Lockman, *Comrades and Enemies: Arab and Jewish Workers in Palestine, 1906–1948* (Berkeley: University of California Press, 1996), 99–102.

121. Arlosoroff, *Jews, Arabs and Great Britain*, 42.

122. Arlosoroff, "Ha-pekidut ha-Britit ve-ha-bayit ha-le'umi," 80.

123. In the months leading up to the publishing of the Passfield White Paper, Zionists worked to secure the support of Sidney Webb (Lord Passfield) (1859–1947), who replaced

Leo Amery as colonial secretary two months before the 1929 riots and maintained hope that the Labour Government would reaffirm British support for the Jewish national home. For instance, Dov Hoz (1894–1940), then the Poale Zion and Histadrut emissary in London (and also the brother-in-law of Moshe Shertok), urged fellow Zionists to trust Webb, a position he maintained into the spring of 1930. Hoz noted that Webb himself had made sure Labour's 1917 platform had included a clause about the right of Jews to settle in Palestine. Weizmann, too, believed that Webb would affirm Britain's commitment to a Jewish home in Palestine. Webb even pledged to Weizmann that he would meet with John Hope-Simpson before the latter traveled to Palestine in order to convey Weizmann's concerns (a meeting that ultimately never took place). See Gorny, *The British Labour Movement and Zionism*, 54–55. Arlosoroff also held Sidney Webb in high esteem, particularly as a socialist thinker, and included his book *The Decay of Capitalist Civilisation* (coauthored with his wife, Beatrice Webb) among a selection of proposed titles to translate and publish in Hebrew for a forthcoming 1931 series. Sidney Webb and Beatrice Webb, *The Decay of Capitalist Civilisation* (London: George Allen and Unwin, 1923).

124. Arlosoroff, *Jews, Arabs and Great Britain*, 42.

125. Those articles would be translated into Hebrew.

126. Originally a member of the Liberal Party, Joseph Kenworthy (1886–1953) joined the Labour Party in 1926 after David Lloyd George assumed the head of the Liberal Party. Kenworthy succeeded his father as Lord Strabolgi in 1934. In the 1940s, Kenworthy worked to revive the dominion idea through the Jewish Dominion of Palestine League, for which he served as chairman.

127. "Emanuel Neumann Predicts Success for United Palestine Appeal in 1927," *Jewish Telegraphic Agency* (hereafter *JTA*), Dec. 28, 1926.

128. Susan Lawrence (1871–1947), who visited Palestine in 1935 and was particularly impressed by the socialist societies created on the kibbutzim, went on to become a supporter of Zionism. At the Labour Party Conference in Edinburgh the following year, Lawrence met with Berl Katznelson, who observed that her "humanist" Labour politics had fallen out of fashion in a political party increasingly committed to "extreme radicalism." Quoted in Anita Shapira, *Berl: The Biography of a Socialist Zionist* (Cambridge: Cambridge University Press, 1984), 260.

129. Charles Roden Buxton (1875–1942) published an article in the *Daily Herald* in February 1918 in support of Zionism. See Gorny, *The British Labour Movement and Zionism*, 20–22.

130. For more on Harold Laski (1893–1950) and Zionism, see Yosef Gorny, "The Jewishness and Zionism of Harold Laski," *Midstream* 23, no. 9 (1977): 72–77.

131. G. T. Garratt was a Labour politician who had served as a colonial civil servant in India for eleven years. He criticized British histories of India that ignored the existence of Indian nationalism, a position that earned him the enmity of conservative leaders in Britain. Sabyasachi Bhattacharya, "A Brief Survey of Colonial Historiography in India," in *Different Types of History*, ed. Bharati Ray (Delhi: Pearson, 2009), 80.

132. Chaim Arlosoroff to G. T. Garratt, July 8, 1930, CZA A44/5/1.

133. Chaim Arlosoroff to G. T. Garratt, Sept. 8, 1930, CZA A44/5/1.

134. Basil Williams, *The British Empire* (Oxford: Oxford University Press, 1928).

135. Basil Williams, *Ha-Imperiah ha-Britit*, trans. Chaim Arlosoroff (Tel Aviv: Hevra, 1930), n.p.

136. George Fiddes, *The Dominions and Colonial Offices* (London: Putnam's Sons, 1926). Fiddes (1858–1936) served as permanent under-secretary of state for the colonies from 1916 to 1921 in David Lloyd George's government.

137. Arlosoroff, "Ha-misrad la-moshavot," in *Kitve Hayim Arlozorov*, 1:143–53, 143.

138. Chaim Arlosoroff to Sima Arlosoroff, August 17, 1929, London, CZA A44/11.

139. Chaim Arlosoroff to Alexander Astor, May 14, 1930, CZA A44/5/1.

140. The family firm, Isaac and Samuel, conducted business primarily in Latin America. Vogel's maternal uncle Benjamin Isaac served as consul for the short-lived Granadine Confederation (comprising mainly present-day Colombia and Panama) and consul general for Guatemala. Raewyn Dalziel, *Julius Vogel: Business Politician* (Auckland: Auckland University Press, 2013), 12.

141. Chaim Arlosoroff to Alexander Astor, May 14, 1930, CZA A44/5/1.

142. Chaim Arlosoroff to Alexander Astor, May 14, 1930, CZA A44/5/1.

143. Chaim Arlosoroff to Sima Arlosoroff, Nov. 21, 1930, CZA A44/11.

144. Though his Zionist political convictions were very much the product of his youth in Germany, Arlosoroff was born in the multiethnic space of the Russian Empire, where nationalism and socialism were synthesized by both Jewish and non-Jewish political actors. On the relationship between nationalism and socialism among Russian Jews, as manifested in their diverse and multitudinous cultural, political, and social projects, see Kenneth B. Moss, *Jewish Renaissance in the Russian Revolution* (Cambridge, MA: Harvard University Press, 2009); Frankel, *Crisis, Revolution, and Russian Jews*; and Jonathan Frankel, *Prophecy and Politics: Socialism, Nationalism, & the Russian Jews, 1862–1917* (Cambridge: Cambridge University Press, 1981).

145. Gorny, *The British Labour Movement and Zionism*, 75.

146. George Bernard Shaw articulated this Fabian position, shared by Webb, in George Bernard Shaw, *Fabianism and Empire: A Manifesto by the Fabian Society* (London: Grant Richards, 1900).

147. Gorny, *The British Labour Movement and Zionism*, 71. Elleke Boehmer notes that George Bernard Shaw and Sidney and Beatrice Webb opposed nationalism at home but did not object to imperial expansion in the name of socialism. See Elleke Boehmer, *Colonial and Postcolonial Literature: Migrant Metaphors*, 2nd ed. (Oxford: Oxford University Press, 2005), 42.

148. Jawaharlal Nehru (1889–1964) is perhaps the most famous independence leader who was also a follower of Fabian socialism, to which he was introduced during his time in London as a law student before World War I. A *London Times* magazine article published in 1951 (and critical of Nehru's politics) stated, "Beatrice and Sidney Webb, the godparents of

Fabian Socialism, are in a truer sense his creators than Vishnu and Siva." Harold Laski was, in fact, probably the English Fabian with the greatest influence on Nehru's political thinking. Though Fabian socialism would come to be associated with the anticolonial movement by the 1940s, in the early 1930s, Webb's socialist imperialism was still mainstream in Fabian circles. The (London) *Times* article is quoted in Lawrence H. White, *The Clash of Economic Ideas: The Great Policy Debates and Experiments of the Last Hundred Years* (Cambridge: Cambridge University Press, 2012), 249. For more on Nehru's socialist politics, see Sobhag Mathur, "Nehru: The Evolution of His Thought in the Pre-Independence Decades," in *Spectrum of Nehru's Thought*, ed. Sobhag Mathur and Shankar Goyal (New Delhi: Mittal, 1994), 33–50.

Chapter 3

1. See Aviva Halamish, *Be-merutz kaful neged ha-zman: mediniyut ha-'aliyah ha-Tziyonit bi-shnot ha-shloshim* (Jerusalem: Yad Ben-Zvi, 2006).

2. Gershon Agronsky (1894–1959), later Agron, was born in Ukraine and spent his childhood in Philadelphia. During World War I, he served in the Jewish Legion of the British Army in Palestine. After the war, Agronsky worked for the press office of the Jewish Agency and for the Jewish Telegraphic Agency. In 1932, he founded and served as editor of the English-language daily the *Palestine Post* (which later became the *Jerusalem Post*). He served as mayor of Jerusalem from 1955 until his death. See Gershon Agron, *Asir ha-ne'emanut* (Jerusalem: M. Nyuman, 1964). For more on Agronsky's work with the *Palestine Post*, see Erwin Frenkel, *The Press and Politics in Israel: The "Jerusalem Post" from 1932 to the Present* (Westport, CT: Greenwood Press, 1994).

3. Labour politician J. H. Thomas (1874–1949) succeeded Sidney Webb as colonial secretary. The Labour politicians who supported the National Government were expelled alongside MacDonald; they reconstituted themselves as a new political group, known as National Labour.

4. Martin Kolinsky suggests a parallel between Zionist pressure to remove Luke and Arab pressure to remove Bentwich; see Martin Kolinsky, *Law, Order and Riots in Mandatory Palestine, 1928–35* (London: St. Martin's, 1993), 106–9.

5. Bentwich and Bentwich, *Mandate Memories*, 146–47.

6. Bentwich, *Wanderer between Two Worlds*, 202.

7. Bentwich, 203. Helen supported her brother Hugh Franklin's unsuccessful bid for Parliament in 1931 and ran unsuccessfully herself the following year. Beginning in 1934, she served on the education committee of the London County Council (LCC). She was elected as a member of the LCC in 1938, serving until her retirement in 1965.

8. Norman Bentwich to Chaim Arlosoroff, Sept. 9, 1931, CZA A44/4. The "three sides of the triangle" refers to the Jews, Arabs, and British in Palestine.

9. Chaim Arlosoroff, *Yoman Yerushalayim* (Tel Aviv: Mifleget Po'ale Eretz-Yisrael, 1949), 8.

10. Arlosoroff, 11. The book, written by a Dutchman, offered a humorous analysis of

the Englishman's character and his attitude toward religion, sex, law, and education. G. J. Renier, *The English: Are They Human?* (London: Williams & Norgate, 1931).

11. Chancellor referred to the pre–World War I Jewish economic practice of employing Arab workers in Jewish agricultural settlements (especially in the citrus industry). The Shaw Commission had held up this example as a model beneficial to Jewish-Arab relations, in contrast to the Labor Zionist tenet of employing only Jewish workers.

12. Arlosoroff, *Yoman Yerushalayim*, 17–18.

13. Arlosoroff, 18.

14. Arlosoroff, 19.

15. "Outline of the Programme of the Jewish Agency," *Palestine Bulletin*, Sept. 1, 1931, 2; "Sir John Chancellor Leaves Palestine: Sailing for England on Relinquishing High Commissionership," *JTA*, Sept. 3, 1931.

16. "Outline of the Programme of the Jewish Agency," 2.

17. "Outline," 2.

18. "Outline," 2.

19. By "populations ... purely British by race and speech," Arlosoroff means white settler colonies, including Australia and New Zealand. "Outline," 2.

20. "Outline," 2.

21. Max Nurock (1893–1978), Herbert Samuel's private secretary and the Bentwiches' close friend who had been appointed assistant chief secretary of the Palestine government, was out of the country when Arlosoroff began his tenure as head of the Political Department. Edwin Samuel (1898–1978) spent 1931 and 1932 at Columbia University on a Commonwealth Fund fellowship with plans to study the American administration in the Philippines or, as he put it, an "effort to be imperial by a non-imperial Power." Samuel, *A Lifetime in Jerusalem*, 121.

22. Chaim Arlosoroff to Norman Bentwich, Sept. 28, 1931, CZA A255/650. Albert Montefiore Hyamson served as chief immigration officer from 1921 to 1934, but he was out of the country at the beginning of Arlosoroff's tenure as Political Department head. John Bernard Barron served as director of revenue and customs until 1924.

23. Arlosoroff, *Yoman Yerushalayim*, 57–58.

24. For more on daily life and urban culture in mandate-era Tel Aviv, see Anat Helman, *Young Tel Aviv: A Tale of Two Cities* (Waltham, MA: Brandeis University Press, 2010).

25. Quoted in Maoz Azaryahu, *Tel Aviv: Mythography of a City* (Syracuse, NY: Syracuse University Press, 2007), 58. For more on the ways that Tel Aviv was envisioned and constructed in opposition to Jaffa, see Mark LeVine, *Overthrowing Geography: Jaffa, Tel Aviv, and the Struggle for Palestine, 1880–1948* (Berkeley: University of California Press, 2005).

26. Arlosoroff, *Yoman Yerushalayim*, 46.

27. Arlosoroff, 16–17.

28. Arlosoroff, 8.

29. Arlosoroff, 86.

30. Arlosoroff, 91. Ruhi Abdel Hadi (1885–1954) was born in Jenin and studied law in Istanbul before World War I. During the British mandate period, he held various posts in the Palestine government, including assistant district officer of Jerusalem, assistant secretary of the government, and senior assistant secretary of the government.

31. The congress was also referred to as the "Pan-Islamic Conference."

32. Krämer, *A History of Palestine*, 257.

33. Arlosoroff, *Yoman Yerushalayim*, 36–37.

34. The dispute between Jews and Muslims over access to the Western Wall had been a key factor in the escalation of violence during the August 1929 riots. The mufti had convened an international conference to discuss protecting the wall and had alleged that Jews intended to take over the Al-Aqsa Mosque in the months leading up to the riots. Segev, *One Palestine Complete*, 306–7.

35. Arlosoroff, *Yoman Yerushalayim*, 56.

36. After his tenure in Jerusalem, Herbert Danby (1889–1953) returned to Britain in 1936 to serve as Regius Professor of Hebrew at Oxford.

37. Arlosoroff, *Yoman Yerushalayim*, 58–59. By "satanic policy," Arlosoroff refers to the notion in some Zionist circles that British policy in Palestine was uniformly and intentionally anti-Zionist.

38. Gershon Agronsky, "Notes on Visit to Bombay on Behalf of the Jewish Agency," April 17–May 2, 1930, CZA Z4/4129.

39. Meyer Nissim had also served as general manager of David Sassoon and Company.

40. Agronsky, "Notes on Visit." For a comparison of Israel and Pakistan, see Faisal Devji, *Muslim Zion: Pakistan as a Political Idea* (Cambridge: Harvard University Press, 2013).

41. Arlosoroff, *Yoman Yerushalayim*, 127–30.

42. Arlosoroff, *Jews, Arabs and Great Britain*, 38.

43. "Outline," 2.

44. Gorny, From Binational Society to Jewish State, 57–59.

45. David Werner Senator (1896–1953) joined the Jewish Agency as a non-Zionist, serving on the Jerusalem Executive from 1930 to 1935 and as treasurer and head of the immigration department. Senator was also a member of Brit Shalom and served as an administrator of the Hebrew University. While Ruppin eventually abandoned the principles of Brit Shalom, Bergmann remained committed to the idea of binationalism. For more on Senator, see Adi Livny, "Fighting Partition, Saving Mount Scopus: The Pragmatic Binationalism of D. W. Senator (1930–1949)," in *Textual Transmission in Contemporary Jewish Cultures*, ed. Avriel Bar-Levav and Uzi Rebhun (New York: Oxford University Press, 2020), 225–46.

46. Arlosoroff, *Yoman Yerushalayim*, 122.

47. Arlosoroff, 137.

48. Arlosoroff, 136.

49. Habima, one of the first Hebrew-language theaters, was founded in 1917 in Moscow. Members of the theater moved the company to Palestine in 1928. See Shlomo Shva, ed.,

Shiv'im ha-shanim ha-rishonot: Sipur ha-Bima (Tel Aviv: Keter, 1987); and Emanuel Levy, *The Habima, Israel's National Theater, 1917–1977: A Study of Cultural Nationalism* (New York: Columbia University Press, 1979).

50. Arlosoroff, *Yoman Yerushalayim*, 144–45.

51. The conflict stemmed from two fundamentally different perspectives on land rights. Traditional Palestinian Arab notions of land rights stemmed from occupancy, whereas the mandatory authorities and Jewish settlers maintained that rights stemmed from documented ownership.

52. For more on the coverage of the conflict in the Palestinian press, see R. Michael Bracy, *Printing Class: 'Isa al-'Isa, Filastin, and the Textual Construction of National Identity, 1911–1931* (Lanham, MD: University Press of America, 2011), 99–106.

53. For more on the conflict over Wadi al-Hawarith, see Muhammad Suwaed, "The Wadi al-Hawarith Affair (Emek Hefer): Disputed Land and the Struggle for Ownership: 1929–1933," *Middle Eastern Studies* 52, no. 1 (2016): 135–52. For more on Jewish National Fund land purchases and the issue of land ownership more broadly, see Yossi Katz, *The Land Shall Not Be Sold in Perpetuity: The Jewish National Fund and the History of State Ownership of Land in Israel* (Jerusalem: Magnes, 2016); Aida Essaid, *Zionism and Land Tenure in Mandate Palestine* (Abingdon, UK: Routledge, 2014); Yossi Katz, *The Battle for the Land: The History of the Jewish National Fund (KKL) before the Establishment of the State of Israel* (Jerusalem: Magnes, 2005); and Kenneth W. Stein, *The Land Question in Palestine, 1917–1939* (Chapel Hill: University of North Carolina Press, 1987). On British land policy in Mandate Palestine, see Martin P. Bunton, *Colonial Land Policies in Palestine, 1917–1936* (Oxford: Oxford University Press, 2007).

54. Arlosoroff, *Yoman Yerushalayim*, 157–58.

55. Arlosoroff, 158.

56. Arlosoroff, 158–59.

57. Arlosoroff, 159–60.

58. In the American South, for instance, New Deal policies that restricted tenant farming were opposed by socialist and labor activists, culminating in the 1934 founding of the Southern Tenant Farmers' Union.

59. Bentwich, *Wanderer between Two Worlds*, 203–4.

60. Helen Bentwich to Caroline Franklin, Jan. 25, 1932, WL 7HBE2/12.

61. Helen supported her brother, the suffragist Hugh Franklin, when he unsuccessfully stood as the Labour candidate for Hornsey in the general election in October 1931.

62. Bentwich, *Wanderer between Two Worlds*, 203.

63. Bentwich, 204. "Wandering between two worlds, one dead, the other powerless to be born" is taken from the poem "Stanzas from the Grande Chartreuse" by Matthew Arnold (1822–88).

64. Government House, now the headquarters of the United Nations Truce Supervision Organization, sits atop Abu Tor's Jebel Deir Abu Tor, also known as the "Hill of Evil Counsel."

65. Liora Halperin shows how Jewish multilingualism persisted into and beyond the mandate era. While Hebrew's dominance was "real and powerful," its limits demonstrated how deeply the Yishuv and Zionist culture were bound up in "outside entities," including Britain, the Arab world, and the non-Hebrew-speaking Jewish diaspora. Halperin, *Babel in Zion*, 10.

66. Helen Bentwich to Caroline Franklin, Feb. 6, 1932, WL 7HBE/2/12.

67. Helen Bentwich to Caroline Franklin, Feb. 11, 1932, WL 7HBE/2/12.

68. Arlosoroff, *Yoman Yerushalayim*, 206.

69. "Disturbances at Hebrew University When Norman Bentwich Delivers First Lecture," *JTA*, Feb. 12, 1932.

70. Helen Bentwich to Caroline Franklin, Feb. 11, 1932, WL 7HBE/2/12.

71. Brit HaBirionim translates as "Alliance of Thugs." When Arlosoroff was assassinated the following year, Abba Ahimeir (1897–1962) was arrested and charged with inciting the murder. He had fiercely opposed the Haavara (Transfer) Agreement, negotiated by Arlosoroff. Though he was cleared of the charge before the trial began, Ahimeir remained in prison until 1935. For more on Ahimeir, see Peter Bergamin, "An Intellectual Biography of Abba Ahimeir" (PhD diss., University of Oxford, 2016); and Joseph Nedava, ed., *Abba Ahimeir: ha-ish she-hitah et ha-zerem: li-demuto, le-torato, li-khetavav u-le-ma'avakav* (Tel Aviv: Hotza'at ha-'amutah le-hafatzat toda'ah le'umit, 1987).

72. The Sicarii, known as such because they carried small daggers called *sicae*, were an extremist group of Jewish Zealots who attacked Roman rulers and their allies in the first century CE. While Brit HaBirionim drew inspiration from the Sicarii, Ehud Sprinzak argues that "Birionim's ennoblement of the Jewish past was neither halakhic nor historical. It was above all a mythological rediscovery of the glorious tales of the nation, a romantic glorification of the old days of blood, soil, heroism, and conquest." Ehud Sprinzak, *The Ascendance of Israel's Radical Right* (Oxford: Oxford University Press, 1991), 25.

73. While *birionim* can translate as "hooligans," Arlosoroff used *huliganim* here.

74. Arlosoroff, *Yoman Yerushalayim*, 206–7.

75. Gordon, "'Nothing but a Disillusioned Love'?"

76. Bentwich, *Wanderer between Two Worlds*, 206–7.

77. Arlosoroff, *Jews, Arabs and Great Britain*, 25–26.

78. See Arlosoroff, "Ha-pekidut ha-Britit ve-ha-bayit ha-le'umi."

79. Quoted in Anita Shapira, *Berl: The Biography of a Socialist Zionist* (Cambridge: Cambridge University Press, 1984), 171.

80. Arlosoroff, *Yoman Yerushalayim*, 216.

81. Arthur Wauchope to Chaim Arlosoroff, Dec. 29, 1931, CZA S25/30–111.

82. On Arlosoroff's understanding of the rise of Nazism, see Zeev Tzahor, "Chaim Arlosoroff and His Attitude toward the Rise of Nazism," *Jewish Social Studies* 46, no. 3/4 (1984): 321–30.

83. Shapira, *Israel: A History*, 80–81. See also Anita Shapira, "Zionism in the Age of Revolution," *Modern Judaism* 18, no. 3 (1998): 217–26; and Shapira, *Land and Power*, 206–10.

84. Shapira, *Land and Power*, 207.
85. Chaim Arlosoroff diary notes, Feb. 14, 1932, CZA A123/19.
86. Arlosoroff, "The Ninth Dominion," 293.
87. Arlosoroff diary notes, Feb. 14, 1932, CZA A123/19.
88. Arlosoroff, *Yoman Yerushalayim*, 259–60.
89. Arlosoroff, "The Future of Zionist Policy (1932)," in Kaplan and Penslar, *The Origins of Israel*, 231–32.
90. Arlosoroff, 235–36.
91. Arlosoroff, 237.
92. Shlomo Avineri writes, "That Arlosoroff never proposed anything on these lines on any other occasion, nor tried this line of argument on any member or leader of his own party, clearly suggests that the 'fourth option' cannot be construed as a clear-cut policy choice." Avineri, *Arlosoroff*, 96. In fact, Arlosoroff sent a copy of the confidential letter to David Ben-Gurion with a note reading "Ben-Gurion, just for you . . . C.A." Quoted in Anita Shapira, *Ben-Gurion: Father of Modern Israel* (New Haven, CT: Yale University Press, 2014), 91. Arlosoroff, "The Future of Zionist Policy (1932)," 237.
93. Gad Frumkin (1887–1960), who was raised in the Muslim quarter of Jerusalem's Old City, was the only Jewish jurist to serve on the Palestine Supreme Court. On Frumkin's formative interactions with Arab neighbors in Ottoman Palestine, see Menachem Klein, *Lives in Common: Arabs and Jews in Jerusalem, Jaffa, and Hebron* (Oxford: Oxford University Press, 2014), esp. 43–45.
94. Mustafa Al-Khalidi (1878–1944), referred to by Arlosoroff as El Khaldi, was a Palestinian jurist and member of the Supreme Court who later served as mayor of Jerusalem until his death in 1944. Al-Khalidi approached Frumkin in 1936, following the Arab strike and revolt, to try to negotiate a Jewish-Arab accord. See Neil Caplan, *Futile Diplomacy*, vol. 2, *Arab-Zionist Negotiations and the End of the Mandate* (Abingdon, UK: Routledge, 2015), 35–40.
95. Francis Khayat, a member of Jerusalem's Arab Christian community, served on the Supreme Court.
96. Ali bey Jarallah, along with Gad Frumkin, had been one of only two lawyers in Jerusalem in 1917. Both he and Frumkin had studied law in Constantinople.
97. Chaim Arlosoroff diary notes, Feb. 16, 1932, CZA A123/19. On legal history in Mandate Palestine, see Likhovski, *Law and Identity in Mandate Palestine*.
98. Arlosoroff, *Yoman Yerushalayim*, 253.
99. Chaim Arlosoroff diary notes, Feb. 22, 1932, CZA 123/19.
100. Chaim Arlosoroff to Wellesley Aron, May 29, 1932, CZA S25/7753.
101. Eva Violet Mond Isaacs (1895–1973) was styled Lady Erleigh and, after 1935, the Marchioness of Reading. Isaacs's mother, Violet Goetz, was a devout Anglican of Huguenot ancestry. As an adult, after the death of her father in 1930, Isaacs converted to Judaism and later published an autobiography; see Eva Isaacs, *For the Record: The Memoirs of Eva, Marchioness of Reading* (London: Hutchinson, 1973).
102. Chaim Arlosoroff diary notes, Feb. 25, 1932, CZA 123/19.

103. Arlosoroff, *Yoman Yerushalayim*, 246.

104. Percival David did, indeed, endow a chair at the Hebrew University the following year: the Sir Sassoon David Chair of Near Eastern Art and Archaeology in memory of his father. Ironically, the Indian Jewish newspaper the *Jewish Advocate* proudly held up the founding of the chair as evidence of Baghdadi Jewish engagement with Zionism. Joan G. Roland, *The Jewish Communities of India: Identity in a Colonial Era* (New Brunswick, NJ: Transaction, 1998), 163.

105. Arlosoroff, *Yoman Yerushalayim*, 237.

106. Leon Pinsker (1821–91), a physician, was born in Russian Poland and initially supported Jewish emancipation, believing it would solve the Jewish condition in Europe. The Odessa Pogrom in 1871 and the wave of pogroms that began in 1881 convinced Pinsker that antisemitism would remain eradicable as long as Jews lacked a nation of their own. In 1884, he founded Hibbat Zion (Chovevei Zion), one of the forerunners of the modern Zionism movement.

107. Leon Pinsker, "Auto-Emancipation: An Appeal to His People by a Russian Jew (1882)," in *The Zionist Idea*, ed. Arthur Hertzberg (New York: Atheneum, 1970), 198.

108. Leon Pinsker, *Auto-Emancipation*, trans. D. S. Blondheim (New York: Maccabean Publishing, 1906).

109. Chaim Arlosoroff to Arthur Wauchope, May 13, 1932, CZA S25/30/78.

110. Arthur Wauchope to Chaim Arlosoroff, May 15, 1932, CZA S25/30/79.

111. Pinsker, "Auto-Emancipation," (1970 edition), 187.

112. Arthur Wauchope to Chaim Arlosoroff, May 15, 1932, CZA S25/30/79.

113. Chaim Arlosoroff to Arthur Wauchope, May 25, 1932, CZA S25/30/74–75.

114. Arlosoroff to Wauchope.

115. Arlosoroff to Wauchope.

116. This refers to the fifth wave of Jewish immigration to Palestine, generally considered to have lasted from 1932 to 1939.

117. While German Jewish immigration to Palestine increased significantly in this period, and the Fifth Aliyah is often labeled the "German Aliyah," the majority of Jews who immigrated to Palestine between 1932 and 1939 came from Poland. See Irith Cherniavsky, *Be'or shineihem: 'al 'aliyatam shel yehudei polin lifnei hashoah* (Tel Aviv: Resling, 2015).

Chapter 4

1. An earlier version of this chapter was published as "A Late Imperial Elite Jewish Politics: Baghdadi Jews in British India and the Political Horizons of Empire and Nation," *Jewish Social Studies* 23, no. 2 (Feb. 2018): 48–85.

2. The term *memorial*, as used by David Ezra and members of his community, refers to a written petition presented to a government or authority.

3. "Memorial to the Viceroy and Governor General of India in Council from the Members of the Jewish Community of Calcutta," August 1929, National Library of Israel (NLI), Sassoon Archive (SA), arc. 4°1790, box 46C.

4. For more on the Government of India Act of 1919, see Rohit De, "Constitutional Antecedents," in *The Oxford Handbook of the Indian Constitution*, ed. Sujit Choudhry, Madhav Khosla, and Pratap Bhanu Mehta (Oxford: Oxford University Press, 2016), 17–37, esp. 26–27.

5. Roland, *Jewish Communities of India*, 116.

6. Bill Schwartz has commented on the challenges faced both by British officials in navigating and by historians in writing about a complex, constantly shifting imperial legal system. Bill Schwartz, *The White Man's World* (Oxford: Oxford University Press, 2011), 345.

7. "Memorial to the Viceroy and Governor General."

8. Rachel Ezra to Solomon Sassoon, August 26 (letter also dated August 25), 1931, NLI, SA, arc. 4°1790, box 49.

9. Rachel Ezra to Solomon Sassoon, March 19, 1931, NLI, SA, arc. 4°1790, box 49.

10. Joan Roland, whose book constitutes the most comprehensive historical research on Indian Jewry, argues that Baghdadi Jews' "struggle to escape their marginal status and be considered fully European constitutes a main theme of the Baghdadis' sojourn in India; their relationship with government and their political affiliations and attitudes must be examined in this context." Roland, *Jewish Communities of India*, 57. See also Yulia Egorova, *Jews and India: Perceptions and Image* (London: Routledge, 2006). For other histories of Baghdadi Jews and other Jewish communities (principally the Bene Israel and Cochin Jews) in India, see Shalva Weil, ed. *The Baghdadi Jews in India: Maintaining Communities, Negotiating Identities and Creating Super-Diversity* (Abingdon, UK: Routledge, 2019); Nathan Katz, ed., *Studies of Indian Jewish Identity* (New Delhi: Manohar, 2011); Cernea, *Almost Englishmen*; Anil Bhatti and Johannes H. Voight, eds., *Jewish Exile in India: 1933–1945* (New Delhi: Manohar, 2005); Jael Silliman, *Jewish Portraits, Indian Frames: Women's Narratives from a Diaspora of Hope* (Hanover, NH: Brandeis University Press/University Press of New England, 2001); Dalia Ray, *The Jewish Heritage of Calcutta* (Calcutta: Minerva, 2001); Mavis Hyman, *Jews of the Raj* (Calcutta: Hyman, 1995); Esmond David Ezra, *Turning Back the Pages: A Chronicle of Calcutta Jewry* (London: Brookside, 1986); Ezekiel N. Musleah, *On the Banks of the Ganga: The Sojourn of the Jews in Calcutta* (North Quincy, MA: Christopher Publishing House, 1975); and Flower Elias and Judith Elias Cooper, *The Jews of Calcutta: The Autobiography of a Community, 1792–1972* (Calcutta: Jewish Association of Calcutta, 1974). On the transnational identity of Baghdadi Jews in Iraq and beyond, see S. R. Goldstein-Sabbah, *Baghdadi Jewish Networks in the Age of Nationalism* (Leiden: Brill, 2021).

11. The Baghdadi community in India, and the Sassoons in particular, were highly endogamous. Cousin-marriage was common and considered ideal because it kept the family fortune intact. See Roland, *Jewish Communities of India*, 19. Rachel Ezra was descended from David Sassoon through both parents—her mother, Flora Sassoon (1859–1936), was the great-granddaughter of David Sassoon (through his first wife), and her father, Solomon Sassoon (1841–94), was David Sassoon's son with his second wife Farha Hyeem. The pairing between half-great-uncle and niece surprised even the extremely endogamous Sassoon family. David Ezra, through his mother, Mozelle, was a great-grandson of David Sassoon.

David and Rachel Ezra were thus related through a dense and complex web of endogamy. Most basically, they were both half-first cousins and first cousins once removed, as David was also Rachel's mother's first cousin. Stanley Jackson, *The Sassoons* (New York: Dutton, 1968), provides a family tree. For more on the Sassoon family, see Esther da Costa Meyer and Claudia J. Nahson, *The Sassoons* (New Haven, CT: Jewish Museum and Yale University Press, 2023); Joseph Sassoon, *The Global Merchants: The Enterprise and Extravagance of the Sassoon Dynasty* (London: Allen Lane, 2022); Cecil Roth, *The Sassoon Dynasty* (London: Robert Hale, 1941); Peter Stansky, *The Worlds of Philip and Sybil* (New Haven, CT: Yale University Press, 2003); and Eilat Negev and Yehuda Koren, *The First Lady of Fleet Street* (London: JR Books, 2011). See also my article, on which this chapter is based: Elizabeth E. Imber, "A Late Imperial Elite Jewish Politics: Baghdadi Jews in British India and the Political Horizons of Empire and Nation," *Jewish Social Studies* 23, no. 2 (Winter 2018): 48–85.

12. Musleah, *On the Banks of the Ganga*, 352–53.

13. Roland, *Jewish Communities of India*, 22.

14. Edward Judah, "Classification of the Jewish Sephardic Community of Bengal," speech delivered at the Judean Club, Calcutta, Jan. 16, 1934, NLI, SA, arc. 4°1790, box 46c.

15. It is unclear precisely why the status was revoked in 1885. See Roland, *Jewish Communities of India*, 58–60.

16. Judah, "Classification of the Jewish Sephardic Community of Bengal."

17. On the Armenian community of Calcutta, see Susmita Bhattacharya, "The Armenians of Calcutta," in *Calcutta Mosaic: Essays and Interviews on the Minority Communities of Calcutta*, ed. Himadri Banerjee, Nilanjana Gupta, and Sipra Mukherjee (London: Anthem, 2009), 70–85.

18. Stein, "Protected Persons," 87–88. The tenuousness of the assertion of Iberian heritage was acknowledged by Edward Judah, one of the Baghdadi memorialists, when he said in a public lecture in Calcutta in 1934 that "it is difficult for our community as a whole to prove Spanish descent as can be done by most Sephardic Jews in Europe." Judah, "Classification of the Jewish Sephardic Community of Bengal."

19. Roland, *Jewish Communities of India*, 115.

20. Maria Misra, *Business, Race, and Politics in British India, c. 1850–1960* (Oxford: Oxford University Press, 1999), 164.

21. According to the Bengal electoral rules, a European was defined as "any person of European descent in the male line being a British subject and resident in British India, who either was born in or has a domicile in the British Isles, Canada, Newfoundland, Australia, New Zealand, or the Union of South Africa, or whose father was so born or has or had up to the date of the birth of the person in question such a domicile." An Anglo-Indian was defined as anyone of "European descent in the male line who is not a European, or of mixed Asiatic and non-Asiatic descent, whose father, grandfather or more remote ancestor in the male line was born in the Continent of Europe, Canada, Newfoundland, Australia, New Zealand, the Union of South Africa or the United States of America, and who is not a European." William Marris and James Wilford Garner, *Civil Government for Indian Students*

(Calcutta: S. C. Sanial, 1921), 337–38; Roland, *Jewish Communities of India*, 54, 116.

22. Copies of the memorial were also sent to the members of the Simon Commission (Indian Statutory Commission) and to Rufus Isaacs, the Anglo-Jewish Liberal statesman and former viceroy and governor general of India.

23. "Memorial to the Viceroy and Governor General."

24. The Marathi people, who speak the Marathi language, are an ethnic group from the western Indian state of Maharashtra.

25. "Memorial to the Viceroy and Governor General." Note the mention of "pre-war Asiatic Turkey." Baghdadi Jews who had not become British subjects before World War I were considered enemy aliens under the Aliens Restriction (Amendment) Act of 1919. With regard to the assertion of Sephardi identity, in addition to the link it established with Europe, Sephardi heritage also struck a significant chord in the British sociopolitical consciousness. Sephardi Jews had long distinguished themselves in western Europe in trade and business, and Britain's most prominent Jews of the past century—Benjamin Disraeli and Moses Montefiore—had come from Sephardi families.

26. "Memorial to the Viceroy and Governor General."

27. "Memorial to the Viceroy and Governor General."

28. "Memorial to the Viceroy and Governor General."

29. Stansky, *Worlds of Philip and Sybil*, 1. Philip Sassoon's father, Edward Sassoon (1856–1912), had held the seat from 1899 until his death.

30. For more on Philip Sassoon, see Damian Collins, *Charmed Life: The Phenomenal World of Philip Sassoon* (London: Harper Collins, 2017); and Stansky, *Worlds of Philip and Sybil*.

31. "Memorial to the Viceroy and Governor General."

32. Unlike other Jewish politicians in Britain, including the Ezras' relative Philip Sassoon, who tended to abstain from Jewish issues, Isaacs openly sympathized with Zionist causes (though more earnestly later on) and involved himself in development projects in Palestine. Though he had overseen the implementation of the Montagu-Chelmsford reforms (in the Government of India Act of 1919), seen by many in Britain as an unwise introduction of self-rule to India, Isaacs clashed with Indian supporters of self-governance and civil disobedience. In 1922, he ordered the arrest and imprisonment of Gandhi.

33. David Ezra to Rufus Isaacs, August 20, 1929, NLI, SA, arc. 4°1790, box 46c.

34. Mitchell B. Hart, "Jews and Race: An Introductory Essay," in *Jews and Race: Writings on Identity and Difference, 1880–1940*, ed. Mitchell B. Hart (Waltham, MA: Brandeis University Press, 2011), xiii–xxxix, esp. xvii.

35. David Ezra to S. H. Haskell, Sept. 12, 1929, NLI, SA, arc. 4°1790, box 46C.

36. David Ezra to S. H. Haskell, Sept. 12, 1929, NLI, SA, arc. 4°1790, box 46C.

37. Edward Judah to Joseph Judah, Dec. 1929, NLI, SA, arc. 4°1790, box 46C.

38. Silliman, *Jewish Portraits, Indian Frames*, 18.

39. Schwartz, *White Man's World*, 292.

40. Joseph Judah to Edward Judah, May 8, 1930, NLI, SA, arc. 4°1790, box 46C.

41. Joseph Judah to Edward Judah, June 9, 1930, NLI, SA, arc. 4°1790, box 46C.
42. Edward Judah to Joseph Judah, May 15, 1930, NLI, SA, arc. 4°1790, box 46C.
43. Edward Judah to Joseph Judah, June 17, 1930, NLI, SA, arc. 4°1790, box 46C.
44. Parliamentary Debates, Commons, 5th series (1909–81), vol. 301, May 7, 1935, col. 906.
45. Vernon Dawson to Edward Judah, June 4, 1935, NLI, SA, arc. 4°1790, box 46c.
46. Edward Judah to Rachel and David Ezra, July 25, 1935, NLI, SA, arc. 4°1790, box 46c.
47. Elizabeth Buettner, "Riding the Elephant or Riding the Bus: Britons, India, and Elite Status in the Late Imperial Era," in *At the Top of Empire*, ed. Claire Laux, François-Joseph Ruggiu, and Pierre Singaravélou (Brussels: Peter Lang, 2009), 219–35, esp. 220.
48. For more on the relationship between the Sassoon family and the British royal family, see Jackson, *The Sassoons*, 67–122.
49. "King's Birthday Honours: Departmental Lists," *Manchester Guardian*, June 3, 1927, 6.
50. Though selected to represent Iran in India, Rustomjee was born in India and was a member of the Parsi community that had resided in India since the tenth century. For more on the Parsi community in India, see Mitra Sharafi, *Law and Identity in Colonial South Asia: Parsi Legal Culture, 1772–1947* (Cambridge: Cambridge University Press, 2014); and John R. Hinnells and Alan Williams, eds., *Parsis in India and the Diaspora* (London: Routledge, 2008).
51. *Yearbook of the Royal Asiatic Society of Bengal* 5 (1939): 91; *Journal and Proceedings of the Asiatic Society of Bengal* (1935): lxxv.
52. King Emperor's Anti-tuberculosis Fund for India to Rachel Ezra, April 26, 1938, NLI, SA, arc. 4°1790, box 72.
53. Indian Science Congress Association, *The Shaping of Indian Science*, 3 vols. (Hyderabad: Universities Press, 2003), 1:100.
54. Rachel Ezra diary, Feb. 5, 1926, NLI, SA, arc. 4°1790, box 38.
55. Rachel Ezra diary, March 10, 1924, NLI, SA, arc. 4°1790, box 20.
56. Barbara N. Ramusack, *The Indian Princes and Their States* (Cambridge: Cambridge University Press, 2004), 136.
57. Silliman, *Jewish Portraits, Indian Frames*, 75.
58. R. Ezra to Sassoon, August 26, 1931, NLI, SA, arc. 4°1790, box 49.
59. Rachel Ezra to Solomon Sassoon, Sept. 2, 1931, NLI, SA, arc. 4°1790, box 49.
60. Henry Gidney to Rufus Isaacs, July 25, 1933, London Metropolitan Archives, ACC/3121/E3/512, File 1, Gidney.
61. "Memorial to the Viceroy and Governor General."
62. Roland, *Jewish Communities of India*, 126. On the similarities between the dominion idea as a path toward self-determination in the Indian and Zionist cases, see Dubnov, "Notes on the Zionist Passage to India."
63. Roland, *Jewish Communities of India*, 126; K. K. Chaudhari, "Modern Period," *Maharashtra State Gazetteers: Greater Bombay District*, ed. K. K. Chaudhari, 3 vols. (Mumbai:

Government of Maharashtra, 1986), 1:499. For more on the subcommittee of the FICCI and elite Indian approaches to swadeshi more broadly, see David Lockwood, *The Indian Bourgeoisie: A Political History of the Indian Capitalist Class in the Early Twentieth Century* (London: I.B. Tauris, 2012), esp. chapter 6, 126–48.

64. Chaudhari, Maharashtra State Gazetteers, 499.

65. Mohandas Gandhi to Gangaram M. Thaware, Feb. 12, 1933, in *The Collected Works of Mahatma Gandhi*, 100 vols. (New Delhi: Publications Division, Ministry of Information and Broadcasting, Government of India, 1972), 53:278–79.

66. Mohandas Gandhi to Ghanshyam D. Birla, March 2, 1933, in *Collected Works*, 53:445–46; Mohandas Gandhi, "Higher Education for the Harijans," Feb. 25, 1933, in *Collected Works*, 53:392–94.

67. Eleanor Zelliot, "Experiments in Dalit Education: Maharashtra, 1850–1947," in *Education and the Disprivileged: Nineteenth and Twentieth Century India*, ed. Sabyasachi Bhattacharya (Hyderabad: Orient Longman, 2002), 35–49, esp. 48.

68. "The New Year Honours: Appointments and Promotions in the Orders of Chivalry," *Manchester Guardian*, Jan. 1, 1947, 6.

69. Pradip Sinha, *Calcutta in Urban History* (Calcutta: Firma KLM, 1978), 31.

70. For more on the social, cultural, and racial geography of Calcutta, see Keya Dasgupta, "Mapping the Spaces of Minorities," in Banerjee, Gupta, and Mukherjee, *Calcutta Mosaic*, 22–68; and Swati Chattopadhyay, *Representing Calcutta: Modernity, Nationalism, and the Colonial Uncanny* (New York: Routledge, 2005).

71. Ezra, *Turning Back the Pages*, 242, 264. Ezra claims that by the 1930s, Baghdadi Jewish women in Calcutta had long since abandoned the practice of ritual immersion following menstruation. In addition to a rare conversion to Judaism, the Ezras' mikvah was most likely used for *tevilat kelim*, the ritual purification of utensils for eating, and by brides and grooms before their wedding.

72. Ezra, *Turning Back the Pages*, 42.

73. Ezra Yehezkel-Shaked, *Jews, Opium, and the Kimono* (Jerusalem: Rubin Mass, 2003), 179.

74. Elia Etkin, "The Ingathering of (Non-human) Exiles: The Creation of the Tel Aviv Zoological Garden Animal Collection, 1938–1948," *Journal of Israeli History* 35, no. 1 (2016): 57–74.

75. Rachel Ezra diary, May 15, 1926, NLI, SA, arc. 4°1790, box 38.

76. Rachel Ezra diary, Sept. 22, 1926, NLI, SA, arc. 4°1790, box 38.

77. For more on the WJC, see Leon Kubowitzki, *Unity in Dispersion: A History of the World Jewish Congress* (New York: World Jewish Congress, 1948).

78. "Memorial to the Viceroy and Governor General."

79. Sheffer, *Moshe Sharett*, 21–23; Shapira, *Ben-Gurion*, 31–36.

80. For more on Ottoman Zionism, see Michelle Campos, "Between 'Beloved Ottomania' and 'The Land of Israel': The Struggle over Ottomanism and Zionism among Palestine's Sephardi Jews, 1908–1913," *International Journal of Middle East Studies* 37, no. 4 (2005):

461–83; Esther Benbassa, "Zionism in the Ottoman Empire at the End of the 19th and the Beginning of the 20th Century," *Studies in Zionism* 11, no. 2 (1990): 127–40; and Sarah Abrevaya Stein, *Making Jews Modern: The Yiddish and Ladino Press in the Russian and Ottoman Empires* (Bloomington: Indiana University Press, 1990), esp. chapter 2.

81. Rachel Ezra diary, August 24, 1913, NLI, SA, arc. 4°1790, box 69.

82. David Sassoon to Rachel Ezra, Dec. 12, 1917, NLI, SA, arc. 4°1790, box 40a.

83. Musleah, *On the Banks of the Ganga*, 356.

84. Roland, *Jewish Communities of India*, 151.

85. Israel Cohen, *The Journal of a Jewish Traveller* (London: John Lane, 1925), 233–34. *Mincha* is the Jewish afternoon prayer service.

86. Cohen, 235.

87. Cohen, 240. A lakh is 100,000 rupees; a crore is 10,000,000 rupees.

88. Ray, *Jewish Heritage of Calcutta*, 105.

89. "The Fifth Annual General Meeting of the Bombay Zionist Association," *Zion's Messenger*, Oct. 1923, 15.

90. Israel Zangwill (1864–1926), the Anglo-Jewish writer and founder of the Jewish Territorialist Organization, made the notorious speech at Carnegie Hall in New York City in October 1923.

91. "Mr. Israel Zangwill in America," *Zion's Messenger*, Jan. 1924, 1.

92. It is unclear if the Ezras and Herbert Samuel had previously met, but it is very likely that Rachel Ezra had known Samuel when she lived in Britain with her mother, brother, and sister following the death of her father. Flora Sassoon, Rachel Ezra's mother, took over the leadership of David Sassoon & Company when her husband died. She was a noted Hebraist and supporter of scientific research who operated in the same social and familial network of elite British Jews as did Herbert Samuel.

93. Frederick Kisch, then head of the Jewish Agency's Political Department, described the content of these Zionist speeches, which he said were mostly "personally addressed" to Herbert Samuel: "We have criticized you, we shall criticize you again, but you are one of us and we want you to stay." Kisch, *Palestine Diary*, 115.

94. Rachel Ezra diary, April 18–20, 1924, NLI, SA, arc. 4°1790, box 20.

95. Ray, *Jewish Heritage of Calcutta*, 105; Hyman, *Jews of the Raj*, 192.

96. Henry Near, *The Kibbutz Movement: A History*, 2 vols. (Oxford: Littman Library of Jewish Civilization, 1992), 1:282.

97. Gideon Shimoni, *Jews and Zionism: The South African Experience (1910–1967)* (Cape Town: Oxford University Press, 1980), 32.

98. Ray, *Jewish Heritage of Calcutta*, 105, 216.

99. Roland, *Jewish Communities of India*, 178.

100. For more on Indian attitudes toward the refugees, see Egorova, *Jews and India*, 31–60.

101. Roland, *Jewish Communities of India*, 178.

102. Meir Benayahu, "Ha-leydi Rahel David 'Ezra," *Hed Ha-Mizrach*, July 29, 1949, 7, 15; see also L. Bein, "Plite Yisrael be-rahave ha-'olam," *Ha-Tzofeh*, June 2, 1944, 6.

103. According to Ezra Yehezkel-Shaked, one of the refugees was Max Hodorovski, who later changed his name to Menachem Savidor and went on to become the chairman of the Knesset. See Yehezkel-Shaked, *Jews, Opium, and the Kimono*, 179–80.

104. Yehezkel-Shaked, 179.

105. Benayahu, "Ha-leydi Rahel David 'Ezra," 15.

106. Benayahu, 15.

107. Benayahu, 15.

108. C. Warren-Boulton was a London-born officer in the Calcutta and Presidency Battalion of the Indian Auxiliary Force.

109. Roland, *Jewish Communities of India*, 216.

110. Documentary proof of European descent could not be provided because it did not exist. A synagogue's word, nevertheless, sufficed to satisfy the AFI; Roland, *Jewish Communities of India*, 216.

Chapter 5

1. For more on Hermann Kallenbach (1871–1944), see Shimon Lev, *Soulmates: The Story of Mahatma Gandhi and Hermann Kallenbach* (Telangana: Orient Blackswan, 2012); James D. Hunt and Surendra Bhana, "Spiritual Rope-Walkers: Gandhi, Kallenbach, and the Tolstoy Farm, 1910–13," *South African Historical Journal* 58 (2007): 174–202; David Y. Saks, "Right-Hand Man of the Mahatma: Hermann Kallenbach, Gandhi and Satyagraha," *Jewish Affairs* (Autumn 1998): 45–48; Isa Sarid and Christian Bartolf, *Hermann Kallenbach: Mahatma Gandhi's Friend in South Africa: A Concise Biography* (Berlin: Gandhi-Informations-Zentrum, 1997). Much attention has been paid recently to the nature of the relationship between Kallenbach and Gandhi. Joseph Lelyveld's 2011 biography *Great Soul* closely examines the relationship, highlighting the homoerotic content of the pair's letters and the intimate nature of their partnership. The book was received with controversy in India and was banned in Gujarat. See Joseph Lelyveld, *Great Soul: Mahatma Gandhi and His Struggle with India* (New York: Alfred A. Knopf, 2011). Further speculation about the relationship was raised when the Indian government purchased Gandhi's letters to Kallenbach in 2012. A selection of those letters went on display in New Delhi in 2013. A significant portion of the letters was published in earlier editions of Gandhi's collected works: *The Collected Works of Mahatma Gandhi*, 100 vols. (New Delhi: Publications Division, Ministry of Information and Broadcasting, Government of India, 1994), vol. 96. The later revised edition edited out many of the more intimate letters from Gandhi to Kallenbach. On this redaction, see Tridip Suhrud, "'Re-editing' Gandhi's Collected Works," *Economic and Political Weekly*, Nov. 20, 2004, 4967–69.

2. Meaning "holding firmly to the truth," *satyagraha* refers to Gandhi's campaign of nonviolent resistance that he first launched during his time in South Africa and that later became a cornerstone of the Indian independence movement. See M. K. Gandhi, *Satyagraha in South Africa* (1928; reprint, Ahmedabad: Navajivan Publishing House, 1972).

3. The home was called the "Kraal," the Afrikaans word that refers to a Nguni homestead, because Kallenbach had incorporated elements of African architecture into its design.

4. Kallenbach was born in Lithuania, close to the Prussian border. His family crossed the border, settling in the East Prussian town of Russ when Kallenbach was a child.

5. Moshe Sharett to Hermann Kallenbach, July 15, 1936, CZA S25/3239.

6. "Mr. Gandhi and the Jews," *Jewish Chronicle*, Oct. 2, 1931, 17. On Gandhi's time in South Africa, see Ashwin Desai and Goolam Vahed, *The South African Gandhi: Stretcher-Bearer of Empire* (Stanford, CA: Stanford University Press, 2016); Ramachandra Guha, *Gandhi before India* (New York: Vintage, 2013). On Gandhi's Jewish friends in South Africa, see Margaret Chatterjee, *Gandhi and His Jewish Friends* (London: Macmillan, 1992); Gideon Shimoni, *Gandhi, Satyagraha and the Jews: A Formative Factor in India's Policy Towards Israel* (Jerusalem: Leonard Davis Institute for International Relations, Hebrew University, 1977). On Gandhi's attitude toward the Jewish national home, see P. R. Kumaraswamy, *Squaring the Circle: Mahatma Gandhi and the Jewish National Home* (New Delhi: KW Publishers, 2018).

7. The majority of Indians in Natal arrived beginning in the mid-nineteenth century as indentured laborers. A minority came later as traders. By 1904, the Indian population in South Africa had reached 122,734. Uma Shashikant Mesthrie, "From Advocacy to Mobilization: *Indian Opinion*, 1903–1914," in *South Africa's Alternative Press: Voices of Protest and Resistance, 1880s–1960s*, ed. Les Switzer (Cambridge: Cambridge University Press, 1997), 100. On the history of indentured Indians in South Africa, see Ashutosh Kumar, *Coolies of the Empire: Indentured Indians in the Sugar Colonies, 1830–1920* (Cambridge: Cambridge University Press, 2017).

8. Theosophy, an esoteric religious movement that emerged in the late nineteenth century and drew much of its philosophy from Hinduism, was—like the Tolstoyan movement—part of a cluster of new-age spiritual movements. Gandhi drew inspiration from Tolstoy, and although he never considered himself to be a theosophist, he operated in theosophist circles as a law student in England.

9. For more on Henry Polak, see Jane Haggis, Clare Midgley, Margaret Allen, and Fiona Paisley, *Cosmopolitan Lives on the Cusp of Empire: Interfaith, Cross-Cultural and Transnational Networks, 1860–1950* (London: Palgrave, 2017), esp. 37–61; and S. Durai Raja Singam, "The Polaks and Gandhiji," *Indian Review* 63, no. 5/6 (1964): 173–77. For Polak's retrospective writings on Gandhi, see H. S. L. Polak, "Memories of Gandhi," *Contemporary Review* 173 (1948): 134–37; H. S. L. Polak, "Gandhi: Saint and/or Politician," *Christianity and Crisis* 2, no. 24 (1943): 3–6; and H. S. L. Polak, "Mr. Gandhi and Non-violence," *Asiatic Review*, 37, no. 130 (1941): 354–57.

10. On Gandhi's readings of Max Nordau, see Margaret Chatterjee, *Studies in Modern Jewish and Hindu Thought* (London: Macmillan, 1997), esp. 1–22.

11. Jan Smuts agreed to release the three men in an effort to quell the protests and strikes. Subsequently, Gandhi and Smuts reached an agreement in 1914 that abolished a punitive tax on Indians in South Africa, recognized Hindu and Muslim marriages, eased immigration restrictions on Indians, and repealed the Transvaal Asiatic Registration Act (the "Black Act").

12. On Sonja Schlesin (1888–1956), see Harriet Feinberg, "With Gandhi in South Africa: Sonja Schlesin," *Jewish Affairs* 27, no. 1 (2017): 6–11; and George Paxton, *Sonja Schlesin: Gandhi's South African Secretary* (Glasgow: Pax, 2006).

13. On L. W. (Louis Walter) Ritch (d. 1952), see Guha, *Gandhi before India*, esp. 163; and Shimoni, *Gandhi, Satyagraha and the Jews*, 11.

14. Morris Alexander (1878–1946), a barrister and long-serving MP, founded the Jewish Board of Deputies for the Cape Colony. He married Ruth Schechter (1888–1942), daughter of Solomon Schechter (1847–1915), in 1907. On Morris Alexander, see Gustav Saron, *Morris Alexander: Parliamentarian and Jewish Leader* (Johannesburg: South African Jewish Board of Deputies, 1966); and Enid Alexander, *Morris Alexander: A Biography* (Cape Town: Juta, 1953). On Ruth Schechter Alexander (later Farrington), see Baruch Hirson, *The Cape Town Intellectuals: Ruth Schechter and Her Circle, 1907–1934* (Cape Town: Merlin, 2001); and Baruch Hirson, "Ruth Schechter: Friend to Olive Schreiner," *Searchlight South Africa* 3, no. 1 (August 1992): 47–71.

15. See H. S. L. Polak, "Racial Discrimination in South Africa," *Jewish Chronicle*, Nov. 9, 1934, 34; "Racial Discrimination in South Africa: Jewish Anti-Indianism Denied," *Jewish Chronicle*, Dec. 21, 1934, 10; and H. S. L. Polak, "Racial Discrimination in South Africa," *Jewish Chronicle*, Dec. 28, 1934, 20.

16. See Sarah Azaransky, *This Worldwide Struggle: Religion and the International Roots of the Civil Rights Movement* (Oxford: Oxford University Press, 2017), 39–43; and Desai and Vahed, *The South African Gandhi*, esp. chapter 2, 30–48.

17. Shimoni, *Gandhi, Satyagraha and the Jews*, 19.

18. Shimoni, 12. See Isaac Deutscher, *The Non-Jewish Jew and Other Essays* (Oxford: Oxford University Press, 1968). This category was not applicable to all Jews who associated with Gandhi, especially those who had less intimate relationships with Gandhi than did Kallenbach and Polak. Morris Alexander, for instance, was a "Jewish Jew." Ruth Schechter Alexander, though her second marriage to a non-Jew isolated her from the South African Jewish community, was certainly born into a family fully immersed in Judaism and the Jewish community.

19. On the history of South African Zionism, see Shimoni, *Jews and Zionism*.

20. The Jewish population in South Africa totaled 59,741 by 1918, 4.1 percent of the total white population. By 1936, the year Kallenbach received the letter from Shertok asking him to go to India, South Africa's Jewish population had risen to 90,645, representing 4.5 percent of the white population. Allie A. Dubb, *The Jewish Population of South Africa: The 1991 Sociodemographic Survey* (Cape Town: Kaplan Center, University of Cape Town, 1994), 7.

21. For instance, the Conjoint Foreign Committee of British Jewry (formed by the Board of Deputies of British Jews and the Anglo-Jewish Association) published an anti-Zionist letter in the *Times* in May 1917. See "The Future of the Jews," (London) *Times*, May 24, 1917, 5.

22. Shimoni, *Jews and Zionism*, 27.

23. The reach and impact of South African nationalist politics extended to the British metropole. As a boy in London, Henry Polak developed early anti-British imperial convic-

tions, influenced by his father's work as an agent for a pro-Boer newspaper. Haggis et al., *Cosmopolitan Lives on the Cusp of Empire*, 39.

24. On Naidu's visit to South Africa, see Goolam Vahed, "Race, Empire, and Citizenship: Sarojini Naidu's 1924 Visit to South Africa," *South African History Journal* 64, no. 2 (2012): 319–42.

25. H. S. L. Polak, "Early Memories of Gandhi," *Hindustan Review*, March 1948, 142, quoted in Shimoni, *Gandhi, Satyagraha and the Jews*, 6–7.

26. For more on Polak's work with the Indian Overseas Association, see Robert P. Gregory, "H.S.L. Polak and the Indian Overseas Association," *Vivekananda Kendra Patrika*, Feb. 1973, 33–38.

27. H. S. L. Polak, "A South African Problem," *Jewish Chronicle*, Sept. 5, 1913, 14.

28. Polak, 14.

29. H. S. L. Polak, "Jews and Indians in South Africa," *Jewish Chronicle*, Jan. 15, 1923, 18.

30. Percy Cowen, "Jews and Indians in South Africa," *Jewish Chronicle*, April 2, 1923, 18. As a Unionist MP, Morris Alexander opposed anti-Indian legislation in the House of Assembly of South Africa.

31. Selig Brodetsky, *Memoirs: From Ghetto to Israel* (London: Weidenfeld and Nicolson, 1960), 121. For more on Brodetsky, see Louis Rosenhead, *Professor Selig Brodetsky: Scholar, Dreamer, Man of Action* (Leeds: Leeds University Press, 1963).

32. "Mr. Gandhi and the Jews," *Jewish Chronicle*, Oct. 2, 1931, 17.

33. "Mr. Gandhi and the Jews," 17.

34. "Mr. Gandhi's Message," *Jewish Chronicle*, Oct. 2, 1931, 5.

35. "The Palestine Movement," *Jewish Chronicle*, Oct. 30, 1931, 20.

36. Hugh Harris, "Books Reviewed," *Jewish Chronicle*, Oct. 2, 1931, 11.

37. After her initial contact with Gandhi in 1909, Maud Polak worked with L. W. Ritch, who had by then settled in London, on the South African British Indian Committee. She had wanted to return to South Africa with Gandhi in 1909 but did not visit the country until 1912, when she accompanied Gokhale on his trip there. For more on Maud Polak, see Guha, *Gandhi before India*, esp. 330–31 and 357–60.

38. Selig Brodetsky, "Note of Interview with the Mahatma Gandhi," Oct. 15, 1931, CZA F38/1283.

39. Brodetsky.

40. "The Palestine Movement," *Jewish Chronicle*, Nov. 13, 1931, 17.

41. Lev, *Soulmates*, 57, 61.

42. Louis Lewin to Hermann Kallenbach, Oct. 27, 1912, quoted in Lev, *Soulmates*, 74.

43. Mohandas Gandhi to Hermann Kallenbach, Feb. 25, 1913, in *Collected Works*, 96:112.

44. Hermann Kallenbach to Louis Lewin, July 27, 1913, quoted in Lev, *Soulmates*, 78.

45. Arthur Ruppin to Hermann Kallenbach, Sept. 3, 1913, quoted in Lev, *Soulmates*, 79.

46. For instance, Rev. A. P. Bender, leader of the Cape Town Hebrew Congregation, refused to support Zionism until after the Balfour Declaration. He had felt that Jewish nationalism was an affront to British imperial loyalty. Shimoni, *Jews and Zionism*, 52.

47. On the history of antisemitism in South Africa, see Milton Shain, *The Roots of Antisemitism in South Africa* (Charlottesville: University Press of Virginia, 1994); and Milton Shain, *A Perfect Storm: Antisemitism in South Africa, 1930–1948* (Johannesburg: Jonathan Ball, 2015).

48. On Shertok's time in London, see his diaries, in Sharett, *Yeme London*, vols. 1–3; and Sheffer, *Moshe Sharett*, 37–41.

49. On this cohort of imperial elites at British universities, see Colin Shindler, *Israel and the European Left: Between Solidarity and Delegitimization* (London: Bloomsbury, 2012), 80; and Shompa Lahiri, *Indians in Britain: Anglo-Indian Encounters, Race and Identity, 1880–1930* (London: Frank Cass, 2000).

50. Moshe Shertok diary, June 17, 1937, CZA A245/6.

51. Arlosoroff, *Yoman Yerushalayim*, 16–17.

52. Moshe Shertok to Hermann Kallenbach, July 15, 1936, CZA S25/3239.

53. Moshe Shertok to Hermann Kallenbach, July 15, 1936, CZA S25/3239.

54. Hermann Kallenbach to Moshe Shertok, July 25, 1936, CZA S25/3239.

55. Agronsky, "Notes on Visit to Bombay"; Immanuel Olsvanger, "The Diary at the Central Zionist Archives, Jerusalem" (hereafter Olsvanger diary), trans. Edelgaard David, in *Indo Judaic Studies: Some Papers*, ed. Yohanan ben David (New Delhi: Northern Book Center, 2002), August 19, 1936, 17. The original diary is held at the Central Zionist Archives, CZA S25/3583.

56. Roland, *Jewish Communities of India*, 125.

57. See Mrinalini Sinha, "Suffragism and Internationalism: The Enfranchisement of British and Indian Women under an Imperial State," in *Women's Suffrage in the British Empire: Citizenship, Nation, and Race*, ed. Ian Christopher Fletcher, Laura E. Nym Mayhall, and Philippa Levine (London: Routledge, 2000), 224–40.

58. Olsvanger diary, August 19, 1936, 17–18.

59. David, *Indo Judaic Studies*, 67–68; Egorova, *Jews and India*, 27–28.

60. Olsvanger diary, August 19, 1936, 18. When Naidu visited South Africa in 1924, she caused an upset in the Jewish community by arguing that Jews had a "duty to display no racial arrogance or superiority toward Indians in South Africa just because they happened to be classed as Europeans." Naidu argued that Jews were "in reality of Asiatic descent." This conception of Jews likely contributed to her approval of Jewish settlement in Palestine. "Sarojini Naidu and the Jews," *Cape Argus*, March 3, 1924, in clippings in the Morris Alexander Papers, University of Cape Town Libraries Special Collections, BC 160, List I C, box 36, folder 12.

61. Olsvanger makes no mention of Polak's role in connecting Brodetsky and Sokolow with Gandhi in 1931.

62. Olsvanger diary, Sept. 13, 1936, 27.

63. Shimoni, *Gandhi, Satyagraha and the Jews*, 31.

64. Olsvanger diary, Sept. 19, 1936, 29–30.

65. Shimoni, *Gandhi, Satyagraha and the Jews*, 31.

66. On ties between Palestinian Arab nationalists and the Nazi Party in the interwar period, see Barry Rubin and Wolfgang G. Schwanitz, *Nazis, Islamists, and the Making of the Modern Middle East* (New Haven, CT: Yale University Press, 2014).

67. Olsvanger diary, Sept. 22, 1936, 34.

68. Olsvanger, 34.

69. Jawaharlal Nehru to Immanuel Olsvanger, Sept. 25, 1936, CZA S25/3583.

70. Elias M. Epstein (sometimes referred to Eliahu M. Epstein) (1895–1958) was born in Liverpool, was founding editor of the *Palestine Weekly*, and worked for the Jewish National Fund in Jerusalem. He should not be confused with Eliahu Epstein (later Elath) (1903–1990), born in Snovsk (present-day Ukraine), who headed the Middle East section of the Jewish Agency from 1934 to 1945 and later served as the first Israeli ambassador to the United States. This Epstein was also involved in Yishuv-India relations and served as the chief Palestine contact of A. E. Shohet, the Jewish Agency representative in India.

71. Elias M. Epstein to Yusuf Meherally, Sept. 27, 1936, CZA S25/3239.

72. Jawaharlal Nehru, *Eighteen Months in India, 1936–37, Being Further Essays and Writings* (Allahabad: Kitabistan, 1938), 132–39.

73. These units included the Jewish Settlement Police, the Jewish Supernumerary Police, and the joint British-Jewish Special Night Squads, commanded by the Christian Zionist British military officer Orde Wingate (1903–44). These units were sourced from the Haganah, the Jewish paramilitary organization founded after the Jaffa riots in 1921. Although British authorities neither recognized nor sanctioned the Haganah, their cooperation with these Jewish units—an "informal legitimation"—represented a significant political achievement for leaders of the Yishuv. See Sheffer, *Moshe Sharett*, 81; and Uri Ben-Eliezer, *The Making of Israeli Militarism* (Bloomington: Indiana University Press, 1998), esp. 1–50.

74. Sheffer, *Moshe Sharett*, 83–87.

75. Moshe Sharett, *Yoman Medini*, vol. 2, March 11, 1937 (Tel Aviv: Am Oved, 1968), 58–59.

76. Quoted in Lev, *Soulmates*, 123.

77. Hermann Kallenbach to Moshe Shertok, June 1, 1937, in David, *Indo Judaic Studies*, 64.

78. Hermann Kallenbach to Pekez, July 8, 1937, quoted in Lev, *Soulmates*, 124.

79. Hermann Kallenbach to Moshe Shertok, June 1, 1937, in David, *Indo Judaic Studies*, 64–65.

80. Moshe Sharett to Hermann Kallenbach, July 15, 1936, CZA S25/3239.

81. Mohandas Gandhi to Hermann Kallenbach, July 4, 1937, *Collected Works*, 96:287–88.

82. "Mr. Gandhi and the Jews," *Jewish Chronicle*, Oct. 2, 1931, 17.

83. Statement given by Mahatma Gandhi to Mr. Kallenbach on Zionism in July 1937, CZA S25/3587.

84. Mohandas Gandhi to Hermann Kallenbach, July 20, 1937, *Collected Work*, 96:289.

85. Monograph on Zionism prepared for Mohandas Gandhi, CZA S25/3587.

86. Mohandas Gandhi to Hermann Kallenbach, Feb. 28, 1938, *Collected Works*, 96:292.

87. Gandhi made the statement on November 20, 1938, in Segaon, a village in Madhya Pradesh; it was published in *Harijan* on November 26, 1938.

88. M. K. Gandhi, "The Jews," *Harijan*, Nov. 26, 1938, 352.

89. Gandhi, 353.

90. Shimoni, *Gandhi, Satyagraha and the Jews*, 40.

91. Gandhi, "The Jews," 352.

92. Gandhi, 352–53.

93. Gandhi, 353.

94. Pyarelal, "Non-Violence and World Crisis," *Harijan*, Dec. 24, 1937, 392–95.

95. Scholars disagree on the precise date of Ha-'Ol's founding, dating it sometime between January 1939 and July 1939. Ha-'Ol literally means "the yoke"—a reference to the rabbinic idea of the "yoke of the kingdom of heaven" (i.e., service to God)—but the group translated the word as "the Bond" in the publication of Buber and Magnes's letters to Gandhi. For more on Ha-'Ol, see Noam Zadoff, *Gershom Scholem: From Berlin to Jerusalem and Back*, trans. Jeffrey Green (Waltham, MA: Brandeis University Press, 2017), 65–69; Kotzin, *Judah L. Magnes*, 277–79; and Paul Mendes-Flohr, "The Yoke of the Kingdom in Jerusalem," in *The Jewish Legacy and the German Conscience: Essays in Memory of Rabbi Joseph Asher*, ed. Moses Rischin and Raphael Asher (Berkeley: Judah L. Magnes Museum, 1991), 233–45.

96. See Martin Buber and Judah Magnes, *Two Letters to Gandhi from Martin Buber and J. L. Magnes* (Jerusalem: Rubin Mass, 1939).

97. Buber and Magnes, 21.

98. Buber and Magnes, 23.

99. Buber and Magnes, 5–6.

100. Buber and Magnes, 5.

101. Buber and Magnes, 25.

102. Bentwich, *For Zion's Sake*, 112.

103. Buber and Magnes, *Two Letters to Gandhi*, 29–30.

104. Buber and Magnes, 30.

105. Buber and Magnes, 30–31.

106. Buber and Magnes, 32–33.

107. Buber and Magnes, 19.

108. Buber and Magnes, 18–19.

109. Buber and Magnes, 36.

110. Buber and Magnes, 12.

111. Buber and Magnes, 37–38.

112. Shimoni, *Gandhi, Satyagraha and the Jews*, 47.

113. Kumaraswamy, *Squaring the Circle*, 152.

114. The successor of *Zion's Messenger* (1921–24), the *Jewish Advocate* was the organ of the Bombay Zionist Association, published from 1931 to 1953.

115. A. E. Shohet, "Gandhi and the Jews," *Jewish Advocate*, Dec. 2, 1938, 3.

116. Hermann Kallenbach to Mohandas Gandhi, Dec. 28, 1938, quoted in Lev, *Soulmates*, 141.

117. A. E. Shohet to Eliahu Epstein, March 7, 1939, CZA S25/3587.

118. A. E. Shohet to Eliahu Epstein, March 24, 1939, CZA S25/3586.

119. A. E. Shohet to Eliahu Epstein, March 24, 1939, CZA S25/3586.

120. Gregory, "H.S.L. Polak and the Indian Overseas Association," 36.

121. Gupta, *Imperialism and the British Labour Movement*, 118, 225, 227.

122. Shimoni, *Gandhi, Satyagraha and the Jews*, 54.

123. M. K. Gandhi, "No Apology," *Harijan*, Feb. 18, 1939, 24.

124. Gandhi, 24.

125. Quoted in Shimoni, *Gandhi, Satyagraha and the Jews*, 55.

126. Quoted in Shimoni, 55.

127. Philip Hartog (1864–1947) was an educationalist and supporter of Zionism who was instrumental in the founding of the School of Oriental Studies, what became the School of Oriental and African Studies (SOAS), in 1938.

128. Mohandas Gandhi, "Withdrawn," *Harijan*, May 27, 1939, 139.

129. Gandhi, 139.

Chapter 6

1. Bentwich, *Wanderer between Two Worlds*, 281.

2. Bentwich, *My 77 Years*, 148. The Jewish Agency memorandum to the Évian Conference can be found in Arieh Tartakower and Kurt R. Grossman, *The Jewish Refugee* (New York: Institute of Jewish Affairs of the American Jewish Congress and World Jewish Congress, 1944), appendix I, 538–45. On the history of the Évian Conference, see Paul R. Bartrop, *The Evian Conference of 1938 and the Jewish Refugee Crisis* (Cham: Palgrave Macmillan, 2018). See also Norman Bentwich, "The Evian Conference and After," *Fortnightly* 144 (Sept. 1938): 287–95.

3. Bentwich, *Wanderer between Two Worlds*, 263.

4. Bentwich, 262.

5. Bentwich, 271.

6. Bentwich, 274–275.

7. Bentwich, 283.

8. Bentwich, 295.

9. Jehuda Reinharz and Yaacov Shavit, *The Road to September 1939: Polish Jews, Zionists, and the Yishuv on the Eve of World War II* (Waltham, MA: Brandeis University Press, 2018), 127. I use the term *territorialist* here to describe schemes for Jewish settlement beyond Palestine. Supporters of these schemes, as had been the case for members of the original Jewish Territorialist Organization, saw these options as more practical solutions to the Jewish question than Palestine. Unlike many earlier territorialist schemes, however, support in the 1930s for these non-Palestine destinations was generally not motivated by a desire to build a

thriving Jewish nation in those spaces. Zionist leaders, including Ben-Gurion, also used the term *territorialism* to describe these schemes.

10. "Ne'umo shel D. Ben-Gurion ba-khinus ha-yishuvi she-nitkayem bi-yerushalayim," Dec. 12, 1938, Ben-Gurion Archive (hereafter BGA) 87949.

11. On the history of Jewish refugee settlement in British Guiana, and in the British West Indies more broadly, see Joanna Newman, *Nearly the New World: The British West Indies and the Flight from Nazism, 1933–1945* (New York: Berghahn, 2019).

12. Chaim Weizmann to Herbert Speyer, Nov. 17, 1938, in Chaim Weizmann, *The Letters and Papers of Chaim Weizmann*, ed. Barnet Litvinoff and Aaron Klieman, ser. A, vol. 18, Jan. 1937–Dec. 1938 (New Brunswick, NJ: Transaction, 1979), 488.

13. Sharett, *Yoman Medini*, vol. 4, Feb. 24, 1939, 90.

14. As a result, Norman Bentwich was sometimes misidentified as a non-Zionist at the time; some historiography replicates this misnomer. The reason for this misidentification stems from the role he played in averting a non-Zionist exodus from the Jewish Agency during the 1937 Zionist Congress in Zurich, where delegates debated the extremely divisive matter of partition. Norman achieved this by arranging a compromise in the Congress's resolution: the Congress would further explore the possibility of an independent Jewish state created by partition but would also undertake negotiations with Arabs to see if peace in an unpartitioned Palestine were possible—a non-Zionist goal.

15. Moss, *An Unchosen People*.

16. The Arab delegation consisted both of Palestinian representatives and delegates from other Arab countries, including Egypt, Iraq, Saudi Arabia, Yemen, and Transjordan. Palestinian delegates did not take part in the two tripartite meetings.

17. There are notable exceptions to this, particularly Reinharz and Shavit, *The Road to September 1939*; Abraham J. Edelheit, *The Yishuv in the Shadow of the Holocaust: Zionist Politics and Rescue Aliya, 1933–1939* (New York: Routledge, 2018); and Caplan, *Futile Diplomacy*, vol. 2.

18. Bentwich, *Wanderer between Two Worlds*, 300–301.

19. The Adeni Jewish community was historically distinct from the Yemenite Jewish community of the region's hinterlands; however, a majority of the Jewish community by the 1930s was Yemenite, having fled to the Port of Aden.

20. Bentwich, *Wanderer between Two Worlds*, 301–2.

21. Bentwich, 301.

22. Ernest Bevin, "Impressions of the British Commonwealth Relations Conference of 1938," *International Affairs* 18, no. 1 (1939): 56.

23. Cited in K. Sarwar Hasan, "The Commonwealth—Whither?" *Pakistan Horizon* 18, no. 1 (1965): 29.

24. Bentwich, *Wanderer between Two Worlds*, 308.

25. Helen Bentwich, 1938 diary, Sept. 13, 1938, WL 7HBE/4

26. Bentwich, *Wanderer between Two Worlds*, 310.

27. On the place of moderates in Indian nationalism, see Ray T. Smith, "The Role of

India's 'Liberals' in the Nationalist Movement, 1915–1947," *Modernization in South Asian Studies: Essays in a Changing Field* 8, no. 7 (1968): 607–24.

28. Bentwich, *Wanderer between Two Worlds*, 304.

29. Helen Bentwich, 1938 diary, Sept. 8, 1938, WL 7HBE/4.

30. Bentwich, August 24, 1938.

31. Bentwich, August 28, 1938.

32. Bentwich, *Wanderer between Two Worlds*, 305–6. On the history of Youth Aliyah, see Hacohen, *To Repair a Broken World*, esp. chapter 13; and Brian Amkraut, *Between Home and Homeland: Youth Aliyah from Nazi Germany* (Tuscaloosa: University of Alabama Press, 2006).

33. Helen Bentwich, 1938 diary, Sept. 22, 1938, WL 7HBE/4.

34. Helen Bentwich, Sept. 22, 1938.

35. Helen Bentwich, Sept. 27, 1938.

36. Helen Bentwich, Oct. 2, 1938.

37. Bentwich, *Wanderer between Two Worlds*, 311.

38. Bentwich, *Wanderer between Two Worlds*, 319.

39. Helen Bentwich, 1938 diary, Oct. 20, 1938, WL 7HBE/4.

40. Helen Bentwich, 1938 diary, Oct. 20, 1938, WL 7HBE/4.

41. Sharett, *Yoman Medini*, vol. 4, Feb. 7, 1939, 24.

42. Y. Netz, "*Mikhtavim mi-London*," *Ha-Mashkif*, Feb. 17, 1939, 5.

43. On the impact of British immigration policy on youth aliyah, see Dvora Hacohen, "British Immigration Policy to Palestine in the 1930s: Implications for Youth Aliyah," *Middle Eastern Studies* 37 no. 4 (2001): 206–18.

44. See Shapira, *Ben-Gurion*, 112–14; and Sheffer, *Moshe Sharett*, 94–95.

45. Sharett, *Yoman Medini*, vol. 4, Feb. 4, 1939, 16–17.

46. Sharett, *Yoman Medini*, vol. 4, Jan. 19, 1939, 13.

47. The educator Benzion Mossinson (1878–1942) was a member of the General Zionist Council, president of Keren Hayesod, and principal of the Herzliya Hebrew High School.

48. Sharett, *Yoman Medini*, vol. 4, Feb. 7, 1939, 24.

49. Sharett, 24.

50. Sharett, *Yoman Medini*, vol. 4, Feb. 6, 1939, 23.

51. Quoted in Shapira, *Berl*, 275.

52. Quoted in Reinharz and Shavit, *The Road to September 1939*, 180.

53. Charles V. Reed, *Royal Tourists, Colonial Subjects and the Making of a British World, 1860–1911* (Manchester: Manchester University Press, 2016), 124.

54. The stretch of buildings from 74 to 77 Great Russell Street, with their white Georgian facades, was later known as Bloomsbury House but should not be confused with another nearby Bloomsbury House, the former Palace Hotel on Bloomsbury Street, which served beginning in early 1939 as the headquarters for various refugee organizations, including the Council for German Jewry.

55. Sharett, *Yoman Medini*, vol. 4, Feb. 7, 1939, 24–25.

56. Sharett, 26.

57. It is commonly, though incorrectly, recorded in the historiography that Gerald Isaacs's father Rufus Isaacs, 1st Marquess of Reading and former viceroy of India, was at the St James's Palace Conference. In fact, the senior Isaacs had died in 1935. See, for example, Howard M. Sacher, *A History of Israel: From the Rise of Zionism to Our Time* (Ann Arbor: University of Michigan Press, 1996), 220.

58. Arlosoroff, *Yoman Yerushalayim*, 246.

59. On the trend from anti-Zionism toward non-Zionism in the Anglo-Jewish elite, see Shimoni, "From Anti-Zionism to Non-Zionism in Anglo-Jewry."

60. "Agency Adopts Compromise Resolution on Palestine; Two Non-zionists Added to Executive," *JTA*, August 23, 1937; Harry Schneiderman, "Palestine," *The American Jewish Year Book*, vol. 40 (Sept. 26, 1938, to Sept, 13, 1939), 310–32; Menahem Kaufman, *An Ambiguous Partnership: Non-Zionists and Zionists in America, 1939–1948* (Jerusalem: Magnes Press, 1991), 34–45.

61. The other drafters of the memorandum included Neville Laski, then president of the Board of Deputies of British Jews, Osmond d'Avigdor-Goldsmid, and Lionel Cohen. All three had also been appointed months earlier as non-Zionist members of the Jewish Agency Political Advisory Committee in London.

62. Chaim Weizmann to Arthur Lourie, Nov. 20, 1937, in Weizmann, *The Letters and Papers of Chaim Weizmann*, ser. A, vol. 18, 246.

63. Sharett, *Yoman Medini*, vol. 4, Feb. 7, 1939, 26.

64. Frederick Kisch to Robert Szold, May 8, 1931, CZA F38\479.

65. Sharett, *Yoman Medini*, vol. 4, Feb. 14, 1939, 52.

66. Sharett, 52–53.

67. Sharett, *Yoman Medini*, vol. 4, Feb. 17, 1939, 62.

68. Sharett, *Yoman Medini*, vol. 4, Feb. 14, 1939, 53–54.

69. Sharett, 52–53.

70. Sharett, 54.

71. Sharett, 54.

72. Sharett, *Yoman Medini*, vol. 4, Feb. 15, 1939, 56.

73. Sharett, 56–58.

74. Sharett, 58.

75. Sharett, *Yoman Medini*, vol. 4, Feb. 16, 1939, 59.

76. Sharett, *Yoman Medini*, vol. 4, Feb. 20, 1939, 67.

77. Sharett, *Yoman Medini*, vol. 4, Feb. 21, 1939, 73.

78. Sharett, *Yoman Medini*, vol. 4, Feb. 20, 1939, 68.

79. Sharett, *Yoman Medini*, vol. 4, Feb. 24, 1939, 88.

80. Sharett, 90.

81. Sharett, *Yoman Medini*, vol. 4, Feb. 25, 1939, 91.

82. "No Ghetto in Palestine," *Palestine Post*, Feb. 27, 1939, 1.

83. "The Jews Will Not Submit to Position of Minority," *Palestine Post*, Feb. 27, 1939, 1.

84. Shapira, *Land and Power*, 228–29.

85. Sharett, *Yoman Medini*, vol. 1, June 9, 1936, 159. The speech is also cited in Shapira, *Land and Power*, 228.

86. Sharett, *Yoman Medini*, vol. 4, March 4, 1939, 107.

87. Malcolm MacDonald had even served at the time as a supportive mediator between the Zionist camp and his father's government, a fact that only heightened the sense of betrayal felt by many Zionists in 1939. Norman Rose, *Chaim Weizmann: A Biography* (New York: Elisabeth Sifton, 1986), 279–80.

88. For example, see Sharett, *Yoman Medini*, vol. 4, March 2, 1939, 103.

89. Sharett, *Yoman Medini*, vol. 4, March 10, 1939, 135.

90. Sharett, *Yoman Medini*, vol. 4, March 6, 1939, 111.

91. Sharett, *Yoman Medini*, vol. 4, March 10, 1939, 132–33.

92. Sharett, *Yoman Medini*, vol. 4, March 6, 1939, 111.

93. Vera Weizmann, *The Impossible Takes Longer: The Memoirs of Vera Weizmann as Told to David Tutaev* (New York: Harper & Row, 1967), 140.

94. Sharett, *Yoman Medini*, vol. 4, March 14, 1939.

95. Sharett, *Yoman Medini*, vol. 4, March 15, 1939.

96. Bentwich, *Wanderer between Two Worlds*, 321.

97. Bentwich, *My 77 Years*, 155–56.

98. On Jewish immigration to South Africa during the 1930s, see Jocelyn Hellig, "German Jewish Immigration to South Africa during the 1930s: Revisiting the Charter of the SS *Stuttgart*," *Jewish History and Culture* 11, nos. 1–2 (2009): 124–38.

99. On the rise of antisemitism in South Africa, see Shain, *A Perfect Storm*.

100. Bentwich, *Wanderer between Two Worlds*, 328.

101. Mike Levy, *Get the Children Out! Unsung Heroes of the Kindertransport* (London: Lemon Soul, 2021), 224–25; Judith Tydor Baumel-Schwartz, *Never Look Back: The Jewish Refugee Children in Great Britain, 1938–1945* (West Lafayette, IN: Purdue University Press, 2012), 55–56.

102. Anne Summers notes that Gladys Skelton may also have been connected to the Bentwiches through Norman's late sister Rosalind Lange, with whom she attended Girton College. See Anne Summers, *Christian and Jewish Women in Britain, 1880–1940: Living with Difference* (Cham: Palgrave Macmillan, 2017), 185.

103. Elaine Laski's first husband was Norman Laski, cousin of Neville and Harold Laski. After her divorce, she married a cousin of the Laskis, Neville Blond.

104. Norman Bentwich noted that the Central British Fund for German Jewry was created "to avoid the endemic trouble of duplication in Jewish philanthropic efforts at times of great emergency and public emotion." Norman Bentwich, *They Found Refuge* (London: Cresset, 1956), 20.

105. Helen Bentwich, "Warning against Unorganized Effort," *Jewish Chronicle*, Dec. 16, 1938, 32.

106. "On 25 December 1938 youngsters from a Kindertransport report on their reception

in Britain," Dec. 25, 1938, doc. 213, published in Susanne Heim, ed., *The Persecution and Murder of the European Jews by Nazi Germany, 1933–1945*, vol. 2, *German Reich 1938–August 1939* (Berlin: de Gruyter, 2019), 585–87.

107. Bentwich, "Warning against Unorganized Effort."

108. Claudia Curio, "'Invisible' Children: The Selection and Integration Strategies of Relief Organizations," *Shofar* 23, no. 1 (2004): 41–56.

109. Quoted in Curio, 49.

110. Quoted in Curio, 49.

111. Helen Bentwich to Judah Magnes, Jan. 31, 1939, CAHJP, Judah Magnes Papers P3/201. On the history of the rescue of Jewish men from Nazi Europe, see Clare Ungerson, *Four Thousand Lives: The Rescue of German Jewish Men to Britain, 1939* (Cheltenham, UK: History Press, 2014). "Young" men were limited to those between the ages of eighteen and forty.

112. Bentwich, *Wanderer between Two Worlds*, 289.

113. Bentwich, *They Found Refuge*, 104–5.

114. Helen Bentwich, 1939 diary, Sept. 18, 1939, 7HBE/4

115. Bentwich, *They Found Refuge*, 107.

116. Rachel Pistol, *Internment during the Second World War: A Comparative Study of Great Britain and the USA* (London: Bloomsbury, 2017), 79–81; Wendy Ugolini, *Experiencing War as the 'Enemy Other': Italian Scottish Experience in World War II* (Manchester: Manchester University Press, 2011): 160–62.

117. On Jewish refugees in Portugal, see Marion Kaplan, *Hitler's Jewish Refugees: Hope and Anxiety in Portugal* (New Haven, CT: Yale University Press, 2020).

118. Norman Bentwich, *Wanderer in War* (London: Victor Gollancz, 1946), 22–24.

119. Bentwich, 24.

120. On the broader history of internment during World War II, see David Cesarani and Tony Kushner, *The Internment of Aliens in Twentieth Century Britain* (London: Routledge, 1993).

121. Sharett, *Yoman Medini*, vol. 4, March 20, 1939, 184. "Political maximum" was the term used by the British and mandatory governments beginning in 1937 to refer to the maximum number of Jews permitted to immigrate to Palestine independent of the economic absorptive capacity.

122. Sharett, *Yoman Medini*, vol. 4, March 20, 1939, 333.

123. Yoav Gelber, "The Meeting between the Jewish Soldiers from Palestine Serving in the British Army and She'erit Hapletah," in *She'erit Hapletah, 1944–1948: Rehabilitation and Political Struggle*, ed. Gutman Yisrael and Drechsler Adina (Jerusalem: Yad Vashem, 1990): 60–79.

124. Cited in Daphna Sharfman, *Palestine in the Second World War: Strategic Plans and Political Dilemmas—The Emergence of a New Middle East* (Eastbourne: Sussex Academic Press, 2014), 58.

125. Moshe Shertok, "The Jewish Battalions: Demand for Jewish Army Not Relinquished," *Palestine and Middle East Monthly* 14 (August 1942): https://www.sharett.org.il/

cgi-webaxy/sal/sal.pl?lang=en&ID=880900_sharett_new&act=show&dbid=MS_articles_eng&dataid=20.

126. Moshe Shertok to General Pat Wilson, June 19, 1942, in Moshe Sharett, *Ma'avak Medini*, vol. 1, part 2, ed. Yaakov Sharett and Rina Sharett (Tel Aviv: ha-'Amutah le-moreshet Moshe Sharett), 35.

127. "Short Minutes of Meeting Held on Wednesday, February 23rd, 1944 at 77 Great Russell Street, London," London Jewish Agency Executive, BGA 228379; Sharfman, *Palestine in the Second World War*, 136.

128. Chaim Weizmann to James Grigg, March 28, 1944, in Chaim Weizmann, *The Letters and Papers of Chaim Weizmann*, vol. 21, ser. A, *January 1943–May 1945*, ed. Michael J. Cohen (New Brunswick, NJ: Transaction, 1979), 151.

129. Moshe Shertok, "Main Factors in Zionist Politics," *Jewish Frontier*, August 1, 1944, 9–10.

130. Shertok, 10–11.

131. Shertok, 12.

132. Shertok, 10–11.

133. Shertok, 11.

134. Shertok, 13.

135. "A Jewish Brigade Group," (London) *Times*, Sept. 20, 1944, 3.

136. Judith Tydor Baumel, *The "Bergson Boys" and the Origins of Contemporary Zionist Militancy*, trans. Dena Ordan (Syracuse, NY: Syracuse University Press, 2005), 133; Derek J. Penslar, *Jews and the Military: A History* (Princeton, NJ: Princeton University Press, 2015), 221.

137. "Front-Line Ceremony for Brigade Flag," *Palestine Post*, April 6, 1945, 3.

138. "Blue-and-White Flag of Palestine Presented to Jewish Brigade at Moving Ceremony in Italy," *JTA*, April 4, 1945.

139. "Front-Line Ceremony for Brigade Flag," *Palestine Post*, April 6, 1945, 3.

140. Idith Zertal, *From Catastrophe to Power: The Holocaust Survivors and the Emergence of Israel* (Berkeley: University of California Press, 1998), esp. chapter 1.

141. "People's Call from Mt. Scopus: Mr. Shertok's Keynote: Let My People Go," *Palestine Post*, May 14, 1945, 1.

Chapter 7

1. *Protokol mi-yeshivat hanhalat ha-Sokhnut ha-Yehudit*, March 18, 1947, BGA 227528.

2. *Anglo-American Committee of Inquiry Report on Jewish Problems in Palestine and Europe* (Washington, DC: United States Government Printing Office, 1946), 5.

3. Sheffer, *Moshe Sharett*, 185; "Terms of Reference Nullified Inquiry Findings," *Palestine Post*, May 9, 1946, 1.

4. Sheffer, *Moshe Sharett*, 178–79.

5. Moshe Shertok to the Standing Committee of Mapai, Sept. 3, 1946, in Moshe Sharett, *Yerehim be-'emek Ayalon*, ed. Pinhas Ofer (Tel Aviv: ha-'Amutah le-moreshet Moshe Sharett, 2011), 306.

6. On the challenges of identifying parallels and analogies between Israel/Palestine and India/Pakistan, see Rephael G. Stern, "Uncertain Comparisons: Zionist and Israeli Links to India and Pakistan in the Age of Partition and Decolonization," *Law and History Review* 39, no. 3 (August 2021): 451–78.

7. *Protokol mi-yeshivat hanhalat ha-Sokhnut ha-Yehudit*, March 18, 1947, BGA 227528.

8. On this latter point, see Rephael G. Stern and Arie M. Dubnov, "A Part of Asia or Apart from Asia? Zionist Perceptions of Asia, 1947–1956," in *Unacknowledged Kinships: Postcolonial Studies and the Historiography of Zionism*, ed. Stefan Vogt, Derek J. Penslar, and Arieh Bruce Saposnik (Waltham, MA: Brandeis University Press, 2023), 233–71. For work placing the Asian Relations Conference in the context of broader Israel-India relations, see Kumaraswamy, *India's Israel Policy*, 183–88; and Yulia Egorova, *Jews and India*, 54–55.

9. Sarojini Naidu to the Hebrew University, Oct. 2, 1946, CZA S25/7483/125.

10. David Werner Senator to Sarojini Naidu, Nov. 7, 1946, CZA S25/7483/128.

11. A. Appadorai to the Hebrew University, Jan. 30, 1947, CZA S25/7483/45.

12. Benny Morris, *Righteous Victims: A History of the Zionist-Arab Conflict, 1881–2001* (New York: Vintage, 2001), 106.

13. Gerb Korman, "New Jewish Politics for an American Labor Leader: Sidney Hillman, 1942–1946," *American Jewish History* 82, no. 1 (1994): 195.

14. Sharett, *Yeme London*, 1:26n6 (my emphasis).

15. Sarojini Naidu to the Hebrew University, Oct. 2, 1946, CZA S25/7483/125.

16. Bentwich, *My 77 Years*, 216–17.

17. "True Character of 'Asian Conference' Exposed: League Assembly Rejects Invitation," *Dawn*, March 20, 1947, 8. Quoted in Gopa Sabharwal, "In Search of an Asian Vision: The Asian Relations Conference of 1947," in *Imagining Asia(s): Networks, Actors, Sites*, ed. Andrea Acri, Kashshaf Ghani, Murai K. Jha, and Sraman Mukherjee (Singapore: ISEAS, 2019), 62–63.

18. Bracha Habas and David Hacohen, *'Esrim yom be-Hodu* (Tel Aviv: Am Oved, 1948), 65–66.

19. Habas and Hacohen, 8.

20. Habas and Hacohen, 8–9.

21. David Hacohen to Jawaharlal Nehru, March 31, 1947, CZA S25/7485/45–46.

22. Moshe Ya'akov Ben-Gavriel to the Organizing Committee of the Inter-Asian Relations Conference, March 7, 1947, CZA S25/7483/22.

23. On British clubs in India, see Sinha, "Britishness, Clubbability, and the Colonial Public Sphere."

24. Habas and Hacohen, *'Esrim yom be-Hodu*, 18–27.

25. Habas and Hacohen, 28

26. Habas and Hacohen, 24.

27. Habas and Hacohen, 41–43

28. Hacohen did not acknowledge that Indians, in fact, spoke hundreds of languages and that the country was home to many ethnic groups. Perhaps Hacohen meant here that Muslim and Hindu Indians could come from the same ethnolinguistic group.

29. Habas and Hacohen, *'Esrim yom be-Hodu*, 53–54.
30. Habas and Hacohen, 55.
31. Ya'akov Shimoni, "Report on the Inter-Asian Conference," CZA S25/7485/87.
32. Hacohen and Habas, *'Esrim yom be-Hodu*, 68.
33. Shimoni, "Report on the Inter-Asian Conference," CZA S25/7485/89.
34. Bergmann quoted in A. Appadorai, *Asian Relations: Being [a] Report of the Proceedings and Documentation of the First Asian Relations Conference, New Delhi, March–April, 1947* (New Delhi: Asian Relations Organization, 1948), 57.
35. Takieddin el-Solh, quoted in Appadorai, 63–64.
36. Appadorai, 64.
37. Appadorai, 64–65.
38. Shimoni, "Report on the Inter-Asian Conference," CZA S25/7485/91.
39. Hugo Bergmann to Martin Buber, April 10, 1947, in Martin Buber, *The Letters of Martin Buber: A Life of Dialogue*, ed. Nahum N. Glatzer and Paul Mendes-Flohr, trans. Richard and Clara Winston and Harry Zohn (Syracuse, NY: Syracuse University Press, 1996), 518.
40. Appadorai, *Asian Relations*, 70.
41. Shimoni, "Report on the Inter-Asian Conference," CZA S25/7485/90.
42. Hacohen to Nehru, March 31, 1947, CZA S25/7485/45–46.
43. Shimoni, "Report on the Inter-Asian Conference," CZA S25/7485/92.
44. Shimoni, "Report on the Inter-Asian Conference," CZA S25/7485/95.
45. Alfred Bonné, "Supplementary Notes to the Report of the Delegation on the Inter-Asian Conference in New Delhi," CZA S25/7485.
46. Ya'akov Shimoni, "Asian Relations Conference Publicity Section," CZA S25/7485/264.
47. Hacohen and Habas, *'Esrim yom be-Hodu*, 71.
48. Bergmann to Buber, April 10, 1947, in Glatzer and Mendes-Flohr, *The Letters of Martin Buber*.
49. "Translation from the Hebrew, Moral Stature, Marginal Note in *'Davar'* of 27.4.1947," CZA S25/7485/31.
50. Caroline Elkins, *Legacy of Violence: A History of the British Empire* (New York: Knopf, 2022), 413–44.
51. H. G. Reissner, "An Eastern Declaration?" *AJR Information*, May 1947, 1.
52. Shimoni, "Report on the Inter-Asian Conference," CZA S25/7485/90.
53. Gandhi, "The Jews," 352.
54. Elkins, *Legacy of Violence*, 447–52.

Conclusion

1. David Werner Senator to Norman Bentwich, Feb. 27, 1948, CZA A255/75.
2. Norman Bentwich to David Werner Senator, March 11–12, 1948, CZA AK100/1.
3. Bentwich, *My 77 Years*, 226.

Bibliography

Primary Sources
I. Archives
Ben-Gurion Archive (BGA)
Central Archives for the History of the Jewish People (CAHJP)
Central Zionist Archives in Jerusalem (CZA)
Jabotinsky Institute in Israel (JI)
London Metropolitan Archives
Middle East Centre Archive, St Antony's College, University of Oxford
National Library of Israel (NLI)
University of Cape Town Libraries Special Collections
Women's Library, London School of Economics (WL)

II. Newspapers and Periodicals
AJR Information
American Jewish Yearbook
Cape Argus
Davar
Doar Hayom

Fortnightly
Ha-Mashkif
Hapoel Hatzair
Harijan
Ha-Tzofeh
Hed Ha-Mizrach
Israel Digest
Jewish Advocate
Jewish Chronicle
Jewish Frontier
Jewish Telegraphic Agency (JTA)
Manchester Guardian
New Palestine
Palestine and Middle East Monthly
Palestine Bulletin
Palestine Post
Sentinel
Spectator
Times (London)
Zion's Messenger

III. Diaries, Memoirs, and Other Published Sources

Agron, Gershon. *Asir ha-ne'emanut*. Jerusalem: M. Nyuman, 1964.

Ahad Ha'am. "Pinsker and Political Zionism." Translated by Leon Simon. *Zionist Pamphlets*, 2nd series. London: The Zionist, 1916.

Anglo-American Committee of Inquiry Report on Jewish Problems in Palestine and Europe. Washington, DC: United States Government Printing Office, 1946.

Appadorai, A. *Asian Relations: Being [a] Report of the Proceedings and Documentation of the First Asian Relations Conference, New Delhi, March–April, 1947*. New Delhi: Asian Relations Organization, 1948.

Arlosoroff, Chaim. *Am, hevrah, u-medinah*, edited by Ascher Maniv. Tel Aviv: Yad Tabenkin, 1984.

———. "The Future of Zionist Policy (1932)." In Kaplan and Penslar, *The Origins of Israel*, 219–38.

———. *Jews, Arabs and Great Britain: A Study of Zionism in the Light of Recent Events*. Winnipeg: Israelite Press, 1930.

———. *Kitve Hayim Arlozorov*. 7 vols. Tel Aviv: A. J. Stybel, 1934–35.

———. *Yoman Yerushalayim*. Tel Aviv: Mifleget Po'ale Eretz-Yisrael, 1949.

"The Balfour Declaration (November 2, 1917)." In *The Jew in the Modern World: A Documentary History*. 3rd ed., edited by Paul Mendes-Flohr and Jehuda Reinharz, 660. Oxford: Oxford University Press, 2011.

Bentwich, Helen. *If I Forget Thee: Some Chapters of Autobiography, 1912–1920.* London: Paul Elek, 1979.
Bentwich, Norman. *England in Palestine.* London: Kegan Paul, Trench, Trubner, 1932.
———. *My 77 Years.* Philadelphia: Jewish Publication Society of America, 1961.
———. *They Found Refuge.* London: Cresset, 1956.
———. *Wanderer between Two Worlds.* London: Kegan Paul, Trench, Trubner 1941.
———. *Wanderer in War.* London: Victor Gollancz, 1946.
Bentwich, Norman, and Helen Bentwich. *Mandate Memories, 1918–1948.* London: Hogarth, 1965.
Bevin, Ernest. "Impressions of the British Commonwealth Relations Conference of 1938." *International Affairs* 18, no. 1 (1939): 56–76.
Brodetsky, Selig. *Memoirs: From Ghetto to Israel.* London: Weidenfeld and Nicolson, 1960.
Buber, Martin. *The Letters of Martin Buber: A Life of Dialogue.* Edited by Nahum N. Glatzer and Paul Mendes-Flohr. Translated by Richard and Clara Winston and Harry Zohn. Syracuse, NY: Syracuse University Press, 1996.
———. *On Judaism.* Edited by Nahum Glatzer. New York: Schocken, 1967.
Buber, Martin, and Judah Magnes. *Two Letters to Gandhi from Martin Buber and J. L. Magnes.* Jerusalem: Rubin Mass, 1939.
Cohen, Israel. *The Journal of a Jewish Traveller.* London: John Lane, 1925.
Committee for Assisting the Defence. *The Arlosoroff Murder Trial: Speeches and Relevant Documents.* Jerusalem: Hassolel Partnership, 1934.
Executive Committee of the General Federation of Jewish Labour in Palestine. *Documents and Essays on Jewish Labour Policy in Palestine.* Westport, CT: Greenwood Press, 1975.
Fiddes, George. *The Dominions and Colonial Offices.* London: Putnam's Sons, 1926.
Gandhi, M. K. *The Collected Works of Mahatma Gandhi.* 100 vols. New Delhi: Publications Division, Ministry of Information and Broadcasting, Government of India, 1958–1994.
———. *Satyagraha in South Africa.* 1928. Reprint, Ahmedabad: Navajivan Publishing House, 1972.
Garratt, G. T., and Edward Thompson. *Rise and Fulfillment of British Rule in India.* London: Macmillan, 1934.
Habas, Bracha, and David Hacohen. *'Esrim yom be-Hodu.* Tel Aviv: Am Oved, 1948.
Hyamson, Albert Montefiore. *Palestine: A Policy.* London: Methuen, 1942.
Inter-imperial Relations Committee. *Imperial Conference 1926: Report, Proceedings and Memoranda.* Nov. 1926.
Isaacs, Eva. *For the Record: The Memoirs of Eva, Marchioness of Reading.* London: Hutchinson, 1973.
Jabotinsky, Vladimir. "On the Iron Wall (1923)." In Kaplan and Penslar, *The Origins of Israel*, 257–63.
Journal and Proceedings of the Asiatic Society of Bengal (1935).
Kaplan, Eran, and Derek J. Penslar, eds. *The Origins of Israel, 1882–1948: A Documentary History.* Madison: University of Wisconsin Press, 2011.

Kisch, Frederick. *Palestine Diary*. London: Victor Gollancz, 1938.

Marris, William, and James Wilford Garner. *Civil Government for Indian Students*. Calcutta: S. C. Sanial, 1921.

Nehru, Jawaharlal. *Eighteen Months in India, 1936–37, Being Further Essays and Writings*. Allahabad: Kitabistan, 1938.

Olsvanger, Immanuel, "The Diary at the Central Zionist Archives, Jerusalem." Translated by Edelgaard David. In *Indo Judaic Studies: Some Papers*, edited by Yohanan ben David, 17–44. New Delhi: Northern Book Center, 2002.

Parliamentary Debates, Commons, 5th series (1909–81), vol. 301.

Philips, P. D., and Gordon Leslie Wood, eds. *The Peopling of Australia*. Melbourne: Macmillan, 1928.

Pinsker, Leon. "Auto-Emancipation: An Appeal to His People by a Russian Jew (1882)." In *The Zionist Idea*, edited by Arthur Hertzberg, 181–98. New York: Atheneum, 1970.

———. *Auto-Emancipation*. Translated by D. S. Blondheim. New York: Maccabean Publishing, 1906.

Polak, H. S. L. "Gandhi: Saint and/or Politician." *Christianity and Crisis* 2, no. 24 (1943): 3–6.

———. "Memories of Gandhi." *Contemporary Review* 173 (1948): 134–37.

———. "Mr. Gandhi and Non-violence." *Asiatic Review*, 37, no. 130 (1941): 354–57.

Renier, G. J. *The English: Are They Human?* London: Williams & Norgate, 1931.

Samuel, Edwin. *A Lifetime in Jerusalem: The Memoirs of the Second Viscount Samuel*. Jerusalem: Israel Universities Press, 1970.

Samuel, Herbert. *Grooves of Change: A Book of Memoirs*. Indianapolis, IN: Bobbs-Merrill, 1946.

Sharett, Moshe. *Ma'avak Medini*. Vol. 1, part 2. Edited by Yaakov Sharett and Rina Sharett. Tel Aviv: ha-'Amutah le-moreshet Moshe Sharett, 2014.

———. *Nitra'eh ve-ulai lo: mikhtavim min ha-tsava ha-'Otomani, 1916–1918*. Tel Aviv: ha-'Amutah le-moreshet Moshe Sharett, 1998.

———. *Yeme London: mikhteve Moshe Sharett mi-yeme ha-limudim*. 3 vols. Tel Aviv: ha-'Amutah le-moreshet Moshe Sharett, 2003–8.

———. *Yerehim be-'emek Ayalon*. Edited by Pinhas Ofer. Tel Aviv: ha-'Amutah le-moreshet Moshe Sharett, 2011.

———. *Yoman Medini*. 5 vols. Tel Aviv: Am Oved, 1968–79.

Shaw, George Bernard. *Fabianism and Empire: A Manifesto by the Fabian Society*. London: Grant Richards, 1900.

Sokolow, Nahum. *History of Zionism: 1600–1918*. Vol. 1. London: Longmans, Green, 1919.

Storrs, Ronald. *The Memoirs of Ronald Storrs*. New York: G. P. Putnam's Sons, 1937.

Webb, Sidney, and Beatrice Webb. *The Decay of Capitalist Civilisation*. London: George Allen and Unwin, 1923.

Wedgwood, Josiah. *The Seventh Dominion*. London: Labour Publishing, 1928.

Weizmann, Chaim. *The Letters and Papers of Chaim Weizmann*. Edited by Barnet Litvinoff. Ser. B, vol. 1, August 1898–July 1931. New Brunswick, NJ: Transaction, 1983.

———. *The Letters and Papers of Chaim Weizmann*. Edited by Barnet Litvinoff and Aaron Klieman. Ser. A, vol. 18, Jan. 1937–Dec. 1938. New Brunswick, NJ: Transaction, 1979.

———. *The Letters and Papers of Chaim Weizmann*. Edited by Michael J. Cohen. Ser. A, vol. 21, Jan. 1943–May 1945. New Brunswick, NJ: Transaction, 1979.

Weizmann, Vera. *The Impossible Takes Longer: The Memoirs of Vera Weizmann as Told to David Tutaev*. New York: Harper & Row, 1967.

Williams, Basil. *The British Empire*. Oxford: Oxford University Press, 1928.

———. *Ha-imperiah ha-Britit*. Translated by Chaim Arlosoroff. Tel Aviv: Hevra, 1930.

Yearbook of the Royal Asiatic Society of Bengal 5 (1939).

Secondary Sources

Adlington, Lucy. *Great War Fashion: Tales from the History Wardrobe*. Gloucestershire: History Press, 2013.

Alexander, Enid. *Morris Alexander: A Biography*. Cape Town: Juta, 1953.

Amkraut, Brian. *Between Home and Homeland: Youth Aliyah from Nazi Germany*. Tuscaloosa: University of Alabama Press, 2006.

Aschheim, Steven E. *Beyond the Border; The German-Jewish Legacy Abroad*. Princeton, NJ: Princeton University Press, 2007.

Avineri, Shlomo. *Arlosoroff*. New York: Grove Weidenfeld, 1989.

Azaransky, Sarah. *This Worldwide Struggle: Religion and the International Roots of the Civil Rights Movement*. Oxford: Oxford University Press, 2017.

Azaryahu, Maoz. *Tel Aviv: Mythography of a City*. Syracuse, NY: Syracuse University Press, 2007.

Banerjee, Himadri, Nilanjana Gupta, and Sipra Mukherjee, eds. *Calcutta Mosaic: Essays and Interviews on the Minority Communities of Calcutta*. London: Anthem, 2009.

Barak-Gorodetsky, David. *Judah Magnes: The Prophetic Politics of a Religious Binationalist*. Lincoln: Jewish Publication Society and University of Nebraska Press, 2021.

Bartley, Paula. "Preventing Prostitution: The Ladies' Association for the Care and Protection of Young Girls in Birmingham, 1887–1914." *Women's History Review* 7, no. 1 (1998): 37–60.

Bartrop, Paul R. *The Evian Conference of 1938 and the Jewish Refugee Crisis*. Cham: Palgrave Macmillan, 2018.

Bar-Yosef, Eitan. "Bonding with the British: Colonial Nostalgia and the Idealization of Mandatory Palestine in Israeli Literature and Culture after 1967." *Jewish Social Studies* 22, no. 3 (2017): 1–37.

———. "'The Horror' in Hebrew: *Heart of Darkness* in Israeli Culture." *Interventions: International Journal of Postcolonial Studies* 18, no. 3 (2016): 319–34.

Bar-Yosef, Eitan, and Nadia Valman, eds. *"The Jew" in Late-Victorian and Edwardian Culture: Between the East End and East Africa*. London: Palgrave Macmillan, 2008.

Baskin, Judith R., ed. *Jewish Women in Historical Perspective*. 2nd ed. Detroit, MI: Wayne State University Press, 1998.

Baumel-Schwartz, Judith Tydor. *The "Bergson Boys" and the Origins of Contemporary Zionist Militancy*. Translated by Dena Ordan. Syracuse, NY: Syracuse University Press, 2005.

———. *Never Look Back: The Jewish Refugee Children in Great Britain, 1938–1945*. West Lafayette, IN: Purdue University Press, 2012.

Bear, Laura. *Lines of the Nation: Indian Railway Workers, Bureaucracy, and the Intimate Historical Self*. New York: Columbia University Press, 2007.

Beizer, Michael. "Who Murdered Professor Israel Friedlander and Rabbi Bernard Cantor: The Truth Rediscovered." *American Jewish Archives* 55, no. 1 (2003): 63–114.

Ben-Avram, Baruch. "*Ha-Po'el Ha-Tza'ir ha-Germani—parashah shel kevutzat intelektualim 1917–1929*." *Ha-Tziyonut* 7 (1981): 80–85.

Benbassa, Esther. "Zionism in the Ottoman Empire at the End of the 19th and the Beginning of the 20th Century." *Studies in Zionism* 11, no. 2 (1990): 127–40.

Ben-Eliezer, Uri. *The Making of Israeli Militarism*. Bloomington: Indiana University Press, 1998.

Ben-Gurion, David, and Moshe Pearlman. *Ben Gurion Looks Back in Talks with Moshe Pearlman*. New York: Simon and Schuster, 1965.

Bentwich, Margery. *Thelma Yellin: Pioneer Musician*. Jerusalem: Rubin Mass, 1964.

Bentwich, Norman. *Brigadier Frederick Kisch: Soldier and Zionist*. London: Vallentine Mitchell, 1966.

———. *For Zion's Sake: A Biography of Judah Magnes*. Philadelphia: Jewish Publication Society of America, 1954.

Bentwich, Norman, and Margery Bentwich. *Herbert Bentwich: The Pilgrim Father*. Jerusalem: Hotza'ah Ivrith, 1940.

Ben-Zvi, Abraham, and Aharon Klieman, eds. *Global Politics: Essays in Honor of David Vital*. London: Frank Cass, 2001.

Bergamin, Peter. "An Intellectual Biography of Abba Ahimeir." PhD diss., University of Oxford, 2016.

Bernstein, Deborah. "Gender, Nationalism and Colonial Policy: Prostitution in the Jewish Settlement of Mandate Palestine, 1918–1948." *Women's History Review* 21, no. 1 (2012): 81–100.

Bhabha, Homi. "Of Mimicry and Man: The Ambivalence of Colonial Discourse." *October* 28 (1984): 125–33.

Bhattacharya, Sabyasachi. "A Brief Survey of Colonial Historiography in India." In *Different Types of History*, edited by Bharati Ray, 71–86. Delhi: Pearson, 2009.

Bhatti, Anil, and Johannes H. Voight, eds. *Jewish Exile in India: 1933–1945*. New Delhi: Manohar, 2005.

Biger, Gideon. *An Empire in the Holy Land: Historical Geography of the British Administration in Palestine, 1917–1929*. Jerusalem: Magnes Press, 1994.

———. *Moshevet keter o bayit le'umi: hashpa'at ha-shilton ha-Briti 'al Eretz-Yisrael, 1917–1930*. Jerusalem: Yad Ben-Zvi, 1983.

Bilitzki, Eliyahu. *Hayim Arlozorov*. Tel Aviv: Tarbut V'hinukh, 1966.

Birnbaum, Pierre, and Ira Katznelson, eds. *Paths of Emancipation: Jews, States, and Citizenship*. Princeton, NJ: Princeton University Press, 1995.

Bloom, Cecil. "The British Labour Party and Palestine, 1917–1948." *Jewish Historical Studies* 36 (1999–2001): 141–71.

———. "Josiah Wedgwood and Palestine." *Jewish Historical Studies* 42 (2009): 147–72.

Blunt, Alison. *Domicile and Diaspora: Anglo-Indian Women and the Spatial Politics of Home*. Malden: Wiley, 2005.

———. "Imperial Geographies of Home: British Domesticity in India, 1886–1925." *Transactions of the Institute of British Geographies* 24, no. 4 (1999): 421–40.

Boehmer, Elleke. *Colonial and Postcolonial Literature: Migrant Metaphors*. 2nd ed. Oxford: Oxford University Press, 2005.

Bowden, Tom. *The Breakdown of Public Security: The Case of Ireland, 1916–1921, and Palestine, 1936–1939*. Beverly Hills, CA: Sage, 1977.

Bracy, R. Michael. *Printing Class: 'Isa al-'Isa, Filastin, and the Textual Construction of National Identity, 1911–1931*. Lanham, MD: University Press of America, 2011.

Brown, Michael. "A Tale of Two Bad Trips: Chaim Arlosoroff in America." In *Between History and Literature: Studies in Honor of Isaac Barzilay/Ben historyah le-sifrut: sefer yovel le-Yitzhak Barzilay*, edited by Stanley Nash, 7–35. Tel Aviv: Hakibbutz Hameuchad, 1997.

Brubaker, Rogers. "Myths and Misconceptions in the Study of Nationalism." In *The State of the Nation: Ernest Gellner and the Theory of Nationalism*, edited by John Hall, 233–65. Cambridge: Cambridge University Press, 1998.

Buettner, Elizabeth. *Empire Families: Britons and Late Imperial India*. Oxford: Oxford University Press, 2004.

———. "Riding the Elephant or Riding the Bus: Britons, India, and Elite Status in the Late Imperial Era." In *At the Top of Empire*, edited by Claire Laux, François-Joseph Ruggiu, and Pierre Singaravélou, 219–35. Brussels: Peter Lang, 2009.

Bunton, Martin P. *Colonial Land Policies in Palestine, 1917–1936*. Oxford: Oxford University Press, 2007.

Burton, Antoinette. *Dwelling in the Archive: Women Writing House, Home, and History in Late Colonial India*. Oxford: Oxford University Press, 2003.

Campos, Michelle. "Between 'Beloved Ottomania' and 'The Land of Israel': The Struggle over Ottomanism and Zionism among Palestine's Sephardi Jews, 1908–1913." *International Journal of Middle East Studies* 37, no. 4 (2005): 461–83.

Caplan, Neil. *Futile Diplomacy*. Vol. 2, *Arab-Zionist Negotiations and the End of the Mandate*. Abingdon, UK: Routledge, 2015.

Cernea, Ruth Fredman. *Almost Englishmen: Baghdadi Jews in British Burma*. Lanham, MD: Lexington Book, 2006.

Cesarani, David, and Tony Kushner. *The Internment of Aliens in Twentieth Century Britain*. London: Routledge, 1993.

Chasin, Stephanie M. *British Jews and Imperial Service: Nationalism, Pan-Islamism, and Zionism in Mandate Palestine and Colonial India*. London: I.B. Tauris, 2024.

Chatterjee, Margaret. *Gandhi and His Jewish Friends.* London: Macmillan, 1992.
——. *Studies in Modern Jewish and Hindu Thought.* London: Macmillan, 1997.
Chatterjee, Partha. *The Nation and Its Fragments: Colonial and Postcolonial Histories.* Princeton, NJ: Princeton University Press, 1994.
Chattopadhyay, Swati. *Representing Calcutta: Modernity, Nationalism, and the Colonial Uncanny.* New York: Routledge, 2005.
Chaudhari, K. K., ed. *Maharashtra State Gazetteers: Greater Bombay District.* 3 vols. Mumbai: Government of Maharashtra, 1986.
Chazan, Meir. "The Dispute between Aharonovitch and Arlosoroff over the Zionist Stance on the 'Arab Question.'" *Middle Eastern Studies* 43, no. 6 (2007): 983–96.
——. *Metinut: ha-gishah ha-metunah be-ha-Po'el ha-Tza'ir u-ve-Mapai, 1905–19.* Tel Aviv: Am Oved, 2009.
Cherniavsky, Irith. *Be'or shineihem: 'al 'aliyatam shel yehudei polin lifnei hashoah.* Tel Aviv: Resling, 2015.
Chester, Lucy. "Factors Impeding the Effectiveness of Partition in South Asia and the Palestine Mandate." In *Order, Conflict, and Violence,* edited by Stathis N. Kalyvas, Ian Shapiro, and Tarek Masoud, 75–96. Cambridge: Cambridge University Press, 2008.
Choudhry, Sujit, Madhav Khosla, and Pratap Bhanu Mehta, eds. *The Oxford Handbook of the Indian Constitution.* Oxford: Oxford University Press, 2016.
Cohen, Benjamin B. *In the Club: Associational Life in South Asia.* Oxford: Oxford University Press, 2015.
Cohen, Julia Phillips. *Becoming Ottomans: Sephardi Jews and Imperial Citizenship in the Modern Era.* Oxford: Oxford University Press, 2014.
Cohen, Michael J. *Britain's Moment in Palestine: Retrospective and Perspectives, 1917–48.* London: Routledge, 2014.
Cohen, Stuart A. *English Zionists and British Jews: The Communal Politics of Anglo-Jewry, 1895–1920.* Princeton, NJ: Princeton University Press, 1982.
Collins, Damian. *Charmed Life: The Phenomenal World of Philip Sassoon.* London: Harper Collins, 2017.
Conrad, Eric. *Lily H. Montagu, Prophet of a Living Judaism.* New York: National Federation of Temple Sisterhoods, 1953.
Constantine, Stephen. "The Buy British Campaign of 1931." *European Journal of Marketing* 21, no. 4 (1987): 44–59.
Cornfield, Giveon, with Max Seligman. *Zion Liberated: Jewish Nation Building under the British Mandate in Palestine.* Bloomington, IN: Xlibris, 2013.
Curio, Claudia. "'Invisible' Children: The Selection and Integration Strategies of Relief Organizations." *Shofar* 23, no. 1 (2004): 41–56.
Dalziel, Raewyn. *Julius Vogel: Business Politician.* Auckland: Auckland University Press, 2013.
Darwin, John. "A Third British Empire? The Dominion Idea in Imperial Politics." In *The Oxford History of the British Empire.* Vol. 4, *The Twentieth Century,* edited by Judith Brown and Wm Roger Louis, 64–87. Oxford: Oxford University Press, 1999.

Davidoff, Leonore, and Catherine Hall. *Family Fortunes: Men and Women of the English Middle Class, 1780–1850*. London: Routledge, 2002.
Desai, Ashwin, and Goolam Vahed. *The South African Gandhi: Stretcher-Bearer of Empire*. Stanford, CA: Stanford University Press, 2016.
Deutscher, Isaac. *The Non-Jewish Jew and Other Essays*. Oxford: Oxford University Press, 1968.
Devji, Faisal. *The Impossible Indian: Gandhi and the Temptation of Violence*. Cambridge, MA: Harvard University Press, 2012.
——. *Muslim Zion: Pakistan as a Political Idea*. Cambridge, MA: Harvard University Press, 2013.
Diner, Hasia, and Gennady Estraikh. *1929: Mapping the Jewish World*. New York: New York University Press, 2013.
Dolev, Diana. *The Planning and Building of the Hebrew University, 1919–1948: Facing the Temple Mount*. Lanham, MD: Lexington Books, 2016.
Dubb, Allie A. *The Jewish Population of South Africa: The 1991 Sociodemographic Survey*. Cape Town: Kaplan Center, University of Cape Town, 1994.
Dubnov, Arie. " 'Ha-medinah she-ba-derekh' o ha-imperiah makeh shenit? imperializem federativi ve-le'umiut yehudit be-ikbot milhemet ha-olam ha-rishonah." *Yisrael* 24 (2016): 5–36.
——. "Notes on the Zionist Passage to India, or: The Analogical Imagination and Its Boundaries." *Journal of Israeli History* 35, no. 2 (2016): 177–214.
Dubnov, Arie, and Hanan Harif. "Zionisms: Roads Not Taken on the Journey to the Jewish State." *Ma'arav*, April 29, 2012. http://maarav.org.il/english/2012/04/29/zionisms-roads-not-taken-on-the-journey-to-the-jewish-state-arie-dubnov-hanan-harif/.
Dubnov, Arie, and Laura Robson, eds. *Partitions: A Transnational History of Twentieth-Century Territorial Separatism*. Stanford, CA: Stanford University Press, 2019.
Edelheit, Abraham J. *The Yishuv in the Shadow of the Holocaust: Zionist Politics and Rescue Aliya, 1933–1939*. New York: Routledge, 2018.
Egorova, Yulia. *Jews and India: Perceptions and Image*. London: Routledge, 2006.
Elias, Flower, and Judith Elias Cooper. *The Jews of Calcutta: The Autobiography of a Community, 1792–1972*. Calcutta: Jewish Association of Calcutta, 1974.
Elkins, Caroline. *Legacy of Violence: A History of the British Empire*. New York: Knopf, 2022.
Endelman, Todd. *The Jews of Britain, 1656–2000*. Berkeley: University of California Press, 2002.
Essaid, Aida. *Zionism and Land Tenure in Mandate Palestine*. Abingdon, UK: Routledge, 2014.
Etkin, Elia. "The Ingathering of (Non-human) Exiles: The Creation of the Tel Aviv Zoological Garden Animal Collection, 1938–1948." *Journal of Israeli History* 35, no. 1 (2016): 57–74.
Eyal, Eya. *The Disenchantment of the Orient: Expertise in Arab Affairs and the Israeli State*. Stanford, CA: Stanford University Press, 2006.

Ezra, Esmond David. *Turning Back the Pages: A Chronicle of Calcutta Jewry*. London: Brookside, 1986.

Feinberg, Harriet. "With Gandhi in South Africa: Sonja Schlesin." *Jewish Affairs* 27, no. 1 (2017): 6–11.

Feldman, David. "Jews and the British Empire c. 1900." *History Workshop Journal* 63, no. 1 (2007): 70–89.

Fink, Carole. *Defending the Rights of Others: The Great Powers, Jews, and International Minority Protection, 1878–1938*. Cambridge: Cambridge University Press, 2004.

Fischer, Hadas. "Tokhnit 'to'elet': tzarkhanut milhamtit ha-monit be-hasut memshelet ha-mandat, 1942–1946." *Zion* 79 (2014): 201–30.

Frank, Billy, Craig Horner, David Stewart, eds. *The British Labour Movement and Imperialism*. Newcastle upon Tyne: Cambridge Scholars, 2010.

Frankel, Jonathan. *Crisis, Revolution, and Russian Jews*. Cambridge: Cambridge University Press, 2009.

———. *The Damascus Affair: "Ritual Murder," Politics, and the Jews in 1840*. Cambridge: Cambridge University Press, 1997.

———. *Prophecy and Politics: Socialism, Nationalism, & the Russian Jews, 1862–1917*. Cambridge: Cambridge University Press, 1981.

Frenkel, Erwin. *The Press and Politics in Israel: The "Jerusalem Post" from 1932 to the Present*. Westport, CT: Greenwood Press, 1994.

Gal, John, Stefan Köngeter, and Sarah Vicary, eds. *The Settlement House Movement Revisited: A Transnational History*. Bristol: Bristol University Press, 2020.

Gelber, Yoav. "The Meeting between the Jewish Soldiers from Palestine Serving in the British Army and She'erit Hapletah." In *She'erit Hapletah, 1944–1948: Rehabilitation and Political Struggle*, edited by Gutman Yisrael and Drechsler Adina, 60–79. Jerusalem, Yad Vashem, 1990.

Getter, Miriam. *Hayim Arlozorov: Biografiah politit*. Tel Aviv: Hakibbutz Hameuchad, 1977.

Ghosh, Durba. *Sex and the Family in Colonial India: The Making of Empire*. Cambridge: Cambridge University Press, 2006.

Gist, Noel P., and Roy Dean Wright. *Marginality and Identity: Anglo-Indians as a Racially Mixed Minority in India*. Leiden: Brill, 1973.

Glynn, Jennifer, ed. *Tidings from Zion: Helen Bentwich's Letters from Jerusalem, 1919–1931*. London: I.B. Tauris, 2000.

Goldstein-Sabbah, S. R. *Baghdadi Jewish Networks in the Age of Nationalism*. Leiden: Brill, 2021.

Gordon, Adi, ed. *"Berit shalom" ve-ha-Tziyonut ha-du-le'umit: 'ha-She'elah ha-'Aravit' ke-she'elah Yehudit*. Jerusalem: Carmel, 2008.

———. "'Nothing but a Disillusioned Love'? Hans Kohn's Break with the Zionist Movement." In *Against the Grain: Jewish Intellectuals in Hard Times*, edited by Ezra Mendelsohn, Stefani Hoffman, and Richard I. Cohen, 117–42. New York: Berghahn, 2014.

Gorny, Yosef. *Ahdut ha-'Avodah, 1919–1930: ha-yesodot ha-ra'ayonim ve-ha-shitah ha-medinit.* Tel Aviv: Tel Aviv University Press, 1973.

———. *From Binational Society to Jewish State: Federal Concepts in Zionist Political Thought, 1920–1990, and the Jewish People.* Leiden: Brill, 2006.

———. *The British Labour Movement and Zionism, 1917–1948.* Abingdon, UK: Routledge, 1983.

———. "The Jewishness and Zionism of Harold Laski." *Midstream* 23, no. 9 (1977): 72–77.

———. *Zionism and the Arabs, 1882–1948.* Oxford: Oxford University Press, 1987.

Granick, Jaclyn. *International Jewish Humanitarianism in the Age of the Great War.* Cambridge: Cambridge University Press, 2021.

Granick, Jaclyn, and Abigail Green, eds. "Gendering Jewish Inter/Nationalism," special issue. *Journal of Modern Jewish Studies* 21, no. 2 (2022)

Green, Abigail. *Moses Montefiore: Jewish Liberator, Imperial Hero.* Cambridge: Cambridge University Press, 2012.

Gregory, Robert P. "H. S. L. Polak and the Indian Overseas Association." *Vivekananda Kendra Patrika*, Feb. 1973, 33–38.

Guha, Ramachandra. *Gandhi before India.* New York: Vintage, 2013.

Gupta, Partha Sarathi. *Imperialism and the British Labour Movement, 1914–1964.* New Delhi: Sage, 2002.

Hacohen, Dvora. "British Immigration Policy to Palestine in the 1930s: Implications for Youth Aliyah." *Middle Eastern Studies* 37 no. 4 (2001): 206–18.

———. *To Repair a Broken World: The Life of Henrietta Szold, Founder of Hadassah.* Cambridge. MA: Harvard University Press, 2021.

Haggis, Jane, Clare Midgley, Margaret Allen, and Fiona Paisley. *Cosmopolitan Lives on the Cusp of Empire: Interfaith, Cross-Cultural and Transnational Networks, 1860–1950.* London: Palgrave, 2017.

Halamish, Aviva. *Be-merutz kaful neged ha-zman: mediniyut ha-'aliyah ha-Tziyonit bi-shnot ha-shloshim.* Jerusalem: Yad Ben-Zvi, 2006.

Halkin, Hillel. *Jabotinsky: A Life.* New Haven, CT: Yale University Press, 2014.

Hall, John, ed. *The State of the Nation: Ernest Gellner and the Theory of Nationalism.* Cambridge: Cambridge University Press, 1998.

Halperin, Liora. *Babel in Zion: Jews, Nationalism, and Language Diversity in Palestine, 1920–1948.* New Haven, CT: Yale University Press, 2015.

———. *The Oldest Guard: Forging the Zionist Settler Past.* Stanford, CA: Stanford University Press, 2021.

Hart, Mitchell B., ed. *Jews and Race: Writings on Identity and Difference, 1880–1940.* Waltham, MA: Brandeis University Press, 2011.

Hasan, K. Sarwar. "The Commonwealth—Whither?" *Pakistan Horizon* 18, no. 1 (1965): 28–37.

Hattis, Susan Lee. *The Bi-national Idea in Zionism during Mandatory Times.* Haifa: Shikmona, 1970.

Heim, Susanne, ed. *The Persecution and Murder of the European Jews by Nazi Germany, 1933–1945.* Vol. 2, *German Reich 1938–August 1939.* Berlin: de Gruyter, 2019.

Heller, Joseph. *Mi-Berit Shalom le-Ihud: Yehuda Leib Magnes ve-ha-ma'avak li-medinah du-le'umit.* Jerusalem: Magnes Press, 2003.

Hellig, Jocelyn. "German Jewish Immigration to South Africa during the 1930s: Revisiting the Charter of the SS *Stuttgart,*" *Jewish History and Culture* 11, nos. 1–2 (2009): 124–38.

Helman, Anat. *Young Tel Aviv: A Tale of Two Cities.* Waltham, MA: Brandeis University Press, 2010.

Hinnells, John R., and Alan Williams, eds. *Parsis in India and the Diaspora.* London: Routledge, 2008.

Hirsch, Dafna. *Banu henah le-havi et ha-ma'arav : hanhalat higyenah ve-beniyat tarbut be-hevrah ha-Yehudit bi-tekufat ha-Mandat.* Sde Boker: Ben-Gurion Research Institute for the Study of Israel and Zionism, 2014.

———. "'Interpreters of Occident to the Awakening Orient': The Jewish Public Health Nurse in Mandate Palestine." *Comparative Studies in Society and History* 50, no. 1 (2008): 227–55.

———. "'We Are Here to Bring the West, Not Only to Ourselves': Zionist Occidentalism and the Discourse of Hygiene in Mandate Palestine." *International Journal of Middle East Studies* 41, no. 4 (2009): 577- 94.

Hirsch, Luise. *From the Shtetl to the Lecture Hall: Jewish Women and Cultural Exchange.* Lanham, MD: University Press of America, 2013.

Hirson, Baruch. *The Cape Town Intellectuals: Ruth Schechter and Her Circle, 1907–1934.* Cape Town: Merlin, 2001.

———. "Ruth Schechter: Friend to Olive Schreiner." *Searchlight South Africa* 3, no. 1 (August 1992): 47–71.

Hoffman, Stefani, and Ezra Mendelsohn, eds. *The Revolution of 1905 and Russia's Jews.* Philadelphia: University of Pennsylvania Press, 2008.

Horev, Shai. *Ideolog u-medina'i: hashkafat 'olamo u-mekomo ha-ideologi shel Hayim Arlozorov be-misgeret ha-manhigut ha-ideologit shel Tenu'at ha-'Avodah.* Haifa: Duhifat, 2015.

Hughes, Matthew. *Britain's Pacification of Palestine: The British Army, the Colonial State, and the Arab Revolt, 1936–1939.* Cambridge: Cambridge University Press, 2019.

Huneidi, Sahar. *A Broken Trust: Sir Herbert Samuel, Zionism and the Palestinians, 1920–1925.* London: I.B. Tauris, 2001.

Hunt, James D., and Surendra Bhana. "Spiritual Rope-Walkers: Gandhi, Kallenbach, and the Tolstoy Farm, 1910–13." *South African Historical Journal* 58 (2007): 174–202.

Hyman, Mavis. *Jews of the Raj.* Calcutta: Hyman, 1995.

Imber, Elizabeth E. "A Late Imperial Elite Jewish Politics: Baghdadi Jews in British India and the Political Horizons of Empire and Nation." *Jewish Social Studies* 23, no. 2 (Winter 2018): 48–85.

Indian Science Congress Association. *The Shaping of Indian Science.* 3 vols. Hyderabad: Universities Press, 2003.

Jackson, Stanley. *The Sassoons*. New York: Dutton, 1968.

Jacobson, Abigail. *From Empire to Empire: Jerusalem between Ottoman and British Rule*. Syracuse, NY: Syracuse University Press, 2011.

———. "Negotiating Ottomanism in Times of War: Jerusalem during World War I through the Eyes of a Local Muslim Resident." *International Journal of Middle East Studies* 40, no. 1 (2008): 69–88.

Jones, Helen. "National, Community and Personal Priorities: British Women's Responses to Refugees from the Nazis, from the Mid-1930s to Early 1940s." *Women's History Review* 21, no. 1 (2012): 121–51.

Kalmar, Ivan Davidson, and Derek J. Penslar. *Orientalism and the Jews*. Waltham, MA: Brandeis University Press, 2005.

Kalyvas, Stathis N., Ian Shapiro, and Tarek Masoud, eds. *Order, Conflict, and Violence*. Cambridge: Cambridge University Press, 2008.

Kaplan, Eran. *Beyond Post-Zionism*. Albany: State University of New York Press, 2015.

———. *The Jewish Radical Rights: Revisionist Zionism and Its Ideological Legacy*. Madison: University of Wisconsin Press, 2005.

———. "Post-Post-Zionism: A Paradigm Shift in Israel Studies?" *Israel Studies Review* 28, no. 1 (2013): 142–55.

Kaplan, Marion. *Hitler's Jewish Refugees: Hope and Anxiety in Portugal*. New Haven, CT: Yale University Press, 2020.

Karlinsky, Nahum. *California Dreaming: Ideology, Technology, and Society in the Citrus Industry in Palestine, 1890–1939*. Albany: State University of New York Press, 2005.

Karlip, Joshua. *The Tragedy of a Generation: The Rise and Fall of Jewish Nationalism in Eastern Europe*. Cambridge, MA: Harvard University Press, 2013.

Katz, Ethan B., Lisa Moses Leff, and Maud S. Mandel, eds. *Colonialism and the Jews*. Bloomington: Indiana University Press, 2017.

Katz, Nathan, ed. *Studies of Indian Jewish Identity*. New Delhi: Manohar, 2011.

Katz, Shmuel. *Lone Wolf: A Biography of Vladimir (Ze'ev) Jabotinsky*. 2 vols. New York: Barricade, 1996.

Katz, Yossi. *The Battle for the Land: The History of the Jewish National Fund (KKL) before the Establishment of the State of Israel*. Jerusalem: Magnes Press, 2005.

———. *The Land Shall Not Be Sold in Perpetuity: The Jewish National Fund and the History of State Ownership of Land in Israel*. Jerusalem: Magnes Press, 2016.

Kaufman, Menahem. *An Ambiguous Partnership: Non-Zionists and Zionists in America, 1939–1948*. Jerusalem: Magnes Press, 1991.

Khalidi, Rashid. *The Hundred Years' War on Palestine: A History of Settler Colonialism and Resistance, 1917–2017*. New York: Macmillan, 2020.

Khiterer, Victoria. "The October 1905 Pogroms and the Russian Authorities." *Nationalities Papers* 45, no. 5 (2015): 788–803.

Kimmerling, Baruch. *Zionism and Territory: The Socio-territorial Dimensions of Zionist Politics*. Berkeley, CA: Institute of International Studies, 1983.

Klausner, Margot. *Sufat Sivan: parashah aharonah be-haye Hayim Arlozorov*. Tel Aviv: Sifre Gadish, 1956.

Klein, Menachem. *Lives in Common: Arabs and Jews in Jerusalem, Jaffa, and Hebron*. Oxford: Oxford University Press, 2014.

Klier, John Doyle, and Shlomo Lambroza, eds. *Pogroms: Anti-Jewish Violence in Modern Russian History*. Cambridge: Cambridge University Press, 1992.

Kling, Simha. "Chaim Arlozorov." In *Fields of Offering: Studies in Honor of Raphael Patai*, edited by Victor Sanua, 243–63. Cranbury, NJ: Associated University Presses, 1983.

Kolinsky, Martin. *Law, Order and Riots in Mandatory Palestine, 1928–35*. London: St. Martin's, 1993.

Korman, Gerb. "New Jewish Politics for an American Labor Leader: Sidney Hillman, 1942–1946." *American Jewish History* 82, no. 1 (1994): 195–214.

Kotzin, Daniel P. *Judah L. Magnes: An American Jewish Nonconformist*. Syracuse, NY: Syracuse University Press, 2010.

Kozma, Liat. *Global Women, Colonial Ports: Prostitution in the Interwar Middle East*. Albany: State University of New York Press, 2017.

Krämer, Gudrun. *A History of Palestine: From the Ottoman Conquest to the Founding of the State of Israel*. Princeton, NJ: Princeton University Press, 2008.

Krischer, Ofri, and Arie Dubnov. "Ha-sagah le-vet Bentwich." *Yisrael* 27–28 (2021): 271–312.

Kubowitzki, Leon. *Unity in Dispersion: A History of the World Jewish Congress*. New York: World Jewish Congress, 1948.

Kumar, Ashutosh. *Coolies of the Empire: Indentured Indians in the Sugar Colonies, 1830–1920*. Cambridge: Cambridge University Press, 2017.

Kumaraswamy, P. R. *Israel's India Policy*. New York: Columbia University Press, 2010.

———. *Squaring the Circle: Mahatma Gandhi and the Jewish National Home*. New Delhi: KW Publishers, 2018.

Kurz, Nathan. *Jewish Internationalism and Human Rights after the Holocaust*. Cambridge: Cambridge University Press, 2021.

Lahiri, Shompa. *Indians in Britain: Anglo-Indian Encounters, Race and Identity, 1880–1930*. London: Frank Cass, 2000.

Lavsky, Hagit. *Before Catastrophe: The Distinctive Path of German Zionism*. Detroit, MI: Wayne State University Press, 1996.

———, ed. *Toldot ha-Universitah ha-'Ivrit bi-Yerushalayim: hitbasesut u-tzemihah*. Jerusalem: Magnes Press, 2005.

Leff, Lisa. "Trusting Adolphe Crémieux: Jews and Republicans in Nineteenth-Century France." In *On the Word of a Jew: Religion, Reliability, and the Dynamics of Trust*, edited by Nina Caputo and Mitchell B. Hart, 101–16. Bloomington: Indiana University Press, 2019.

Lelyveld, Joseph. *Great Soul: Mahatma Gandhi and His Struggle with India*. New York: Alfred A. Knopf, 2011.

Lev, Shimon. *Soulmates: The Story of Mahatma Gandhi and Hermann Kallenbach*. Telangana: Orient Blackswan, 2012.

LeVine, Mark. *Overthrowing Geography: Jaffa, Tel Aviv, and the Struggle for Palestine, 1880–1948*. Berkeley: University of California Press, 2005.

Levine, Philippa. *Prostitution, Race & Politics: Policing Venereal Disease in the British Empire*. New York: Routledge, 2003.

Levy, Emanuel. *The Habima, Israel's National Theater, 1917–1977: A Study of Cultural Nationalism*. New York: Columbia University Press, 1979.

Levy, Mike. *Get the Children Out! Unsung Heroes of the Kindertransport*. London: Lemon Soul, 2021.

Likhovski, Assaf. *Law and Identity in Mandate Palestine*. Chapel Hill: University of North Carolina Press, 2006.

———. "Post-Post-Zionist Historiography." *Israel Studies* 15, no. 2 (2010): 1–23.

Livny, Adi. "Fighting Partition, Saving Mount Scopus: The Pragmatic Binationalism of D. W. Senator (1930–1949)." In *Textual Transmission in Contemporary Jewish Cultures*, edited by Avriel Bar-Levav and Uzi Rebhun, 225–46. New York: Oxford University Press, 2020.

———. "The Hebrew University in Mandatory Palestine: A Relational History (1918–1948)." PhD diss., Hebrew University of Jerusalem, 2021.

Lockman, Zachary. *Comrades and Enemies: Arab and Jewish Workers in Palestine, 1906–1948*. Berkeley: University of California Press, 1996.

Lockwood, David. *The Indian Bourgeoisie: A Political History of the Indian Capitalist Class in the Early Twentieth Century*. London: I.B. Tauris, 2012.

Loeffler, James. *Rooted Cosmopolitans: Jews and Human Rights in the Twentieth Century*. New Haven, CT: Yale University Press, 2018.

Loeffler, James, and Moira Paz, eds. *The Law of Strangers: Jewish Lawyers and International Law in the Twentieth Century*. Cambridge: Cambridge University Press, 2019.

Martin, Jane. "Beyond Suffrage: Feminism, Education and the Politics of Class in the Interwar Years." *British Journal of Sociology of Education* 29, no. 4 (2008): 411–23.

Mathur, Sobhag. "Nehru: The Evolution of His Thought in the Pre-Independence Decades." In *Spectrum of Nehru's Thought*, edited by Sobhag Mathur and Shankar Goyal, 33–50. New Delhi: Mittal, 1994.

Meacham, Standish. *Toynbee Hall and Social Reform*. New Haven, CT: Yale University Press, 1987.

Meiton, Fredrik. *Electrical Palestine: Capital and Technology from Empire to Nation*. Berkeley: University of California Press, 2019.

Melzer, Emmanuel. *No Way Out: The Politics of Polish Jewry*. Cincinnati, OH: Hebrew Union College Press, 2013.

Mendelsohn, Adam D. *The Rag Race: How Jews Sewed Their Way to Success in America and the British Empire*. New York: New York University Press, 2014.

Mendelsohn, Ezra. *The Jews of East Central Europe between the World Wars*. Bloomington: Indiana University Press, 1983.

———. *On Modern Jewish Politics*. Oxford: Oxford University Press, 1993.

Mendes-Flohr, Paul. "The Yoke of the Kingdom in Jerusalem." In *The Jewish Legacy and the German Conscience: Essays in Memory of Rabbi Joseph Asher*, edited by Moses Rischin and Raphael Asher, 233–45. Berkeley, CA: Judah L. Magnes Museum, 1991.

Mendes-Flohr, Paul, and Anya Mali, eds. *Gustav Landauer: Anarchist and Jew*. Berlin: De Gruyter Oldenbourg, 2015.

Mesthrie, Uma Shashikant. "From Advocacy to Mobilization: Indian Opinion, 1903–1914." In *South Africa's Alternative Press: Voices of Protest and Resistance, 1880s–1960s*, edited by Les Switzer, 99–126. Cambridge: Cambridge University Press, 1997.

Metzer, Jacob, and Oded Kaplan. *Meshek Yehudi u-meshek 'Aravi be-Eretz-Yisrael*. Jerusalem: Falk Institute for Economic Research, 1991.

Meyer, Esther da Costa, and Claudia J. Nahson. *The Sassoons*. New Haven, CT: Jewish Museum and Yale University Press, 2023.

Michels, Tony. *A Fire in Their Hearts: Yiddish Socialists in New York*. Cambridge, MA: Harvard University Press, 2009.

Miller, Rory, ed., *Britain, Palestine, and Empire: The Mandate Years*. London: Ashgate, 2010.

Misra, Maria. *Business, Race, and Politics in British India, c. 1850–1960*. Oxford: Oxford University Press, 1999.

Morris, Benny. *Righteous Victims: A History of the Zionist-Arab Conflict, 1881–2001*. New York: Vintage, 2001.

Moss, Kenneth B. *Jewish Renaissance in the Russian Revolution*. Cambridge, MA: Harvard University Press, 2009.

———. *An Unchosen People: Jewish Political Reckoning in Interwar Poland*. Cambridge, MA: Harvard University Press, 2021.

Mulvey, Paul. *The Political Life of Josiah C. Wedgwood: Land, Liberty, and Empire, 1872–1943*. Woodbridge, UK: Boydell, 2010.

Musleah, Ezekiel N. *On the Banks of the Ganga: The Sojourn of the Jews in Calcutta*. North Quincy, MA: Christopher Publishing House, 1975.

Myers, David N. *Between Jew & Arab: The Lost Voice of Simon Rawidowicz*. Waltham, MA: Brandeis University Press, 2008.

Naar, Devin E. *Jewish Salonica: Between the Ottoman Empire and Modern Greece*. Stanford, CA: Stanford University Press, 2016.

Near, Henry. *The Kibbutz Movement: A History*. 2 vols. Oxford: Littman Library of Jewish Civilization, 1992, 1997.

Nedava, Joseph, ed. *Abba Ahimeir: ha-ish she-hitah et ha-zerem: li-demuto, le-torato, li-khetavav u-le-ma'avakav*. Tel Aviv: Hotza'at ha-'amutah le-hafatzat toda'ah le'umit, 1987.

Negev, Eilat, and Yehuda Koren. *The First Lady of Fleet Street*. London: JR Books, 2011.

Newman, Joanna. *Nearly the New World: The British West Indies and the Flight from Nazism, 1933–1945*. New York: Berghahn, 2019.

Norris, Jacob. *Land of Progress: Palestine in the Age of Colonial Development, 1905–1948*. Oxford: Oxford University Press, 2013.

Oz, Amos. *The Hill of Evil Council*. Translated by Nicholas de Lange. Orlando, FL: Harcourt, 1976.

Paxton, George. *Sonja Schlesin: Gandhi's South African Secretary*. Glasgow: Pax, 2006.

Pedersen, Susan. *The Guardians: The League of Nations and the Crisis of Empire*. Oxford: Oxford University Press, 2015.

Peleg, Yaron. *Orientalism and the Hebrew Imagination*. Ithaca, NY: Cornell University Press, 2005.

Penslar, Derek J. *Jews and the Military: A History*. Princeton, NJ: Princeton University Press, 2015.

———. *Zionism: An Emotional State*. New Brunswick, NJ: Rutgers University Press, 2023.

Pianko, Noam. *Zionism and the Roads Not Taken: Rawidowicz, Kaplan, Kohn*. Bloomington: Indiana University Press, 2010.

Pistol, Rachel. *Internment during the Second World War: A Comparative Study of Great Britain and the USA*. London: Bloomsbury, 2017.

Procida, Mary A. *Married to the Empire: Gender, Politics and Imperialism in Colonial India*. Manchester: Manchester University Press, 2002.

Rabinovitch, Simon. *Jewish Rights, National Rites: Nationalism and Autonomy in Late Imperial and Revolutionary Russia*. Stanford, CA: Stanford University Press, 2014.

———, ed. *Jews & Diaspora Nationalism: Writings on Jewish Peoplehood in Europe and the United States*. Waltham, MA: Brandeis University Press, 2012.

Radice, Lisanne. *Beatrice and Sidney Webb: Fabian Socialists*. London: Macmillan, 1984.

Ramusack, Barbara N. *The Indian Princes and Their States*. Cambridge: Cambridge University Press, 2004.

Rappaport, Erika, Mark J. Crowley, and Sandra Trudgen Dawson, eds. *Consuming Behaviours: Identity, Politics and Pleasure in Twentieth-Century Britain*. London: Bloomsbury Academic, 2015.

Ratzabi, Shalom. *Between Zionism and Judaism: The Radical Circle in Brith Shalom, 1925–1933*. Leiden: Brill, 2002.

Razi, Tammy. *Yalde ha-hefker: he-hatzer ha-ahorit shel Tel Aviv ha-Mandatorit*. Tel Aviv: Am Oved, 2009.

Ray, Dalia. *The Jewish Heritage of Calcutta*. Calcutta: Minerva, 2001.

Reed, Charles V. *Royal Tourists, Colonial Subjects and the Making of a British World, 1860–1911*. Manchester: Manchester University Press, 2016.

Reinharz, Jehuda, and Motti Golani. *Chaim Weizmann: A Biography*. Waltham, MA: Brandeis University Press, 2024.

Reinharz, Jehuda, and Yaacov Shavit. *Glorious, Accursed Europe: An Essay on Jewish Ambivalence*. Waltham, MA: Brandeis University Press, 2010.

———. *The Road to September 1939: Polish Jews, Zionists, and the Yishuv on the Eve of World War II*. Waltham, MA: Brandeis University Press, 2018.

Renton, James. *The Zionist Masquerade: The Birth of the Anglo-Zionist Alliance 1914–1918*. New York: Palgrave, 2007.

Robson, Laura. *Colonialism and Christianity in Mandate Palestine*. Austin: University of Texas Press, 2011.
Roland, Joan G. *The Jewish Communities of India: Identity in a Colonial Era*. New Brunswick, NJ: Transaction, 1998.
Rose, Norman. *Chaim Weizmann: A Biography*. New York: Elisabeth Sifton, 1986.
———. *The Gentile Zionists: A Study in Anglo-Zionist Diplomacy, 1929–1939*. Abingdon, UK: Routledge, 1973.
———. "The Seventh Dominion." *Historical Journal* 14, no. 2 (1971): 397–416.
Rosenhead, Louis. *Professor Selig Brodetsky: Scholar, Dreamer, Man of Action*. Leeds: Leeds University Press, 1963.
Roth, Cecil. *The Sassoon Dynasty*. London: Robert Hale, 1941.
Rubin, Barry, and Wolfgang G. Schwanitz. *Nazis, Islamists, and the Making of the Modern Middle East*. New Haven, CT: Yale University Press, 2014.
Rubin, Gil. "From Federalism to Binationalism: Hannah Arendt's Shifting Zionism." *Contemporary European History* 24, no. 3 (2015): 393–414.
———. "The End of Minority Rights: Jacob Robinson and the Jewish Question in World War II." *Simon Dubnow Institute Yearbook* 11 (2012): 55–71.
Ruderman, David. *Jewish Enlightenment in an English Key: Anglo-Jewry's Construction of Modern Jewish Thought*. Princeton, NJ: Princeton University Press, 2002.
Rudolph, Lloyd I., and Susanne Hoeber Rudolph. *Postmodern Gandhi and Other Essays: Gandhi in the World and at Home*. Chicago: University of Chicago Press, 2006.
Russell, David. "'The Jolly Old Empire': Labour, the Commonwealth and Europe, 1945–51." In *Britain, the Commonwealth and Europe*, edited by Alex May, 9–20. London: Palgrave, 2001.
Sabbagh-Khoury, Areej. *Colonizing Palestine: The Zionist Left and the Making of the Palestinian Nakhba*. Stanford, CA: Stanford University Press, 2023.
Sabharwal, Gopa. "In Search of an Asian Vision: The Asian Relations Conference of 1947." In *Imagining Asia(s): Networks, Actors, Sites*, edited by Andrea Acri, Kashshaf Ghani, Murai K. Jha, and Sraman Mukherjee, 60–90. Singapore: ISEAS, 2019.
Sacher, Howard M. *A History of Israel: From the Rise of Zionism to Our Time*. Ann Arbor: University of Michigan Press, 1996.
Saks, David Y. "Right-Hand Man of the Mahatma: Hermann Kallenbach, Gandhi and Satyagraha." *Jewish Affairs* (Autumn 1998): 45–48.
Salzmann, Philip Carl and Donna Robinson Divine, eds. *Postcolonial Theory and the Arab-Israel Conflict*. London: Routledge, 2008.
Sarid, Isa, and Christian Bartolf. *Hermann Kallenbach: Mahatma Gandhi's Friend in South Africa: A Concise Biography*. Berlin: Gandhi-Informations-Zentrum, 1997.
Saron, Gustav. *Morris Alexander: Parliamentarian and Jewish Leader*. Johannesburg: South African Jewish Board of Deputies, 1966.
Sassoon, Joseph. *The Global Merchants: The Enterprise and Extravagance of the Sassoon Dynasty*. London: Allen Lane, 2022.

Schechtman, Joseph B. *Fighter and Prophet: The Jabotinsky Story, the Last Years*. New York: A. S. Barnes, 1961.

———. *Rebel and Statesman: The Vladimir Jabotinsky Story, the Early Years*. New York: T. Yoseloff, 1956.

Schneider, Fred D. "British Labour and Ireland, 1918–1921: The Retreat to Houndsditch." *Review of Politics* 40, no. 3 (July 1978): 368–91.

Schor, Laura S. *The Best School in Jerusalem: Annie Landau's School for Girls, 1900–1960*. Waltham, MA: Brandeis University Press, 2013.

Schreier, Joshua. *Arabs of the Jewish Faith: The Civilizing Mission in Colonial Algeria*. New Brunswick, NJ: Rutgers University Press, 2010.

———. *The Merchants of Oran: A Jewish Port at the Dawn of Empire*. Stanford, CA: Stanford University Press, 2017.

Schwartz, Bill. *The White Man's World*. Oxford: Oxford University Press, 2011.

Segev, Tom. *One Palestine Complete: Jews and Arabs under the British Mandate*. New York: Metropolitan, 2000.

Shafir, Gershon. *Land, Labor and the Origins of the Israeli-Palestinian Conflict, 1882–1914*. Berkeley: University of California Press, 1996.

Shain, Milton. *A Perfect Storm: Antisemitism in South Africa, 1930–1948*. Johannesburg: Jonathan Ball, 2015.

———. *The Roots of Antisemitism in South Africa*. Charlottesville: University Press of Virginia, 1994.

Shaltiel, Eli. *Pinhas Rutenberg: 'aliyato u-nefilato shel "ish hazak" be-Eretz-Yisrael, 1879–1942*. 2 vols. Tel Aviv: Am Oved, 1990.

Shamir, Ronen. *The Colonies of Law: Colonialism, Zionism, and Law in Early Mandate Palestine*. Cambridge: Cambridge University Press, 2000.

———. *Current Flow: The Electrification of Palestine*. Stanford, CA: Stanford University Press, 2013.

Shanes, Joshua. *Diaspora Nationalism and Jewish Identity in Habsburg Galicia*. Cambridge: Cambridge University Press, 2012.

Shapira, Anita. *Ben-Gurion: Father of Modern Israel*. New Haven, CT: Yale University Press, 2014.

———. *Berl: The Biography of a Socialist Zionist*. Cambridge: Cambridge University Press, 1984.

———. *Israel: A History*. Waltham, MA: Brandeis University Press, 2012.

———. *Land and Power: The Zionist Resort to Force, 1881–1948*. Stanford, CA: Stanford University Press, 1992.

———. "Zionism in the Age of Revolution." *Modern Judaism* 18, no. 3 (1998): 217–26.

Shapiro, Joseph. *Hayim Arlozorov*. Tel Aviv: Am Oved, 1975.

Shapiro, Yonathan. *Ahdut ha-'Avodah ha-historit*. Tel Aviv: Am Oved, 1975.

Sharafi, Mitra. *Law and Identity in Colonial South Asia: Parsi Legal Culture, 1772–1947*. Cambridge: Cambridge University Press, 2014.

Sharfman, Daphna. *Palestine in the Second World War: Strategic Plans and Political Dilemmas—The Emergence of a New Middle East*. Eastbourne: Sussex Academic Press, 2014.

Shavit, Yaacov. *Jabotinsky and the Revisionist Movement: 1925–1948*. Abingdon, UK: Frank Cass, 1988.

Sheffer, Gabriel. *Moshe Sharett: Biography of a Political Moderate*. Oxford: Clarendon, 1996.

Sherman, A. J. *Mandate Days: British Lives in Palestine, 1918–1948*. New York: Thames and Hudson, 1997.

Shilo, Margalit. "Women as Victims of War: The British Conquest (1917) and the Blight of Prostitution in the Holy City." *Nashim* no. 6 (2003): 72–81.

———. "Zanutan shel banot Yerushalayim motza'e Milhemet ha-'Olam ha-Rishonah: mabat gavri ve-mabat nashi." *Yerushalayim ve-Eretz-Yisrael* 1 (2003): 173–96.

Shimoni, Gideon. "From Anti-Zionism to Non-Zionism in Anglo-Jewry, 1917–1937." *Jewish Journal of Sociology* 28, no. 1 (1986): 19–47.

———. *Gandhi, Satyagraha and the Jews: A Formative Factor in India's Policy toward Israel*. Jerusalem: Leonard Davis Institute for International Relations, Hebrew University, 1977.

———. *Jews and Zionism: The South African Experience (1910–1967)*. Cape Town: Oxford University Press, 1980.

———. "The Non-Zionists in Anglo-Jewry, 1937–1948." *Jewish Journal of Sociology* 28, no. 2 (1986): 89–115.

Shindler, Colin. *Israel and the European Left: Between Solidarity and Delegitimization*. London: Bloomsbury, 2012.

Shumsky, Dimitry. *Ben Prag li-Yerushalayim: Tziyonut Prag ve-ra'ayon ha-medinah ha-du-le'umit be-Eretz-Yisrael*. Jerusalem: Leo Baeck Institute, 2010.

———. *Beyond the Nation-State*. New Haven, CT: Yale University Press, 2018.

———. "Brith Shalom's Uniqueness Reconsidered: Hans Kohn and Autonomist Zionism." *Jewish History* 25, no. 3/4 (2011): 339–53.

Shva, Shlomo, ed. *Shiv'im ha-shanim ha-rishonot: Sipur ha-Bima*. Tel Aviv: Keter, 1987.

Silliman, Jael. *Jewish Portraits, Indian Frames: Women's Narratives from a Diaspora of Hope*. Hanover, NH: Brandeis University Press/University Press of New England, 2001.

Sinanoglou, Penny. *Partitioning Palestine: British Policymaking at the End of Empire*. Chicago: University of Chicago Press, 2019.

Singam, S. Durai Raja. "The Polaks and Gandhiji." *Indian Review* 63, no. 5/6 (1964): 173–77.

Sinha, Mrinalini. "Britishness, Clubbability, and the Colonial Public Sphere: The Genealogy of an Imperial Institution in Colonial India." *Journal of British Studies* 40, no. 4 (2001): 489–521.

———. "Suffragism and Internationalism: The Enfranchisement of British and Indian Women under an Imperial State." In *Women's Suffrage in the British Empire: Citizenship, Nation, and Race*, edited by Ian Christopher Fletcher, Laura E. Nym Mayhall, and Philippa Levine, 224–40. London: Routledge, 2000.

Sinha, Pradip. *Calcutta in Urban History*. Calcutta: Firma KLM, 1978.

Smith, Ray T. "The Role of India's 'Liberals' in the Nationalist Movement, 1915–1947." *Modernization in South Asian Studies: Essays in a Changing Field* 8, no. 7 (1968): 607–24.

Spence, Jean. "Working for Jewish Girls: Lily Montagu, Girls' Clubs and Industrial Reform 1890–1914." *Women's History Review* 13, no. 3 (2004): 491–510.

Sprinzak, Ehud. *The Ascendance of Israel's Radical Right*. Oxford: Oxford University Press, 1991.

Stansky, Peter. *The Worlds of Philip and Sybil*. New Haven, CT: Yale University Press, 2003.

Stein, Joshua B. "Josiah Wedgwood and the Seventh Dominion Scheme." *Studies in Zionism* 11, no. 2 (1990): 141–55.

———. *Our Great Solicitor: Josiah C. Wedgwood and the Jews*. Selinsgrove, PA: Susquehanna University Press, 1992.

Stein, Kenneth W. *The Land Question in Palestine, 1917–1939*. Chapel Hill: University of North Carolina Press, 1987.

Stein, Sarah Abrevaya. *Extraterritorial Dreams: European Citizenship, Sephardi Jews, and the Ottoman Twentieth Century*. Chicago: University of Chicago Press, 2016.

———. *Making Jews Modern: The Yiddish and Ladino Press in the Russian and Ottoman Empires*. Bloomington: Indiana University Press, 1990.

———. "Modern Jewries and the Imperial Imagination." *AJS Perspectives* (Fall 2005): 14–16.

———. *Plumes: Ostrich Feathers, Jews, and a Lost World of Global Commerce*. New Haven, CT: Yale University Press, 2010.

———. "Protected Persons? The Baghdadi Jewish Diaspora, the British State, and the Persistence of Empire." *American Historical Review* 16, no. 1 (2011): 80–108.

———. *Saharan Jews and the Fate of French Algeria*. Chicago: University of Chicago Press, 2014.

Stern, Rephael G. "Uncertain Comparisons: Zionist and Israeli Links to India and Pakistan in the Age of Partition and Decolonization." *Law and History Review* 39, no. 3 (August 2021): 451–78.

Sufian, Sandra M. *Healing the Land and the Nation: Malaria and the Zionist Project in Palestine, 1920–1947*. Chicago: University of Chicago Press, 2008.

Sugarman, Martin. "The Zion Muleteers of Gallipoli, March 1915–May 1916." *Jewish Historical Studies* 36 (1999–2001): 113–39.

Suhrud, Tridip. "'Re-editing' Gandhi's Collected Works." *Economic and Political Weekly*, Nov. 20, 2004, 4967–69.

Summers, Anne. *Christian and Jewish Women in Britain, 1880–1940: Living with Difference*. Cham: Palgrave Macmillan, 2017.

Suwaed, Muhammad. "The Wadi al-Hawarith Affair (Emek Hefer): Disputed Land and the Struggle for Ownership: 1929–1933." *Middle Eastern Studies* 52, no. 1 (2016): 135–52.

Tartakower, Arieh, and Kurt R. Grossman. *The Jewish Refugee*. New York: Institute of Jewish Affairs of the American Jewish Congress and World Jewish Congress, 1944.

Teveth, Shabtai. *Retzah Arlozorov*. Jerusalem: Schocken, 1982.

Thynne, Jane. *Black Roses*. London: Simon & Schuster, 2013.

Tzahor, Zeev. "Chaim Arlosoroff and His Attitude toward the Rise of Nazism." *Jewish Social Studies* 46, no. 3/4 (1984): 321–30.

Ugolini, Wendy. *Experiencing War as the "Enemy Other": Italian Scottish Experience in World War II*. Manchester: Manchester University Press, 2011.

Ulrichsen, Kristian. *The First World War in the Middle East*. Oxford: Oxford University Press, 2014.

Umansky, Ellen M. *Lily H. Montagu and the Advancement of Liberal Judaism: From Vision to Vocation*. Lewiston, NY: Edwin Mellen, 1983.

Ungerson, Clare. *Four Thousand Lives: The Rescue of German Jewish Men to Britain, 1939*. Cheltenham, UK: History Press, 2014.

Vahed, Goolam. "Race, Empire, and Citizenship: Sarojini Naidu's 1924 Visit to South Africa." *South African History Journal* 64, no. 2 (2012): 319–42.

Vernon, James. *The Cambridge History of Britain: Modern Britain, 1750 to the Present*. Cambridge: Cambridge University Press, 2017.

Vogt, Stefan. "The Postcolonial Buber: Orientalism, Subalternity, and Identity Politics in Martin Buber's Political Thought." *Jewish Social Studies* 22, no. 1 (Fall 2016): 161–86.

Vogt, Stefan, Derek Penslar, and Arieh Saposnik, eds. *Unacknowledged Kinships: Postcolonial Studies and the Historiography of Zionism*. Waltham, MA: Brandeis University Press, 2023.

Walkowitz, Judith R. *Nights Out: Life in Cosmopolitan London*. New Haven, CT: Yale University Press, 2012.

———. *Prostitution and Victorian Society: Women, Class, and the State*. Cambridge: Cambridge University Press, 1980.

Wallach, Yair. "The Racial Logic of Palestine's Partition." *Ethnic and Racial Studies* 48, no. 8 (2023): 1576–98.

Weil, Shalva, ed. *The Baghdadi Jews in India: Maintaining Communities, Negotiating Identities and Creating Super-Diversity*. Abingdon, UK: Routledge, 2019.

Wendehorst, Stephan E. C. *British Jewry, Zionism, and the Jewish State, 1936–1956*. Oxford: Oxford University Press, 2012.

Wheatley, Natasha. "Mandatory Interpretation: Legal Hermeneutics and the New International Order in Arab and Jewish Petitions to the League of Nations." *Past & Present* 227, no. 1 (2015): 205–48.

White, Lawrence H. *The Clash of Economic Ideas: The Great Policy Debates and Experiments of the Last Hundred Years*. Cambridge: Cambridge University Press, 2012.

Yehezkel-Shaked, Ezra. *Jews, Opium, and the Kimono*. Jerusalem: Rubin Mass, 2003.

Zadoff, Noam. *Gershom Scholem: From Berlin to Jerusalem and Back*. Translated by Jeffrey Green. Waltham, MA: Brandeis University Press, 2017.

Zelliot, Eleanor. "Experiments in Dalit Education: Maharashtra, 1850–1947." In *Education and the Disprivileged: Nineteenth and Twentieth Century India*, edited by Sabyasachi Bhattacharya, 35–49. Hyderabad: Orient Longman, 2002.

Zertal, Idith. *From Catastrophe to Power: The Holocaust Survivors and the Emergence of Israel*. Berkeley: University of California Press, 1998.

Zipperstein, Steven J. *Elusive Prophet: Ahad Ha'am and the Origins of Zionism*. Berkeley: University of California Press, 1993.

Index

Page numbers in *italics* refer to illustrations.

Acre prison break (1947), 274
Aden, 207, 276–77
Adler-Rudel, Salomon, 233
Agronsky (Agron), Gershon, 127, 150; Indian Muslim support sought by, 19–20, 98, 108–9, 170, 176, 178, 296n31
Ahad Ha'am, 25, 29, 46, 48, 84, 121, 171
Aharonivitch, Yosef, 60, 61
Ahdut ha-Avodah, 41, 59, 60–61, 90, 256
Ahdut ha-Avodah (journal), 90–91
Ahimeir, Abba, 119
Al-Aqsa Mosque, 104, 110
Alexander, Morris, 164, 169
Alexander (Farrington), Ruth (Schechter), 164, 320nn14, 18
Alfred (major general), 32
al-Husseini, Amin (grand mufti), 106, 107, 108, 170, 174
Ali, Shaukat, 107, 170, 172
Aliens Act (South Africa, 1937), 233
aliyah. *See* immigration
Al-Khalidi, Mustafa, 127
Allenby, Edmund, 25, 30
All-India Depressed Classes Association, 151
All-India Muslim League, 175, 182
American Jewish Committee, 46
American Jewish Congress, 156
American Jewish Joint Distribution Committee, 41, 202, 248
American Red Cross, 30, 39
American Zionist Organization, 30

Amery, Leo, 298n50, 302–3n123
Andrews, Lewis Yelland, 188
Angell, Norman, 91
Anglo-American Committee of Inquiry, 251, 252, 253
Anglo-Iraqi Treaty (1922), 66
Anglo-Jews. *See* British Jews
Angola, 233
Anno Domini 2000 (Vogel), 93
antisemitism, 6, 15, 131, 187; Arlosoroff's charges of, 119, 230; among British in Palestine, 18, 24, 27, 36, 39, 40, 41, 53, 73; Chancellor's reputation for, 85, 99; concern in Britain over backlash of, 146, 236, 237; Pinsker's view of, 129, 130, 131; in South Africa, 174, 233
Appadorai, A., 255
Arab League, 253, 258, 263, 264–65
Arab Revolt in Palestine (1936–1939), 174, 175, 184, 188, 203, 204, 212, 228, 229, 271
Arandora Star, SS, 240
Arlosoroff, Chaim, 5, 21, 48, *71*; Arab nationalism acknowledged by, 61, 111; at Norman Bentwich's lecture, 118, 119; binationalism condemned by, 120–21; British administration in Palestine viewed by, 70–74, 90, 104, 128; British Conservatives mistrusted by, 64; British culture and institutions admired by, 55–56, 67, 82, 85, 95, 127–28; British Labour politics and, 90–91, 116; British views of Arabs and Jews contrasted by, 70, 74; Chancellor viewed by, 101–2; dominion status viewed by, 13, 56, 57, 67, 70, 75, 77–82, 86, 123, 157, 222, 278; early life of, 58–59; evolutionary Zionism abandoned by, 122–23, 125; French imperialism criticized by, 65–66; as intellectual, 59–60, 62, 82; ideas on labor practices, 61, 87–89; Eva Isaacs and, 128–29; Jaffa riots (1921) and, 60, 70; Jerusalem viewed by, 105; Jewish affinity for Britain noted by, 85; Jewish Agency's Political Department led by, 97, 99, 105–6, 110, 111, 115, 116; Julius Vogel planned biography by, 54–55, 92–93; letter to Weizmann from, 56–57, 97, 116, 122, 124–26, 132; murder of, 58, 133; in London, 54–55, 82–83; pacifists criticized by, 84, 116, 120; Pan-Islamic politics viewed by, 108, 111; the Permanent Mandates Commission and, 62–66; social anarchism's influence on, 60; as statist, 56–57, 59, 280; time pressures viewed by, 97, 125, 131–32; Wauchope and, 112–15, 121–24, 129–32, 278; World Islamic Congress feared by, 107–12, 123, 170, 220; Zionist-British partnership viewed by, 9, 19, 66, 75, 84, 85, 89, 90, 97–98, 101–3, 113–16, 122, 128, 133, 136, 278
Arlosoroff, Gerda (Goldberg), 62, 294n1
Arlosoroff, Saul, 58–59, 294n1
Arlosoroff, Shulamit, 62, 294n1
Arlosoroff, Sima (Rubin), 54, 55, 106, 123, 127, 128, 133, 294n1
Aron, Wellesley, 128, 157
Ashbee, C. R., 36
Asian Relations Conference (1947), 22, 250, 253–75
Atlee, Clement, 251, 253, 274
Australia, 8, 13, 48, 67, 76, 88, 92, 206–12, 240
Austria, 188–89, 193, 201, 234, 248
Auto-Emancipation (Pinsker), 129–32, 188
autonomism, 13, 18, 25, 29, 48, 56, 61, 111, 157
Avineri, Shlomo, 59, 310n92
'avodah 'ivrit (Hebrew labor), 48, 61, 87–89, 302n117

Baghdadi Jews, 7, 20, 134, 207; Anglo-Indians and, 149–50; British classification of, 138–46, 149–50, 178; European

identity and, 8–9, 278; Gandhi and, 195–196; Indian nationalism and, 135, 148, 149, 150–51, 159–60; memorial campaign for European classification and, 134–35, 136, 138–46; refugees aided by, 34, 153, 158–60; Sephardi identity and, 139–40, 142–43; wealth of, 11, 138, 146–47, 207; World War II and, 160–61; Zionism and, 12, 153–58
Baldwin, Stanley, 64
Balfour, Arthur, 1, 50, 67
Balfour Declaration (1917), 1, 19, 43, 46, 69, 94, 109, 130, 153, 166, 174, 187, 214, 272–73, 298n50, 298n52
Balfour Declaration (1926), 67, 68, 103
Balosher, Moshe Moisei, 294n1
Balosher, Nava, 294n1
Banerjee, Amiya Charan, 148
Banerjee, Mrinalini, 148
Basque region, 234
Bedouins, 50
Belgium, 202, 239, 248
Bell, Gertrude, 72
Bene Israel, 140, 144, 150, 159, 179, 207
Ben-Gavriel, Moshe Ya'akov, 260
Ben-Gurion, David, 2, 21, 203, 205, 225, 232, 246, 252; attitudes toward nonstatist visions for Palestine, 56, 79; immigration limits opposed by, 214; independence backed by, 226, 228; Ottoman Empire and Zionism viewed by, 153–54; Palestinian Arab nationalism and, 60; partition backed by, 184; Herbert Plumer viewed by, 69; at St James's Palace Conference, 215, 221–22, 229–30; talks with Britain opposed by, 240; territorialism opposed by, 202; on the use of force, 227; Col. Josiah Wedgwood viewed by, 82
Bennett, Ernest, 76
Bentwich, Helen (Franklin), 5, 18, 21, 49, 138, 203, 258; appeasement of Hitler viewed by, 208, 212; in Australia, 206–13; British officials and policy in Palestine critiqued by, 37, 40, 42, 70, 87; critiques of Zionism by, 35–36; Curtin viewed by, 211; ethnonationalism opposed by, 24, 46; as feminist, 18; at Hebrew University opening, 50; hostess role resented by, 33–34, 138; immigration limits assailed by, 209–10; Jerusalem social life of, 44–47, 126–27, 152; in Labour Party, 100, 117; as Ladies' Club founder, 38–40; as Kindertransport organizer, 21, 26, 201, 213, 233–38; Kisch viewed by, 45; letters of, 26–27, 33–34, 35, 38, 39, 42; as non-Zionist, 18, 24, 26, 29–30, 279; Norman's lecture controversy recalled by, 118–19; Palestine residence dreaded by, 116–18; as relief worker, 51–53, 84–85; religious beliefs of, 46–47; Richmond viewed by, 72–73; Shaw Commission dismissed by, 87; as socialist, 23, 26, 27, 33, 45, 52; as social worker, 27–28, 30–36, 38, 39, 52–53; Wedgwood viewed by, 67; during World War I, 23–24; Zionism increasingly admired by, 24, 29, 45–46
Bentwich, Herbert, 24
Bentwich, Joseph (José), 51, 213
Bentwich, Lilian. *See* Friedlander, Lilian
Bentwich, Norman, 5, 18–19, 21, 23, 39, 49, 67, 72, 104, 127, 138, 169, 180, 218, 250, 258; in Aden, 207, 276–77; African refugee scheme explored by, 213, 232–33; in Australia, 206–13; as attorney general, 25–26, 48, 72, 100, 104; as binationalist and supporter of Brit Shalom and Ihud, 25, 47–49, 53, 111, 120, 127, 248, 277, 280; in civilian administration, 38, 42, 43; criticisms of, 26, 44; dominion status viewed by, 13, 48; Évian Conference viewed by, 200; in exile from

Bentwich, Norman (*cont.*)
　Palestine, 99–100, 116; friendship with Judah Magnes, 46–47; at Hebrew University opening, 50; isolationism resented by, 210; Jerusalem social life of, 44–47, 126–27, 152; as law professor, 117–19; and lecture controversy, 117–21, 123; as Magnes's biographer, 193; overlapping worlds of, 277–78; on Reform Judaism, 46–47; partition opposed by, 184, 205; refugees aided by, 201–3, 205, 233–35, 236, 238–40; in settlement movement, 25, 33–34; South Africa visited by, 233; Weizmann and, 35; women's equality backed by, 28; as Zionist, 24, 29–30, 47–48, 98, 205

Bentwich, Thelma. *See* Yellin, Thelma
Ben-Yehuda, Eliezer, 41
Ben-Zvi, Yitzhak, 215, 216–17, 219, 287n3
Berger (Mohl), Sophia, 39, 51
Bergmann, Hugo, 48–49, 112, 120, 192, 255–56, 264–71
Besant, Annie, 72
Betterton, Henry, 301–2n103
Bevin, Ernest, 207–8, 251
Bhabha, Homi, 287n28
binationalism, 10, 13, 17, 18, 28, 29, 44, 48–49, 53, 56, 111, 120–21, 124, 157, 248, 253, 271, 277, 283n15; Anglo-American Committee's embrace of, 251; mainstream Zionists vs., 119, 121, 127, 253. *See also* Brit Shalom; Ihud
Birla, G. D., 150
Blau, Moshe, 213, 226
Blond, Neville, 329n103
Blunt, Wilfrid Scawen, 72
Boer War, 95
Bombay, 11, 34, 135, 137–38, 150, 178–79, 185, 196; Jewish Agency representative in, 195; memorial campaign for European categorization submitted by Baghdadi Jews in, 143–45; Norman Bentwich's remarks about poverty in, 207; Zionist association in, 154, 155–56

Bombay Municipal Council, 109
Bonné, Alfred, 256, 268
Brachyahu, Anna, 256; relationship with Moshe Shertok, 257.
Brahmachari, Upendranath, 147
Braude, Isaiah, 83
Brit HaBirionim, 119
Britain. *See* Great Britain
"British Clerks and the National Home" (Arlosoroff), 70–75
British Empire, The (Williams), 92
Brit Shalom, 25, 48–49, 53, 120–21, 125, 191, 194, 248, 256. *See also* binationalism; Ihud
British Commonwealth, 26, 91, 102; creation of, 67; Palestine's potential inclusion in, 8, 56, 57, 68, 76, 77, 79, 96, 123, 157, 278; state-like power of dominions in, 13, 48
British Empire: anticolonialism and nationalist movements in 7–9, 12, 14, 17, 22, 108, 116, 164, 166, 167, 175, 182–83, 204, 260, 261, 263–70, 278; in contrast to Great Britain, 146–47, 238; as model for Jewish political life, 17, 26, 48, 88, 95; modern Jewish historiography, 14–15; Muslims in, 8, 20, 40, 63, 73, 86, 98, 105, 107–12, 139–40, 163, 170, 175, 176, 178, 182, 196, 220–21, 224, 242, 253, 258, 260, 262, 270, 273, 275, 276; as a refuge for Jews fleeing Nazism, 21, 158–60, 201–3, 207, 209–10, 232–33, 240, 257, 272, 277; self-government, 11, 38, 87, 95, 102, 134, 139, 148, 150, 207, 243. *See also* British Commonwealth; Great Britain
British Jews, 6, 11, 23, 28, 34, 46, 51–52, 127, 131, 167, 205, 218, 234, 237, 274
Brodetsky, Selig, 169–72, 176, 180

Brown, Percy, 148
Buber, Martin, 48, 59, 120, 192–95, 270, 273
"Buffs" (Royal East Kent Regiment), 241
Bullitt, William Christian, 230
Bulwer-Lytton, Victor, 148
Burma, 68, 263
Butler, Josephine, 31–32
Butler, Rab, 225
Buxton, Charles, 91

Calcutta, 8, 11, 20, 34; Jewish institutions in, 151–53, 154–57; memorial campaign for European categorization led by Baghdadi Jews in, 134–35, 136, 138–46; neighborhoods of, 152; as seat of Baghdadi Jewish leadership in India, 138; social world of Jewish elites in, 147–49
Campbell, J. E. F., 72
Canada, 8, 13, 67, 68, 76, 79, 103, 187, 240; in comparison to Palestine, 124
Canberra, 210
Cantonization, 125, 184
Cantor, Bernard, 41
caste system, 142, 150. *See also* Dalits ("untouchables")
Central British Fund for German Jewry, 235
Chagla, M. C., 109
Chamberlain, Joseph, 231, 232
Chamberlain, Neville, 208, 210–12, 217, 225, 230, 231, 242
Chancellor, John, 69, 83, 87, 99, 107, 123, 129; antisemitism ascribed to, 85; Arlosoroff's meetings with, 101–2
Chatterji, Mrs. J. C., 148
Chichele-Plowden, Pamela, 148
China, 137, 263, 270
Chovevei Zion movement, 24
Churchill, Winston, 27, 242–43, 247
Churchill White Paper (1922), 43
Clayton, Gilbert, 72

"Cleared!" (Kipling), 37, 42, 53
Cochin Jews, 159
Cohen, Dennis, 234
Cohen, Israel, 154–55
Cohen, Lionel, 328n61
Collings, Joe, 210
Colonial Office (Great Britain), 15, 26, 43, 83, 92, 99–100, 184, 277
Commonwealth Relations Conference (1938), 206–9, 250
Constitutional Act (Canada, 1791), 124
Contagious Diseases Acts, 31–32
Council for German Jewry, 26, 200–202, 206, 213, 233–34, 236, 238
Cowen, Percy, 169
Cox, Percy, 72
Crémieux, Adolphe, 6
Curtin, John, 211
Czechoslovakia, 8, 106, 189, 208, 211, 232, 248

Dada Abdulla and Sons, 163
Dagan, Peretz, 76, 80
Dalits ("untouchables"), 150–51, 273
Damascus Affair, 6
Danby, Herbert, 108
David, Meyer, 135, 148, 150–51, 178
David, Percival, 129
d'Avigdor-Goldsmid, Osmond, 328n61
Deedes, Wyndham, 72, 201, 213, 232–34
Deutscher, Isaac, 166
Delgrada, Anita, 148
Desai, Mahadev, 180, 186, 198
diaspora: concern over reproducing Jewish diaspora conditions in Palestine, 111, 125; Jewish advocacy for Indian diaspora, 164, 168, 197; Jewish and Indian diasporic experiences compared and contrasted, 169, 195; Zionism in relation to the Jewish diaspora, 11, 80
diaspora nationalism, 6

Disraeli, Benjamin, 93, 314n25
Dizengoff, Meir, 62, 64, 105
The Dominions and the Colonial Offices (Fiddes), 92
dominion status, 8, 10, 11, 13–14, 67, 76–77, 91, 92, 95, 96, 102, 103, 148, 150, 157, 207, 211, 274; Arlosoroff's view of, 13, 19, 56–57, 70, 75, 77–82, 86–88, 123–24, 222, 278; Asian outreach likened to, 260–61; Norman Bentwich's view of, 48; Jabotinsky's view of, 75–77; statist and nonstatist elements of, 13–14, 19, 57, 96, 280; Wedgwood's proposal for, 29, 67–70, 83. *See also* Seventh Dominion Scheme
Dovercourt Camp, 235
Duval, Elsie, 27

Eder, David, 34–35
Edward VII, king of Great Britain, 146–47
Egypt, 23, 60, 72, 74, 86, 87, 221–22, 225, 226, 232, 247, 258, 263, 265
Egyptian Expeditionary Forces, 1
el-Said, Karima, 265–66
el-Solh, Takieddin, 264–66
Epstein, Eliahu (Elath), 323n70
Epstein, Elias M., 183
Epstein, Mortimer, 287–88n6
Etzel. *See* Irgun
Évian Conference (1938), 200–203, 207
Exodus, SS, 274
Ezra, David, 20, 178, 278; as animal lover, 152; Arms Act exemption sought by, 139, 142; in Calcutta Jewish community, 138, 155; club memberships of, 148–49; elite social ties of, 135, 147–48, 151, 152–53; in Jewish and Indian cultures, 136, 146–47, 149, 151–53, 155, 158, 159–61, 159–60; Jewish organizations led by, 153, 154, 155, 158; Jewish refugees and, 158–59; knighthood bestowed on, 147;

memorial campaign for European classification and, 134, 140–46, 151, 160–61; Ottoman rule and, 153; in Palestine, 154, 156; Zionism and, 154–58
Ezra, Mozelle, 312–13n11
Ezra, Rachel, 20, 137, 150, 155–59, 178, 278; attitudes toward Indian self-rule of, 135, 149–50; in Calcutta Jewish community, 138, 155; devoutness of, 151, 154; elite social ties of, 135, 147–48, 151, 152–53; as hostess, 138, 152–53, 159–60; Jewish and Indian futures linked by, 159–60; Jewish organizations led by, 151–52, 155; in Palestine, 154, 156; in prewar London, 137–38, 146–47; Zionism and, 154–58

Faisal I, king of Iraq, 66, 87, 104
federalism, 10, 13, 29, 56, 61, 79, 157, 220, 224, 244, 252–54
Federation of Indian Chambers of Commerce and Industry (FICCI), 150
Feinberg, Avshalom, 300n81
Feinberg, Tzila, 300n81
Feldman, David, 15
Fiddes, George, 92
Filastin (newspaper), 43, 113
Finkelstein, Ze'ev, 77
France, 44, 78, 189–90, 193, 201, 211–12, 230, 239, 241; and its mandate over Lebanon and Syria, 62–64, 66
Franklin, Alice, 27
Franklin, Arthur, 38, 41
Franklin, Caroline (Helen Bentwich's mother), 26–27, 33, 34, 38, 41, 42, 52, 291n55
Franklin, Hugh, 27, 28, 305n7, 308n61
French Empire. *See* France
Friedlander, Israel, 41, 288n8
Friedlander, Lilian (Bentwich), 41, 288n8
Frumkin, Gad, 127

INDEX

Gallipoli campaign, 68
Gandhi, Indira, 266
Gandhi, Mohandas, 8, 109, 135, 145, 149–51, 159–60, *165*, 185, 204, 254, 268, 273–74; attitudes toward Jews and Judaism of, 166, 170; appeasement analogy of, 273–74; Brodetsky and Sokolow's meeting with, 171–73; dominion status backed by, 14; Jews' repudiation of, 171, 191–196; Kallenbach's friendship with, 20–21, 162–69, 173, 176–77, 186–88, 279; Nazism viewed by, 190–91; noncooperation policy of, 180, 197; outreach by Olsvanger to, 167, 174–85; Palestine mediation offered by, 187; Polak's friendship with, 20–21, 164, 166, 167–71, 279; retraction published by, 198; satyagraha movement of, 162, 164, 166, 191, 269; in South Africa, 9, 11, 20, 162–68; "spiritual" Zionism proposed by, 170–71; Zionism opposed by, 189–91, 196–98
Gandhi, Ramdas, 185
Garratt, G. T., 91
Gaster, Moses, 24
General Zionism, 12
George V, king of Great Britain, 147
Germany, 2, 6, 7, 19, 46, 58–59, 78, 97, 112, 122, 124, 133, 142, 158, 162, 174, 181, 187–93, 195, 197–98, 200–206, 207, 208, 212, 232, 233–39, 248, 260, 274
Gidney, Henry, 149
Goetz, Violet, 310n101
Good Will Movement (Welfare of India League; Progressive League), 150, 178
Gordon, A. D., 59
Gordon, Joshua, 24
Government of India Act (1919), 134–35, 139–40, 142, 146
Government of India Act (1935), 146, 178
Grasovsky (Samuel), Hadassah, 41, 47

Grasovsky (Gur), Yehuda, 41
Great Britain: antisemitism in, 131, 274; Balfour Declaration (1917) by, 1, 19, 43, 46, 166, 174; Balfour Declaration (1926) by, 67, 68, 103; children's emigration from, 237; immigration restrictions in, 131; immigration to Palestine limited by, 16, 21, 42–43, 76, 94, 157, 185, 202, 214, 224, 229, 232, 248–49, 270; and India, 134–35, 139, 203, 253; Indian Jews and, 138–46; in international politics, 15, 63, 64, 66, 81, 154, 211–12; and Ireland, 37–38; Labour politics in, 29, 37, 38, 53, 57, 64, 67, 69, 83–84, 87, 90–91, 94, 99, 106, 175, 210–11; mandate for Palestine assigned to, 4–5, 25, 174; as model for Jewish political life, 8, 19, 56, 57, 278; in modern Jewish historiography, 15, 29; Orientalism in, 72, 74; Palestine policy and, 42–43, 64, 89, 94; Palestine riots and, 36–38, 42, 87; press in, 80, 168–73, 213, 216, 217, 219, 232, 239; refugee children and, 214, 219, 233–36, 237–38, 239; refugee adults and, 236–40; as Zionist center, 11; Zionist relations with, 9, 10, 17, 19, 21, 56, 57, 64, 66, 67, 83, 97, 102–4, 114–16, 127, 198–99, 203–6, 222–32, 243, 245–49, 251–53, 254, 280. *See also* British Empire
Grierson, Jane Hope, 40
Grigg, James, 243

Haavara (Transfer) Agreement (1933), 133
Habas, Bracha, 256, 257, 259, 264, 270, 274
Habima, 112–13
Habonim, 128, 157
Hacohen, David, 256–63, 267, 273
Hadassah (the Women's Zionist Organization of America), 39, 51–52, 85
Hadi, Ruhi Abdel, 106
Haganah, 36–37, 42, 188, 204, 249, 252, 256

Haifa, 2, 39, 51, 77, 79, 102, 175, 212, 228
Halifax, Edward Wood, Earl of (formerly Lord Irwin), 145, 223
Ha-'Ol, 192
Ha-Or (newspaper), 125
Hapoel Hatzair, 59–61, 62, 90
Harijan (newspaper), 189, 194–98
Hart, Mitchell, 143
Hartog, Philip, 198
Haskell, Florence E., 155
Haycraft, Thomas, 42
Haycraft Commission, 42, 70
Hebrew University, 18, 26, 49–50, 117–21, 129, 130, 249, 255, 263
Hechalutz movement, 256
Heifetz, Jascha, 127
Heine, Heinrich, 179
Henriques, Cyril, 52
Herzl, Theodor, 29, 215, 231
Hindus, 8, 109, 135, 140, 142, 147, 150, 159, 161, 176, 177, 178, 179–80, 196, 262, 268, 275
Histadrut, 48, 62, 257
Hitler, Adolf, 130, 133, 158, 174, 180, 181, 191, 193–94, 197, 208, 210–11, 223, 273
Hoare, Samuel, 234
Hodorovski, Max (Menachem Savidor), 318n103
Holocaust, 5, 22, 248, 260, 271, 274. *See also* World War II
Holocaust survivors, 10, 243, 245, 247–49, 271, 274
Hoofien, Marianne, 32, 35–36, 39
Hope-Simpson, John, 302–3n123
Hoz, Dov, 302–3n123
Hungary, 247
Hutheesing, Gunottam, 179
Hutheesing, Krishna, 179
Hyamson, Albert, 51, 306n22
Hyamson, Marie, 51
Hyeem, Farha, 312–13n11

Ihud Party, 25, 49, 248, 255. *See also* binationalism; Brit Shalom
Ilan, Ben-Zion, 256
immigration: of Arabs into Palestine, 188; British limits on, 16, 21, 42–43, 76, 94, 157, 185, 202, 214, 224, 229, 232, 240, 248–49, 270; of Jewish refugees, 10, 13, 19, 21, 26, 34, 97, 158–59, 200–202, 207–10, 214, 219, 223–24, 233; South African limits on, 233; U.S. limits on, 6
imperialism: British critiques of, 72, 175; and British Labour, 69, 81, 175; in its British vs. French manifestations, 65–66; compared and contrasted to Nazism on the eve of WWII, 190–94; Nehru's assessment of, 181–83; and its relationship to Jews and Zionism in scholarship, 14–17; *See* British Empire, French Empire
India, 7–8, 22, 44–45, 67, 95, 134–61, 162–63, 253; Agronsky's trip to, 108–9; anticolonialism and nationalism in, 9, 10, 17, 20, 60, 68, 95, 103, 108, 135–136, 150–51, 203–4; Baghdadi Jews in, *see* Baghdadi Jews; class and racial discrimination in, 142, 148–49, 261; compared to Palestine, 10, 22, 145–46, 254, 262–63; Crown rule in, 11; dominion status proposed for, 13–14, 67, 87; Jewish refugees in, 34, 153, 158–60, 207, 272; immigration to British Commonwealth from, 208–9; independence of, 253, 258–59, 274–75; Muslims in, 20, 86, 98, 108–9, 111, 139–40, 170, 175, 176, 182, 196, 224, 253, 258, 260, 262, 268, 270, 275; partition of, 22, 190, 262, 274–75; poverty in, 207, 261–62; Round Table Conferences on, 91, 94–95, 107, 135, 145, 149, 169, 171–73, 179; Zionism in, 12, 153–58, 257; Zionist relations with, 164, 166–67, 170–99, 250–75

Indian Arms Act (1878), 139
Indian Auxiliary Force (AIF), 160
Indian Council of World Affairs, 250, 255
Indian National Congress, 109, 145, 167, 179, 180, 183, 185, 253
Indian Overseas Association, 168, 197
Indian Rebellion (1857), 138
Indonesia, 263
Inquisition, 140, 262
Inter-Aid Committee for Children from Germany and Austria, 234
Iran, 147, 270
Iraq, 64, 66, 73–74, 87, 104, 123–24, 138, 221, 225, 258
Irgun, 188, 212, 228, 242, 251–52, 271, 274
Ireland, 35, 67, 68, 207; in comparison to Palestine, 37–38, 42, 271
Ironside, Edmund, 241
Isaacs, Eva, 128–29, 218
Isaacs, Gerald, 2nd Marquess of Reading, 218–19, 231, 238
Isaacs, Rufus, 1st Marquess of Reading, 128, 142, 144, 146, 218, 328n57
Isle of Man, 162, 239
Israel, Wilfred, 233
Israeli independence, 277
Italy, 60, 72, 78, 119, 212, 222, 232, 241–42, 247–48

Jaffa, 1–2, 123, 173; in the British Orientalist imagination, 74; education in, 40; Irgun attack against Palestinians in, 212; during WWI, 30, 79; Zionist comparison to Tel Aviv of, 105. *See also* Jaffa riots (1921); Tel Aviv
Jaffa riots (1921), 41–43, 60–61, 70, 73
Jabotinsky, Ze'ev, 29, 36–37, 42, 56, 61, 75–82, 157, 280
Jerusalem, 28; education in, 30–31; as a focus of Pan-Islamism, 107–8, 170; during the Nebi Musa riots (1920), 36–37, 41–42; prostitution in, 31–32; as a site of elite cross-cultural socialization, 20, 38, 105–6, 127, 278; social work and welfare services in, 32–35, 36, 50–52; in the wake of WWI, 30
Jerusalem Ladies' Club, 38–39
Jewish Agency for Palestine, 11, 20, 56, 58, 99, 108, 128, 195, 205, 213–16, 226, 248, 250, 251–53, 255–56, 274; British talks boycotted by, 252–53; at Évian Conference, 200; formation of, 82; inclusion of non-Zionists in, 82, 218–19; in Passfield White Paper, 94; Peel Commission's partition plan backed by, 202, 222; Political Department of the, 96, 97, 98, 163, 175, 220. *See also* Zionist Commission; Palestine Zionist Executive
Jewish Agency Political Advisory Committee, 218
Jewish Brigade (WWII), 203, 214, 241–43, 246–49
Jewish Chronicle (newspaper), 163, 166, 168–73, 187, 190, 235
Jewish National Fund (JNF), 52, 113, 115, 118
Jewish Relief Association (JRA), 153, 158
Jinnah, Muhammad Ali, 109, 258
Joint. *See* American Jewish Joint Distribution Committee
Jordan, 258. *See also* Transjordan
Jouvenel, Henry de, 63, 65–66
Judah, Edward, 143–46
Der jüdische Volkssozialismus (Arlosoroff), 59–60

Kadoorie, Elly, 31
Kallenbach, Hermann, 20–21, *165*, 167–70, 194; Gandhi's friendship with, 162–64, 176–77, 186, 188; Indian outreach by, 20, 163, 174, 176–78, 180–81, 183, 185–88, 195–97, 199, 254, 256, 279; kibbutz

Kallenbach, Hermann (*cont.*)
  movement's influence on, 185; Polak's disagreements with, 166; as Zionist, 173–74, 199, 279
Kaplansky, Shlomo, 56
Katznelson, Berl, 56, 60, 79, 121, 184, 215–16, 226, 303n128
Kenworthy, Joseph, 91
Khayat, Francis, 127
Khilafat movement, 8, 98, 109, 172. *See also* Pan-Islamism
Khmelnitsky massacres, 262
kibbutz movement, 45–46, 47, 59, 60, 157, 173, 185
Kindertransport, 21, 26, 201, 213, 233–39
King David Hotel bombing (1946), 252
Kipling, Rudyard, 37, 42, 53, 74
Kisch, Frederick, 24, 99, 100–2, 317n93; anti-British sentiment criticized by, 220; appointment as head of the Political Department of, 45; Helen Bentwich's view of, 47, 52; early life of, 44; Wedgwood viewed by, 69, 82
Kisch, Hermann, 44
Kitchener Camp, 237–39
Klivnov, Ya'akov, 77
Kohn, Hans, 48–49, 53, 120
Kook, Abraham Isaac, 49, 50, 110
Kristallnacht, 189, 192, 201, 202, 213, 214, 233
Kropotkin, Peter, 54, 59, 60
Kunin, Ben-Zion, 215–16
Kunzru, H. N., 209, 266

Labor Zionists, 2, 12, 28, 45, 62, 83, 102, 119, 158, 209, 256, 271; 'avodah 'ivrit (Hebrew labor) backed by, 87–89; binationalism vs., 121; and British Labour, 84, 90–91, 116; British Labor critiques of, 95; communists vs., 41; and dominion status, 80–82; and Palestinian Arab nationalism, 60–61, 89, 111; statist and nonstatist views among, 53, 56, 59, 280
Landau, Annie, 30–31, 35–36, 127
Landauer, Gustav, 59
Lange, Michael, 24
Lange (Bentwich), Rosalind "Nita," 24, 41
language policy, 38–40
Laski, Elaine (Blond), 234, 237
Laski, Harold, 91, 175, 329n103
Laski, Neville, 91, 328n61, 329n103
Lawrence, Susan, 91
League of Nations, 15, 45, 94, 107, 110, 250; Arlosoroff's early attitudes toward, 67, 68; High Commission for Refugees of, 21, 201; ineffectiveness of, 64, 66, 201; Iraq in, 87; mandates of, 4–5, 11, 43, 62–66, 183; Wedgwood's skepticism toward, 68–69. *See also* Permanent Mandates Commission
Lebanon, 63, 65–66, 258
Lehi, 251–52, 271
Lewin, Louis, 173
Lipsky, Louis, 83
Lloyd George, David, 68, 141, 303n126, 304n136
Lloyd, George, 242
London School of Economics, 175, 209, 256
Lourie, Arthur, 215, 216
Lowestoft Camp, 235
Luft, Zvi, 296n23
Luke, Harry, 51, 69–70, 99, 101
Lunn, William, 301n101

MacDonald, Malcolm, 217, 221–26, 229–30, 232, 242
MacDonald, Ramsay, 64, 83, 94, 99, 106, 217, 230
MacDonald Letter (1931), 94, 100, 230
MacInnes, Janet, 32, 39–40
Madagascar, 233
Magnes, Beatrice, 46–47, 106

Magnes, Judah, 46, 106, 202, 287n3; Bentwiches and, 24, 25, 44, 46–50, 117–19, 236; as binationalist and supporter of Brit Shalom, 48–49, 120, 248; as founder of Ihud, 248; Ha-'Ol founding and, 192; appeal to Gandhi by, 192–95, 273; as pacifist, 193–94, 205

Malaya, 263

Mandate Memories (Bentwich and Bentwich), 27

Mandate Palestine. *See* Palestine

mandate system, 4–5, 11, 25, 43, 62–66, 174, 183. *See also* Permanent Mandates Commission

Mapai, 59, 90, 121, 226, 229, 252

Marx, Karl, 54, 60, 61

May, Doris, 216

Meherally, Yusuf, 183

Mehta, Chunilal V., 150

Meir, Yaakov, *49*

Mereminsky, May Bere, 256–57

Meyerson (Meir), Golda, 252

Millstein, Selene, 51

Mir'at al-Sharq (Mirror of the East; newspaper), 107

Miron, Leah, 215

Mr. Gandhi: The Man (Millie Polak), 171

Mizrachi (Religious Zionists), 98

Moetzet Hapoalot (Council of Women Workers), 256

Mond, Alfred, 128

Money (general), 35

Montagu, Lily, 27

Montefiore, Moses, 6, 92

Moody, Sydney, 104–5

Mookerjee, Rajendra Nath, 147

Morris, Rhys Hopkin, 301–2n105

Moses, E., 150

Mosseri, Jack, 31

Mossinson, Benzion, 215

Motzkin, Leo, 127

Mountbatten, Louis, 253, 274

Movement for the Care of Children from Germany (Refugee Children's Movement), 234–36

Mumbai. *See* Bombay

Munich Agreement (1938), 189, 211–12, 222, 225, 230, 232, 273

Muslims, 50, 63, 73, 86, 105, 107–9, 220–21, 242, 258, 276; in India, 20, 86, 98, 108–9, 111, 139–40, 170, 175, 176, 182, 196, 224, 253, 258, 260, 262, 268, 270, 275

Mussolini, Benito, 68, 119

Myers, Jack, 287–88n6

Naidu, Padmaja, 266

Naidu, Sarojini, 167, 179, 255, 257, 259, 266

Nashashibi family, 107

Native Americans, 266

Nayyar, Pyarelal, 194–95, 208

Nazism, 5, 6, 7, 96, 122, 142–43, 174, 181, 183, 188–89, 199, 212, 232, 238, 242, 279; Afrikaner sympathy toward, 233; Gandhi's reaction to the rise of, 166, 189–98; Haavara (Transfer Agreement) and, 133; refugees from, 13, 19, 21, 26, 34, 97, 158–59, 187, 200–202, 207, 214, 219, 223–24, 233; Zionist sense of time factor linked to, 96, 121, 124–26

Nebi Musa riots, 36–37, 41–42

Nedivi, Joseph, 196

Nehru, Jawaharlal, 204; as anticolonialist, 95, 180, 182, 183; Asian Relations Conference convened and attended by, 22, 250, 254, 259, 260, 263–70; attitudes toward Zionism of, 180, 260; as Fabian socialist, 95; Harold Laski linked to, 175; Olsvanger's meetings with, 179–83, 185, 266–67

Netherlands, 235, 239

Netz, Yosef, 213

Newfoundland, 67

Newton, Effie, 39–40
New York Kehillah, 46
New Zealand, 54, 67, 76, 82, 92–93, 103
Nicholas II, emperor of Russia, 58
Nissim, Meyer, 109, 150, 154, 178
non-Zionism, 9, 17, 20, 21, 50, 164, 166, 199, 202, 204, 213, 218–19, 228, 234, 237, 255, 277, 279; among Baghdadi Jews, 109, 129; and exigency, 5, 7, 10, 12, 205, 206, 280; of Helen Bentwich, 18, 26, 28–30, 44; and the Jewish Agency, 82, 94; Shertok's shifting attitudes toward, 218–19; 231
Nordau, Max, 163
Northern Rhodesia, 233
Nuremberg Laws (1935), 189
Nurock, Max, 24, 127, 232, 287n3, 306n21
Nurock, Mordechai "Max," 287n3

Occupied Enemy Territory Administration (OETA), 31–31, 35
October Manifesto, 58
Old Yishuv, 41, 50
Olsvanger, Immanuel, 167, 174–86, 254, 255–56
Operation Agatha, 252, 271
Operation Pied Piper, 237–38
opium trade, 137
Ormsby-Gore, William, 145–46, 158
Ottoman Empire, 1–2, 15, 30; defeat of (1918), 3, 4; in relation to Zionism, 153–54

Pacifism, 37, 46, 68, 84, 120, 125, 193–94, 205
Pakistan, 109, 262
Palestine: 1929 Palestine riots in, 50–53, 54, 82–85, 205; Arab Revolt (1936–1939), 174–75, 184, 188, 202, 204, 212–13, 228, 229, 271; British officials in, 31, 45, 70–75, 90, 99, 101–2, 104, 128; compared to India, 10, 22, 145–46, 254, 262–63; compared to Ireland, 37–38, 42, 271; compared to South Africa, 88–89; Indian attitudes toward, 109, 170–99, 250–75, 266–68, 273–74; Jaffa riots (1921) in, 41–43, 60–61, 70, 73; Jewish-Arab relations in, 5, 13, 19, 56, 88–89, 97, 116, 117, 120, 124, 129, 175, 184, 192, 202, 218, 260, 277; Jewish Brigade (WWII) from, 203, 214, 240–43, 247–49; Jewish insurgency in, 243, 251, 262, 269, 271, 273; as Jewish national home, 5–6; League of Nation's Permanent Mandates Commission and, 62–66, 94; Nebi Musa riots (1920) in, 36–37, 41–42; non-Zionist attitudes toward, 5, 7, 10, 12, 205, 206, 218, 280; Palestinian Arab nationalism in, 34, 36, 60–61, 79, 83, 89, 111, 116, 175, 181–83, 220; Palestinian Christians in, 32, 40, 105, 107; partition plan for, 10, 16, 21, 22, 184–85, 190, 202, 205, 212, 218–19, 222, 225, 227, 251, 254, 262, 267, 275; as a potential dominion, 8, 10, 13, 29, 48, 67–70, 75–82, 86, 211, 278, 280; social work in, 30–35, 235; St James's Palace Conference (1939) on, 213–32. *See also* Palestinian Arabs
Palestine Regiment, 241, 247
Palestine Zionist Executive, 45, 53, 80, 82. *See also* Zionist Commission; Jewish Agency for Palestine
Palestinian Arabs, 12, 16, 43, 77, 80, 176, 177, 198, 224, 243, 258, 260, 263, 265; in the 1948 Arab-Israeli War, 277; in the British Army during WWII, 241; in the civil war in Mandatory Palestine (1947–1948), 277; Irgun attacks against, 188, 212, 228; nationalist movement of, 34, 36, 60–61, 79, 83, 89, 111, 116, 175, 181–83, 220
Pan-Asianism, 260

Pan-Arabism, 8
Pandit, Vijaya Lakshmi, 266
Panikkar, K. M., 259, 268
Pan-Islamism, 8, 19, 98, 108–9, 111–12, 170, 220. *See also* Khilafat
Parnell, Charles Stewart, 37
Parsis, 135, 145, 147, 152, 161
partition, 185, 212, 219, 222, 225, 227, 251, 267, 274–75, 276; compared in India and Palestine, 10, 22, 190, 254, 258–59, 262; debated among Jewish leaders, 21, 184, 202, 205, 218; as a topic in scholarship, 16
Passfield White Paper (1930), 90–91, 93–94, 100, 230
Peel Commission, 174, 184, 187, 188, 202, 212, 222, 228
Permanent Mandates Commission, 62–66, 94. *See also* League of Nations
Philby, St John, 72
Pinsker, Leon, 129–32, 188
Pioneer Corps, 238–39, 241
Plumer, Herbert Charles Onslow Plumer, 1st Viscount, 47, 69, 72, 76
Polak, Henry, 20–21, 177, 180, 199, 279; as founder of the Indian Overseas Association, 168; relationship with Gandhi, 163–73, 196–97
Polak, Maud, 171–72
Polak, Millie, 168, 171
Poland, 6, 60, 78, 201, 238; Jewish to Palestine from, 133; Jews in, 181, 240
Pollack, Fritz W., 257, 258
Poona Pact, 150
Progressive League (Welfare of India League; Good Will Movement), 150, 178
prostitution, 27, 31–32

Raymond, Albert, 150
Red Cross, 30, 39
Refugee Children's Movement (Movement for the Care of Children from Germany), 234–36
Reissner, Hanns G., 272
Revisionist Zionists, 9, 12, 29, 61, 76, 126, 158, 280; Arlosoroff's view of, 83–84, 119; Norman Bentwich opposed by, 120; dominion status considered by, 75–77, 80, 82; fascist wing (Brit HaBirionim) of, 119; Haavara (Transfer) Agreement opposed by, 133; nonstatist options considered by, 56; paramilitary violence carried out by, 188, 271, 274; in South Africa, 167; St James's Palace Conference opposed by, 213–14; Weizmann opposed by, 98
Rhodesia, 73
Richmond, Ernest, 72–73
Ritch, L. W., 164, 169
Rokach, Israel, 228
Romania, 6
Rommel, Erwin, 214, 242
Roosevelt, Franklin D., 200
Rothschild, Walter, 1
Round Table Conferences on India (1930–1932), 91, 94–95, 107, 135, 145, 149, 169, 171–73, 179
Royal East Kent Regiment ("Buffs"), 241
Ruppin, Arthur, 112, 127, 173
Ruskin, John, 163
Russian Empire, 1, 58, 169, 257. *See also* Soviet Union
Russian Revolution (1917), 6
Russian Revolution of 1905, 58
Rustomjee, Mancherjee, 147
Rutenberg, Pinhas, 24, 36, 212, 218, 287n3

Sacher, Harry, 24, 25, 237, 287n3, 287–88n6
St James's Palace Conference (1939), 195, 206, 213–32, 240, 245; dress and decorum at, 215–16
Salameh, Salmah, 32

Salt March (1930), 179, 193
Samuel, Beatrice (Franklin), 38, 39–40, 41, 156
Samuel, Edwin, 41, 47, 306n21
Samuel, Herbert, 28, 41, 72; in Council for German Jewry, 200–201, 238; Rachel and David Ezra and, 156; Gandhi rebuked by, 198; as high commissioner of Palestine, 36, 38, 39, 44, 61, 69, 234; Jewish immigration to Palestine temporarily suspended by, 42–43; Plumer contrasted with, 69
Samuel, Walter, 2nd Viscount Bearsted, 213, 218, 231
Saphir, Elisabeth Johanna, 298n50
Sassoon, David, 137, 138
Sassoon, Edward, 314n29
Sassoon, Flora (Rachel Ezra's mother), 156, 312–13n11, 317n92
Sassoon, Philip, 141
Sassoon, Solomon (Sulman), 135
Sassoon and Company, 137, 289n31, 307n39, 312–313n11, 317n92
satyagraha, 162, 164, 166, 191, 192, 194, 269
Saudi Arabia, 258
Savidor, Menachem (Max Hodorovski), 318n103
Schechter, Solomon, 24–25, 320n14
Schlesin, Sonja, 164, *165*
Scholem, Gershom, 49, 120, 192
Sebag-Montefiore, Robert, 287–88n6
Senator, David Werner, 112, 255, 276
Sephardi Jews: vs. Baghdadi Jews, 139–40, 142–43; in Britain, 143; in Palestine, 30, 62; and Ottomanism, 154; from Rhodes, 232
settlement movement, 25, 33, 48
settler colonialism, 16–17, 68
Seventh Dominion Scheme, 56, 67–82, 83, 91. *See also* dominion status
Shapira, Anita, 122
Shaw, George Bernard, 304nn146–47

Shaw, Walter, 301–2n105
Shaw Commission, 53, 84, 87–88, 90–91, 94, 101, 110
Shertok (Sharett), Moshe, 5, 9, 21, 268; anticolonial links of, 9; arrest and detention of, 252–53, 256, *257*; Norman Bentwich compared to, 203; Brachyahu and, 257; early life of, 1; images of, *4*, *217*, *257*; Indian outreach by, 163, 174–78, 184–86, 203–4, 209, 250, 253–54, 260, 268; Isaacs viewed by, 219, 231; Jewish Brigade (WWII) and, 203, 214, 241–43, 246–49; Jewish statehood backed by, 249; language study by, 2, 3, 257; Ottoman army service in WWI of, 1–3; Ottoman and Jewish futures considered by, 1–2, 153–54; partition backed by, 184–85, 251; post-WWII outlook analyzed by, 243–47; shifting attitudes toward non-Zionists of, 218–19, 231; at St James's Palace Conference, 206, 213–32; Palestine's place in the British imperial and world order analyzed by 220–23, 229–31, 243–47; time at the London School of Economics of, 175, 256; uncertainty of, 2–4, 227, 279; Zionist-British cooperation pursued by, 203–6, 214, 219–20; 229, 240–1; 245–46, 248–49; 279
Shertok, Tzippora (Meirov), 2, 3, 185
Shimoni, Gideon, 157, 166, 181
Shimoni, Ya'akov, 256, 263–64, 266–71, 273–74
Shohet, A. E., 195–96
Sieff, Rebecca (Marks), 234, 237
Sikhs, 135, 139, 147, 161, 275
Silliman, Jael, 144
Simon, Ernst, 49, 192
Simon, John, 142
Simon, Leon, 25
Simon Commission, 87, 135, 142, 144
Singapore, 80, 87

Singh, Jagatjit, 148
Sinha, Pradip, 152
Skelton, Gladys, 234
Smilansky, Moshe, 302n117
Smuts, Jan, 144, 319n11
Snell, Henry, 301–2n105
Social Service Association (Welfare Society), 32, 35–36, 39
Sokolow, Nahum, 98–99, 171–73, 184
Sombart, Werner, 59, 62
South Africa, 7, 8, 48, 67, 77; Gandhi in, 9, 11, 20, 162–68; immigration limited by, 233; Indians in, 163, 191–92, 195; Jewish-Indian relations in, 163–64, 168–69, 177; Palestine compared by Arlosoroff to, 88; self-government in, 11; Zionism in, 166–67, 177
Southern Rhodesia, 69, 232
Soviet Union, 78, 203, 243–44, 246; relations with Britain, 81; Jewish life in, 113, 130, 132
Spanish Civil War, 234
Special Committee on Palestine (UNSCOP), 274–75, 276
Spicer, Roy G. B., 100–101, 105
Spinoza, Baruch, 179
Steimatzky, Yechezkel, 76
Storrs, Ronald, 30–31, 36
Strathearn (ophthalmologist), 127
Sudan, 74
Suez Canal, 221
swadeshi, 150
swaraj, 142
Syria, 63–64, 65–66, 258
Syrian Relief Fund, 30
Szold, Henrietta, 39

Tel Aviv, 112, 152, 185, 228; during Jaffa Riots (1921), 41; during Jewish insurgency, 252, 274; during WWI, 30; Zionist comparison to Jaffa of, 105. *See also* Jaffa

Territorialism, 202–3, 232
Thakurdas, Purshottamdas, 150
theosophists, 163–64
Tolstoy, Leo, 162–63
Toynbee, Arnold, 208
Toynbee Hall (settlement house), 25, 27
Transjordan, 129. *See also* Jordan
Trotskyites, 125
Trumpeldor, Joseph, 68

Uganda, 232
Uganda Scheme, 202, 287n28
uncertainty: as a central feature of the Jewish political imagination, 2–3, 9–10, 12, 95, 97–98, 115, 133, 136, 227, 254, 272, 279, 280, 282–83n14
United Kingdom. *See* Great Britain
United Nations, 22, 250, 255, 274
Ussishkin, Menachem, 78, 118
Uziel, B. Z., 62, 64

Va'ad Leumi (Jewish National Council), 62, 66, 215, 228, 255, 258, 274
Vester, Bertha Spafford, 32, 39
Vogel, Julius, 54, 82, 84, 92–93

Wadi al-Hawarith, 113, 115–16
Wailing Wall. *See* Western Wall
Waley-Cohen, Robert, 237
Warburg, Felix, 234
Warburg, Lola Hahn, 234
Warren-Boulton, C., 160
Wauchope, Arthur, 99, 101, 127, 184, 225; Arlosoroff and, 9, 98, 112–16, 121–24, 128, 129–33, 278
Webb, H. A., 127
Webb, Beatrice, 288n13, 300n13
Webb, Sidney, 94, 95, 99, 100, 230, 288n13, 302–3n123
Weber, Max, 59
Wedgwood, Florence, 67

Wedgwood, Josiah C., 29, 81, 82, 91; and the Seventh Dominion Scheme, 67–70, 75–80, 83, 240

Weizmann, Chaim, 34, 36, 50, 54, 65, 69, 91, 93, 128, 145, 230, 243, 247, 251–52, 259, 272; "assimilationist" Jews criticized by, 218; Chamberlain's meeting with, 231; as chemist, 290n37; evolutionary Zionism promoted by, 77, 122; letter from Arlosoroff to, 56–57, 97, 116, 122, 125–26, 129–30, 132; partition backed by, 184; prostitution viewed by, 32; at St James's Palace Conference, 215–18, 221, 225–26, 229, 231; territorialism opposed by, 202–3; Wedgwood and, 68; Zionist Organization led by, 45, 94, 98–99, 114, 171, 184

Weizmann, Vera, 231

Welfare of India League (Good Will Movement; Progressive League), 150, 178

Welfare Society (Social Service Association), 32, 35–36, 39

Wells, H. G., 27

Weltsch, Robert, 49

Western Wall, 50, 83, 86, 107, 110, 112

White Paper (1922). *See* Churchill White Paper

White Paper (1930). *See* Passfield White Paper

White Paper (1939), 21, 202, 205, 206, 232, 240, 241, 246, 248, 249, 251, 270

Willcock, John, 210

Williams, Basil, 92

Wingate, Orde, 323n73

Wise, Stephen, 171, 214, 215, 217, 225

Wolf, Lucien, 24

Women's International Zionist Organization, 234

Wood, Edward, 1st Earl of Halifax (formerly Lord Irwin), 145, 223

World Islamic Congress, 104, 107–12, 123, 170, 220

World Jewish Congress (WJC), 153

World War I, 1–3, 5, 6, 7, 11, 21, 24, 27, 44, 46, 58, 62, 79, 85, 87, 98, 139, 154, 256, 257.

World War II, 21, 158, 160, 205, 277. *See also* Holocaust

Yaski, Chaim, 51

Yellin, David, 41, 47

Yellin, Eleazar, 41

Yellin, Thelma (Bentwich), 41, 47, 106

Yemen, 226, 277

Yiddishism, 6

Young, Mark, 101, 107–8, 110, 113–14, 123

Young Turk Revolution (1908), 153

Youth Aliyah, 210

Zangwill, Israel, 24, 34, 156

Zionism: vs. binationalism, 119, 121, 127, 253; cultural Zionism, 11, 12, 17, 28, 29, 121, 171; Gandhi's opposition to, 189–91, 196–98; General Zionism, 12; and Great Britain, 9, 10, 17, 19, 21, 56, 57, 64, 66, 67, 83, 97, 102–4, 114–16, 127, 198–99, 203–6, 222–32, 243, 245–49, 251–53, 254, 280; in India, 12, 153–58, 257; Nehru's attitudes toward, 180, 260; political Zionism, 11, 12, 121, 129, 156; in South Africa, 166–67, 177. *See also* Labor Zionists; Mizrachi (Religious Zionists); Revisionist Zionists

Zionist Actions Committee, 54, 62

Zionist Asianism, 254

Zionist Commission, 3, 32, 34, 36, 41. *See also* Jewish Agency for Palestine; Palestine Zionist Executive

Zionist Congresses, 8, 54, 62, 77, 80, 82, 94, 98, 114, 184, 218, 241, 253, 326n14

Zionist Organization, 19, 45, 56, 67, 83, 94, 154, 169, 171, 173, 184, 213, 237, 244

Zion Mule Corps, 68

STANFORD STUDIES IN JEWISH HISTORY AND CULTURE

Jessica Marglin and Daniel Schwartz, Editors

This series features novel approaches to examining the Jewish past in the form of innovative work that brings the field into productive dialogue with the newest scholarly concepts and methods. Open to a range of disciplinary and interdisciplinary approaches, from history to cultural studies, this series publishes exceptional scholarship balanced by an accessible tone, illustrating histories of difference and addressing issues of current urgency. Books in this list push the boundaries of Jewish Studies and speak compellingly to a wide audience of scholars and students.

Paris Papamichos Chronakis, *The Business of Transition: The Jewish and Greek Merchants of Salonica, 1882-1919*
2024

Naomi Seidman, *Translating the Jewish Freud: Psychoanalysis in Hebrew and Yiddish*
2024

Ariel Evan Mayse, *Laws of the Spirit: Ritual, Mysticism, and the Commandments in Early Hasidism*
2024

Immanuel Etkes, *The Invention of a Tradition: The Messianic Zionism of the Gaon of Vilna*
2024

Viola Alianov-Rautenberg, *No Longer Ladies and Gentlemen: Gender and the German-Jewish Migration to Mandatory Palestine*
2024

Susan Rubin Suleiman, *Daughter of History: Traces of an Immigrant Girlhood*
2023

Sandra Fox, *The Jews of Summer: Summer Camp and Jewish Culture in Postwar America*
2023

David Biale, *Jewish Culture Between Canon and Heresy*
2023

Alan Verskin, *Diary of a Black Jewish Messiah: The Sixteenth-Century Journey of David Reubeni through Africa, the Middle East, and Europe*
2023

Aomar Boum, Illustrated by Nadjib Berber, *Undesirables:
A Holocaust Journey to North Africa*
2023

Dina Porat, *Nakam: The Holocaust Survivors Who Sought Full-Scale Revenge*
2023

Christian Bailey, *German Jews in Love: A History*
2023

Matthias B. Lehmann, *The Baron: Maurice de Hirsch and the Jewish Nineteenth Century*
2022

Liora R. Halperin, *The Oldest Guard: Forging the Zionist Settler Past*
2021

Samuel J. Spinner, *Jewish Primitivism*
2021

Sonia Gollance, *It Could Lead to Dancing: Mixed-Sex Dancing and Jewish Modernity*
2021

Golan Y. Moskowitz, *Wild Visionary: Maurice Sendak in Queer Jewish Context*
2020

Julia Elsky, *Writing Occupation: Jewish Émigré Voices in Wartime France*
2020

Alma Rachel Heckman, *The Sultan's Communists:
Moroccan Jews and the Politics of Belonging*
2020

Clémance Boulouque, *Another Modernity: Elia Benamozgh's Jewish Universalism*
2020

Devi Mays, *Forging Ties, Forging Passports: Migration and the Modern Sephardi Diaspora*
2020

Dalia Kandiyoti, *The Converso's Return: Conversion and Sephardi
History in Contemporary Literature and Culture*
2020

For a complete listing of titles in this series, visit
the Stanford University Press website, www.sup.org.

The authorized representative in the EU for product safety and compliance is:
Mare Nostrum Group B.V.
Mauritskade 21D
1091 GC Amsterdam
The Netherlands
Email address: gpsr@mare-nostrum.co.uk

KVK chamber of commerce number: 96249943

The authorized representative in the EU for product safety and compliance is:
Mare Nostrum Group
B.V Doelen 72
4831 GR Breda
The Netherlands

www.ingramcontent.com/pod-product-compliance
Lightning Source LLC
Chambersburg PA
CBHW030603230426
43661CB00053B/1816